The California Republic

The California Republic

Institutions, Statesmanship, and Policies

Edited By
Brian P. Janiskee and
Ken Masugi

ROWMAN & LITTLEFIELD PUBLISHERS, INC.
Lanham • Boulder • New York • Toronto • Oxford

ROWMAN & LITTLEFIELD PUBLISHERS, INC.

Published in the United States of America
by Rowman & Littlefield Publishers, Inc.
A wholly owned subsidary of The Rowman & Littlefield Publishing Group, Inc.
4501 Forbes Boulevard, Suite 200, Lanham, Maryland 20706
www.rowmanlittlefield.com

PO Box 317
Oxford
OX2 9RU, UK

British Library Cataloguing in Publication Information Available

Library of Congress Cataloging-in-Publication Data

The California republic : institutions, statesmanship, and policies /
    edited by Brian P. Janiskee and Ken Masugi.
        p.   cm.
    Includes bibliographical references.
    ISBN 0-7425-3250-X (hc)—ISBN 0-7425-3251-8 (pbk.)
    1. California—Politics and government.   I. Janiskee, Brian P., 1967–
II. Masugi, Ken.
JK8716.C294 2003
320.9794—dc21   2003013204

Printed in the United States of America

∞ ™ The paper used in this publication meets the minimum requirements
of American National Standard for Information Sciences—Permanence of
Paper for Printed Library Materials, ANSI/NISO Z39.48-1992.

*Dedicated to my mother and the memory of
her departed brothers and sisters*

—KM

Dedicated to Jennifer, Katherine, Alexandra, and Mary

—BPJ

Californians all, in war and in peace, in one way or other

Contents

Preface

This collection has its origins in a scholarly conference and has been enhanced with more recent contributions. The Claremont Institute celebrated California's one hundred fiftieth anniversary of its birth by hosting "Democracy in California: Sesquicentennial Reflections on Equality and Liberty in the Golden State," October 27–28, 2000. The editors of *Nexus*, the law and policy journal of the Chapman University School of Law, graciously offered an issue of their journal for the revised papers from the conference. Many of the articles in this volume first appeared in *Nexus*. We thank them for their generosity, especially editor-in-chief professor Hugh Hewitt, professor John Eastman, and managing editor Jeanette Lee.

The essays presented a political and legal history of the development of a Progressive regime and its conditions of freedom. To this end, the conference sought to emphasize the themes of political philosophers such as Aristotle and Alexis de Tocqueville and the statesmanship of Abraham Lincoln and thus help foster a new generation of scholarship on California. We later obtained the participation of not only established scholars of California but also others whose expertise would profitably be directed to California issues. Obviously, the essays could not cover every important element of its culture or politics, yet we hope nonetheless this collection might guide serious students in the way they study this vital state.

Often lauded as having the fifth (or sixth or seventh, depending on what measure one uses) largest economy in the world, California seems to lead the nation in other measures as well—particularly cultural and political trends. But were it an independent state, it would be one of the world's strangest democracies. Understanding this strangeness, this exoticism, was our task. Even before its national preeminence, and well before the staggering budget crisis, the need to understand California as a necessary part of understanding America was abundantly clear. In order to understand, to quote Abraham Lincoln, "where we are

and whither we are tending," we were forced to reexamine the political principles of the Compromise of 1850, of the early state constitutions, and of the
American founding, just as we must keep in mind the mores and practices of
American citizenship. The essays strive to make these connections and thus lead
us to self-knowledge. They had been organized into four themes: the conditions
of democratic statehood; Progressivism and its statesmen; mores, multicultur-
alism, and citizenship; and the future of Progressive democracy.

We would like to thank the Claremont Institute for its support of the confer-
ence and this collection. All of our Claremont Institute colleagues were of tre-
mendous help as we completed this work. Special thanks go out to president
Brian Kennedy, fellow "Latino" Bob Gransden, Regina Cobb, Jeanette Jaime,
Adam Fuller, Matt Peterson, Lindsay White, and Melanie Marlowe. We wish to
thank Mary Carpenter, Laura Roberts, Terry Fischer and the editorial staff at
Rowman & Littlefield for their support. Special thanks also go out to Debbi
Fox in the Department of Political Science at California State University, San
Bernardino, for her assistance in the production of this manuscript. In addition,
I would like to thank Tresha Vinson.

We would also like to thank professors Charles Kesler and Ralph Rossum of
Claremont McKenna College for the contributions the Henry Salvatori Center
and the Rose Institute of State and Local Government made to the conference.
The Hon. Terry O'Rourke, an old friend of the Claremont Institute, continued
his most welcomed support.

Of course the conference that eventually lead to this collection of readings
would have been impossible without the support of the late Thomas B. Silver,
president of the Claremont Institute. Tom Silver left us on December 26, 2001,
but his vision and integrity are ever present.

Furthermore, our work has been continually inspired by Harry V. Jaffa, Distinguished Fellow of the Claremont Institute and Henry Salvatori, Distinguished Professor Emeritus at Claremont McKenna College, and Howard F.
Ahmanson, president of Fieldstead & Company. Finally, our personal thanks
go out to our families who have endured the travails that come with project
deadlines.

Introduction

Republican Government
in California

Brian P. Janiskee and Ken Masugi

As the companion reader to our textbook, *Democracy in California*, the *California Republic* elaborates on many of our earlier arguments. The coeditors hope the arguments presented will stimulate further thinking on the problem of self-government, especially as it manifests itself in California. These contributions, whether article length or brief, elaborate on the growth of government in public and private life associated with the bipartisan Progressive movement. We see Progressivism behind the controversial issues our authors confront—the tax revolt, civil rights, gun control, and others. Progressivism, whatever its immediate appeal, has eroded the limited government and constitutionalism that California's founders derived from America's founders. Whenever we hear the slogan "reform" today, our Progressive proclivities are being appealed to. The local government in California is nonpartisan—cleansed of the direct influence of political parties—so we must deal with city managers; thus, again, we enjoy the results of Progressivism. When we Californians are incensed about an issue, we can vote directly on it, even putting our desires into the state constitution through those distinctively Progressive tools, the initiative, referendum, and recall. The voters may bypass the legislature and undermine its authority and that of the governor as well. And the universities in which we study and teach receive funding in return for research that benefits the Progressive administrative state. In addition, the academy gains enormously in stature as sources for model legislation and good governance.

The essays collected here explore the evolution of Progressivism in California and its contemporary policy consequences. They consider the real, not theoretical, effects of abandoning natural rights and the limited government that follows from belief in their truth and power. If all men are created equal, as the Declaration of Independence says—and every California Constitution has affirmed this—then certain policy consequences follow. They are obvious for civil rights, in the principle of nondiscrimination and abolition of race-based preferences. Civil rights and all other laws must necessarily *not* violate the very foundation for the rule of law—equal natural rights. This principle establishes the principle of government by consent and hence democratic government, as Abraham Lincoln argued.

Thus, this collection eschews the approach often taken in compiling such editions—a blandness intended to give no offense, a hopeless attempt to strike balances of viewpoint, the rejection of practical lessons to be learned for citizenship and community involvement. We challenge the prevailing view of politics and political scholarship in its shrinking from the workaday world of political life. More so than *Democracy in California*, this volume exemplifies a political approach to contemporary political problems. The central argument here involves the continued relevance of the Declaration of Independence's central proposition—"all men are created equal." Though this may sound cliché, in fact it provides the basis for government by consent—that is, limited government, which is also in need of representation, broad suffrage, and the separation of powers to assure that government remains limited but also sufficient to its tasks.

If Alexis de Tocqueville was the inspiration for our earlier book, Abraham Lincoln inspires our second, for it was Lincoln who maintained that this revolutionary truth was "the father of all moral principle in them"—and by extension in us as well, even though we have no blood connection with those in that distant generation. For we are "blood of the blood and flesh of the flesh of the men who wrote the Declaration," when we grasp the truth of this principle. As Lincoln noted in his speech attacking the proslavery *Dred Scott* opinion and its defenders such as Stephen Douglas, "I had thought the Declaration promised something better than the condition of British subjects; but no, it only meant that we should be *equal* to them in their own oppressed and *unequal* condition. According to that it gave no promise that having kicked off the King and Lords of Great Britain, we should not at once be saddled with a King and Lords of our own."[1] Whereas the American Founders and Lincoln took the equality principle to justify government by consent and American institutions such as the separation of powers and federalism, the Progressives reconceptualized equality and made it the principle to transform these institutions. In science, Darwinian biology replaced "the laws of nature and of nature's God." In politics, the evolution of equality replaced the equality of rights. Thus the role of government became transformed—from the earlier one of protecting equal rights (with all the inequalities that would result) to one of guaranteeing minimum levels of security and comforts for all.

The Progressive reforms all lead in turn to the growth of virtually unchecked government power on the state level. It is increasingly more difficult for an incumbent to be voted out of office, as candidates are restricted in the financing of elections. Even if officeholders change, more decisions are deferred to nonelected bodies, whose members cannot be turned out of office directly by the voters. The South Coast Air Quality Management District (AQMD) is comprised of elected and appointed officials from different counties. The board can make decisions about policies they deem affect the environment. Yet it cannot be replaced directly by the voters, who have no procedure by which they can change policy. All they have left is the politics of protest, where demonstrating replaces deliberation and responsibility. Other seemingly neutral boards such as a Design Review Committee—nonpartisan of course—can require a house of worship to be designed in the way it designates, not the way the worshippers prefer. The length of time it takes a congregation to gather permits and meet city standards (e.g., enough parking space) can actually discourage a religious institution from being built. The rules applying to businesses and other secular activities hamper religious institutions more than profit-making endeavors. Moreover, houses of worship generate no tax revenue, so a city's budget cannot show direct benefit from the growth of churches, whereas it can readily from car dealerships. But the example of the religious institution gives one pause about the legitimacy of the requirement generally—what community standards should any property holder have to meet in order to engage in business? Progressive institutions operate away from the public eye and attempt to appear nonpolitical so as not to draw attention. Thus they seek to distinguish between administration (or good government) and politics (partisanship).

To return to a more explicitly political context for Progressive themes today, let us consider three current issues of California politics—the campaign to recall Governor Gray Davis, the continuing struggle to find a just immigration policy, and tax issues. These issues are linked to the Progressive policy of bypassing elected representatives and officials and going directly to the people—even to repudiate the results of a recent election. While it is tempting to think that the solution to the problems of democracy is more democracy, such a reaction suppresses the main problem of republican government—the application of reason to the passions. As founding father James Madison maintained in *The Federalist*:

"it is the reason, alone, of the public that ought to control and regulate the government. The passions ought to be controlled and regulated by the government."[2] The issue here is how the "reason of the public" can be made to prevail. One cringes at the assault on the passions that initiative and referendum campaigns can generate. Yet one should not cease our deliberation here. One should also consider that the enervated legislature is also a fruit of Progressivism. If they were willing to take on controversial issues in the first place and face the electorate for their judgment, there would be no need for the direct democracy. It might well be the case that the initiative and referendum have become Madisonian "inventions of prudence" in restricting the excesses of the administrative state.[3]

With these issues in mind, consider the keywords from the passion-driven arguments over immigration—open borders and walls; exploitation and amnesty; freedom-seekers and illegals, economic benefit and national security. Yet, despite these formidable rhetorical obstacles to an immigration policy, the rage today can scarcely be compared with what greeted Chinese and other Asian immigrants in the nineteenth century. Lynch mobs competed with anti-Chinese legislation and constitutional provisions.[4] Consider the voters' passage of Proposition 187, in November 1994 by a 59 to 41 percent margin. The constitutional amendment would have barred state benefits (such as public education and health care) to undocumented immigrants and their children. However, a federal court declared it unconstitutional and Governor Gray Davis did not appeal the decision. Davis had initially split the differences on benefits to undocumented immigrants, vetoing a bill to permit them to obtain driver's licenses but supporting in-state tuition rates for undocumented college students. In the throes of the recall campaign, however, Davis retreated and gave his support to driver's licenses for undocumented immigrants. Yet it seems that Proposition 187, or a variant thereof, would pass again today. The fear of taking principled action keeps the issues alive. Marginal policies in the area of immigraton, of whatever merit, are not decisive. Obviously, immigration is ultimately a federal policy and California voters should not be accused of racism or xenophobia; rather, they are insisting that the federal government take decisive action, a course they continue to spurn. The costs of national indecision should not be borne by state governments. The nature of American citizenship is the watershed question that looms in the background and the crabbed policies of the national administrative state cannot deal with such issues of high principle except by smothering them and preventing serious consideration of them.

As California's budget deficit soars (as high as $35 billion, depending on the estimate one believes), desperate legislators look for ways out—issuing bonds that serve as loans, devolving more taxes on local governments, cutting various programs, and so on. A favorite object of blame is the fabled Proposition 13, passed in June 1978, by a 65 to 35 percent margin, following skyrocketing property taxes that caused some homeowners to lose their property. The constitutional amendment reduced current property tax rates on homes, businesses, and farms by over 50 percent. Property tax rates could not exceed 1 percent of the property's assessed value and increases were capped. All state tax rate increases had to be approved by a two-thirds vote of the legislature and local tax rates also required two-thirds voter approval. This sparked a nationwide tax revolt that resulted in similar measures throughout the country.

Thus, Proposition 13 limited the ability of local governments to raise money through *property* taxes. One political effect was to force them to raise money through *sales* taxes and to cede more political power to the state government in Sacramento, which would kick as many tax dollars back to local governments as it felt like sharing. Local governments could raise money through sales taxes not merely by increasing the tax rate, but by encouraging the location of tax-generating businesses in a city or county. (This in turn had perverse effects—churches, apartment buildings, and small shops did not generate as much tax revenue as "big-box" retailers such as Costco and Walmart, and automobile dealerships. Localities competed with each other to attract such businesses.)

Twenty-five years later, some Californians blame Proposition 13 for undermining social services, local government autonomy, and citizen confidence in their local institutions. Others have even attributed a rise in crime and collapsed freeways to Proposition 13. Yet, while legislators have attempted ways around it, few have called for its repeal, for fear that the revenue would be raised in ways even more onerous. Moreover, legislators increased government spending in other ways, actually creating today's budget crisis. Politically, what this means is that Governor Davis and the overwhelmingly Democratic Assembly and Senate must choose the cuts (while appeasing their constituents with spending increases in various services). They would obviously suffer electoral consequences for their actions. As Thomas Krannawitter of the Claremont Institute has noted, the constitutional requirement that a two-thirds majority in both legislative houses pass the budget virtually ensures a bipartisan budget or one that appears bipartisan. This is a Progressive measure that makes it difficult to attribute partisan blame for an improperly drafted budget. The ability to blame a party is essential for responsible government. This in turn has led to the current democratic crisis of recall.

However, within a few months of the reelection of Governor Davis, some Republicans and independents sought to recall him, for hiding the extent of the deficit during his campaign (Article II, sections 13–19). Davis has record low popularity ratings in the polls. While many Republicans would love to replace Davis, and many Democrats would be gleeful at his fall, it is unclear what either party would gain from his replacement. Republicans would be accused of playing politics at a time of fiscal crisis; Democrats would be left with divisions that would lose them the governorship. Republicans might be better off focusing on electing a Republican senator in 2004 and forcing total responsibility for the cuts and tax increases on the Democrats. Democrats might want to rally around Davis and demand concessions from him in return, possibly by conceding more to the more radical wing of the party on moral issues such as capital punishment and gay rights. But could not the size of the deficit have been better understood during the campaign? Were the figures and calculations that arcane? In other words, one wonders whether the administrators of the administrative state, the ultimate fruit of Progressivism, are responsible for hiding the figures. Are they truly to blame for the recall? One element of Progressivism calls forth another, until we have no way back to constitutional government.

These three examples of contemporary political strife in the year 2003 illustrate how deeply Progressivism affects our politics. The essays here explore numerous other consequences of Progressivism. Moreover, we have gone outside the conventional understanding of political issues to present arguments about the Hollywood Western, farming, and California political and constitutional history. Besides political scientists, our contributors include historians, journalists, and political activists.

The first group of essays explores the relationship between the statehood of California and the federal system in which it exists. Constitutional historian Herman Belz uncovers the political theory of the South and its need to object to the admission of California as a free state, in the Compromise of 1850. Political theorist Gordon Lloyd then examines the premises of the 1849 and 1879 Constitutions and uncovers disquieting changes in the latter. Constitutional scholar Ralph Rossum explores the unappreciated effect of the direct election of U.S. Senators through the Seventeenth Amendment on federalism, especially the roots of this amendment as pursued by the kind of Progressivism that thrived in California. Another constitutional scholar, Edward Erler, then offers the provocative idea that the best weapons against Progressivism may indeed be the tools of Progressivism itself: initiatives, referenda, and recalls.

The second group of essays examines the current condition of our major political institutions. Legendary California newspaper columnist Dan Walters offers his reflections on what ails the state's "professional" legislature. Claremont Institute president Brian Kennedy examines the gubernatorial style of Gray

Davis in light of the founding father of California Progressivism, Hiram John-son. Civil rights attorney and former journalist Harold Johnson renders judg-ment on the current California court system. Political scientist and media analyst Richard Reeb wraps up the second section with an update on the 2002 elections.

Contained in the third group of essays are observations on local government in the Golden State. Political scientist Brian Janiskee explores the decline of local government, what for Tocqueville was the school of democracy. Policy analyst and local finance expert Steven Frates establishes the extent to which local gov-ernments are at the financial mercy of the state government. Policy advocate Jon Coupal of the Howard Jarvis Taxpayers Association demonstrates the deep connection between direct democracy and the tax revolt.

The fourth section is taken with an assessment of what are arguably the three most well-known California politicians. Political scientist Scot Zentner offers an account of Hiram Johnson as both a refounder of sorts in California and a national figure in the Progressive movement. Political Scientist Jack Pitney offers a look at the career of Richard Nixon as a bellwether of California's influence on the national political scene. Policy analyst and Reagan biographer Steven Hayward challenges us to appreciate the truly seismic effect of California Gover-nor Ronald Reagan's appearance on the national political stage.

The fifth section of this collection—focused on policy analysis and perspec-tives on current controversies—is in many ways the most dynamic. Modern civil rights pioneer and UC Regent Ward Connerly allows us a glimpse into the early stages of the Proposition 209 movement, an event for which it is still difficult to overestimate the magnitude. With respect to the impact of film on political culture, Political scientist John Marini examines the political teaching of the Hollywood Western. Classical scholar, influential columnist, and fifth-generation farmer Victor Davis Hanson details the deep connection between agriculture and democracy and, in so doing, offers a stark warning for our politi-cal future. Political scientist Larry Peterman provides a case study that convinc-ingly demonstrates the centrality of interest group struggle in current California education policy. Political scientist Daniel Palm assesses the extent to which Cal-ifornians still enjoy, to any meaningful degree, the right to bear arms. Richard Reeb, who analyzed the 2002 elections in this same volume, presents a second essay, the subject of which is a critical analysis of the state's political journalism. Policy analyst Stephen Schwartz gives an account of the lasting effects of Califor-nia's utopian antipoverty campaigns, especially Upton Sinclair's EPIC proposal. Political scientist Ric Williams examines the political toll of California's ubiqui-tous battles over water.

In the five sections our themes range from founding principles to institutions, from local government to statesmanship, and from elections to policy analysis. By daring to use a variety of approaches, we hope the reader will find these essays notable introductions to their particular subject and provocations to explore further the idea of the California Republic and in doing so come to a greater understanding of the polity of the nation's largest state and a deeper appreciation of the nature of republican government.

NOTES

1. Abraham Lincoln, *Collected Works of Abraham Lincoln*, ed. Roy P. Basler, vol. 2 (New Brunswick, N.J.: Rutgers University Press, 1953), 407.

2. James Madison, *Federalist* 49, introduction and notes by Charles R. Kesler, ed. Clinton Rossiter (New York, Mentor, 1999 [1961]), 285.

3. See Edward J. Erler, "Californians and Their Constitution: Progressivism, Direct Democracy, and the Administrative State," in this volume.

4. See Brian P. Janiskee and Ken Masugi, *Democracy in California*, for a brief survey of these issues (Lanham, Md.: Rowman & Littlefield, 2002), 8–9.

I

CALIFORNIA IN A FEDERAL SYSTEM

Popular Sovereignty, the Right of Revolution, and California Statehood

Herman Belz

The history of California statehood in the 1840s illustrates the reciprocal relationship that exists between liberty and union as ends of American constitutionalism under the social contract theory of government. In the era of the American Revolution, the philosophy of social contract provided a language of mutual obligation between citizens and states in the American Union that obviated the traditional doctrine of government sovereignty.[1] After 1789, the conduct of federal-system politics produced rival free labor- and slave labor-based conceptions of popular self-government, which, by 1840, assumed the form of a sectional contest for control of the federal government. The Southern version of social contract and political community formed the basis of slaveholder opposition to the formation of the State of California under an antislavery constitution. When California was admitted into the Union in 1850, in the face of proslavery threats to secede from the Union, the Southern version of social contract theory was shown to be heretical and marked for extinction. California spoke for the nation in affirming liberty and union as the true meaning of the Constitution, informed by the principles of the Declaration of Independence.

Abraham Lincoln's statement on the right of revolution, presented in a speech on the Mexican War in the House of Representatives in January 1848, guides this analysis of California statehood.[2] Examining the boundary dispute that was the ostensible cause of the war with Mexico, Lincoln said that the extent of Texas jurisdiction, and hence of American national territory, depended on revolution. Although it was not pertinent to his purpose of attacking President James K. Polk, Lincoln explained the nature of the right of revolution. "Any people anywhere," he said, "being inclined and having the power, have the *right* to rise up,

3

and shake off the existing government, and form a new one that suits them better. This is a most valuable—a most sacred right—a right, which we hope and believe, is to liberate the world."[3] Lincoln also considered the conditions in which the right of revolution might be exercised. "Nor is this right confined to cases in which the whole people of an existing government, may choose to exercise it. Any portion of such people that *can*, *may* revolutionize, and make their *own*, of so much territory as they inhabit."[4]

More than in Texas, which had revolted against Mexico in 1836, the right of revolution in 1848 was directly pertinent to the attempt by the people of California to form a government for themselves. This fact, and the general significance of California statehood from the standpoint of the social contract philosophy of government, have not been properly understood.[5]

The specific issue that triggered the sectional conflict leading to the Compromise of 1850 concerned the legitimacy of the political community organized by the people of California in the late 1840s. A significant, if not the dominant, historical interpretation of California statehood has generally focused on whether it was a genuinely democratic movement, based on a justifiable exercise of the right of revolution under the principles of the Declaration of Independence. Some writers deny the democratic legitimacy of the statehood movement, viewing it as a project of American Imperialism that imposed a government on a foreign people in disregard of the wishes of the majority of Californians.[6] This view receives support from the historiographical tradition deriving from Josiah Royce and Hubert Howe Bancroft. It depicts the Bear Flag Revolt of 1846—the first clear signal of popular demand for American home rule—as a foolish and fraudulent, if colorful and entertaining, political farce. Sarcastic criticism of the Bear Flag Men tends to corroborate the contemporary judgment of Southerners, that the people of California were not a legitimate people capable of governing themselves.

In contrast to this view, it is the argument of this essay that the statehood movement initiated by the Sonoma Rebels had a *better* grasp of the real meaning of popular self-government than the national policy makers who started the Mexican War, occupied California after the conquest, and imposed military government on the territory. More reliable than the interpretation of the sarcastic school, is the view of Robert Glass Cleland: that without the Mexican War the Bear Flag Revolt would have brought California into the Union.[7]

BEAR FLAGGERS

That California was eligible country in which to exercise the right of revolution is implicit in the observation of New England captain William Shaler in 1804:

"It would be as easy to keep California in spite of the Spaniards, as it would be to win it from them in the first place."[8] Settled in 1769, California was transferred from Spanish imperial to Mexican republican rule in the revolution of 1824. Scholarly opinion concurs that the change was nominal, and that government in the remote province remained that of "petty military despotism."[9] Mexican sovereignty was practically nonexistent. The existing government was indistinguishable from chronic disorder and revolutions, where one set of rulers frequently replaced another. According to historian Frederick Merk, "[t]o the outside world California seemed a derelict on the Pacific . . . considered likely to be towed soon into an American port."[10]

Employing the concepts in a relational normative sense in respect of legal conditions, the inhabitants of California can be thought of as being in a state of nature toward each other, or in a state of war in relation to the Mexican California government.[11] In either view, a growing feeling of independence, based on the indifference (or hostility) of the Mexican government to their interests, was a reasonable response of many native Californians, and most of the American immigrant population that entered the country in the 1840s.

The election of expansionist-minded, proslavery Democrat James K. Polk as president in 1844 brought California into American foreign policy planning. The annexation of Texas having been secured by the pro-Southern Tyler administration in 1845, the Polk administration made acquisition of California and New Mexico its top foreign policy objective.

The Polk administration intended to obtain California by one of three means. In descending order of preference, the methods to be used were: treaty purchase, popular revolt against the Mexican government—leading to annexation on the Texas model—or military conquest. When one considers the relevant demographics—a Mexican California population of seven thousand inured to an authoritarian political culture comprising only one thousand adult males, of whom one hundred were literate—the option of waiting for an indigenous independence movement to develop seems far-fetched. This perception is not contradicted by the opinion of idealistic philosopher-historian Josiah Royce, that "California would have been ready to drop into our basket like a mellow apple" in a year or less if the Mexican War had been avoided.[12] Polk's problem was that the proslavery expansionist bias of his party discouraged—if it did not render impossible—the democratic statesmanship required to support a genuine exercise of the right of revolution in California—either by native Californians or (as proved to be the case) by American settlers who entered the province in large numbers in the 1840s.

In the spring of 1846, the Polk administration, frustrated in its diplomatic maneuvers, tried to decide how to start a war with Mexico. It was at this time, June 1846, with U.S. Army explorer and potential military adventurer Captain John C. Frémont in California, that a small band of American settlers organized the military resistance known as the Bear Flag Revolt. With the exception of Robert Glass Cleland, the academy has generally regarded the Bear Flag Men with more ridicule than admiration. What perplexes scholars is that the Bear Flag rebels took the principles of the Declaration of Independence and the social contract philosophy of government so *seriously!* Their doing so is treated as a kind of pretentious impertinence, deserving of condemnation, but for its manifest folly. Bancroft, for example, judges the political rhetoric of William B. Ide, author of the proclamation declaring the existence of the California Republic, to be below that of the Mexican California leaders Castro and Pico in truthfulness, and midway between them in bombast and absurdity.[13] William Henry Ellison, a twentieth-century historian, says the citizens of the United States who initially attempted to impose their institutions on California "were not greatly concerned with protecting the inalienable rights of life, liberty, and the pursuit of happiness by instituting a government deriving its consent from the consent of the governed." The Sonoma settlers' ideas of democracy "were as yet not developed sufficiently to make them feel obligated to respect the wishes of the majority, the Californians."[14]

Against the tradition of sarcastic criticism, it seems more accurate to say that the instincts of the Bear Flag rebels were good. Their involvement with American Army officer and explorer John C. Frémont was expedient and reasonable, and their grasp of social contract theory and the right of revolution sound. Considered in historical context, Ide's famous proclamation cannot be dismissed as mere rhetorical boilerplate.

Justification for the uprising lay in the fact that settlers had been invited to California by the promises of land and a republican government. Subsequently denied the right to buy or rent land, and feeling oppressed by military despotism, they believed themselves threatened with expulsion by the California government. The purpose of the revolt at Sonoma, according to Ide's proclamation, was to establish a republican government for the promotion of agriculture, commerce, and the mechanical arts, and for the encouragement of virtue and literature. Ide appealed to the bravery of men bound together by principles of self-preservation, love of truth, and hatred of tyranny, urging all persons and citizens of Sonoma to join in making a republican government. When asked by his compatriots to explain by what authority they had occupied General Vallejo's ranch, Ide declared: "We are robbers, or we must be conquerors!"[15] Like Tom Paine advising Americans that a declaration of independence would resolve the paradox of professing loyalty to the crown while engaging in revolutionary resistance, Ide recognized that a proclamation of independence was needed to justify revolutionary action. In an otherwise acerbic account, Bancroft seems to concur, when he observes that the dignity of the revolt and proclamation of the Bear Flag Men consisted in their willingness to fight as well as to talk.[16]

Criticized for their false description of Mexican California policies and for attempting, without justification, to overthrow a foreign government, the Bear Flaggers have been held to a high standard of probity. Their legacy is viewed as one of cultural resentment against Mexican-Californians. This criticism assumes that an effective and legitimate California government existed under Mexican rule. However, revolution was justified under social contract theory, because the condition of the country was that of a state of nature, or state of war.

Southern politicians were so offended by what they saw as the ultimate outcome of the demand for self-government which the Bear Flag Revolt raised, that they would destroy the Union rather than see it augmented by a free state constitution. To understand the nature of the slaveholders' opposition, it is necessary to consider how the statehood movement developed as a form of resistance to the military government imposed on California by the Polk administration after the conquest.

MILITARY GOVERNMENT IN CALIFORNIA

If the purpose of the Mexican War was to expand the area of the national domain that was dedicated to slavery, it would have been illogical for the Polk administration to permit a free-soil constitution to be adopted in the territory that was the principal object of foreign expansion. Yet, remarkably, this is what happened after the conquest of California. This outcome was not ordained by nature; it requires explanation in historical terms. Part of the answer, undoubtedly, lies in the fact that, after the annexation of Texas, the Democratic Party assumed that, under the rules of American politics, serious opposition to slavery was a practical impossibility. Most important in protecting slavery against political attack was the practice of maintaining equilibrium between the slave and free states in the U.S. Senate. Although priding itself on its appeal to the sovereignty of the people, the Democratic Party lacked the political imagination to conceive of a popular free-soil movement emerging anywhere—especially in remote California—to challenge the slave power's invincibility.

But slavery was a distracting afterthought in California statehood politics. The movement for self-government was not conceived as an anti-Southern project. In demanding a social compact government based on consent, American settlers in California put individual liberty and property rights first, placing them in categorical opposition to all forms of dependency and unfreedom. While this caused the movement to be antislavery by definition, in the mid-1840s it meant more specifically that Americans instinctively resisted the military government imposed by the Polk administration.

The occupation government that existed from 1846 to 1850 has been made out to be a more complex phenomenon than it actually was. Confusion is said to have existed concerning whether the government was military or civil in nature.[17] A succession of commanders—Sloat, Stockton, Kearny, Frémont, Mason, Riley—spoke of creating a temporary civil government for the protection of life, liberty, and property, under forms allowing a degree of popular participation. They issued proclamations declaring civil government to be in existence, and assumed the title of civil governor. This was a conceit or a charade; unquestionably the government of occupation was military in nature. It was based on the laws of war under the law of nations, which was applied to conquered Mexican provinces by the executive authority of the president acting as commander-in-chief.[18] Military force, not consent based on popular representation, was the means by which the government of occupation ruled the inhabitants of California.

Under these circumstances, the spirit of resistance expressed in the uprising at Sonoma was revived. The philosophical cause of California statehood was the idea of introducing "home rule" based on American settlers' concept of "natural law."[19] Under social contract theory, as in the untutored way the people of California seem to have considered the matter, it was a category error for a military commander to simultaneously claim authority as a civil governor. Americans in California acted as though instructed in the Lockean doctrine that any government not civil in nature was ipso facto in a state of war with its people.[20]

To appreciate Americans's objections to military government, it is helpful to examine the Polk administration's attempts to justify postconquest imperial rule. Statements of executive branch officials expressed the relationship that existed in the Southern mind between national sovereignty and the slave power—indeed, the slaveholders' reliance on the federal government—notwithstanding rhetorical appeals to state sovereignty, or popular sovereignty, depending on circumstance.

In his annual message to Congress in December 1846, President Polk asserted that under the law of nations, military conquest ended the Mexican civil government in California, conferring on the U.S. government the right and duty to provide for the maintenance of civil order and the rights of the inhabitants. Military and naval commanders were said to be in the process of "assimilating" con quered provinces "as far as practicable to the free institutions of our own country."[21] A year later, the conquest of California and New Mexico having been completed, President Polk recommended that Congress extend the civil jurisdiction and laws of the United States, and establish territorial governments over the former Mexican lands for the protection of person and property. Renewing his recommendation after conclusion of the peace treaty with Mexico, in July 1848 the president acknowledged the controversy over extending slavery into the territories, which had been ignited by the Wilmot Proviso. Warning against geographical divisions and dissensions in organizing territorial governments, he urged Congress to invoke "that spirit of concession, conciliation, and compromise in your deliberations in which the Constitution was framed."[22]

President Polk stressed the political, rather than economic, value of the conquered territories. He noted that "[t]he value of the public lands embraced within the limits of the ceded territory, is far less important to the people of the United States than the sovereignty over the country."[23] Although most states contained no public lands owned by the United States, the sovereignty and jurisdiction over them were of incalculable importance to the nation. Yet, while Mexican sovereignty transferred to the United States upon conclusion of the peace treaty, ambiguity and uncertainty about the locus of sovereignty within American government over the conquered territories threatened to immobilize Congress at the same time that it stimulated the statehood movement in California.

In July 1848, Polk conceded that the executive branch had no constitutional ability to maintain temporary governments under military authority in California and New Mexico. With the end of the war, he said, "these temporary governments necessarily ceased to exist."[24] Authority to govern civil society by martial law could no longer be derived from the law of nations. Hoping for congressional organization of territorial governments, however, Polk took a hard line against home rule by inhabitants of California and New Mexico, who though "entitled to the benefit of our laws and Constitution" were left without any regularly organized government. In this circumstance, in a gesture of constitutional prestidigitation, Polk proposed a new source of authority in the doctrine of "presumptive" popular consent. He claimed legitimacy for the existing military government (which he admitted had legally ceased to exist) as "a de facto government" that might be continued temporarily "by the presumed consent of the inhabitants." He therefore "advised" the people of California "to conform and submit" to the de facto government until Congress could legislate a territorial government for them.[25]

Secretary of State James Buchanan provided a more extensive justification of the doctrine of de facto legality. In October 1848, Buchanan, in an official communication, said that the military government left in existence at the end of the war would continue in full operation "with the presumed consent of the people."[26] "The great law of necessity" justified this conclusion, according to Buchanan. "The consent of the people is irresistibly inferred from the fact that no civilized community could possibly desire to abrogate an existing government, when the alternative would be to place themselves in a state of anarchy, beyond the protection of all laws, and reduce them to the unhappy necessity of submitting to the dominion of the strongest."[27] Royce's comment on this novel theory is apt: "the government of California is denied to be a discoverable actuality, is treated as a mere presumption, and is based upon the notion that California, being between the devil and the deep blue sea, must get out by the one road that providence has kindly opened: namely, the military government."[28]

The theory of de facto government advanced by the Polk administration represented a significant extension of martial law into the regulation of civil society.[29] From the standpoint of traditional limits on executive authority, there was much to criticize in this development, notwithstanding the conclusion of some historians that the people of California suffered no serious oppression or mistreatment under military rule.[30] In relation to the American political tradition, the relevant fact was "the natural odium felt against military authority by civilians."[31] This ingrained disposition produced popular agitation directed against the occupation government, and the retention of elements of Mexican law, most notably the alcalde system of local government.[32]

Accounts of the period of military government establish beyond question that, far from the creature of the federal executive establishment, as Southern opponents of California statehood charged in 1850, the movement for self-government rested on a broad basis of popular support. From the outset there was protest against military rule. The first newspaper in California argued for the convening of a constitutional convention, election of a legislature, and establishment of a provisional government with a view toward sending a delegate to Congress.[33] After the California phase of the war ended in February 1847, friction increased between the people and a succession of military and naval commanders who, unable to communicate readily with their superiors in Washington, D.C., were operating substantially on their own. Facing civil unrest and army desertions in November 1848, the American naval and military commanders agreed to recommend election of delegates to form a provisional constitution and government if Congress failed to create a territorial government for California.[34]

News of Congress's inaction on the matter of territorial government, coinciding with the administration's advice to submit to the de facto government under the doctrine of presumptive popular consent, provoked the home rule movement into action. Throughout 1848, legislative councils and assemblies for the maintenance of civil order were spontaneously organized in the mining district, and in some towns. Additional local councils were formed and a number of mass meetings held in December 1848 and January 1849 demanding a constitutional convention and the establishment of a provisional government. The legislative assembly of San Francisco played a prominent role in the popular resistance. Abolishing the widely resented alcalde's office, the assembly declared the people's intention to withhold the presumed consent that military officials claimed in support of the de facto government.[35]

The provisional government movement justified its action under the theory of social contract and the right of revolution. Peter H. Burnett, the leading theorist of popular self-government, picked up, as it were, where William B. Ide and the Bear Flag rebels left off in 1846, when the Sonoma Uprising was overtaken by the events of the Mexican War.

Burnett was a lawyer, jurist, and politician recently arrived from Oregon, where he was active in forming a compact-based provisional government, the validity of which was confirmed by Congress in the Oregon Territorial Act of August 1848. As the basis of the home rule movement, Burnett asserted the fundamental principle of the Declaration of Independence that governments derive their just powers from the consent of the governed. The people of California had "the right to exercise the power inherent in human nature . . . to institute government for the protection of life, liberty, and the right of property." Insisting that this question was beyond the jurisdiction of the president to decide, Burnett rejected the administration's doctrine of presumed popular consent to the de facto military government, contrary to the manifest will of the people. Declaring that the president could not "presume away the liberties of the people," Burnett argued that if the people had no power to dissent, they had no power to give their consent. They were and must be a free people, not passive instruments to be used by the government.[36]

In May 1849, the home rule movement declared for the first time that its purpose was to form a provisional state, rather than a territorial government.[37] Affirmation of this constitutional objective was in part a response to congressional paralysis blocking the organization of territorial governments for California and New Mexico. Congress saw fit, however, to enact legislation extending the revenue laws to California, designating San Francisco as a port of entry, and authorizing the appointment of customs collectors.[38] In an address to the people of California adopted by the San Francisco legislative council, Burnett attacked the congressional policy. "For the first time in the history of the 'model Republic' and perhaps in any civilized government in the world," he declared, "the Congress of the United States, representing a great nation of more than twenty millions of freemen, have assumed the right, not only to *tax us without representation*, but to *tax us without giving us any government at all*."[39] Not only did the people have a right to form their own government, Burnett asserted, but in writing a state constitution they must also settle the slavery question that Congress seemed incapable of resolving.

Bereft of political, ideological, and material resources, U.S. military officials in California acceded to the statehood movement. Realizing the people were in a rebellious mood, newly appointed commander general Bennet Riley issued a proclamation in June 1849, calling for the election of officers to fill government vacancies, and delegates to a constitutional convention. Still refusing to recognize the authority of the people to form a government, and warning against the evils of "illegal local legislation," Riley cited Mexican-California law as a basis for his action.[40] Although questioning Riley's authority, popular-sovereignty-minded settlers accepted the military governor's election timetable as expedient for their purposes.

The Constitutional Convention met in Monterey in September, 1849. Forty-eight delegates were elected, including twenty-three from northern states, fifteen from southern, and eight native Californians. With respect to the congressional debate over California statehood in 1850, the most significant feature of the Constitution was its prohibition of slavery.[41]

Discussion of the slavery question in the Constitutional Convention seems to have had an abstract quality. Notwithstanding the sectional division in the delegates' political background, no debate over slavery occurred. Nevertheless, slavery was on everyone's mind; it had to be taken into account because of Congressional preoccupation with the subject of territorial slavery. The question of motive and purpose on an issue that threatened to divide the nation cannot be avoided. It is pertinent to ask whether adoption of the free soil principle in the California Convention was a matter of choice or of necessity. Did circumstances of geography, climate, culture, and history—including the strange good fortune of discovering gold at the very moment when the country passed from Mexican to American rule—make the prohibition of slavery an inevitable and foregone conclusion? Or was there a real possibility that slave property could have been introduced into California, in which case adoption of the free soil principle was a matter of moral and political choice? The question is relevant because a free soil constitution based on necessity and inevitability could be seen as nothing more than an attempt to avoid insulting Southern sensibilities, rather than a deliberate moral choice of freedom over slavery.

Slavery did not exist in California; it had been abolished in Mexico in 1829. To become part of California society, it would have to be imported from outside. In an attempt to defuse sectional hostility an argument was made at the time that natural conditions prohibited slave labor from being introduced into territories acquired from Mexico.[42] Against this speculation there is considerable evidence of Southern interest in extending slavery into California and New Mexico under the protection of a Congressionally organized territorial government. Southerners recognized that, historically, slave labor was suitable to mining operations. There were suggestions in the Southern press of plans by armed Southern companies to take their slaves to California. One proposed method of settlement was for slave owners to emancipate their slaves in their state of domicile, sign them to indentured labor contracts, and then transport them to California. Bancroft states that in 1849–1850 many blacks were brought in to work in the mines, were subsequently made free, and maintained their freedom by asserting their rights.[43] Southern interest in California focused not only on the moral offense to Southern values that exclusion from the territories signified, but also on strategic requirements of political and economic expansion to maintain parity with the North.[44]

Cardinal Goodwin tells a fascinating story about a company of Texan slaveholders who unsuccessfully tried to move into the mining district. The incident offers a microcosm of the confrontation between free soil and proslavery conceptions of popular sovereignty that dominated the debate over California's admission in 1850. In the mining area, a system of self-government was created in which miners made rules prescribing district boundaries, and elected governing personnel to record the measurements of settlers' claims. The recorders of claims were authorized to settle disputes over claims, with a provision for appeal to the miners. In July 1849, a company of Texan slaveholders led by Colonel Thomas Jefferson Green entered the district with fifteen Negro slaves. Disregarding the rules for regulating claims, they occupied land and entered claims for themselves and their slaves. The miners objected that this action violated both local rules and federal law, which restricted occupation of public lands to U.S. citizens. Refusing to comply, the Texans threatened to resist by force, whereupon the miners voted to expel the "invaders," and resolved that no slaves or Negroes should own claims, or even work in the mines. The Texans left and their slaves disappeared.[45]

Although it was known that Convention delegates from Southern states wanted to introduce slavery into California, under the circumstances they decided not to object to the Constitutional provision prohibiting slavery. Rather, Southerners anticipated a proslavery strategy in the future, either by extending the eastern boundary to make an extremely large state that could be divided into one or more slave states, or by dividing the state as it then existed, if south California should prove adaptable to slave labor. The free soil interest being dominant, it was feared that a fight over slavery in the convention would harm the chances of Congress granting statehood. Far from a policy determined by preexisting conditions, adoption of the free soil principle expressed both a moral choice of liberty for the sake of Union, and prudent recognition of the need for political unity in the home rule movement.[46]

Of course, where slavery was an issue, the race question was also implicated. Since it was a matter of secondary importance, race relations could be debated. In California, as in other states where the free soil principle was upheld, opposition to slavery rested in part on self-interested motives that do not appear "idealistic" and "humanitarian" to twentieth-century scholars.[47] Most miners who did not want Negro slaves living in the state also did not want free Negroes. In the Constitutional Convention a proposal to exclude free blacks received support, but was rejected because it raised federal constitutional questions about the rights of citizens under the Privileges and Immunities Clause of the Constitution. The racial attitude described by the American alcalde Walter Colton, expressed in the observation that "free white diggers won't dig with slaves," confirms the perception that the fundamental issue was the conflict between conceptions of social contract philosophy based on freedom and slavery.[48] This became apparent in the controversy over the meaning of popular sovereignty that California statehood ignited in Congress.

POPULAR SOVEREIGNTY

Analysis of the debate over self-government in California requires a definition of popular sovereignty, as contemporaries understood it. This would be derived from the American political tradition, and be broad enough to comprehend the sectional points of view that shaped the Compromise of 1850. Abraham Lincoln provided such a definition at the time of the Lincoln-Douglas debates.

"What does Popular Sovereignty mean?" asked Lincoln. "Strictly and literally it means the sovereignty of the people over their own affairs—in other words the right of the people of every nation and community to govern themselves."[49] Lincoln said the idea of popular sovereignty was "floating around the world" for several centuries before it "took tangible form" in the words of the Declaration of Independence:

> We hold these truths to be self-evident: That all men are created equal; That they are endowed by their Creator with certain inalienable rights; That among these are life, liberty, and the pursuit of happiness; That to secure these rights governments are instituted among men, *deriving their just powers from the consent of the governed*. . . . If that is not Popular Sovereignty, then I have no conception of the meaning of words.[50]

Popular sovereignty was the right of self-government—the principle that each man, and every community of men, should do precisely as they please with all which is exclusively their own.[51] This definition was consistent with the view stated by Senator Lewis Cass, Democrat of Michigan, in the debate over California statehood. Cass said popular sovereignty was the right of internal legislation in a community, referred to in the Declaration of Independence as a power belonging to the people at large for their exercise, and incapable of annihilation.[52]

The debate over popular sovereignty in relation to California statehood focused on two basic issues. First was the procedural-formal question of the particular political community within the federal system where the right of self-government was properly exercised. The second question concerned the substantive matters of public policy upon which the popular sovereign could act.

Four theories can be identified in contemporary debates concerning the locus of popular sovereignty in the American Union. One theory posited popular sovereignty exclusively at the state level, in the people as constituent power of the state governments.[53] A second view placed popular sovereignty in the people of the United States, considered as a national political community represented in and acting through the federal government.[54] A third concept held that popular sovereignty resided in the people of the United States as the constituent power of both the federal *and* state governments under a system of divided sovereignty.[55] Still another concept of popular sovereignty identified it with self-government by inhabitants or citizens in national territories.[56]

The second issue in the debate over Californian self-government concerned the things that, jurisdictionally speaking, belonged exclusively to the relevant popular sovereign. To contextualize, where in the constitutional order as a whole did authority over the subject of slavery reside? More specifically in the circumstances of the Mexican War, which of the possible popular sovereigns identified in contemporary constitutional theory had the authority to decide on the matter of slavery in the territories?

Prior to 1846, several rules and practices of popular sovereignty were used to deal with the slavery question, depending on circumstances. A strong rule, universally accepted, was that the sovereign people of each state had authority to decide whether slavery should be recognized or prohibited within their jurisdiction, to the exclusion of claims of other popular sovereigns. A second rule, less universally recognized, was that Congress, as representative of the national popular sovereign, had the power to prohibit slavery in national territory, as in the Northwest Ordinance of 1787 (reenacted by Congress in 1789),[57] and the Missouri Compromise Act of 1820,[58] which prohibited slavery in Louisiana Purchase Territory north of the 36–30 line of latitude. Under this rule, Congress had an implied power to legislate the existence of slavery in national territory, although it had not exercised this power. A corollary practice under this rule was for the people in southerly territories, acting as a territorial popular sovereign, to recognize slavery in the course of forming a state government, as in the organization of the states of Louisiana (1812), Mississippi (1817), Alabama (1819), Missouri (1821), Arkansas (1836), and Florida (1845).

In the Mexican War context, the Republic of Texas, a slaveholding country lying south of the Missouri Compromise line, was annexed to the United States in 1845, by a resolution of Congress which affirmed the 36–30 line and declared that states that might be formed with the consent of Texas were to be admitted into the Union with or without slavery as the people might desire.[59] In 1846 Representative David Wilmot, a Pennsylvania Democrat, introduced in Congress legislation to prohibit slavery in territories that might be acquired from Mexico, whether lying north *or* south of the 36–30 line. In 1848, Congress enacted a law organizing a territorial government and prohibiting slavery in Oregon, which confirmed the free soil principle adopted by the people of the territory in a provisional government. These measures offered precedents possibly relevant to the disposition of the California statehood question.

The proposal to admit California into the Union raised a series of interrelated questions: what *was* California—a national territory, a conquered foreign territory, a state, or an independent republic? Whatever their political and governmental form, did the people of California possess the authority to legislate on the subject of slavery? In the sense of being a matter of exclusive concern to the people of California, did the principle of popular sovereignty have just application to the slavery issue?

Executive branch policy on slavery in the Mexican cession shaped the political situation in which the California statehood question was considered. Seeking to augment the power of the slave states, Polk vacillated between extension of the Missouri line, and the Democrat Party's position of territorial popular sovereignty, as means of achieving this end.[60] In August 1848, in a futile effort to gain support for extending the Missouri line into new territory, Polk cited it as justification for approving the Oregon free soil territorial legislation. Finally, in December 1848, Polk, now a lame duck president, recommended popular sovereignty at the Constitutional Convention stage of territorial development in California and New Mexico.[61]

General Zachary Taylor, a military hero of the Mexican War, was elected as a Whig in 1848, and he reversed executive branch policy by supporting California statehood. In May 1849, with the home rule movement well under way, Taylor sent to California a former Georgia congressman, Thomas Butler King, with advice to bypass territorial government and to organize a state constitution. In January 1850, Taylor said that since congressional proposals to legislate on slavery in the territories had provoked controversy, it was his duty "to endeavor to put it in the power of Congress, by the admission of California and New Mexico as States, to remove all occasion for the unnecessary agitation of the public mind."[62] Affirming the constitutional principle that slavery in a state was a subject of concern exclusively to the people of the state, Taylor advised Congress against making admission to the Union conditional on acceptance of a provision concerning slavery contrary to the wishes of the people. To do so would be to treat the people of California, including many native citizens of the United States, as a conquered people required to submit to the will of their conquerors, rather than as a people possessing a right of self-government in a matter that peculiarly affected them. Such a measure would be regarded as "an invasion of their rights, and, upon the principles laid down in our own Declaration of Independence, they would certainly be sustained by the great mass of the American people."[63]

THE ADMISSION OF CALIFORNIA
AND THE SOUTHERN MIND

In a growing state of alarm at the peril of Wilmot Provisoism, Southerners united in bipartisan condemnation of California statehood as an unconstitutional and unjust assault on Southern rights. Southern arguments revealed the corruption of social contract theory when subordinated to the political requirements of protecting slavery. Confronted with an authentic exercise of the right of revolution and popular self-government, Southerners repudiated the principle of state popular sovereignty. Denying that the principle had any just application in California, they said the people of California were not a people in the constitutional sense required for admission into the Union as a state. Moreover, even assuming they were a people, slavery in California was not a matter of exclusive concern to the people of California.

"It can bring no soothing to me to say the act is that of the people," Mississippi Senator Jefferson Davis said of the California Constitution. Objecting that "there was no organized permanent body of persons, such as constitute a people," Davis distinguished between the organized inhabitants of a territory and the unruly mass of adventurers who acted in California.[64] Senator John M. Berrien of Georgia viewed the inhabitants of California as an unorganized body of transient persons who were incompetent to form a constitution. The majority of the people were mere adventurers digging for gold who intended to return to domiciles in the United States.[65] Senator Jeremiah Clemens of Alabama attacked "the new doctrine of squatter sovereignty . . . the right of a few individuals to seize upon the public domain and erect themselves into a sovereignty."[66]

Southerners viewed the people of California as revolutionists acting in defiance of legitimate authority. According to Davis, the people of an organized national territory could not form a state government without the consent of the United States. It was lawlessness compounded, he argued, for an unorganized band like the inhabitants of California to "set at naught the sovereignty of the United States, convert the public domain to their own use, and claim therefrom the right to be admitted into the Union."[67] "[T]his right of self-government," Berrien exclaimed, "of which we hear so much, is not a thing which a man can carry in his pocket, like a passport, or a certificate of citizenship, to be used and exercised upon any spot of earth on which he may tread." Sovereign power over the territory of the United States resided in Congress. The inhabitants of a territory possessed no right of self-government "except as it is given to them by the transfer of the sovereignty of the United States, and only to the extent that that sovereignty is transferred." Berrien concluded, since no right of self-government was conferred by act of Congress, California state makers occupied the public domain without legitimate authority.[68]

Previously, the Southerners had argued that no constitutional principle was more fundamental than the right of a state to determine the slavery question for itself. Yet when the people of California, denied a conventional territorial government through no fault of their own, in effect attempted to *exercise* this right, Southerners moved immediately to deny them membership in the Union. The slaveholder political class thus turned decisively down the road that led to the repudiation of liberty as the end of the American social compact. Scornful of constitutional distinctions as metaphysical abstractions, the slaveholders could see nothing in California statehood but Wilmot Provisoism. Describing the California admission bill as the "Executive Proviso," Senator John C. Calhoun of South Carolina denounced it as a modification of the Wilmot Proviso that was even more unconstitutional than the original. The California bill assumed that sovereignty over the territory was vested in inhabitants claiming the same inherent right of self-government as the people in the states. On the contrary, Calhoun said, sovereignty over territories was vested in the *several states* composing the Union, to be exercised through congressional legislative power that was limited by property rights guaranties. It followed that "the individuals of California who have undertaken to form a constitution and a state, and to exercise the power of legislating without the consent of Congress, have usurped the sovereignty of the state and the authority of Congress, and have acted in defiance of both of them." Calhoun concluded: "what they have done is revolutionary and rebellious in its character, anarchical in its tendency, and calculated to lead to the most dangerous consequences."[69]

Jefferson Davis asked: "What matters it to me whether Congress has declared that within certain limits of the old territory of California slavery shall be prohibited, or whether Congress shall give validity to an act of an unauthorized people within that territory, and thus exclude us from it?"[70] The result in either case was injustice and oppression—permanently imposed on the South by giving the free states a majority in the Senate that destroyed the principle of sectional equality. California's admission would transform the voluntary compact of states into "a forced Union," with the North "coercing states at the point of a bayonet." Reflecting the concern for national power below the surface of states' rights dogma, Davis said Wilmot Provisoism direct from Congress was preferable to the precedent that California statehood would set. As a practical matter it would be easier to repeal an act of Congress than a provision of a state constitution. More serious from a moral point of view, the admission of California under a free state constitution presented "the outrage of a revolutionary seizure of public domain" justified by the assertion of hostility to slavery. Wilmot Provisoism straight from Congress signified "the fraud or usurpation of an agent." Approval of California statehood was worse, because it amounted to "the seizure [of territory and political power] of another subsequently sustained and justified by the agent." It was infuriating to Southerners that the formation of a free state constitution in California should hand victory to Wilmot Proviso partisans without them lifting a finger. Confident in their ability to carry the bill "by numerical force," complained Berrien, they "sit with folded arms . . . call for the question," and do not deign to answer objections to California admission.[71]

Slaveholder resentment against California statehood was further evident in resolutions adopted by the Southern Convention meeting in Nashville in July

1850, to consider a united sectional strategy. Admission of California was seen as a form of congressional exclusion of the South from national territory, in violation of the Constitution. The mode of legislation used to promote Wilmot Provisoism was irrelevant. The Nashville convention resolved: "When therefore Congress attempts to carry out and confirm the acts of these individuals, erecting California into a state and excluding slavery therefrom, it is the same thing as if Congress had originally passed a law to this effect, without the intervention of these individuals." In the Southern view, "The constitution of California becomes the act of Congress; and the Wilmot Proviso passed and enforced by the legislation of Congress."[72]

Southerners proudly acknowledged slavery as the foundation of their conception of social contract and political society. Delegates to the Nashville Convention declared, "The *one* great difference—the greatest that can exist among a people, is the institution of slavery. This alone sets apart the Southern States as a peculiar people—with whom independence as to their internal policy, is the condition of their existence."[73] Slavery existed in the United States independent of the Constitution. It was recognized as property, as a domestic relation of service or labor under the law of a state, and "as a basis of political power."[74] Jefferson Davis said it was erroneous to regard property in slaves as local in nature and deriving its existence from municipal law alone. "Slavery existed before the formation of the Union," he said, and was given recognition in the Constitution that it would not otherwise have enjoyed. In joining the Union, nonslaveholding states placed themselves under an obligation to acknowledge a "species of property unknown to themselves." The Constitution caused slave property in the southern states to be recognized as property throughout the United States.[75]

The California admission bill, to Southern eyes, destroyed this structure of national constitutional protection for slavery. Senator Thomas G. Pratt of Maryland said the bill made "an odious discrimination . . . against the property of the fifteen slaveholding States of the Union, who are thus deprived of that position of equality which the Constitution so manifestly designs."[76] Virginia Senator R. M. T. Hunter insisted that "It is the constitutional right of the South either to have social possession of all the territory, or an equal division of it between the slaveholding and the nonslaveholding States. Either would satisfy the South."[77] Berrien of Georgia summarized the southern position in stating that submission to the California bill was "degrading to a freeman."[78]

The situation warranted extreme action. While the hope of a Congressional adjustment prevented the Southern Convention from discussing specific methods "for a resistance to measures . . . which might involve a dishonor to the Southern States,"[79] delegates observed that the California bill enforced the exclusion from national territory by act of Congress that almost every southern state said she would not submit to. The convention address admonished: "A sovereign State will disdain to inquire in what manner she is stripped of her property, and degraded from an equality with her sister States." American slavery would be destroyed if the South came "under the dominion of the restless people of the Northern States." The slave states "must rule themselves or perish," the convention declared.[80]

As never before in a practical sense, Southerners could see the political and moral-philosophical relationship between state popular sovereignty and a "national democracy," governed by a constitutional majority under the principles of the Declaration of Independence, to which free soil opinion appealed.[81] Secure in their dependence on slavery, Southerners unhesitatingly rejected the national libertarian conception of popular self-government. Confident of the moral and constitutional ground on which their claim to sovereignty rested, they began to seriously plan a revolutionary secession as an alternative to remaining in the Union.

Social contract theory in general, and the Declaration of Independence in particular, posited the right of the people to alter or abolish any government when it became destructive of the end for which it was instituted—the protection of individual rights. Starting with the Kentucky and Virginia Resolutions of 1798, Northern and Southern states claimed a right of state interposition as a means of resisting unjust, abusive, and unconstitutional measures by the federal government. In the South Carolina nullification crisis of 1832, John C. Calhoun tried to upgrade and transform state interposition from a revolutionary into a constitutional right, conferring legal immunity on disunionist political action. Yet Calhoun's project of constitutional construction was less successful than he hoped. The controversy over California statehood showed that, despite the persistence of disunionist rhetoric and federal-state controversies, secession was not accepted as a legitimate constitutional claim. Opponents of secession, like critics of all forms of state interposition since 1798, viewed it as lawless rebellion. Southerners threatening to break up the Union reflected awareness of the revolutionary nature of secession as a form of state protest.

From the Southern point of view, revolution was in the air with the introduction of the Wilmot Proviso. Contemplating a remedy for the proviso, Calhoun warned in 1847 that, should excluding the South from the territories destroy the balance between the sections, it would bring "political revolution, anarchy, civil war, and widespread disaster."[82] In the debate over California admission, many Southerners viewed secession through the prism of revolution. While disavowing any intent of violence or disunion, Jefferson Davis appealed to the example of the country's revolutionary patriots in warning that Southerners were loyal not merely to the form of Union, but to the spirit of constitutional equality that held the states together.[83] Predicting that admission of California would "result in the disturbance of the public peace," Berrien of Georgia said the South was not interested in nullification, as some charged, but secession. Berrien was indifferent about whether secession was to be considered a right resulting from the nature of the federal compact, "or must be considered as revolutionary in its nature—the ultima ratio of an oppressed people; whether it result from the provisions of the Constitution, or belong to the principles of self-government." Whatever it was, Berrien asserted, whenever a number of states resolved to perform the act, "whether revolution, or constitutional and peaceful retirement from the Union," the Union would be at an end.[84] Clemens of Alabama said: "I do not know what Alabama may do . . . [w]henever she commands I will obey. If she determines to resist this [California admission] law by force, by secession, by any means, I am at her service . . . [i]f this be treason, I am a traitor—a traitor who glories in the name."[85]

To the Southern mind, the admission of California was an oppressive act justifying disunionist revolutionary violence—or the threat of revolutionary violence—for the protection of slavery-based communities. Clemens issued a warning to Unionists: "If any State should secede, let him if he dare attempt to employ military force to compel her return." A seceding state would be supported by sister states, and the powers and resources of the federal government would be wholly inadequate in attempting to keep them in the Union against their will. Clemens was confident that "the denial of State sovereignty, either North or South, can bring to the executive nothing but contempt." While conceding he might be a traitor to the Union, Clemens gave notice that accusing political opponents of treason was a game that states could play too.[86]

BREAKING THE EQUILIBRIUM

The California question challenged lawmakers' epistemological and perceptual powers on two basic issues. Did a state exist in California, and did the attempt of the people of California to assume the identity of a state in the Union— paradoxical though it may appear—constitute a crisis that threatened to destroy the Union?

According to the language and logic of the Constitution, a state must first actually exist in order to be admitted into the Union.[87] But the criteria for determining the existence of a valid state were in dispute. Southerners held a double-consent congressional sovereignty doctrine; unless they already were an independent country, the people of a territory first needed the consent of Congress to govern themselves by their own consent under a state constitution, and second, to be admitted into the Union. Asserting that congressional consent had not been given, Calhoun asked: "Can you believe that there is such a State in reality as the State of California? No there is no such State. It has no legal or constitutional existence."[88] California had no validity as a government because it lacked the sanction of Congress. And it could not be admitted into the Union because the prerequisite to admission was existence as a state, independent of the sanction of Congress.

Free soil-minded Whigs and Democrats were convinced that California *was* a state, the existence of which was justified both by the social contract principle of consent, and practical necessity. Whig Senator Jacob Miller of New Jersey said California "has taken the Wilmot Proviso in her own hands," settling the territorial slavery question "precisely in the way in which we all agree she has a right to settle it—by the formation of a state constitution in which her people had the right to admit or prohibit slavery." "You have, in fact, there—whether organized or not—a State."[89] Michigan Democrat Lewis Cass inquired: ". . . are we to be conducted through some politico-metaphysical process of reasoning, and asked to prove, step by step, the right of 100,000 American citizens to provide for their own social existence, and to apply for admission into this Union, as you would require proof to establish the ownership of a house?" By the principles of American institutions and human nature, Cass argued, California was "as truly a State as any one on the face of the earth."[90] Senator Sam Houston of Texas said it was necessary to organize a republican government in California when the necessity of military government ended. "I contend it is an inherent right in the American people, whenever they are thrown together in sufficient numbers, that they shall establish some government for themselves, provisional, territorial, or whatever they may please."[91] William Henry Seward, New York Whig, stated that the people of California, acting under the law of self-preservation, made a constitution to deal with the problem of anarchy. "California sprang from the head of the nation, not only complete in proportions and full armed, but ripe for affiliation with its members."[92]

Whether, or in what sense, California statehood signified a crisis situation was a second issue on which political perceptions differed. Contemporary observers agreed that California needed a legitimate civil government to deal with political and social conditions that could fairly be described as verging on anarchy. Ratification of the Constitution, and election of legislative and executive officers that, by April 1850, brought the state government into existence, went far toward alleviating the crisis in California. Meanwhile, the Californian Congressional delegation, arriving in Washington in February of 1850, found after initial encouragement that Southerners perceived their petition for admission into the Union as a threat to the existence of the Union. In a memorial to Congress, California Senators- and Representatives-elect defended the state. "The people of California," they wrote, "are neither rebels, usurpers, nor anarchists." They sought neither "to sow the seeds of revolution that they might reap in the harvest of discord," nor expected their admission to be made "the test question on which would hang the preservation of the American Union."[93]

The prospect of losing parity in the Senate as a result of California's admission into the Union posed a long-range threat to the political power of the slave states. Slaveholders reacted, however, as though the destruction of slavery were imminent. To secure and stabilize their position in the Union, they threatened to destroy the Union by revolutionary secession.[94] California must be kept out until new legal protection was given to slavery, especially a guaranty of equal protection for slave property in national territories. This argument—if the threat of disunion can be called an argument in a deliberative sense—was persuasive to most of the Washington political establishment.[95] But it did not move President Zachary Taylor, military hero and Louisiana slaveholder, who rejected outright the slaveholders' assessment of the threat posed by free-state California. Southern perception of being under imminent attack was perhaps mainly an expression of alarm that the power of the executive branch might be used to discredit and obstruct the strategy of disunionist intimidation.

A nonpolitical military man, Taylor's policy for dealing with the sectional conflict over slavery was premised on a repudiation of partisan politics. Disregarding party allegiance and local political considerations, Taylor intended to create a patriotic, nonpartisan party that, by isolating and defusing the territorial slavery issue, would reassure the Southern mind of the permanent existence of slavery within its present boundaries.[96] A possible legislative vehicle for this purpose was suggested by a southern Whig proposal in 1849, based on the idea of natural limits to slavery's expansion, to extend the eastern boundary of California to include the entire Mexican cession, bringing it directly into the Union as a free state.[97] Taylor proposed to avoid the debate over territorial slavery by skipping the territorial stage, and admitting both California and New Mexico as free states.[98] Accordingly, he opposed the compromise bill prepared by Henry Clay and the Senate Committee of Thirteen, which would open Utah and New Mexico to slavery under territorial popular sovereignty, as the price of admitting California.

The most important component of Taylor's policy was his declared willingness, as chief executive, to use military force to defend the Union against Southern threats of revolutionary secession. Referring in his annual message of December 1849 to the prospect of disunion, Taylor said, "Whatever dangers may threaten it, I shall stand by it and maintain it in its integrity to the full extent of the obligations imposed and the powers conferred upon me by the Constitution."[99] In discussions with political associates, he let it be known that he viewed secession as insurrection, and that as commander-in-chief he would personally take the field against any state that tried to withdraw from the Union. Like Andrew Jackson in the nullification controversy, he further specified that he would place an embargo on seceding states and blockade Southern harbors. Taylor was also determined to use force against Texas, should it attempt to occupy the New Mexico territory.[100] To remove any doubt about his commitment to the Union, Taylor told Georgia Whigs Alexander Stephens and Robert Toombs that if they attempted to carry out disunionist action he would hang them as traitors.[101]

The decisive event leading to resolution of the potential disunionist crisis occurred in July 1850, when President Taylor suddenly took ill and died. His death eliminated the near certainty of an executive veto of the comprehensive Senate compromise bill, and elevated compromise-minded Vice President Millard Fillmore to the presidency. Thereafter the specific provisions of the Clay omnibus bill were enacted as separate measures.

Taylor's policy for bringing free-soil California into the Union has been criticized as politically unrealistic, and lacking in national vision. The historical consensus is that a genuine crisis of the Union existed, which required a comprehensive settlement to give security to slavery and prevent secession.[102] In fact, devotion to the Union and the Constitution, and a firm grasp of the rightness and legitimacy of California statehood, based on the principles of the Declaration of Independence, gave Taylor's policy a prudence that confounded political contemporaries and later historians. The sound historical conclusion is that Taylor, correctly and realistically understanding the proslavery political mind, saw that needless compromise on behalf of slavery was more dangerous to liberty and Union than forthright defense against revolutionary secession.

In the Compromise of 1850, Congress placated the South by offering recognition of moral equivalency with the free states, and the hope of perpetuating slavery through territorial popular sovereignty. Yet, not resting on the personal commitment and co-promising that mark genuine compromise, the sectional adjustment proved a temporary palliative, incapable of arresting the disintegrating force inherent in proslavery state sovereignty.[103] California statehood, an exercise of popular self-government under social contract theory, was decisive in clarifying the integrative force of the republican consent principle. The admission of California, observed constitutional historian Andrew C. McLaughlin, "brought the slaveholders face to face with the weakness of their peculiar institution; they saw the need of the artificial aid of the national government if slavery was to maintain itself against the power of free labor and the mighty energy of the North."[104] California's admission broke the equilibrium rule of free and slave state parity in the government of the Union. Inducing a sense of impending doom, it caused slaveholders to commit their communities to a struggle for self-preservation for the sake of slavery. The people of California, claiming the right of self-preservation for the sake of liberty, affirmed the historical purpose and philosophical end of the consent principle under social contract theory. Hubert Howe Bancroft was right in concluding: "The truth will have to be acknowledged that the admission of California as a free state led to the war of the rebellion."[105]

In the nation as a whole, as in the microcosm that California represented, a fundamental moral choice had to be made about the social organization of American society. Ambiguity about the moral basis of popular self-government, a necessary consequence of the compromise over slavery in the framing of the Constitution, could no longer be sustained. The people of California, antislavery by instinct as well as precept, were concerned that even a temporary incursion of slaveholders would discourage the formation of republican society based on free labor.[106] California statehood, an exercise of the right of revolution and popular self-government under social contract theory, showed the practically reciprocal, if not organically symbiotic, relationship between liberty and Union as principles of American nationality. We may conclude that the principle of popular sovereignty, which Lincoln said was given "tangible form in the Declaration of Independence," found just application in the free state constitution movement that brought California into the Union.

NOTES

1. John T. Scott, "The Sovereignless State and Locke's Language of Obligation," *American Political Science Review* 94 (2000): 547–61.

2. Abraham Lincoln, "Speech in United States House of Representatives: The War with Mexico, January 12, 1848," in *Collected Works of Abraham Lincoln*, vol. 1, ed. Roy P. Basler (New Brunswick, N.J.: Rutgers University Press, 1953), 431.

3. Lincoln, in *Collected Works*, 438.

4. Lincoln, in *Collected Works*, 438.

5. See further Bayrd Still, "California's First Constitution: A Reflection of the Political Philosophy of the Frontier," *Pacific Historical Review* 4 (1935): 221–34.

6. See, for example, Glenn W. Price, *Origins of the War with Mexico: The Polk-Stockton Intrigue* (Austin: University of Texas Press, 1967); William Henry Ellison, *A Self-Governing Dominion: California, 1849–1860* (Berkeley: University of California Press, 1950), 1–3.

7. See Robert Glass Cleland, *A History of California: The American Period* (New York: Macmillan, 1922), 205.

8. Walton Bean, *California: An Interpretive History*, 2nd ed. (New York: McGraw-Hill, 1973), 75.

9. Bean, *Interpretive History*, 61.

10. Frederick Merk, *Manifest Destiny and Mission: A Reinterpretation* (New York: Knopf, 1963), 72.

11. Scott, "Sovereignless State," 552.

12. Josiah Royce, *California: From the Conquest in 1846 to the Second Vigilance Committee in San Francisco, A Study of American Character* (New York: Knopf, 1948), 130.

13. See Neal Harlow, *California Conquered: War and Peace on the Pacific 1846–1850* (Berkeley: University of California Press, 1982), 103.

14. Ellison, *Self-Governing Dominion*, 2–3.

15. Royce, *From the Conquest*, 56.

16. See Harlow, *California Conquered*, 103.

17. Bean, *Interpretive History*, 125.

18. Theodore Grivas, *Military Governments in California 1846–1850*, (Glendale, Calif.: A. H. Clark, 1963), 9–10.

19. Harlow, *California Conquered*, 265.

20. See Robert Faulkner, *The First Liberal Democrat: Locke's Popular Government* (forthcoming) manuscript at 14, on file with author. William Henry Ellison, critical of the American settlers, views in much the same terms the philosophical ground of the "home rule" movement that protested military government: "This was in the natural order of things, because Americans are prone to criticize authority, especially if it is military, for they reason that military government has no place in time of peace," Ellison, *Self-Governing Dominion*, 15.

21. James K. Polk, *Messages and Papers of the Presidents, 1789–1908,* vol. 4, ed. James D. Richardson (Washington, D.C.: Bureau of National Literature and Art, 1909), 494.

22. Polk, in *Messages*, 589–90.

23. Polk, in *Messages*, 599.

24. Polk, in *Messages*, 596.

25. Polk, in *Messages*, 638.

26. Grivas, *Military Governments*, 205.

27. James Buchanan, "Letter to W. B. Voorhees, October 7, 1848," in *Cross v. Harrison*, 16 How. (57 U.S.) (1850), 184–85.

28. Royce, *From the Conquest*, 201.

29. See George M. Dennison, "Martial Law: The Development of a Theory of Emergency Powers, 1776–1861," *American Journal of Legal History* 18 (1974): 52.

30. Grivas, *Military Governments*, 224.

31. Grivas, *Military Governments*, 222.

32. An alcalde was something of a combination between a mayor and a justice of the peace; an office which combined judicial and executive power in a manner offensive to American founding principles. See further Myra K. Saunders, "California Legal History: The California Constitution of 1849," *Law Library Journal* 90 (Summer 1998): 448. ("As the sole civil officer in the Spanish colonial scheme, the alcalde functioned in various roles: mayor, arbitrator, justice of the peace, trial judge, and legislator.")

33. Harlow, *California Conquered*, 326. Harlow provides the most thorough and balanced account of government and politics in the period of military rule.

34. Harlow, *California Conquered*, 314–15.

35. Cardinal Goodwin, *The Establishment of State Government in California* (New York: Macmillan, 1914), 66–71.

36. William E. Franklin, "Peter H. Burnett and the Provisional Government Movement," *California Historical Society Quarterly* 40 (1961): 126–29.

37. Franklin, "Peter H. Burnett," 129.

38. Ellison, *Self-Governing Dominion*, 17.

39. Franklin, "Peter H. Burnett, 132.

40. Harlow, *California Conquered*, 325; Franklin, "Peter H. Burnett," 130.

41. For more on the California Constitutional Convention of 1849, see Gordon Lloyd, "Nature and Convention in the Creation of the 1849 California Constitution," in *The California Republic: Institutions, Policies, and Statesmanship*, ed. Brian P. Janiskee and Ken Masugi (Lanham, Md.: Rowman & Littlefield, 2003).

42. President Polk stated in his annual message, December 5, 1848: "The question is believed to be rather abstract than practical, whether slavery ever can or would exist in any portion of the acquired territory even if it were left to the option of the slaveholding states themselves. From the nature of the climate and productions in much the larger portion of it is certain it could never exist, and in the remainder the probabilities are that it would not," Polk, *Messages*, 640. Of course, this question had been central in the debate over annexing Texas, as well.

43. Richard H. Sewell, *Ballots for Freedom: Antislavery Politics in the United States 1837–1860* (New York: Oxford University Press, 1976), 193–94; Hubert Howe Bancroft, *History of California*, vol. 6 (1890): 313; Goodwin, *Establishment of State Government*, 116–17.

44. Nathaniel Wright Stephenson, "California and the Compromise of 1850," *Pacific Historical Review* 4 (1935): 114–22.

45. Goodwin, *Establishment of State Government*, 110–12.

46. Goodwin, *Establishment of State Government*, 132.

47. Ellison, *Self-Governing Dominion*, 2 (Californians's "primary purpose was to govern, to promote and protect their own interests, without regard to the rights of men in general").

48. See Harlow, *California Conquered*, 342.

49. "Speech at Bloomington, Illinois" (Sept. 4, 1848), in *Collected Works*, 90.

50. Lincoln, *Collected Works*, 91.

51. Lincoln, Abraham, "Speech at Peoria, Illinois" (Oct. 16, 1854), in *Collected Works*, 265.

52. *Congressional Globe*, 31st Cong., 1st sess., App. 1531 (August 12, 1850).

53. This view was most closely identified with Senator John C. Calhoun, who, during the Nullification Crisis of the 1830s, argued that the Constitution was a compact between the states, and, therefore, that states had the power to nullify federal laws they deemed unconstitutional. See generally William W. Freehling, *Prelude to Civil War: The Nullification Controversy in South Carolina 1816–1836* (New York: Harper & Row, 1966).

54. The most famous defender of this view was Daniel Webster, who explained it at length in his famous debate with Senator Robert Hayne. See *Congressional Debate*, 1830, vol. 6, 35–41, 58–82, 92–93 ("The Constitution itself, in its very front . . . declares that it is ordained and established by the people of the United States" *Congressional Debate*, 93).

55. James Madison was the leading advocate of this view. See, e.g., "Speech in the Virginia Ratification Convention," (June 6, 1788), in James Madison, *Writings: James Madison*, ed. Jack N. Rakove (New York: Library of America, 1999), 362; "Letter to Edward Everett, August 28, 1830," in Madison, *Writings*, 842; Drew McCoy, *The Last of the Fathers: James Madison and The Republican Legacy* (New York: Cambridge University Press, 1989).

56. It is important to distinguish territorial self-government from the popular sovereignty position adopted by Stephen A. Douglas and the Democrat Party in the 1850s as a means of dealing with the slavery question. A legitimate concept of territorial self-government was grounded on the fact that from the beginning of the American Union national territories were never regarded as mere landed possessions, but rather as republican political communities in process of formation, whose end was admission into the Union as a state on the basis of equality with the original states. Inhabitants of territories described themselves as "citizens of the United States, resident in this Territory." According to constitutional historian Arthur Bestor: "In a very real and compelling though not easily definable sense, territories formed an integral part of the American Union, even though the latter was, by strict letter of the law, a Union of *states.*" Arthur Bestor, "Constitutionalism and the Settlement of the West: The Attainment of Consensus, 1754–1784," in *The American Territorial System*, vol. 13, ed. John Porter Bloom (Athens, Ohio: Ohio University Press, 1973).

57. *An Ordinance for the Government of the Territory of the United States Northwest of the River Ohio*, Art. 3, 1 Stat. 51, 53 n. a (July 13, 1787, reenacted August 7, 1787).

58. *An Act to Authorize the People of Missouri Territory to Form a Constitution . . .* , ch. 22, 3 Stat. 545 (March 6, 1820).

59. Don E. Fehrenbacher, *The Dred Scott Case: Its Significance in American Law and Politics* (New York: Oxford University Press, 1978), 138.

60. David M. Potter, *The Impending Crisis 1848–1861* (New York: Harper & Row, 1976), 71.

61. Richardson, *Messages*, 641.

62. Richardson, *Messages*, vol. 5, 27–29.

63. Richardson, *Messages*, vol. 5, 27–29

64. *Congressional Globe*, 1534 (August 13, 1850).

65. *Congressional Globe*, 1525 (August 13, 1850).

66. *Congressional Globe*, 1535 (August 13, 1850).

67. *Congressional Globe*, 1534 (August 13, 1850).

68. *Congressional Globe*, 1523 (August 13, 1850).

69. Ross M. Lence, ed. *Union and Liberty: The Political Philosophy of John C. Calhoun*, (Indianapolis: Liberty Fund, 1992), 592–94.

70. *Congressional Globe*, 1533 (August 12, 1850).

71. *Congressional Globe*, 1522 (August 12, 1850).

72. *Resolutions and Address Adopted by the Southern Convention*, Nashville, Tenn.: H. M. Watterson, 16.

73. *Resolutions*, 8.

74. *Resolutions*, 13.

75. *Congressional Globe*, 149 (February 13, 1850).

76. *Congressional Globe*, 1550 (August 15, 1850).

77. *Congressional Globe*, 1551 (August 15, 1850).

78. *Congressional Globe*, 1522 (August 12, 1850).

79. *Resolutions*, 13.

80. *Resolutions*, 16.

81. See *Congressional Globe*, 263 (speech of Senator Seward, March 11, 1850).

82. Clyde N. Wilson, ed. *The Essential Calhoun: Selections from Writings, Speeches, and Letters* (New Brunswick, N.J.: Transaction, 1992), 385.

83. *Congressional Globe*, 1534 (August 13, 1850).

84. *Congressional Globe*, 1527 (August 12, 1850).

85. *Congressional Globe*, 1535 (August 13, 1850).

86. *Congressional Globe*, 1535 (August 13, 1850).

87. U.S. Const., Art. IV, § 3 ("New States may be admitted into this Union; but no new State shall be formed or erected within the Jurisdiction of any other State; nor any State be formed by the Junction of two or more States, or parts of States, without the consent of the Legislatures of the States concerned as well as of the Congress.")

88. *Union and Liberty*, 597–98.

89. *Congressional Globe*, 313 (February 25, 1850).

90. *Congressional Globe*, 1529–30 (August 12, 1850).

91. *Congressional Globe* 1536 (August 13, 1850).

92. *Congressional Globe*, 261 (March 11, 1850).

93. Ellison, *Self-Governing Dominion*, 94–95.

94. Potter, *Impending Crisis*, 94.

95. Even Abraham Lincoln, who later described how California was "kept *out* of the Union, because she would not let slavery *into* her borders," felt at the time that "perhaps this was not wrong" because "the Union . . . was thought to be in danger." ("Speech at Peoria, Illinois," [October 16, 1854] in Basler, *Collected Works*, 253.)

96. William J. Cooper, *The South and the Politics of Slavery 1828–1856* (Baton Rouge, La.: Louisiana State University Press, 1978), 275–79.

97. Elbert B. Smith, *The Presidencies of Zachary Taylor and Millard Fillmore* (Lawrence: University of Kansas Press, 1988), 129–30.

98. Cooper, *Politics of Slavery*, 272.

99. Lincoln, *Messages*, vol. 5, 24.

100. K. Jack Bauer, *Zachary Taylor: Soldier, Planter, Statesman of the Old Southwest* (Baton Rouge: Louisiana State University Press, 1985), 303.

101. Smith, *Presidencies*, 104–5.

102. See, e.g., Allan Nevins, *Ordeal of the Union: Fruits of Manifest Destiny 1847–1852*, vol. 1 (New York: Scribner, 1947), 257; Potter, *Impending Crisis*, 96.

103. Cf. Peter B. Knupfer, *The Union as It Is: Constitutional Unionism and Sectional Compromise 1787–1861* (Chapel Hill: University of North Carolina Press, 1991).

104. Andrew C. McLaughlin, *Lewis Cass* (Boston: Houghton Mifflin, 1891), 263.

105. Bancroft, *History*, 344.

106. Daniel J. Elazar, *Building Toward Civil War: Generational Rhythms in American Politics* (Lanham, Md.: Madison Books, 1992), 14.

Nature and Convention in the Creation of the 1849 California Constitution

Gordon Lloyd

THE SPECTER HAUNTING EUROPE

Alexis de Tocqueville agreed with Karl Marx that in February 1848 France was in the midst of a unique and momentous event. He wrote Nassau William Senior in April 1848 that the February Revolution was "the most extraordinary situation into which a great nation has ever been suddenly thrown." In Marx's phrase, "there is a specter haunting Europe—the specter of communism."[1] Tocqueville disagreed profoundly with Marx, however, concerning both the legitimacy and the beneficial consequences of such revolutionary action based on what he called "a sort of revolutionary religion." Writing to Paul Clamorgan and Senior, also in spring 1848, Tocqueville notes that the struggle taking place is "the most terrible of all civil wars, the war of class against class, of those who have nothing against those who have." He concludes: "But what a war! Never in sixty years has such a day been seen. The bloodiest days of the French Revolution compared to this are child's play." Earlier, he expressed deep concern to Clamorgan over the absence of genuine political leadership, one that would found a "republic strongly and regularly constituted like that of the United States." And to his former traveling companion, Gustave de Beaumont, Tocqueville complained that "we are situated between a small minority, which wants the socialist or red republic, and an immense majority, which does not want to hear of any republic whatever."[2]

Soon after the February Revolution in 1848, Tocqueville added a preface to the twelfth edition of *Democracy in America* in which he commented on the "sudden and momentous" events that "have just taken place" and that, furthermore, "have not taken him by surprise."[3] But he reminded the reader that "it is not force alone, but rather good laws, which make a new government secure. After the battle comes the lawgiver. The one destroys; the other builds up."[4] And the key question is whether lawgivers create "a republic which threatens the sacred rights of property and of the family, or one which recognizes and honors them. It is a fearful problem concerning, not France alone, but the whole civilized world." He encouraged French lawgivers to turn to America for guidance on the principles that should undergird constitutions: "the principles of order, balance of powers, true liberty, and sincere and deep respect for law."[5]

Although geographically thousands of miles away, the delegates to the California Constitutional Convention were very much aware of the upheavals taking place in Europe. According to delegate Kimball Dimmick, "the eyes of the world are turned towards us."[6] Edward Gilbert challenged his fellow delegates to "look at the people of Europe. . . . For what are they battling—for what are they shedding their blood?" And Robert Semple reminded the citizens of California that "the eyes of all Europe are now directed at California."

Would California meet the Tocqueville test of "a republic strongly and regularly constituted?" Or would its deliberations be governed by—and its Constitution a product of—class antagonisms, narrow self-interest, and shortsighted considerations? What kind of lawgivers would follow the warriors? Would the California lawgivers incorporate the four principles Tocqueville considered necessary to republican constitutions? To put "the important question" in Hamiltonian terms, would California be able to establish republican government, not to mention good government, from "reflection and choice," or would California join the European nations that seemed "destined to depend for their political constitutions on accident and force?"[7] Although Hamilton had put that momentous challenge to the American people of 1787–1789, the question was of vital importance to the Californian people of 1848–1850.

Associated with these critical times, came unprecedented opportunities, including the opportunity to respond affirmatively to "the important question." This opportunity can be seen, for example, in the dramatic shift of emphasis evident in Marx's understanding of revolutionary change. By the end of 1849, Marx realized that his analysis of revolutionary change expressed in *The Communist Manifesto* had focused exclusively, and thus incompletely, on Europe as the central theater of political and economic action. Unlike Tocqueville, who concluded his first volume of *Democracy in America* (fifteen years earlier) with the observation that the future of the world would rest in the hands of two previously obscure nations, namely America and Russia,[8] Marx failed to even consider America and Russia as actors in 1848.

Writing in the January–February 1850 issue of *Review*, however, Marx turned his gaze toward America and opened with the observation that "the most important thing" to have occurred in America was "the discovery of gold in California."[9] In fact, he saw this discovery as "more important than the February Revolution," which Marx thought central to the specter that was haunting Europe and, therefore, the world.[10] In the process of reconsidering the sources of revolutionary change, Marx builds on the observation first made by Adam Smith that the discovery of America was one of the two most important events in the history of the world. The other one was the discovery of the passage of Good Hope. According to Marx, the discovery of gold in California "will have much more impressive consequences than the discovery of America itself."[11] And, furthermore, the discovery has made "obsolete" the discovery of the Cape of Good Hope and ushered in a revolution in world trade. Marx asks the reader to envision the following picture: "A coastline which stretches across thirty degrees of latitude, one of the most beautiful and fertile in the world and hitherto more or less unpopulated, is now being visibly transformed into a rich, civilized land thickly populated by men of all races, from the Yankee to the Chinese, from the Negro to the Indian and Malay, from the Creole and Mestizo to the European." In short, because of the discovery of gold, "[f]or the second time world trade has found a new direction. What Tyre, Carthage and Alexandria were in antiquity, Genoa and Venice in the Middle Ages, what London and Liverpool have been hitherto, the emporia of world trade—this is what New York, San Francisco, . . . and Panama will now become. The focal point of international traffic."[12]

There were two specters haunting Europe: an internal political and moral convulsion, and an external commercial and industrial challenge. The delegates to the California Constitutional Convention were well aware of the effect of these two events on the nature of their deliberations.

THE SPECTER HAUNTING THE UNITED STATES AND CALIFORNIA

Even before the war with Mexico, and the discovery of gold, Tocqueville foresaw the "inevitable" expansion of the people of the United States into the western regions, thus extending their reach "from the Atlantic to the Pacific." "It will not halt," he predicted, "at lines drawn in treaties, but will flow over such imaginary boundaries in all directions."[13] Among other things, the "taste for well-being" and "the spirit of enterprise" are too strong to be restrained by what

James Madison referred to elsewhere as "parchment barriers." Speaking of Texas, again before the Mexican war, Tocqueville observed how "little by little, the inhabitants of the United States are infiltrating into Texas, acquiring land there, and though submitting to the country's laws, establishing there the empire of their language and laws. The province of Texas is still under Mexican rule, but soon there will, so to say, be no more Mexicans there. The same sort of thing happens in every place where the Anglo-Americans come into contact with populations of different origin."[14] It would come as no surprise to Tocqueville, then, that an accident—the discovery of gold—hastened the inevitable "continuous expansion" and progress of immigration and that, also, the Anglo-Americans would set about in a rapid manner establishing "the empire of their laws." In fact, I suggest that the creation of the state of California represents the fulfillment of Tocqueville's prophecy that North America will fall under the complete sway of Anglo-American laws and mores. "All else is doubtful, but that is sure. And this is something entirely new in the world, something, moreover, the significance of which the imagination cannot grasp."[15]

Alta California was transferred from Mexico to the United States with the adoption of the Treaty of Guadalupe Hidalgo in May 1848. As a consequence, California was no longer under the military-civil rule of Commander General-Governor Riley or under the ultimate jurisdiction of the president of the United States in his constitutional capacity as commander-in-chief. Under the U.S. Constitution, it was now the responsibility of the Congress to provide a territorial government and subsequently to admit California to the union as a state with equal standing.[16] But despite the urging of President Polk, by July 1848, Congress had failed to live up to its constitutional responsibility to provide territorial government during both the 1848 and 1849 sessions.[17] The reason for this inaction was that Congress, representing fifteen northern states and fifteen southern states, was hopelessly divided on the issue of slavery in the territories.

Riley persuaded grassroots movements in Northern California to exercise patience in their quest for a constitutional convention and thus bought time for Congress to exercise its constitutional authority. Upon receiving word of Congress's second failure, however, Riley issued a carefully worded proclamation on June 3, 1849. This authorized elections to be held on August 1, selecting delegates to a constitutional convention, which would begin its deliberations on September 1.

There is a sense in which Riley was the first lawgiver of the new California. He was no longer the military commander, nor was he officially the governor—and yet he constituted "the de-facto government." California, said Riley, was not in a state of nature like Oregon, where the settlers had acted on their own authority and framed their own government upon learning of Congressional inaction in 1848. The new statehood-oriented newspapers—and San Francisco populists Myron Norton and Edward Gilbert—to the contrary, Riley proclaimed, in effect, that California was *not* in a Hobbesian world where human existence was "nasty, poor, solitary, brutish, and short." California had "a system of laws, which, though somewhat defective, and requiring many changes and amendments, must continue in force till repealed by competent legislative power."[18] The situation in California, he continued, "is almost identical with that of Louisiana."[19] Riley was referring to the treaty between the United States and France that transferred the Louisiana territory to the United States. According to that treaty, the existing government and existing laws (not inconsistent with the U.S. Constitution) were to continue to have the force of law until a new government was framed and accepted by the people and by Congress. It was in his capacity, Riley said, as "the executive of the existing civil government," that he authorized the calling of a convention. And it was also in this capacity that he called for the election and appointment of officers to fill existing government positions as well as the publication and distribution of a digest of the Mexican Laws of 1837 "that are supposed to be still in force and adapted to the present condition of California."[20]

This proclamation is remarkable, because Riley simultaneously advances the notion that a state of nature does and does not exist. In order to encourage an attachment to the rule of law and respect for tradition—no small task in a land occupied by the military, and inhabited by gold-diggers—Riley proclaimed that the existing Mexican Laws of 1837 were still in operation. And he did this despite the fact that the reach of Mexican Law had been excluded as a result of the war effort and the signing of the treaty of peace. In many ways, California was not like Louisiana; the latter was a peaceful purchase, not a prize of war. Congress's irresponsible negligence actually placed California in a discontinuous and haunting situation. Thus, despite his deliberate avoidance of the issue, the ultimate justification for Riley's proclamation cannot be an appeal to convention. Although he never appeals to the Declaration of Independence, and the right of the people "to institute new government . . . to effect their safety and happiness" that is what, in effect, he did when he called for the election of a constitutional convention to secure the independence of California in the absence of a directive from Congress.

Despite this effort to provide a coherent constitutional framework, and to enlist widespread agreement, Riley's proclamation actually defined the major issues that were to divide the delegates.

First, he wanted a convention at which "all parts of the Territory are repre-

sented."[21] But what *were* the territorial boundaries of California? Given the
appeal to the Treaty of Guadalupe Hidalgo, the territory of California might
have been seen as including Arizona, Nevada, Colorado, and Utah! Yet in his
provision for the selection of delegates, Riley divided California into ten districts
and defined the "limits" of each district.[22] In particular, no representation was
provided for that part of Alta California east of the Sierra Nevada (where Mormons were attempting to create their own social and political arrangements).
Riley's definition of the eastern boundaries of four districts were critical: the
districts of San Diego and Los Angeles, Riley proclaimed, are bounded "on the
east by the Colorado River;" the district of Sacramento is bounded "on the east
by the Sierra Nevada," and "the District of San Joaquin includes all the country
south of the Sacramento District, and lying between the coast range and the
Sierra Nevada."[23] Put differently, Riley defined "all parts of the Territory" in
"natural" or geographical terms rather than in terms of the treaty, or as Alta
California was understood conventionally. The eastern boundary, however, was
to become a source of dispute at the convention, because the drawing of the
boundary was linked to such moral and political considerations as the extension
of slavery in the territories.[24]

Second, Riley ordered the convention "to meet and frame a state constitution
or territorial organization, to be submitted to the people for their ratification,
and then proposed to Congress for its approval."[25] Thus he left open whether
the task of the delegates was to do what Congress failed to do—frame a territorial organization—or to become lawgivers for California. Riley tipped his hand
in the direction of the former: he thought that a "considerable time will necessarily elapse before any new government can be legitimately organized and put
into operation."[26] The ultimate authorizing agent for Riley was still the U.S.
Congress. But this, too, became a source of contention. Should the delegates
frame a territorial government or a state constitution—and what were the implications of the decision one way or the other? Given the moral and political divisions in Congress, should the delegates frame a constitution designed primarily
to secure congressional approval, or one framed with the best interests of California in mind? Or should the delegates try to solve these dilemmas for the entire
nation by drawing a boundary and adopting a policy toward slavery and free
Blacks that would rid the nation of the divisive question once and for all? And
what would happen to California if Congress should fail, once again, to act—
regardless of whether the delegates interpreted their function to be limited and
practical or expansive and visionary?

Despite Riley's assurances that the citizens of California should conduct
themselves as if conditions of orderly continuity and constitutional precedent

prevailed, delegates of opposite persuasions pointed to the "anomalous" and novel situation of California. On September 13, Wilfred Sherwood stated that "we are an anomalous people. There is no State in the Union like California."[27] He repeated this on September 28. Thomas L. Vermeule observed that "California is a political anomaly; and being anomalous, you must deviate from the fixed usages" found in other states and the nation at large.[28] On September 24, Charles Botts described California's condition as anomalous: "We meet here under no express law."[29] The most important anomaly, agreed Myron Norton, was that "we have no laws here."[30] Convention president Robert Semple concurred. Future senator W. M. Gwin, considered California to be very much in a state of nature: it was "like a blank sheet of paper, upon which we are required to write a system of fundamental laws."[31] On September 27, the delegates unanimously approved Norton's motion that the Constitution would take effect upon ratification by the people rather than upon congressional admission. On this decisive issue, therefore, the delegates unambiguously understood themselves to be lawgivers.

Finally, Riley proclaimed who could vote to select the convention delegates:

> Every free male citizen of the United States and of Upper California, twenty-one years of age, and actually resident in the district where the vote is offered, will be entitled to the right of suffrage. All citizens of Lower California who have been forced to come to this territory on account of having rendered assistance to the American troops during the recent war with Mexico, should also be allowed to vote in the district where they actually reside.[32]

Riley's Proclamation on the suffrage was race-neutral and, therefore, at least arguably, included free persons of color, Indians and descendants of Africans and Indians. Yet the proclamation is silent on slavery. As we shall see, the delegates were unanimous in their decision to prohibit slavery, but were seriously divided on extending the franchise beyond white men. It is clear that as far as Riley was concerned, native Californians may be Mexicans by convention, but they can be Californians by naturalization.

THE CONSTITUTIONAL CONVENTION: THE FIRST READING

Delegate Profiles

Assembling in the Alta California capital of Monterey in the fall of 1849, the membership at the constitutional convention was diverse.[33] There were fourteen

lawyers, twelve farmers, nine merchants, four soldiers, two printers, two survey-
ors, one physician, one banker, one "gentleman," and two of unknown employment, elected to represent the ten districts into which Governor Riley had
divided California. Of the forty-eight members in attendance, twenty-two had
come to California from northern states, fifteen had been born and raised in
slave states, four were foreign-born, and seven were native Californians. Jose
Antonio Carrillo was the eldest at fifty-three and J. M. Jones, at twenty-five, was
the youngest delegate; twelve delegates had been in California less than two years
and five had lived in California all their life. Thirty of the delegates had arrived
since 1846 and twelve since the discovery of gold eighteen months earlier. Nevertheless, there was considerable common ground on which the delegates could
base their deliberations. Given the detached geographical location of California,
its ambiguous legal status, the youthfulness of the delegates—the average age
was thirty-eight—and the large number of immigrants seeking a new life, the
convention was, for the most part, spared the deep-seated divisions and personal
rivalries that often plague deliberative bodies. To be sure, there were outbursts
of ill temper and personal affront, as well as expressions of naked self-interest
and district pride. But there was a remarkable willingness to overcome differences and seek common ground. In this regard, the native Californians—the
most politically experienced of the delegates—willingly participated in the creation of a new constitution for a new California.

Bill of Rights

On Friday, September 7, the twenty-member committee (two from each district) chosen to draft the proposed constitution presented their report on a bill
of rights that contained sixteen sections. The first eight were copied from the
1846 Constitution of New York, and the last eight were lifted from the 1846
Iowa Constitution.

The next day, New York native W. E. Shannon proposed dropping the two
opening sections on due process of law and trial by jury found in New York's
Constitution, and replacing them with the first two entries from the Iowa Bill
of Rights. To Shannon, these two entries summarized the basic commitment to
natural rights as a moral and constitutional restraint on the political conduct
of the people, while simultaneously confirming the ultimate authority of the
people:

SECTION 1. All men are, by nature, free and independent, and have certain
unalienable rights—among which are those of enjoying and defending life and lib-

erty, acquiring, possessing and protecting property, and pursuing and obtaining safety and happiness.

SECTION 2. All political power is inherent in the people. Government is instituted for the protection, security, and benefit of the people, and they have the right, at all times, to alter or reform the same, whenever the public good may require it.[34]

Thus Shannon placed California in the natural rights tradition first begun by the founders of the Virginia Bill of Rights and Constitution in June 1776. A bill of rights, stating the purposes of, and limitations on, government, should precede the institutional framework provided by the Constitution, and in order to emphasize this relationship, a statement concerning natural rights should precede a listing of common law rights.

The delegates continued their discussion of the bill of rights on Monday, September 10. They excluded a New York-inspired provision concerning jury-determined compensation for owners of property taken for local improvements. The delegates agreed with Pacificus Ord and J. M. Jones that "the pages of the Constitution should not be encumbered with regulations . . . [which] belong to the statute books."[35] This was the first of numerous references to the distinction between framing a constitution and writing a code of laws. They also slightly modified Section 22 of the Iowa Bill of Rights that guaranteed property rights to resident aliens living permanently in California.

At this point in the deliberations on the bill of rights, Shannon moved to insert Section 23 of the Iowa Constitution: "Neither slavery nor involuntary servitude, unless for punishment of crimes, shall ever be tolerated in this state."[36] Shannon's fellow delegate from Sacramento, M. M. McCarver, requested that his colleague's motion be amended to include the following: "Nor shall the introduction of free negroes, under indentures or otherwise, be allowed."[37]

McCarver temporarily withdrew his amendment and Shannon's proposal was "unanimously adopted." Even though the convention had *unanimously* agreed that California would be a free state, the acrimonious debate over admitting "free negroes" was postponed. The delegates would find no guidance from Iowa, whose constitution was silent on the issue, nor from New York where free persons of color resided and owned property.

On the following day, McCarver returned to the question of "free persons of color." Instead of incorporating an explicit clause in the constitution that would prohibit immigration and residence, he proposed that the constitution explicitly require the first legislature to "pass such laws as will effectually prohibit free persons of color from immigrating to and settling in this State, and to effectually prevent the owners of slaves from bringing them into this State for the purposes of setting them free."[38]

O. M. Wozencraft, a delegate from San Joaquin, provided the "moral and intellectual" defense of McCarver's proposal. He opposed the immigration of free blacks out of "philanthropic reasons." Africans, he said, would always end up being dominated by whites. Moreover, he wanted to protect Californians's "right to labor." He aimed to "encourage labor and protect the laboring class. . . . [T]he capitalists will fill the land with these laboring machines, with all their attendant evils." Without a prohibition "you will see a greater curse than the locusts of Egypt."[39] Once again, McCarver withdrew his proposal after receiving assurances that it would be discussed when the legislative section on the constitution was reported. At this stage of the deliberations, natural rights had been endorsed, slavery was constitutionally prohibited, but the constitutional status of free blacks was still not be decided. Thus ended the first reading of Article I of the bill of rights.

Suffrage

On Wednesday, September 12, the convention considered suffrage (article II). The committee recommended extending the suffrage to "every white male citizen of the United States, of the age of twenty-one years, who shall have been a resident of the State six months preceding the election, and the county in which he claims his vote, twenty days."[40] This was directly copied from the Iowa constitution, which, like the newer states of Illinois and Indiana, had restricted the franchise to white men. Why Iowa was copied—and not New York, where free black men could vote if they met a more stringent residency requirement than white men—was neither debated nor explained. The convention also had the more liberal models of Massachusetts, New Jersey, and Pennsylvania available. They could have followed Governor Riley's race-neutral directive on suffrage used in the selection of the very convention delegates themselves. But they didn't.

Edward Gilbert attempted to move the delegates toward both the liberal models and Riley's directive. He proposed that suffrage be extended to "every male citizen of Mexico, who shall have elected to become a citizen of the United States" in accordance with the Treaty of Guadalupe Hidalgo. To him, the convention had no authority to make distinctions regarding the color of the Mexican citizens who became American citizens as a result of the treaty. Charles

Botts, formerly of Virginia, insisted that only "white male citizens of Mexico" be included in the suffrage.

An extensive discussion ensued over California's obligations under the Treaty of Guadalupe-Hidalgo, the right of California to determine its own electorate, the definition of the color "white," whether Africans were ever citizens of Mexico and could they vote, the legal status of Indians under Mexican law, and whether Indians with taxable property should be able to vote in California. By the end of the day, the delegates agreed, by the narrow margin of 21–20, to extend the suffrage to every male citizen of Mexico, but to constitutionally exclude Indians, Africans, and descendants of Africans.

Banking and Corporations

On Monday, September 13, the delegates began their third week of deliberations. The subjects which generated the most discussion were the six sections in the legislative article (Article IV) concerning corporations and banking. The Committee on the Constitution had followed the New York model that distinguished between corporations and banking. Opposition quickly developed, however, from the hard-money delegates to adopt the provisions in the Iowa constitution. Rodman Price did not think the committee had gone far enough to prevent "the raising up of any privileged class, or set of men, that may consolidate capital, and thereby monopolize individual capital."[41] Like Price, Gwin aimed to "battle for the rights of the people, against monopoly and the legalized association of wealth to appropriate the labor of the many for the benefits of the few."[42] He reminded the delegates that "this is the only country on the globe where labor has the complete control over capital. Let it remain so, if we are to remain free, independent, and prosperous."[43] Botts thought that the delegates had finally "come to a question of the most vital importance to the interest of the community." His "chief object" was to "crush this bank monster."[44] Kimball Dimmick agreed: "we have now arrived at the main question before the House."[45]

In the end, calmer heads prevailed and the report of the committee, with modifications, was accepted. But the important lesson to be extracted from the exchange was this: the framers of 1849 discussed the dangers of class struggle and—as populists in the Jeffersonian and Jacksonian traditions—all were suspicious of monopolies.[46] But they did not constitutionalize that struggle and consequently control the efforts of subsequent legislatures to govern in changing times.

Boundaries

On September 18, L. W. Hastings presented the report of the Committee on Boundaries. His explanation of the committee's decision to locate the eastern boundary at 42 degrees North, 116 degrees West deserves citation:

> Your committee is of the opinion that the present boundary of California comprehends a tract of country entirely too extensive for one State, and that there are various other forcible reasons why that boundary should not be adopted by this Convention. The area of the tract of country included within the present boundary is estimated to be from one hundred and forty-eight thousand six hundred and ninety-one (148,691) square miles, which is nearly equal to that of all the nonslaveholding States of the Union, and which deducting the area of Iowa, is greater than that of the residue of the nonslaveholding States.[47]

The Hastings proposal would extend the boundary beyond the Sierra Nevada boundary proposed by Riley, but not as far as Salt Lake City or the boundaries of Alta California. Discussion was postponed until the next day in order to consider McCarver's twice-delayed proposal on "free persons of color."

McCarver warned that southern slave owners were planning to bring slaves to California and grant them freedom in exchange for three years labor in the mines. He wanted to avoid a "collision between free negroes and white mine workers."[48] Moreover, he claimed that most state constitutions excluded the immigration of free persons of color (but when this was challenged, he could only think of Illinois). Wozencraft, in support of McCarver, repeated his wish to protect California from "the monopolies of capitalists who would bring their negroes here."[49] Henry Tefft agreed: "negro labor, whether slave or free, when opposed to white labor, degrades it."[50]

McCarver was eventually challenged by his fellow delegates from Sacramento, Shannon and Sherwood, and by Dimmick who reminded the delegates that they were founders with an unique opportunity and obligation: "the eyes of the world are turned towards us . . . let it not be said that we have attempted to arrest the progress of human freedom."[51] Even in Illinois, they reminded McCarver, the delegates at the Constitutional Convention refused to endorse such a proposal; instead it was submitted to and approved by the voters as a separate measure.

The controversy over constitutionalizing the prohibition of "free negroes" continued at the afternoon session. McDougal, Wozencraft, Steuart, Botts, and Semple repeat the same argument—"Africans 'by nature' will always be subservient to the caucasian"—and that "free negroes" will be exploited by capitalists, destroying and degrading white labor.[52] According to delegate J. D. Hoppe, "the two races can never intermingle without mutual injury."[53] Stated convention president Semple, "In God's name, let us make California a place where free white men can live. If [blacks] are to be admitted here at all, let us make slaves of them."[54] In response, Shannon cited examples of prominent free blacks in New York, while Dimmick challenged the claim, by McDougal et al., that Californians wanted a prohibition. Moreover, a constitutional ban would "provoke discussion and hostility in the halls of Congress."[55] Gilbert challenged the delegates to act in accordance with "the principles of liberal and enlightened freedom" declared in the bill of rights.[56] "Look at the people of Europe," he said. "For what are they battling—for what are they shedding their blood? It is to maintain their rights—it is for liberty they contend." Even if the proponents are correct that their constituents demanded a constitutional prohibition, "we must go a little further than our constituents in settling this question."[57]

Of particular interest is the exchange between Gilbert and McCarver that anticipates the later exchanges between Justices Taney and McLean, and between Lincoln and Douglas. According to Gilbert, California had an obligation to abide by the privileges and immunities clause of the U.S. Constitution.[58] When McCarver asked: "Are free negroes citizens of the States?" Gilbert responded: "In the State of New York and in most of the Eastern States they are. . . . We go beyond the bounds of ordinary constitution-making when we attempt to introduce into ours a provision of this character." If we do want to get specific about preventing "evils," added Gilbert sarcastically, why not prohibit the immigration to California of "the degraded wretches that come from Sydney."[59] Despite Gilbert's appeal to what Abraham Lincoln later called the "better angels of our nature," the delegates approved McCarver's constitutional directive that the first legislature prohibit "free persons of color" from immigrating to California.[60]

On September 22, the convention returned to the Hastings Report on the boundary. Hastings again outlined the reasoning of the committee: "[The committee was] very cautious to include as little as possible, and yet omit no portion of the territory that was deemed valuable." On the other hand, if the convention were to follow the Gwin-Halleck proposal, and "leave this question of boundary open, [then] we leave the question of slavery open. If we fix the boundary, we fix that question also."[61] Moreover, he added, the Mormons were not represented in the convention, and it would be wrong to impose a government on them, especially since they were applying for territorial government. The Hastings proposal attempted to reconcile a moral and practical dilemma: how to exclude slavery from California without jeopardizing the chances of admission to the Union.

Gwin and Halleck proposed that the boundary extend all the way past Utah. If Congress refused that proposal, then the legislature could negotiate with Congress on an eastern boundary that would extend to either the Colorado or Gila rivers. This proposal, incorporating all of Alta California, "close[d] forever this agitating question of slavery in all the territory this side of the Rocky Mountains,"[62] leaving it still possible for a smaller California to enter as a free state if Congress did not go along with the Alta California boundary. Sherwood supported the proposal, "we owe it to the country to settle the slavery question with respect to Alta California."[63]

Botts, McDougal, McCarver, Snyder, and Shannon joined forces in opposition to the Alta California boundary and in support of the Hastings Committee Report. Botts objected to the attempt by "the new firm of Gwin and Halleck" to settle the question of slavery for the entire nation. "This is a most unrighteous, unholy, and unconstitutional spirit."[64] The question of slavery should be "settled by the people of the Territories themselves." McDougal accused Gwin and Halleck of deliberately proposing a plan that they knew Congress would reject. Slaves and "free negroes" would then be able to pour into the mines from Kentucky and Maryland. He thought that the delegates should not be held accountable for the subject of slavery in the territories.[65] McCarver wondered how "this convention is able to settle a question which all the talent and wisdom of Congress could not settle."[66] Snyder was eager to draw a reasonable boundary to keep Congress from meddling in the state: "I just don't want slaves in California degrading white labor. We should be debating what does it take to get California admitted."[67] And Shannon thought that they were doing well to prohibit slavery in California; slavery in the territories was up to Congress to decide.

On the other side, Norton and Sherwood forged a strong alliance with native Californians in support of the Gwin-Halleck proposal. "We are representatives of what was Alta California. We have no right to dismember California," said Norton.[68] Carrillo asked, "What is California? It is the territory defined as such by the Government of Spain, and always recognized as such by the Mexican Government."[69] To Carrillo, it was the delegates' duty to form a constitution for all of California. "If you do not, your descendants hereafter will have good cause to complain that you have done them injustice."[70]

The debate lasted late into the night on what Halleck regarded "as the most important question that has yet come up for discussion."[71] The Gwin-Halleck proposal was adopted by a vote of 19–4, with many of the Hastings supporters having retired for the evening.

Closing

The delegates moved easily through the remainder of the proposals and concluded their deliberations on the first reading on September 28. One issue deserves a brief comment, because it is pertinent to the deliberation on constitutionalism. The Committee on the Constitution provided for the protection of the separate property of wives. The discussion on the rights of women paralleled the discussion on slavery and "free negroes." Botts supported "the despotism of the husband. . . . This doctrine of women's rights is the doctrine of those mental hermaphrodites, Abby Folsom, Fanny Wright, and the rest of that tribe."[72] Lippitt feared that the clause would encourage divorce; besides, it "is contrary to nature."[73] Dimmick's argument, however, prevailed. The delegates were defending "the rights of women" as found in the laws of Alta California. Besides, they were living in a new age of enlightenment: "as knowledge has become more generally diffused, as the world has become more enlightened, as the influence of free and liberal principles has extended among the nations of the earth, the rights of woman have become generally recognized."[74]

This provision was in neither the Iowa nor New York Constitutions. Thirty years later, the refounders of 1879 would remove this protection from the California Constitution.

THE CONSTITUTIONAL CONVENTION: THE SECOND READING

Bill of Rights

The second reading began with a reconsideration of the Bill of Rights. Price wondered whether a declaration of rights was even needed; "the people know where to find them if they desire to refer to them,"[75] namely, the U.S. Constitution. Norton reminded Price that the provisions of that Constitution "only apply in the United States Courts."[76] And Lippitt attempted, unsuccessfully, to delete the provision that the people shall "instruct" their representatives. "That clause," stated Lippitt, "transforms a republic into a pure democracy. . . . The representatives are turned into mere delegates."[77] McDougal, in response, regarded the representative "as a mere machine."[78] The instruction provision, he said, reinforced the notion that the representative was to be wholly accountable to the electorate. His argument prevailed. The second conversation on the bill of rights was brief and without any other contention. Most importantly, the delegates had reaffirmed the commitment, secured at the first reading, to the doctrine of natural rights, popular sovereignty, and the prohibition of slavery.

Suffrage

At the first reading, the suffrage had been extended to "every white male citizen of the United States, and every male citizen of Mexico (Indians, Africans, and descendants of Africans excepted)."[79] J. Ross Browne, the official recorder, noted that at the second reading "an animated discussion sprang up, and the same points were reargued in the House that had been so warmly discussed in the Committee."[80] In particular, a concerted effort was made to modify the original article II provision to exclude Indians from the franchise.

On October 1, Noriega addressed the convention (via an interpreter) on behalf of Indians born in California. His comments deserve extensive citation because they appeal to the very doctrine of natural right that informed the entire proceedings :

> The Convention was now treating upon a point of very great importance to himself and to California—a question as interesting as it was important; and he should be doing a very great injustice to his constituents, did he not speak upon the subject. By the proposed amendment, all Indians were excluded, while at the same time it allowed all foreigners who might choose to come to California and reside for a few years, to become citizens. You allow the Kanaka to come within your territory and admit them to citizenship, when he is as ignorant and as foolish as any Indian in California. And yet you exclude the native Indians from enjoying equal privileges with him. It had been asserted by some members that Indians are brutal and irrational. Let those gentlemen cast their eyes back for three hundred years and say who were the Indians then. They were a proud and gifted race, capable of forming a government for themselves. If they were not so much enlightened as now, it was not for want of *natural* gifts, but because the lights of science were not then so bright as now, even in Europe; and they could fall but dimly upon the natives of the soil. And he would say to those gentlemen who had sneered at the Indian race, that there might still be Indians in the Territory of California who were equally as rational and gifted as highly by *nature* as those who had depreciated them. He would not carry their recollections back three centuries, but bid them look back but for half a century. All the work that was seen in California, was the work of Indians left by some foreigners. If they were not cultivated and highly civilized, it was because they had been ground down and made slaves of.[81]

Noriega offered an honorable constitutional alternative if the delegates declined to take the highest natural road: "If it was the will of the Convention to exclude the body of Indians, he hoped exceptions might be made, and that those who were the holders of property and had heretofore exercised all the rights and privileges of freemen, might still be permitted to continue in the exercise of those rights."[82]

Halleck, Lippitt, Shannon, and Dent supported Noriega's compromise to secure the right to vote for Indians who were taxed. Their efforts fell short by one vote, 21–22. On October 2, however, de la Guerra requested a reconsideration of the Indian question: He proposed that the following proviso be added: "but this section shall not be construed to prevent the Legislature from admitting such Indians to the elective franchise as they may in future deem capable thereof."[83] The next day, the delegates unanimously concurred with a slightly altered version offered by Noriega and Vermeule.

At the end of the second reading, therefore, the vote was constitutionally guaranteed to "every white male citizen of the United States, and every white male of Mexico who shall have elected to become a citizen of the United States,"[84] but the legislature was empowered to extend the vote to Indians. Here, the California Constitution deviated from the Iowa and New York Constitutions.

The Freedom to Travel

Norton proposed that the constitutional directive to the first legislature, adopted during the first reading, to "effectually prohibit free persons of color from immigrating to and settling in this State," be deleted.[85] He again appealed to moral principles and to the constitutional obligations of every state in the union to obey the privileges and immunities clause of the U.S. Constitution. McCarver repeated his contention that "we are well aware that negroes are not regarded as citizens" entitled to protection under the U.S. Constitution. Thus he felt that the delegates were free from the outside constitutional restraints suggested by Norton. The real issue, said McCarver, was this: shall the delegates constitutionalize the prohibition now—or leave it up to the people to decide by ordinary legislation in the future? He chose the former because he did not want to leave this question to be settled by "a vacillating legislature."[86] Jones supported McCarver: in 1787 "there was not one single State of the Union which endowed the African race with the rights of citizenship."[87] Besides, he did not want to "degrade the white labor of the mines."

Hastings, supported by Steuart and Botts, proposed a compromise between Norton's constitutional principle of racial inclusion and McCarver's doctrine of racial exclusion. Since no one knew for sure what Californians thought about "free negroes," said Hastings, and the delegates were there to frame an organic law and not specific public policy, why not direct the legislature to "pass such laws as may be deemed necessary."[88] The McCarver proposal was defeated and the Hastings compromise passed 33–9. This was an indirect victory for Gilbert and Norton because it removed a constitutional prohibition on immigration. The victory was made complete when the convention proceeded to remove this compromise. The Hastings measure was defeated 27–6, thus completely deleting any mention of constitutionally prohibiting or regulating the immigration of free persons of color.

Amendments

Jones objected to the proposed amending process, because it required a supermajority vote of subsequent legislatures and the electorate to change a document that was to go into effect only by means of a majority vote in the convention and ratification by a majority of the voters.

> I do not think this proposition is democratic, I do not think it is republican. I think the true democratic rule is that the majority shall rule. In all States of the union you will find no restriction so stringent as these, for not only do you have two separate Legislatures to pass upon it, but the last Legislature must pass it by a two-thirds vote. If gentlemen preach that up as democratic or republican doctrine, I must say I do not know what the doctrine is. If they preach it up as a specimen of liberal principles, I know not what liberalist is.[89]

Lippitt reminded his younger colleague that they were writing organic law, and not a legal code. To him, founders have an obligation to create a framework empowering majorities to rule in ordinary situations, but protecting the constitutional framework from the designs of transient majorities influenced by political partisans:

> That is just the difference between the Constitution, and fundamental law of the land, and an ordinary law of the Legislature. Let the will of a majority of the people always make and unmake laws; they are changing from year to year; but do not let these changes—these transient changes, which are brought about by politicians for party purposes, party majorities in favor of a particular measure—affect your fundamental law. It would greatly mitigate against the permanent prosperity of the people. The laws of the State can be repealed at any time if they work badly; but if an alteration made in your Constitution is found to work badly, it will take years to correct it. Whether it be democratic, or republican, or otherwise, I would not

leave it to the mere transient majority of the people; I would not leave the future interests of the whole people dependent upon that majority.[90]

Norton supported the distinction between the creation of organic law and the passing of a specific legislative act. A super-majority vote should be required to amend the constitution, as opposed to a simple majority to pass legislation. He also echoed Madison's argument that the mutability and injustice of the laws are evils to be avoided. Above all, we must avoid revising the constitution for political purposes:

> Sir, in the case of a political party in power, they have the majority in the Legislature, and amendments or revision of the Constitution might be made for political purposes. That is what it is necessary to guard against; that no amendment shall be made for merely political purposes. . . . The great evil of the day is too much legislation and too much constitution making. For this reason, after you have once adopted a Constitution, submitted it to the people, and it is ratified by them, you should abide by that Constitution.[91]

Boundaries

On October 8 and 9, the location of the eastern boundary was discussed for a second time. Sherwood argued that "slavery is the demon question" seizing the nation, and the main reason why the convention was meeting in Monterey. Accordingly, he continued to support the Gwin-Halleck Alta California measure, because if "we can forever prevent discussion in Congress on the subject—prevent a settled division between the North and South, it is our bounden duty to do so." There was also an immediate political consideration, he said, that the convention and the concerned citizens of the nation ought to address: the upcoming 1852 presidential election. In other words, Sherwood wanted to exclude the slavery question from presidential politics as well as congressional politics. He prophesied that "the moment the North, which is the strongest, vote for their own presidential candidate, and the south for theirs—that moment your union is lost."[92] Tefft agreed that no other deliberative assembly in "the past fifty years . . . met together under circumstances of greater responsibility—circumstances which place it in their power to work great weal or woe, not only to themselves and those whom they represent, but to the whole Confederacy of which they form a part, than the Convention."[93] Thus, he supported Gwin-Halleck. On the other hand, Botts and Steuart reminded the delegates that their primary purpose was to secure admission of California as a free state—not to act like Wilmot abolitionists from the North.

Despite the eloquent defense of the Gwin-Halleck boundary proposal, the convention voted, 24–16, to reconsider the two-part measure. Recall that this measure passed by a vote of 19–4 on the first reading. It proposed that the eastern boundary include all of Alta California and that, if Congress didn't agree, the first legislature would have power to secure, through negotiation with Congress, the Sierra Nevada and the Colorado or Gila Rivers as the eastern boundaries. After more spirited discussion, the vote was taken: 24–22 in favor of Gwin-Halleck. This close vote produced considerable disorder in the convention, and after order was restored, an abrupt adjournment was agreed to. Even with so much accomplished, the fate of the convention still hung in the balance over the "demon question": the moral and constitutional issue of slavery.

The delegates sought a compromise on October 10, but seeking common ground in light of a national division was difficult. In the end, they settled for a fixed, natural boundary along the Sierra Nevada and the Colorado River that was likely to secure congressional approval. The delegates reasoned that neither the North nor the South would object; nor would the Mormons. It was this compromise which prevented the 36–30 line from extending to the Pacific Ocean, and thus excluded slavery from America's west coast.

The work of the convention was over. On October 13, the delegates signed the constitution and submitted it to the people for ratification. The voters ratified it by a vote of 12,064 to 811 on November 13, 1850.

REVISITING THE ORIGINAL FOUNDING

The Basic Literature

A reconsideration of the principles behind the 1849 Constitution might well be valuable in the continuing debate over the refounding of California institutions. There is a tendency among both academics and citizens to equate the *new* with the *improved*. But the reverse is a more accurate picture of constitutional development in California; the older may well be superior.

Unfortunately, political scientists and historians tell us little about the 1849 convention and the original founding of the California Republic in their basic coverage of California government and history. What coverage there is does not portray the California Constitutional Convention as a particularly unique or important event. Nor are the framers portrayed as innovative, or even moral— nor the times presented as critical. For example, according to Bernard Hyink and David H. Provost, "the proposed constitution was largely a prefabricated structure combining planks from the U.S. Constitution and the State Constitutions of New York and Iowa."[94] In addition to the ordinariness of the event—the issue of slavery is hardly even mentioned—they emphasize the rapidity with which the delegates put together the document. Since it took "only" six weeks to frame, the implication is that the framers did not put much thought into the creation of the institutional framework. Actually, it took less than six weeks to create most of the original thirteen state constitutions. In fact, the 1846 Iowa Constitution was framed in just over three weeks! It took the New York delegates of 1846 four months to refound their constitution, but that was due in large part to the decision to carve up the document into sections and distribute the work on each section to separate committees. This made coordination difficult to achieve, and the California delegates made a conscious decision to avoid the sort of delays that occurred in New York. So perhaps the more pertinent question should be: why did it take so long to create the California Constitution, and why was it necessary to extend several sessions late into the night? After all, there was a rich and established constitutional tradition to which they could appeal, and there was unanimous agreement that there should be a bill of rights, a bicameral legislature, an elected governor, and an independent judiciary. The answer is that, unlike Iowa and New York, the California delegates elected to engage in an extensive discussion about slavery and boundaries.

A unique feature mentioned in the literature is that the delegates from Southern California—with its contingent of long-term residents—wanted to create a territorial government, while the more populated northern half of the state wanted to pursue statehood. But this misses the extent to which the "native California" delegates considered themselves to be Californians. True, Carrillo did propose on September 5 that a line be drawn near San Luis Obispo "so that all north of that line might have a State government, and all south thereof a Territorial government. He and his colleagues were under instructions to vote for a Territorial organization."[95] But Carrillo, and other native Californians, soon warmed to the idea of a state constitution, and participated fully in its creation. Carrillo, P. N. de la Guerra, Jacinto Rodriguez, and M. G. Vallejo were on the committee that presented the draft of the constitution and they were adamant that California not be divided by Congress to accommodate the national dispute over slavery. By the last week of the convention, the Southern California delegates were arguing for a state government that would encompass all of the former Alta California.

One serious criticism of the 1849 founders does appear in the literature. Hyink and Provost, like Syer and Culver, state that the franchise was limited to "only white males over twenty-one."[96] But they read this suffrage provision from the twentieth century backward rather than from the nineteenth century forward. Syer and Culver go so far as to state that "native Californians were denied this right pending a two-thirds vote of the legislature granting them the franchise." But the nomenclature "native Californian" as used in 1849 pertained to Mexican citizens born in Alta California and Article II of the 1849 Constitution explicitly includes this indigenous group in the suffrage. True, if we consider the Indian tribes to have exclusive claim to the nomenclature "native Americans"—as we are today inclined to do—then they were excluded "pending a two-thirds vote of the legislature."[97] As we have seen, however, a number of delegates, especially native Californians, wanted to open the suffrage to Indians, and the effort failed by one vote.

The basic literature on California is long on explaining the contemporary California political process, and provides, at best, a truncated inquiry of institutional design. As a result, it overlooks the extensive and unsettling discussions that took place at the convention on such enduring public policy issues as racial relations, ethnic diversity, and class conflict. Also overlooked is the insight that we might gain from exploring the larger political question of what it means to found (or refound) and maintain a regime. Many of the forty-eight delegates considered themselves to be founders, and saw the California situation as extraordinary and the "historical moment" to be decisive. They were willing to educate the California electorate while at the same time recognizing that the people were the ultimate sovereign. They distinguished between creating "an organic law" and establishing a legal code or a document containing public policy matters. They viewed a constitution as an empowering—as well as a restraining—document and they were aware that their creation might well have a profound impact on subsequent "political and economic development."

The Refounders of 1879

There was a degree of public spirit, liberality, civility, and enlightenment in 1849 that is missing from subsequent discourses on the ends of constitutionalism. This is perhaps most evident when the 1849 Constitution is compared with the 1879 attempt to constitutionalize class conflict and racial relations, and subsequent attempts in the twentieth century to substitute direct democracy for deliberative democracy. Studies of California politics would be enhanced by paying more attention to the original debates and to the "moral, political, and intellectual" defense of liberal democracy articulated by the founders of 1849. Nevertheless, contemporary scholarship has accepted uncritically the complaints against the original constitution articulated by the refounders of 1879, namely, that California needed "a constitution peculiarly her own, suited to the geography, topography, resources, commercial requirements, and the character of population, and not to the wants of the purely agricultural states after which the constitution of 1849 was copied."[98]

In many ways, the refounding of 1879 constitutionalized the politics of class and race, and was less inclusive and liberal than the first. Moreover, by placing constitutional restrictions on the scope of legislative action, the refounders altered the established constitutional relationship between citizens and their elected leaders.

First, there were no native Californians in attendance and the 1879 Constitution explicitly stated that "all laws of the State of California, and all official writings, and the executive, legislative, and judicial proceedings, shall be conducted, preserved, and published in no other than the English language."[99] This replaced the 1849 constitutional directive[100] that "all laws, decrees, regulations and provisions, which from their nature require publication, shall be published in English and Spanish."[101] The original convention also provided interpreters for the Spanish-speaking delegates, translated all resolutions into Spanish, and alternated the daily prayer between a Protestant minister, Reverend S. M. Willey, and a Roman Catholic priest, Padre Antonio Ramirez. Copies of the original debates and the 1849 Constitution were published in both English and Spanish in quantities that reflected the distribution of the population between native Californians and immigrant Americans.

The 1879 Constitution's explicit restrictions on the ability of Chinese to vote, own property, work in either public or private employment, immigrate to and live in California, constitutionalized race relations. According to Article II, "no native of China, no idiot, insane person, or person convicted of any infamous crime . . . shall ever exercise the privilege of an elector in this State."[102] Article XIX was devoted explicitly to the "Chinese problem." Among other things, the new constitution declared that "Asiatic coolieism is a form of human slavery, and is forever prohibited in this State, and all contracts for coolie labor shall be void."[103] These provisions were the result of the decision of the Workingmen's Party not to "degrade white labor," and were not removed until the twentieth century. To be sure, the 1849 requirement that only white males could vote was removed, but this was a result of the Civil War amendments, not the work of the 1879 convention. In fact, the refounding made it more difficult for males of *any* color to vote than earlier; state residency requirements were increased from six months to one year and county residency requirements were increased from thirty to ninety days.

And this prompts a return to Tocqueville. Does California 1849 represent an exception to Tocqueville's prediction that, in effect, Californians of Anglo-American descent[104] would establish, along with their "empire of laws," the "empire of their language" and that "soon there will, so to say, be no more Mexicans there?" Tocqueville predicted that "the time must come when there will be in North America 150 million people all equal to the other, belonging to the same family, having the same point of departure, the same civilization, language, religion, habits, and mores, and among whom thought will circulate in similar forms and with like nuances. All else is doubtful, but that is sure."[105] Is California 1879 closer to Tocqueville's prediction than California 1849? In this regard, is 2001 California closer to the spirit of 1849 or the spirit of 1879? And how would Tocqueville view the relationship between the multiple races that inhabit California?

Second, the 1879 Constitution exacerbated the class conflict between capital and labor implicit in the original founding. The addition of over thirty restrictions on the legislature, prohibiting it from passing special laws in enumerated cases, and the empowering of an extensive regulatory bureaucracy in the areas of education and corporations, reflect the clash between the Workingmen's Party and corporate interests over the direction of economic policy. The debate over the incidence of taxation and the control of the railroad influence occupied the largest portion of the convention's time and revealed that the delegates were far more interested in providing immediate policy relief to their constituents than thinking about the long-run interests of California. The 1879 refounders consciously attempted to constitutionalize the conflict between capital and labor.

This finally prompts a return to Marx. Marx saw the revolutionary potential of 1849 because he saw—in the discovery of gold, the enterprising spirit of the Yankees, and the birth of a multiracial society made up of immigrants from all over the globe—a profound shrinking and reshaping of the world. He did not comment in late 1849 on what effect this unique situation would have on what he saw just a year earlier as the mortal combat between capital and labor. Not only does he fail to address the issue of class politics in this new situation, he does not address the issue of race relations. Things seem somewhat idyllic; perhaps California 1849 was the place where one could "hunt [for gold] in the morning, fish in the afternoon, rear cattle in the afternoon, criticise after dinner, just as I have a mind, without ever becoming hunter, fisherman, shepherd or critic."[106] And yet we are all aware of Marx's writing on the importance of "winning the battle of democracy" through a politics of "revolution in permanence" in which the forces of capital are subdued by the forces of labor. Is California 1849 close to Marx's vision of a society without the constraints of a division of labor, and, by the way, without communism, and is California 1879 close to his prediction of class politics? And what are we to make of the fact that it was the proletarian-inclined politicians of 1879—and not the forces of established capitalism—who wanted constitutionally to exclude the Chinese and other people of color?

Finally, the founders of 1879 were in fact closer to ordinary politicians than they were to remarkable lawgivers; they turned the "organic law" into a legal code and constitutionalized specific policy matters, in addition to constitutionalizing class conflict and race relations. The attempt to enshrine policy proposals in the form of constitutional amendments became a common theme over the next hundred years.[107] As Bruce Cain's studies have shown, over half of all amendments to the constitution adopted during the twentieth century in California have focused on the following policy topics: taxation, energy, public utilities, water, highways, and fiscal matters.[108] This institutional design, in turn, has shaped twentieth-century constitutional politics in California, one that relies on supermajorities, rotation, and term limits to restrain both the electorate and the representatives from abuse of power.

THE LEGACY OF 1849

The debates of 1849 are, of course, not in the same league as the debates of 1787. Nor are Norton, Gilbert, Halleck, and Shannon of the same stature as Madison, Hamilton, Wilson, and Morris. McCarver, Wozencraft, Jones, and Botts are not direct replicas of Pinkney, Rutledge, Yates, and Lansing. But the debates are most certainly informed by the conversation that took place at the American founding, along with the restraints and opportunities that faced the creators of new state constitutions during the decades of western expansion. And the debates were uniquely informed by the specter of class politics in nineteenth-century Europe and the specter of slavery and disunion that came to haunt America since the original founding.

The arguments of 1849 were conducted very much within—and yet very far removed from—the national disputes. At times, the 1849 deliberations replayed the earlier—and anticipated the subsequent—debates over slavery in the territories. To be sure, the delegates were not of the same status as Hayne, Calhoun, Webster, and Clay, if for no other reason than that they weren't seasoned statesmen wrestling with the daily problems of the regime. And yet the arguments of those with national status are discernible in the debates. One might even claim that they accomplished more toward settling the slavery and boundary issues than their more illustrious national counterparts.

Table 2.1 1849 Convention Delegates

Name	Age	Where born	Of what state as a resident	District (in CA)	Town/P.O. (in CA)	How long? (CA resident)	Profession
Joseph Aram	39	Oneida, NY	IL	San Jose	San Jose	3 yrs.	Farmer
Charles T. Botts	40	Spotsylvania, VA	VA	Monterey	Monterey	16 mos.	Lawyer
Elam Brown	52	Herkimer, NJ	MO	San Jose	Benicia	3 yrs.	Farmer
Jose Antonio Carrillo	53	San Francisco	CA	Los Angeles	Los Angeles	Toda la Vida	Labrador
J. M. Covarrubias	40	CA	CA	San Luis Obispo	San Luis Obispo	?	?
E. O. Crosby	34	Tompkins, NY	NY	Sacramento	Vernon	7 mos.	Lawyer
P. N. de la Guerra	36	CA	CA	Santa Barbara	Santa Barbara	?	?
Miguel de Pedrorena	41	Spain	CA	San Diego	San Diego	12 yrs.	Merchant
Lewis Dent	26	St. Louis County, MO	MO	Monterey	Monterey	3 yrs.	Lawyer
Kimball H. Dimmick	34	Chenango, NY	NY	San Jose	San Jose	3 yrs.	Lawyer
Manual Dominguez	46	San Diego	CA	Los Angeles	Los Angeles	"All my life"	Banker
A. J. Ellis	33	Oneida County, NY	NY	San Francisco	San Francisco	2.5 yrs.	Merchant
Stephen C. Foster	28	East Machias, ME	MO	Los Angeles	Los Angeles	3 yrs.	Agriculturist
Edward Gilbert	27	Dutchess County, NY	NY	San Francisco	San Francisco	2.5 yrs.	Printer
W. M. Gwin	44	Sumner County, TN	LA	San Francisco	San Francisco	4 mos.	Farmer
H. W. Halleck	32	Oneida County, NY	NY	Monterey	Monterey	3 yrs.	U.S. Engineer
Julian Hanks	39	Tolland, CT	CT	San Jose	San Jose	10 yrs.	Farmer
L. W. Hastings	30	Knox County	OH	Sacramento	Sutter	6 yrs.	Lawyer
Henry Hill	33	VA	VA	San Diego	Monterey	1 yr., 5 mos.	U.S. Army
Joseph Hobson	39	Baltimore	MD	San Francisco	San Francisco	5 mos.	Merchant
J. M. Hollingsworth	25	Baltimore	MD	San Joaquin	San Joaquin	3 yrs.	Lieut. Volunteers
J. D. Hoppe	35	Carroll County, MD	MO	San Jose	San Jose	3 yrs.	Merchant
J. M. Jones	25	Scott, KY	LA	San Joaquin	San Francisco	4 mos.	Lawyer

Thomas O. Larkin	47	Charlestown	MA	Monterey	Monterey	16 yrs.	Trader
B. S. Lippincott	34	New York	NJ	San Joaquin	Stockton	3.5 yrs.	Trader
Francis J. Lippitt	37	Rhode Island	NY	San Francisco	San Francisco	2 yrs., 7 mos.	Lawyer
M. M. McCarver	42	Madison, KY	OR	Sacramento	Sacramento	1 yr.	Farmer
John McDougal	32	OH	IN	Sacramento	Sutter	7 mos.	Merchant
B. F. Moore	29	FL	TX	San Joaquin	Stockton	1 yr.	"Elegant leisure"
Myron Norton	27	Birmington, VT	NY	San Francisco	San Francisco	1 yr.	Lawyer
Pacificus Ord	34	Allegany County, MD	LA	Monterey	Monterey	8 mos.	Lawyer
Antonio M. Pico	40	Monterey, CA	CA	San Jose	San Jose	"All my life"	Agriculturist
Rodman M. Price	30	Orange, NY	NJ	San Francisco	San Francisco	4 yrs.	U.S. Navy
Hugo Reid	38	Cardross	Scotland	Los Angeles	San Gabriel	16 yrs.	Farmer
Jacinto Rodriguez	36	Monterey	CA	Monterey	Monterey	"All my life"	Agriculturist
Pedro Sansevaine	31	Bordeaux	Bordeaux	San Jose	San Jose	11 yrs.	"Negotiant"
R. Semple	42	KY	MO	Sonoma	Benicia	5 yrs.	Printer
W. E. Shannon	27	Ireland (Mayo)	NY	Sacramento	Columa	3 yrs.	Lawyer
W. S. Sherwood	32	Sandy Hill, NY	NY	Sacramento	Mormon Island	4 mos.	Lawyer
Jacob R. Snyder	34	Philadelphia, PA	PA	Sacramento	Sacramento	4 yrs.	Surveyor
Abel Stearns	51	MA	MA	Los Angeles	Los Angeles	22 yrs.	Merchant
W. M. Steuart	49	Montgomery County, MD	MD	San Francisco	San Francisco	1 yr.	Lawyer
J. A. Sutter	47	Switzerland	MO	Sacramento	Sutter	10 yrs.	Farmer
Henry A Tefft	26	Washington, NY	WI	San Luis Obispo	Nipomo	4 mo.	Lawyer
M. G. Vallejo	42	Monterey, CA	CA	Sonoma	Sonoma	"All my life"	Military
Thomas L. Vermeule	35	NJ	NY	San Joaquin	Stockton	3 yrs.	Lawyer
J. P. Walker	52	Goochland, VA	MO	Sonoma	Sonoma	13 mos.	Farmer
O. M. Wozencraft	34	Clermont City, OH	LA	San Joaquin	San Francisco	4 mos.	Physician

Source: J. Ross Browne, *Report of the Debates in the Convention of California on Formation of the State Constitution in September and October 1849* (1850).

However imperfect their work, at least the founders of 1849 aimed at securing the well-being of the political community, and they created institutions that had sufficient power and authority to actually govern while trusting the election mechanism to control the abuse of power. Instead of relying on term limits, rotation in office, recall, and supermajorities in the legislature, they relied on the electorate having sufficient public virtue to restrain their elected representatives. If anything, they placed considerable trust in the collective wisdom of the electorate and their representatives. The 1849 framers followed the teaching of the early American republicans (Anti-Federalists) and later Jacksonian Democrats by equating the "accountability" of the representatives with their "dependency on the people." They accordingly emphasized the importance of frequent elections, as well as the provision for annual sssembly elections, and biannual elections for the Senate and governor.

The original framers saw frequent elections as a vital institutional expression of the primacy of the educated citizen in a representative form of government. In fact, they operated under a concept of "the people" which we have unfortunately abandoned. They also recognized the need for "responsible" leadership. To that end, they adopted a version of bicameralism that recognized the importance of the Senate as a moderating influence, while restraining the reach of its influence in the governmental system. Put differently, they did not create the subsequent controversy surrounding the "one man one vote" decisions of the 1960s[109] because they did not adopt the so-called federal model of representation in the Senate. Also instructive is that, unlike the later Progressives, the 1849 framers did not provide for the direct election of the administrative offices within the executive branch. The appointment of administrative officers was deemed to be the function of elected representatives. The framers of 1849 showed a remarkable suspicion for the judicial branch by making it a constitutional requirement that the principle of election pervade the entire judicial structure from justices of the peace to coroners to the clerk of the Supreme Court. Thus the complaint of the 1879 refounders, that the 1849 Constitution placed uncontrolled authority in the hands of the Supreme Court, sounds at best strange.

The address of the delegates to the people of California, upon the completion of their labors on October 13, contains an important message of enduring importance. It is well worth the effort to retrieve the original arguments in order to recapture their sense of the *uniqueness* of California; to revisit the genuine debate that took place between newcomers and old-timers, and to converse with the delegates as they balanced the moral and practical dimensions of politics.

The delegates recognized their own diversity and differences, but still appealed to something called a Californian·

> Although born in different climes, coming from different States, imbued with local feelings, and educated perhaps with predilections for peculiar institutions, laws, and customs, the delegates assembled in Convention *as Californians*, and carried on their deliberations in a spirit of amity, compromise, and mutual concession for the public weal.[110]

Even though the Californian delegates in 1849 had diverse backgrounds, they were confident that the deliberative process would, in time, secure the common good. The alternative to that was the convulsion then plaguing Europe The delegates claimed to have founded institutions based "on the eternal principles of equity and Justice" and derived from deliberation and reflection while "all Europe is agitated with the convulsive efforts of nations battling for liberty."[111] In this regard, they lived up to the Tocquevillean test for lawgivers. Robert Semple expressed the importance of the occasion in his acceptance speech on being named President of the Convention on September 4:

> We are now, fellow-citizens, occupying a position to which all eyes are turned. The eyes not only of our sister and parent States are upon us, but the eyes of all Europe are now directed toward California. I am satisfied that we can prove to the world that California has not been settled entirely by [the] unintelligent and unlettered.[112]

NOTES

1. Karl Marx, "The Communist Manifesto," in *The Marx-Engels Reader*, ed. Robert C. Tucker (New York: Norton, 1978 [1848]), 473.

2. This is a compilation of remarks made in a series of letters reprinted in Alexis de Tocqueville, *Selected Letters on Politics and Society*, ed. Roger Boesche (Berkeley: University of California Press, 1985), 199–225.

3. Alexis de Tocqueville, *Democracy in America*, ed. J. P. Mayer, trans. George Lawrence (New York: Harper Perennial, 1969), xii.

4. Tocqueville, *Democracy*, xii–xiv.

5. Tocqueville, *Democracy*, xiv.

6. The material quoted in this paper from the discussions at the California Constitutional Convention are taken from J. Ross Browne, *Report of the Debates in the Convention of California on Formation of the State Constitution in September and October 1849* (1850) (hereafter *Debates*). Unfortunately, the five hundred-page book containing Riley's Proclamation, the records of the debates, and a digest of Mexican laws is out of print,

and is now considered to be a rare book. Two copies available in the Ahmanson Rare Book Room at the Huntington Library, San Marino, California. The coverage here of Riley's Proclamation, as well as the subsequent sections dealing with the debates of the 1849 convention, the comparison of the 1849 Constitution with the refounded Constitution of 1879, as well as the treatment of the 1849 convention in the basic political science and history literature, is an adaptation of an earlier paper, "The Question of Refounding California Government," prepared for delivery by Gordon Lloyd and Margie Lloyd at the annual meeting of the American Political Science Association, Washington, D.C., August 28–31, 1977. A shorter version of the above-mentioned APSA paper can also be found in an editorial, "The Brilliance of California's Founders," *The Riverside Press-Enterprise*, December 15, 1997, A23. See also Margie Lloyd, "California's Golden Moment: The Latest Lost Opportunity to Heal Constitutional Ills," *California Politics and Policy* 49 (November 1996): 57, for a critique of contemporary proposals to reform, and refound, California's Constitution that ignore the original debates.

7. Alexander Hamilton, "The Federalist No. 1," in *The Federalist Papers*, ed. Clinton Rossiter 33 (New York: Mentor, 1961), 31.

8. See Tocqueville, *Democracy*, 412–13.

9. See Karl Marx and Friedrich Engels, *Reviews from the Neue Rheinische Zeitung Revue, 1850* www.marxists.org/archive/marx/works/1850-nrr.htm (visited April 4, 2003).

10. See, for example, Karl Marx, "The Eighteenth Brumaire of Louis Bonaparte," in *The Marx-Engels Reader*, ed. Robert C. Tucker (New York: Norton, 1978), 594, 599 (seeing February Revolution as the first coalescence of Revolutionary Fervor in Europe).

11. Marx and Engels, *Reviews*, 9.

12. Marx and Engels, *Reviews*, 9.

13. Tocqueville, *Democracy*, 410.

14. Tocqueville, *Democracy*, 409–10.

15. Tocqueville, *Democracy*, 408–13, contains Tocqueville's "Conclusion" to volume one.

16. U.S. Const., Art. IV, § 3.

17. There were three identifiable positions on the constitutional role of Congress with respect to slavery in the territories. The Wilmot Northerners claimed that Congress had the authority, and obligation, to exclude slavery from the territories. In this regard, they appealed to the principles undergirding the Northwest Ordinance, and anticipated the position adopted by the yet-to-be-created Republican Party (after the Kansas-Nebraska Act of 1854) and by Abraham Lincoln in the Lincoln-Douglas debates. The Calhounite Southerners argued that slaveowners had the right to travel with their property to the territories and Congress should protect this right. This was the argument behind Taney's 1857 decision in *Dred Scott v. Sanford*, 19 How. (60 U.S.) 393 (1857), declaring unconstitutional the Missouri Compromise of 1820. In 1849, however, the Calhoun faction was willing to settle for extending the 36–30 line of the Missouri Compromise out to the Pacific Ocean. (The 36–30 line hits the Pacific Ocean just south of

Monterey.) The third faction was a coalition of northerners and southerners who argued that the inhabitants of each territory should decide the question of slavery for itself. This is the position associated later with Stephen Douglas and identified as the doctrine of "popular sovereignty." See generally Harry V. Jaffa, *Crisis of the House Divided* (Garden City, N.Y.: Doubleday, 1959).

18. *Debates*, 3.

19. *Debates*, 3.

20. *Debates*, Appendix.

21. *Debates*, 3.

22. *Debates*, 4.

23. *Debates*, 4.

24. It is truly remarkable today to reflect on how thoroughly the slavery question penetrated into every detail of American political life at the time. Stephen Ambrose points out that even the construction of the transcontinental railroad was delayed because of the effect its location would have on the boundary between slave and free states. See Stephen Ambrose, *Nothing Like It in the World: the Men Who Built the Transcontinental Railroad 1863–1869* (New York: Simon & Schuster, 2000). John Quincy Adams rightly used this fact to demonstrate that the triumph of the Slave Power would have meant the eventual eradication of all civil liberties. See generally William Lee Miller, *Arguing about Slavery* (New York: Knopf, 1996).

25. *Debates*, 4.

26. *Debates*, 4.

27. *Debates*, 80.

28. *Debates*, 330.

29. *Debates*, 193.

30. *Debates*, 77.

31. *Debates*, 116.

32. *Debates*, 6.

33. See the Appendix to this paper for a table summarizing the background of the delegates. This is an adaptation of the original found in *Debates*.

34. F. N. Thorpe, *The Federal and State Constitutions, Colonial Charters, and Other Organic Laws of the States, Territories, and Colonies*, vol. 2 (Washington, D.C.: Government Printing Office, 1993), 1123.

35. *Debates*, 41.

36. *Debates*, 43.

37. *Debates*, 44.

38. *Debates*, 47.

39. *Debates*, 49.

40. *Debates*, 61.

41. *Debates*, 114.

42. *Debates*, 116.

43. *Debates*, 117.

44. *Debates*, 124.

45. *Debates*, 134.

46. A good discussion of the Jeffersonian-Jacksonian tradition of free labor, and particularly its evolution in early California, is to be found in Paul Kens, *Justice Stephen J. Field: Shaping Liberty from the Gold Rush to the Gilded Age* (Lawrence: University of Kansas Press, 1997).

47. *Debates*, 123.

48. *Debates*, 138.

49. *Debates*, 140.

50. *Debates*, 143.

51. *Debates*, 141.

52. *Debates*, 145.

53. *Debates*, 149.

54. *Debates*, 146.

55. *Debates*, 146.

56. *Debates*, 149.

57. *Debates*, 149.

58. U.S. Const., Art. IV, § 2, cl. 1 ("The Citizens of each State shall be entitled to all Privileges and Immunities of citizens in the several States.")

59. *Debates,* 150.

60. The next three days went smoothly as the delegates made their way through the Executive branch and articles on the militia, state debt, and amending the constitution. Shannon and Norton argued successfully against Wozencraft's motion to subject the governor to term limits, and McDougal's attempt to introduce a stringent residency qualification on candidates for governor was also defeated.

61. *Debates*, 173.

62. *Debates*, 175.

63. *Debates*, 181.

64. *Debates*, 178.

65. *Debates*, 199.

66. *Debates*, 183.

67. *Debates*, 183.

68. *Debates*, 184.

69. *Debates*, 193.

70. *Debates*, 193.

71. *Debates*, 188.

72. *Debates*, 260. The Women's Movement, to which Folsom and Wright belonged, emerged as a force of its own, separate from the movement to abolish slavery, in 1848 at Seneca Falls. At the convention declaring their independence, the Women's Movement reaffirmed the centrality of the principles of the enlightenment.

73. *Debates*, 260.

74. *Debates*, 263.

75. *Debates*, 294.

76. *Debates*, 294.

77. *Debates*, 295.

78. *Debates*, 296.

79. *Debates*, 305.

80. *Debates*, 305.

81. *Debates*, 305 (emphasis added).

82. *Debates*, 305.

83. *Debates*, 323.

84. Thorpe, *Constitutions*, vol. 1, 393.

85. *Debates*, 330.

86. *Debates*, 331.

87. *Debates*, 333. Snyder, Lippitt, and Semple agreed.

88. *Debates*, 340.

89. *Debates*, 354.

90. *Debates*, 355.

91. *Debates*, 356–57.

92. *Debates*, 419.

93. *Debates*, 424.

94. See Bernard Hyink and David H. Provost, *Politics and Government in California*, 13th ed. (New York: HarperCollins, 1996). John C. Syer and John H. Culver do recognize the immense geographical and international diversity of the forty-eight delegates along with their youthfulness and varied lengths of residence in California. But instead of emphasizing this unique feature of diversity and immigration—no other state Constitutional Convention in the history of America had to contend with such differences—they too point to the studied lack of originality in the document: "Largely due to the presence of a delegate who earlier had participated in Iowa's constitutional convention, the 137 sections of the California document contain 66 sections taken from basic Iowa law. Probably as a result of the fact that 12 former New Yorkers were convention delegates, 19 sections of the constitution of California originated in the Empire State." John C. Syer and John H. Culver, *Power and Politics in California*, 4th ed. (Toronto: Maxwell Macmillan, 1992), 30.

95. Hyink and Provost, *Politics and Government*, 21.

96. Hyink and Provost, *Politics and Government*, 18.

97. Thorpe, *Constitutions*, vol. 1, 393.

98. H. H. Bancroft, *History of California*, vol. 7 (San Francisco: The History Company, 1888), 371.

99. Cal. Const. of 1879, Art. IV, § 24; Thorpe, *Constitutions*, vol. 1, 419.

100. Cal. Const. of 1849, Art. XI, § 21

101. Thorpe, *Constitutions*, vol. 1, 404.

102. See Carl Brent Swisher, *Motivation and Political Technique in the California Constitutional Convention 1878–1879* (New York: Da Capo, 1969), for an explanation of the alliances that were formed with and against The Workingmen's Party.

103. Thorpe, *Constitutions*, vol. 1, 415–46.

104. Tocqueville's specific focus in the text was on Texas.

105. Tocqueville, *Democracy in America*, 408–13. This Conclusion, in length, is roughly one quarter of the entire first volume and is entitled, "The Three Races That Inhabit the United States."

106. Karl Marx, "The German Ideology," in *The Marx-Engels Reader*, ed. Robert C. Tucker (New York: Norton, 1978) 160. This is one of the few places where Marx outlines what life without the division of labor would look like.

107. See Lawrence Friedman, *A History of American Law* (New York: Simon & Schuster, 1973), 346–54 (describing "the trend toward the inflation of constitutional texts," *id.* at 347).

108. See Bruce E. Cain, et al., "Constitutional Change: Is It Too Easy to Amend Our State Constitution?" in *Constitutional Reform in California: Making State Government More Effective and Responsive*, eds. Bruce E. Cain and Roger G. Noll (Berkeley, Calif.: Institute of Governmental Studies Press, 1995), 288.

109. See, for example, *Baker v. Carr*, 369 U.S. 186 (1962); *Reynolds v. Sims*, 377 U.S. 533 (1964).

110. *Debates*, 474–75 (emphasis in original).

111. *Debates*, 474–75.

112. *Debates*, 18.

California and the Seventeenth Amendment

Ralph A. Rossum

This chapter is largely derived from a larger project I have nearly completed on the consequences on federalism of the Seventeenth Amendment.[1] The general argument of the larger project can be stated briefly.

The founding generation clearly understood that federalism would be protected primarily by the mode of electing the U.S. Senate. The adoption and ratification of the Seventeenth Amendment, providing for direct election of the Senate,[2] changed all that. The Seventeenth Amendment was ultimately approved by the U.S. Congress and ratified by the states to make the Constitution more democratic. Progressives argued forcefully, persistently, and successfully that the democratic principle required the Senate to be elected directly by the people rather than indirectly through their state legislatures. The consequences of the ratification of the Seventeenth Amendment on federalism, however, went completely unexplored, and the people, in their desire to make the Constitution more democratic, inattentively abandoned what the framers regarded as the crucial constitutional means for protecting the federal/state balance and the interests of the states as states.[3] The people inattentively eliminated the primary structural support for federalism and, by so doing, fundamentally altered the very meaning of federalism itself.

Following ratification of the Seventeenth Amendment, there was a rapid growth of the power of the national government, with the Congress enacting measures that adversely affected the states as states[4]—measures that quite simply the Senate previously would never have approved.[5] Initially (during the period from the amendment's ratification in 1913 to *N.L.R.B. v. Jones & Laughlin Steel Corporation*[6] in 1937, and then again since *National League of Cities v. Usery*[7] in

1976) the U.S. Supreme Court's frequent reaction to this congressional expansion of national power at the expense of the states was and has been to attempt to fill the gap created by the ratification of the Seventeenth Amendment and to protect the original federal design. It has done so by invalidating these congressional measures on the grounds that they violate the principles of dual federalism; go beyond the Court's narrow construction of the commerce clause; "commandeer" state officials to carry out certain federal mandates; or, most recently, trench on the states' sovereignty immunity. In so doing, it has repeatedly demonstrated its failure to appreciate that the Seventeenth Amendment not only eliminated the primary structural support for federalism but, in so doing, altered the very nature and meaning of federalism itself.

There is irony in all of this. An amendment, intended to promote democracy, even at the expense of federalism, has been undermined by an activist Supreme Court, intent on protecting federalism, even at the expense of the democratic principle. The irony is heightened when it is recalled that federalism was originally protected both structurally and democratically—the Senate, after all, was elected by popularly elected state legislatures. Today, federalism is protected neither structurally nor democratically—the ratification of the Seventeenth Amendment means that the fate of traditional state prerogatives depends entirely on either congressional sufferance (what the Supreme Court occasionally calls "legislative grace") or whether an occasional Supreme Court majority can be mustered.

In this chapter, I will first summarize the reasons the framers regarded the mode of electing the Senate as the crucial constitutional means for protecting federalism. I will then inventory the various political and social factors that led the public to reject that mode and demand instead direct election of the Senate. As I address each of these factors, I will weave into that narrative the significant role that California played in bringing about the adoption and ratification of the Seventeenth Amendment.

THE FRAMERS' RELIANCE ON THE
MODE OF ELECTING THE SENATE
TO PROTECT FEDERALISM

The framers understood that federalism would be structurally protected by the composition and manner of election of the Senate.[8] On May 31, 1787, very early in the Federal Convention, the delegates rejected Resolution 5 of the Virginia Plan that proposed that the "second branch of the National Legislature ought to be elected by those of the first," doing so by a vote of seven states "no," three states "yes."[9] Instead on June 7, they accepted by a vote of ten states "yes," zero states "no," a motion by John Dickinson and seconded by Roger Sherman providing for the appointment of the Senate by the state legislatures.[10] They were apparently persuaded by Dickinson's argument that the "sense of the States would be better collected through their Governments than immediately from the people at large"[11] and by George Mason's observation that election of the Senate by state legislatures would provide the states with "some means of defending themselves against encroachments of the National Government. In every other department, we have studiously endeavored to provide for its self-defense. Shall we leave the States alone unprovided with the means for this purpose?"[12] Even when the delegates subsequently agreed on June 11 to some form of proportional representation in the Senate,[13] they still remained firmly committed to the election of the Senate by the state legislatures.

On June 20, James Wilson, a passionate nationalist,[14] warned his fellow delegates "a jealousy would exist between the State Legislatures and the General Legislature." He observed "that the members of the former would have views and feelings very distinct in this respect from their constituents. A private Citizen of a State is indifferent whether power be exercised by the General or State Legislatures, provided it be exercised most for his happiness. His representative has an interest in its being exercised by the body to which he belongs."[15] On June 25, he continued his attack on the election of the Senate by state legislatures, charging that "the election of the second branch by the Legislatures will introduce and cherish local interests and local prejudices."[16] Wilson's attack, however, utterly failed, not because the delegates disputed his analysis, but because they approved of the outcome.[17] Since they were committed to preserving the states as political entities, they found persuasive Mason's assertions that the states would need the "power of self-defense"[18] and that "the only mode left of giving it to them was by allowing them to appoint the second branch of the National Legislature."[19] Accordingly, on that day, the convention reaffirmed its previous decision to elect the Senate by state legislatures by a vote of nine states "yes," two states "no."[20]

The service rendered to federalism by the mode of electing the Senate was also repeatedly acknowledged and proclaimed during the ratification debates. Thus, in "An Examination of the Constitution of the United States," Tench Coxe, writing under the pseudonym of "An American Citizen" in Philadelphia's *Independent Gazetteer*, noted that the members of the Senate will "feel a considerable check from the constitutional powers of the state legislatures, whose rights they will not be disposed to infringe, since they are the bodies to which they owe their existence."[21] In the Massachusetts Ratifying Convention, Fisher Ames described senators elected by their state legislatures as "ambassadors of the states,"[22] and Rufus King declared that "the senators will have a powerful check in those men [i.e., those state legislators] who wish for their seats, who will watch their whole conduct in the general government, and will give alarm in case of misbehavior."[23]

In *Federalist* 45, Madison declared that since "[t]he Senate will be elected absolutely and exclusively by the State Legislatures," it "will owe its existence more or less to the favor of the State Governments, and must consequently feel a dependence" on them.[24] In *Federalist* 46, he further noted that if the House of Representatives were to sponsor legislation that encroached on the authority of the states, "a few representatives of the people would be opposed to the people themselves; or rather one set of representatives would be contending against thirteen sets of representatives, with the whole body of their common constituents on the side of the latter."[25] The Senate, he assured his readers, would be "disinclined to invade the rights of the individual States, or the prerogatives of their governments."[26] In *Federalist* 59, Alexander Hamilton likewise emphasized that the appointment of senators by state legislatures secured "a place in the organization of the National Government" for the "States in their political capacities."[27] He continued:

> So far as [the mode of electing the Senate] . . . may expose the Union to the possibility of injury from the State Legislatures, it is an evil; but it is an evil which could not have been avoided without excluding the States, in their political capacities, wholly from a place in the organization of the national government. If this had been done, it would doubtless have been interpreted into an entire dereliction of the federal principle; and would certainly have deprived the State governments of that absolute safeguard which they will enjoy under this provision.[28]

Finally, in *Federalist* 62, Madison praised "the appointment of senators by state legislatures" as not only "the most congenial with the public opinion" but also "giving to state governments such an agency in the formation of the federal government, as must secure the authority of the former."[29]

During the New York Ratifying Convention, Hamilton explicitly connected the mode of electing the Senate with the protection of the interests of the states as states. "When you take a view of all the circumstances which have been recited, you will certainly see that the senators will constantly look up to the state governments with an eye of dependence and affection. If they are ambitious to continue in office, they will make every prudent arrangement for this purpose, and, whatever may be their private sentiments or politics, they will be convinced that the surest means of obtaining reelection will be a uniform attachment to the interests of their several states."[30] He also declared: "Sir, the senators will constantly be attended with a reflection, that their future existence is absolutely in the power of the states. Will not this form a powerful check?"[31] Finally, in the North Carolina Ratifying Convention, James Iredell also noted that "[t]he manner in which our Senate is to be chosen gives us an additional security. . . . There is every probability that men elected in this manner will, in general, do their duty faithfully. It may be expected, therefore, that they will cooperate in every laudable act, but strenuously resist those of a contrary nature."[32]

This same argument was also made repeatedly in the early days of the new republic. For example, in a July 1789 letter to John Adams, Roger Sherman emphasized that "[t]he senators, being eligible by the legislatures of the several states, and dependent on them for reelection, will be vigilant in supporting their rights against infringement by the legislative or executive of the United States."[33] In his 1803 edition of *Blackstone's Commentaries*, St. George Tucker declared that if a senator abuses the confidence of "the individual state which he represents," he "will be sure to be displaced."[34] James Kent in his *Commentaries on American Law* noted that "[t]he election of the Senate by the state legislatures is also a recognition of their separate and independent existence, and renders them absolutely essential to the operation of the national government."[35] And Joseph Story in his *Commentaries on the Constitution of the United States* observed that one of the "main grounds" for the mode of appointing the Senate was that it "would introduce a powerful check upon rash legislation" and "would increase public confidence by securing the national government from undue encroachments on the powers of the states."[36]

THE FRAMERS' RELIANCE ON THE MODE OF ELECTING THE SENATE AS A MEANS OF DEMARCATING NATIONAL AND STATE POWERS

The framers favored election of the Senate by state legislatures not simply because it was "the most congenial with the public opinion"[37] and not simply because it provided incentives for senators to remain vigilant in their protection of the "States in their political capacities."[38] They also favored this structural device because it avoided the need to rely on "parchment barriers" and helped them sidestep what Madison described in *Federalist* 37 is the "arduous" task of "marking the proper line of partition, between the authority of the general, and that of the State governments."[39]

An episode at the very outset of the convention is most telling on this point. On May 31, the convention, meeting as a committee of the whole, had just taken up Resolution 6 of the Virginia Plan that proposed, inter alia, that "the National Legislature ought to be empowered . . . to legislate in all cases to which the separate States were incompetent." Charles Pinckney and John Rutledge "objected to the vagueness of the term *incompetent,* and said they could not well decide how to vote until they should see an exact enumeration of the powers comprehended by this definition."[40] Interestingly, Madison responded by candidly expressing his "doubts concerning [the] practicality" of "an enumeration and definition of the powers necessary to be exercised by the national Legislature." While he said he had come to the convention with a "strong bias in favor of an enumeration," he confessed that, during the weeks before a quorum gathered in Philadelphia (during which he and his fellow Virginia delegates drafted the Virginia Plan, including the language in Resolution 6), "his doubts had become stronger." He declared that he would "shrink from nothing," including, he implied, abandoning any attempt to enumerate the specific powers of the national government, "which should be found essential to such a form of Government as would provide for the safety, liberty, and happiness of the community. This being the end of all our deliberations, all the necessary means for attaining it must, however reluctantly, be submitted to."[41]

Madison's speech merely foreshadowed the argument he would later develop more fully in *Federalist* 51—that the power of the new federal government was to be controlled, not through the "cloudy medium" of words and not through the use of "parchment barriers," but by "so contriving the interior structure of the government, as that its several constituent parts may, by their mutual relations, be the means of keeping each other in their proper places."[42] Nonetheless, his words that day were obviously reassuring, for the convention voted at the conclusion of his speech to accept that portion of Resolution 6 by a vote of nine states "yes," one state "divided."[43]

The convention apparently shared Madison's doubts about the "practicality" of partitioning power between the federal government and the states through an enumeration of the powers of the former. Spending almost no time debating what specific powers the federal government should have, it focused instead and almost exclusively on the question of constitutional structure. Not even when the Committee of Detail created out of whole cloth what ultimately became article I, section 8,[44] did the convention systematically scrutinize the powers enumerated therein; it did not even object to the proposed Necessary and Proper

Clause.[45] The conclusion is clear: Rather than attempt to draw precise lines between the powers of the federal and state governments, the framers preferred to rely instead on such structural arrangements as the election of the Senate by the state legislatures to ensure that the vast powers they provided to the national government would not be abused and that the federal design would be preserved.

THE FRAMERS' REJECTION OF THE
SUPREME COURT AS A MEANS OF
PROTECTING FEDERALISM

The framers relied on constitutional structure to protect the interests of the states as states. The Supreme Court has frequently overturned Congress's decisions of where to draw the line between federal and state powers based solely on its assertion that the framers intended for it to be the branch responsible for protecting their original federal design.[46] The framers, however, had no such intention, for they recognized that they could not make it in the Court's self-interest to assume that responsibility. As the Anti-Federalist Brutus had shrewdly remarked, it would never be in the self-interest of the Court to strike down federal laws trenching on the residuary sovereignty of the states, because "[e]very extension of the power of the general legislature, as well as of the judicial powers, will increase the powers of the courts." Brutus insisted that it will be in the interest of the judges "to extend their power and to increase their rights; this of itself will operate strongly upon the courts to give such a meaning to the constitution in all cases where it can possibly be done as will enlarge the sphere of their own authority," and he concluded: "From these considerations the judges will be interested to extend the powers of the courts, and to construe the constitution as much as possible in such a way as to favour it."[47] The framers made no effort to contradict Brutus's assessment and thus concurred *sub silentio*. In fact, the framers went further; while Brutus pointed out that it would not be in the self-interest of the Court to protect federalism, the framers argued that it was not in the best interest of federalism for it to be protected by the Court. The framers wanted the people to have maximum flexibility to draw the line between federal and state powers where they wished. They recognized, as Madison argued in *Federalist* 46, that the people might "in [the] future become more partial to the federal than to the State governments . . . and in that case, the people ought not surely to be precluded from giving most of their confidence where they may discover it to be most due." They were confident that such a "change [could] only result from such manifest and irresistible proofs of a better administration [by the federal government], as will overcome all [the people's] antecedent propensities";[48] nevertheless, if such a change of public attitude did come about, they wanted to accommodate the people's wishes to draw the line between federal and state power where their representatives in the House and states' representatives in the Senate wanted them, not where the Supreme Court might determine.

ALTERING THE ORIGINAL FEDERAL DESIGN: THE FACTORS THAT LED TO THE ADOPTION AND RATIFICATION OF THE SEVENTEENTH AMENDMENT

The framers' original understanding of how federalism would be protected succeeded admirably for the first century.[49] The measures that the Congress passed were understood, even by the Senate, to be consistent with the original federal design and as serving those interests that prompted the adoption and ratification of the Constitution in the first place.[50] With the *Dred Scott* decision as the principal exception,[51] the Supreme Court similarly understood them as well.[52] Over time, however, the public became increasingly dissatisfied with the indirect election of the Senate and unappreciative of the protection it rendered to federalism. Henry Randolph Storrs, a Federalist from New York, introduced the first joint resolution aimed at altering the election of the Senate by state legislatures in the House of Representatives on February 14, 1826.[53] From then until May 13, 1912, when the Congress submitted to the states for their ratification a proposed constitutional amendment providing for direct election of senators, an additional 187 resolutions seeking to alter the means by which the Senate was elected were also introduced in Congress.[54] The House approved six of these proposals before the Senate reluctantly gave its consent in 1912.[55] The factors that led to the Seventeenth Amendment's adoption and ratification need explanation.

LEGISLATIVE DEADLOCK

One factor was legislative deadlock over the election of senators. Deadlocks commonly occurred when one party controlled the state assembly or house and another the state senate, although in California, that was never the case, as the two legislative deadlocks that each time left the state with only one senator for an entire Congress were caused by other factors. In 1855, the deadlock resulted from a split between the northern (or "Tammany") and southern (or "Chivalry") factions[56] of the Democratic Party; in 1899, the deadlock came about when the Republicans divided in "a contest between Los Angeles and San Francisco."[57]

The difficulties began even prior to statehood. On December 20, 1849, Peter H. Burnett was sworn in as the first American civil governor of California, whereupon General Bennett Riley, by proclamation, recognized the new government and resigned as military governor. On that same day, the legislature proceeded to elect California's first two U.S. Senators: John C. Frémont (hero of the Bear Flag Revolt) was elected on the first ballot and William M. Gwin on the third.[58] (Gwin was a southern professional politician who, while in Washington, D.C., for President Zachary Taylor's inauguration, in 1849 told Senator Stephen A. Douglas that he was going to California and that he would be back within a year as a senator from the new state.)[59] Frémont and Gwin set off immediately for Washington, D.C., where, from January through September 9, when California entered the Union, they spent their time successfully lobbying for statehood—the fact that Frémont was a Free Soiler and Gwin was a Chivalry Democrat made their task easier. On September 11, 1850, they were seated as members of the U.S. Senate, with Frémont, by lot, drawing the short term which expired March 4, 1851, and Gwin receiving the long term running through until March 4, 1855.[60]

Frémont's career as a Senator lasted only 175 days, and he spent a portion of that time back in California seeking reelection.[61] Frémont's efforts in late February of 1851 to be reelected, however, were frustrated by the Chivalry Democrats who dominated the California Legislature. Several from their ranks vied to succeed him, but none could gain a majority of the votes, and so, after 142 ballots, the legislature adjourned, having failed to elect a senator to succeed Frémont and thereby leaving California for the next year with only one senator in Washington (and placing in the hands of the pro-Southern Gwin the sole control of federal patronage in the state).[62]

California's first deadlock was subsequently broken early in the third legislature when, on January 28, 1852, the two houses met in joint session and, on the eighth ballot, elected John B. Weller, another Chivalry Democrat and an ally of Gwin. Weller prevailed over David Colberth Broderick, president of the state Senate. Broderick was an Irish stonecutter and Tammany politician who left New York for California in 1849. In a mirror image of Gwin's promise to Douglas, Broderick swore to his Tammany colleague, General Daniel E. Sickles, that if he ever returned to the East it would be as senator from California.[63]

While Gwin and the Chivalry Democrats defeated Broderick in 1852, Broderick was far from vanquished. He set his eye on taking Gwin's seat when his term expired in 1855, and, in fact, in 1854, he pursued a bold scheme to secure that seat by catching other likely aspirants off-guard by attempting to force the legislature to elect Gwin's successor more than a year before his term would expire. As Hubert Howe Bancroft wrote: "There was no precedent for an election by a legislature not the last before the expiration of a senatorial term; but Broderick was of the order of men who made precedents."[64] Broderick defended his proposal on several grounds: First, given the distance of California from Washington, and the uncertainties of travel, it might not be possible for a new senator to reach the capital in time for a special session of Congress in case one should be called; second, if the election were left to the next session, the legislature might deadlock, leaving the state with only one senator as it had before; and third, nothing in federal or state law forbid what was proposed.[65] Broderick's scheme, however, failed on a tie vote, thus setting up an intense showdown between the Broderick Tammany faction and the Gwin Chivalry faction in the 1855 legislature. The result of that showdown was another deadlock; after thirty-eight ballots cast by the legislature in joint session, the legislature adjourned, leaving Gwin's seat in the U.S. Senate vacant for the next two years.[66]

When the legislature convened in January 1857, its first item of business was to elect two senators—one to fill the seat left vacant as a result of the deadlock two years before and the other to replace Weller, whose term expired in March of that year. Broderick was virtually assured one of the seats; many were in his debt as a result of the great political skill he had displayed in the 1856 state Democratic convention, where he welded together the Chivalry and Tammany factions and thus secured the election that fall of a Democratic legislature and Democratic presidential electors.[67] Broderick was not content, however, with mere election; he not only wanted Weller's long-term seat, but he also wanted to determine who would get the short-term seat. His strategy to accomplish this was to have the legislature reverse the standard procedure and elect a successor to the senator still in office before filling the senate seat that had been vacant for two years. The Democratic caucus agreed to Broderick's plan and elected him to the six-year term on the first ballot. Broderick was then in the position to dictate the terms for whoever would be elected to the short term. His price was high; in return for his endorsement, the successful aspirant would have to yield to him control of all federal patronage. Gwin reluctantly acquiesced to the endorsement, and secured his old seat, but now for a shortened term.[68] Gwin put a brave face on his surrender of patronage, claiming that it was voluntary and that the privilege of dispensing patronage had brought him only ingratitude and anxiety.[69] The big losers, however, were the Chivalry Democrats. Broderick used Gwin's concession to shift federal patronage toward northern rather than southern Democrats, a major change in California politics, which, while under the dominant influence of the Chivalry Democrats, had come to be known as a "Virginia poor house."[70]

Broderick's victory over Gwin, distribution of federal patronage to northern Democrats, and Anti-Lecomptonite sentiments did not set well with Chivalry Democrats in general and David S. Terry in particular. Terry was a close friend and political ally of Gwin and chief justice of the California Supreme Court. When on June 26, 1859, Broderick was overheard at breakfast at the International Hotel in San Francisco making a disparaging remark about Terry, the hotheaded Kentucky native resigned from the Court, a position he was about to lose since he had failed to win renomination at the Democratic Convention, and wrote to Broderick demanding a retraction or satisfaction. Broderick refused to retract his statement, and on September 13 on the shores of Lake Merced, Broderick and Terry met in a duel at dawn. Broderick's pistol had a hair-trigger and went off accidentally before he could take proper aim. Terry's well-aimed bullet struck Broderick in the chest, and he fell mortally wounded, dying three days later at the age of forty.

The Broderick-Terry duel added to the tension between the North and the South and, in California, proved the undoing of the Chivalry Democrats. With the advent of the Civil War, both Gwin and Terry obtained commissions in the Confederate Army, and by the war's end, both had gone into exile in Mexico.[71] The story, however, would not be complete without adding one final detail.

Terry eventually returned to California, settled in Stockton where he practiced law, and married Sarah Althea Hill, onetime mistress of William Sharon, millionaire banker, owner of the Palace Hotel in San Francisco, and U.S. Senator from Nevada. Following her affair, Miss Hill had sued Sharon for alimony, claiming she was his common-law wife. She won her suit in state court, but suffered reversals in the federal courts and ultimately at the hands of the U.S. Supreme Court in a decision written by Justice Stephen J. Field.

Field[72] was a member of the second California Legislature, where he was a supporter of Broderick; he had also served on the California Supreme Court with Terry, becoming chief justice when Terry resigned prior to his duel. Abraham Lincoln subsequently appointed Field in 1863 as the first Californian to the U.S. Supreme Court where he served for thirty-four years. When Terry learned that Field had ruled against the legal claims of his new wife, he made repeated threats against Field, prompting W. H. Miller, attorney general of the

United States, to appoint David S. Neagle, a U.S. deputy marshall, as Field's personal bodyguard. On August 14, 1889, Field, who was traveling to San Francisco under the protection of Neagle, left the train at Lathrop, near Stockton, and entered the station for breakfast. Terry, who had also been on the train, did likewise. When Terry spotted Field, he lunged at him and smashed him twice in the face before Neagle intervened, firing twice and hitting Terry both times in the chest. Terry died instantly, thirty years after the day he shot Broderick.[73]

To return to legislative deadlocks as one of the major factors leading to the adoption and ratification of the Seventeenth Amendment, Article I, Section 3 of the Constitution provided that senators shall be chosen by state legislatures. However, it did not provide, in the words of Joseph Story, "for the manner, in which the choice shall be made by the state legislatures, whether by a joint, or by a concurrent vote; the latter is, where both branches form one assembly, and give a united vote numerically; the former is, where each branch gives a separate and independent vote."[74] As a consequence, states adopted different practices to suit themselves. Chancellor Kent notes that in New York State, the legislature initially chose senators by concurrent vote (as initially did most states) but subsequently moved to joint vote (along with about half the states). The reason was clear; in Kent's words, "As the legislature may prescribe the manner, it has been considered and settled in this state, that the legislature may prescribe that they shall be chosen by joint vote or ballot of the two houses," because otherwise, if the two houses could not separately concur in a choice, the "weight" of the state in the U.S. Senate would be "dissipated."[75] Kent personally took exception to electing senators by a joint vote; while he conceded that this practice "has been too long settled . . . to be now disturbed," he insisted that, "if the question was a new one, that when the Constitution directed that the senators should be chosen by the legislature, it meant not the members of the legislature per capita, but the legislature in the true technical sense, being the two houses acting in their separate and organized capacities, with the ordinary constitutional right of negative on each other's proceedings."[76] Story, however, challenged Kent's logic. Story argued that if the election of a senator was a legislative act, then it would be subject to the veto of the governor, but universal practice had been against recognizing any such executive participation in the choice of senators. "The executive," Story wrote, "constitutes a part of the legislature for such a purpose, in cases where the state constitution gives him a qualified negative upon the laws. But this has been silently and universally settled against the executive participation in the appointment."[77]

Varied and changing state practices regarding the election of senators posed a variety of "annoying" problems for the Senate.[78] Article I, section 4 of the

Constitution specifies that "each House shall be the Judge of the Elections, Returns, and Qualifications of its own Members"; it thereby imposed on the Senate the onerous burden of determining whether a state's senators had, in fact, been properly elected. The Senate was forced, for example, to deal with the unusual election of an Indiana senator in 1857.[79] Throughout the thirty-fifth Congress, only one senator had represented Indiana. With less than a month to go before that Congress was to adjourn sine die, a minority of the Indiana Senate, which had been in deadlock with the House, met with a majority (but not a legal quorum) of the House members and proceeded to elect one senator to fill the existing vacancy and another to succeed the senator whose term was about to expire. The individuals elected as a result of this questionable joint vote presented themselves to the U.S. Senate, which accepted their credentials. Formal protests were made by a majority of the Indiana Senate, who contended that the joint session was not legally summoned and was therefore not competent to elect senators. These protests were unavailing, and the U.S. Senate refused to reverse its decision. In its next session, the Indiana Legislature, which had come under Republican control in both houses, treated both seats as vacant and proceeded by concurrent vote to elect two senators to fill the alleged vacancies. The Senate, however, excluded these newly elected senators on the ground that the legislature of a state had no authority to revise the decision of the Senate under its constitutional authority to judge the qualifications of its own members.

While the Indiana case was before the Senate, Simon Cameron's election in Pennsylvania in 1857 was also contested on the ground that there had not been a concurrent majority of each house in his favor. The Senate in this instance rejected the challenge as untenable under both Pennsylvania law and "the uniform practical construction of the Federal Constitution for the last half-century."

Legislation was introduced in the Senate that would have allowed it to avoid such questions in the future by prescribing the time and manner of electing senators, but with the onset of the Civil War, the Congress was occupied with weightier matters. Upon the war's conclusion, troubling questions concerning senatorial elections again embroiled the Senate when John Stockton's election as senator in New Jersey in 1866 was challenged. It was contended that the joint assembly that elected him had exceeded its powers by declaring that Stockton was elected when he had received only a plurality of the votes cast (40 votes out of 81). Initially, by a vote of 22 to 21, with Stockton himself voting, the Senate accepted a committee report that held that the joint assembly was, for purposes of electing senators, the legislature and that it was entitled to lay down the plurality rule. But three days later, it reconsidered, held that Stockton should not have voted on the question of his own seat, and voted to unseat him. Not only had the Senate exhausted its patience addressing such issues, but Stockton was a Democrat and the Senate Republicans saw his expulsion as increasing the likelihood that they would be able to overturn President Andrew Johnson's veto of the Civil Rights Act of 1866.[80] The Senate then proceeded to approve legislation (which was subsequently agreed to by the House) regulating the time and manner of holding senatorial elections. This 1866 law provided, in brief, that on the second Tuesday after the meeting and organization of a legislature, when a senator is to be elected, the two houses shall meet separately and openly, and by a voice vote, "name one person for senator." On the following day "at twelve o'clock meridian," the members of the two houses shall meet in joint assembly and the results of the previous day's vote shall be canvassed. If each house has given a majority vote to the same person, that person is elected senator. If not, "the joint assembly shall then proceed to choose, by a viva voce vote of each member present a person for the purpose aforesaid, and the person having a majority of all the votes of the said joint assembly, a majority of all the members elected to both houses being present and voting, shall be declared duly elected." If no person received a majority vote on that first day, "the joint assembly shall meet at twelve o'clock, meridian, of each succeeding day during the session of the legislature, and take at least one vote until a senator shall be elected."[81]

This legislation interestingly included provisions for both concurrent and joint voting. As Haynes had written, "In order to lessen the chances of a failure to elect . . . it was felt that some provision must be made for a joint vote; yet, out of deference to the predilections for a concurrent vote—a concession, it is said, to the practice in New York and in New England—the law was made to provide that the first vote should be taken by the two houses separately, with a resort to a joint convention, in case the concurrent vote failed to elect."[82] But, what protection the legislation offered against deadlock by its provision for joint voting, it took away through its requirement for an open voice vote during the first day of voting when the two houses met separately. The legislation provided for the disclosure of the preference of each member and the difference between the two houses; it thereby revealed at the outset what a small minority would need to know to prevent, if it could not control, the election. The legislation thus imposed procedures on the states that not only dramatically increased the prospects for deadlock but also ensured that these deadlocks would consume an enormous amount of valuable state legislative time by requiring that a majority of both houses of a state legislature must agree in the election of a senator and that they must do so by meeting daily in joint assembly.

Thanks in no small part to Congress's passage of the law of 1866, the number of legislative deadlocks began to soar. In 1885, the Oregon Legislature failed, after sixty-eight ballots, to elect a senator and eventually did so only in a special session. Two years later, West Virginia failed to elect anyone. In 1892, Louisiana failed to elect a senator. In 1893, the legislatures in Montana, Washington, and Wyoming deadlocked and failed to elect senators, whereupon the governors of these states filled the vacancies by appointment, only to have the Senate deny them their seats on the grounds that only the state legislatures could elect senators. Kentucky failed to elect a senator in 1896; Oregon in 1897; California, Utah, and Pennsylvania in 1899; Rhode Island in 1907; and Colorado in 1911. Deadlock was perhaps most evident and embarrassing in Delaware; it was represented by only one senator in three Congresses and was without any representation at all from 1901 to 1903.[83] From the passage of the 1866 act until the adoption of the Seventeenth Amendment, there were seventy-one such legislative deadlocks, resulting in seventeen senate seats going unfilled for an entire legislative session or more. These protracted deadlocks deprived the affected states of representation in the Senate, consumed a great deal of state legislative time that was therefore not spent on other important state matters, and served to rally the proponents of direct election. Elihu Root's argument in the Senate in 1911 that legislative deadlocks could be eliminated without the need for a constitutional amendment by the simple expedient of changing the law of July 25, 1866, fell on deaf ears.[84]

BRIBERY AND CORRUPTION

A second factor undermining support for the election of senators by state legislatures often followed on the heels of the first: Scandal resulted when deadlocks were occasionally loosened by the lubricant of bribe money. Prior to the passage of the 1866 act, the Senate had investigated only one case of alleged bribery in the election of a senator.[85] However, between 1866 and 1900, the Senate was called on nine times to investigate alleged bribery in Senate election cases;[86] by 1912, that number had increased to fifteen.[87] In the Fifty-ninth Congress alone, 10 percent of the Senate's entire membership was put on trial or subjected to legislative investigation.[88] Two of the most infamous cases involved the elections of Montana Senator William A. Clark in 1899 and Illinois Senator William Lorimer a decade later. Clark confessed to a "personal disbursement" of over $140,000 to the legislators of Montana and resigned his seat during floor deliberations of a unanimous Senate committee report recommending his expulsion on the grounds that he was not "legally elected" since over half of his majority

(8 of 15) had been obtained through bribery.[89] Lorimer, a dark-horse candidate acceptable to both parties, was elected in 1909 by a bipartisan coalition in the Illinois legislature, thereby breaking a protracted stalemate; however, a year later, the *Chicago Tribune* broke the story of how four state legislators were bribed to change their vote on his behalf, and in 1912, nearly half-way through the completion of his term, Lorimer was expelled by the Senate.[90] Instances of bribery and corruption were, in truth, few in number. As Zwicki has pointed out, "Of the 1,180 senators elected from 1789 to 1909, only fifteen were contested due to allegations of corruption, and only seven were actually denied their seats. Corruption was proved to be present in approximately one-half of one percent of the elections during that period."[91] Nonetheless, these instances were much publicized and proved crucial in undermining support for the original mode of electing senators.

POPULISM AND PROGRESSIVISM

A third factor, closely related to the second, was the growing strength of the populist movement and its deep-seated suspicion of wealth and influence. It presented the Senate as "an unrepresentative, unresponsive 'millionaires club,' high on partisanship but low in integrity."[92] In the House, proponents of direct election proclaimed a need to "awaken . . . in the Senators . . . a more acute sense of responsibility to the people."[93] And in the Senate, they proclaimed the Senate to be "a sort of aristocratic body—too far removed from the people, beyond their reach, and with no especial interest in their welfare."[94]

While populism waned, progressivism waxed in its place, providing still a fourth factor: Progressivism's belief in "the redemptive powers of direct democracy,"[95] i.e., its conviction that the solution to all the problems of democracy was more democracy.[96] The people could be trusted to act for themselves; in Woodrow Wilson's words, government was to be not only "of, by, and for" the people, but "through the people."[97] Thus, Senator William Jennings Bryan argued on the floor that "if the people of the United States have enough intelligence to choose their representatives in the State legislature . . . they have enough intelligence to choose the men who shall represent them in the United States Senate."[98] Senator David Turpee agreed: however valid the reasons might have been for the framers' original mode of electing senators, the people at the end of the nineteenth century were "a new people living and acting under an old system."[99]

POLITICAL FORCES AT WORK
AT THE STATE LEVEL

Over time, election of senators by state legislatures came to be associated with stalemate, corruption, plutocracy, and reaction; by contrast, direct election of senators was associated with reform, integrity, democracy, and progress. The public demanded change and repeatedly carried this message to the Congress itself through direct petitions. Beginning with a petition from the citizens of Kendall and LaSalle, Illinois, dated January 18, 1886, and continuing through the day the Seventeenth Amendment received congressional approval, the Congress received a total of 238 petitions from farmers' associations, labor groups, and other citizens' groups calling for direct election of the Senate.[100]

The politicians also demanded change. Beginning with the Nebraska Republican Party in 1872 and continuing until the ratification of the Seventeenth Amendment, a total of 239 party platforms called for direct election of the Senate, including 220 state party platforms, and nineteen national party platforms.[101]

Even the states themselves demanded change. Beginning with a memorial from the California State Legislature on February 18, 1874, and continuing through congressional adoption of the Seventeenth Amendment in 1912, the Congress received a total of 175 memorials from state legislatures urging adoption of direct election of the Senate.[102] State legislatures did more, however, than merely demand change by sending memorials to the Congress; they took other steps as well to bring it about. Thus, by 1912, thirty-three states had introduced the use of direct primaries,[103] and twelve states had adopted some form of what was known as the "Oregon system."[104]

South Carolina was the first state to introduce the direct primary in 1888.[105] The direct primary democratized the election of senators in the same way that the election of the president had been democratized. As Alan Grimes explains, "[I]n the same fashion in which state members of the Electoral College cast their votes for the presidential candidate who had received the greatest popular vote in the state, so the state legislatures were asked to elect that candidate for senate who had received the greatest popular vote in a preferential primary."[106]

The direct primary, however, shared the same problem as the democratized Electoral College: the faithless elector. State legislators were not legally bound to abide by the results of the primary and could ignore the wishes of the voters. In an attempt to solve this problem, the state of Oregon passed by initiative in 1904 the "Oregon system." Under this system, a general election runoff was held between the primary nominees for the Senate of the major parties, and candidates for the state legislature were "permitted" to include in their platform one of two statements regarding their views on the election of senators. Statement number one pledged the candidate to abide by the results of the general election and, regardless of party affiliation, to vote "for that candidate for United States Senator in Congress who has received the highest number of the people's vote for that position at the general election." Statement number two declared that the candidate would treat the results of the general election "as nothing more than a recommendation" and would vote according to his personal discretion.[107]

Eleven other states (Idaho, Nebraska, Nevada, Colorado, California, Kansas, Minnesota, New Jersey, Ohio, Montana, and Arizona) quickly imitated the Oregon system, with many going even further. Nebraska, for example, required that, after each candidate's name on the primary ballot for the state legislature the following words would appear: "Promises to vote for people's choice for United States Senator" or "Will not promise to vote for people's choice for United States Senator."[108]

The states took another decisive step as well to bring about direct election of the Senate; they exercised their power under Article V of the Constitution and called for a convention to consider amending the Constitution to provide for direct election of the Senate. Calling for a constitutional convention was a high-risk strategy. Article V of the Constitution makes no provision for the manner of selecting and apportioning the delegates to such a constitutional convention, for the place of holding such a convention, for the rules of its proceedings, or for the scope of its authority. As a consequence, many argue that once a convention is called, there is no way to confine its deliberations; such a convention might consider itself authorized to propose other amendments to the Constitution as well—or even to propose an entirely new Constitution organized on completely different principles.[109] Nevertheless, the states seemed willing "to risk opening Pandora's Box for the sake of securing the popular election of senators."[110] In 1893, California became the first state to apply to Congress for such a convention; the people of the state had given their approval—by a vote of 187,987 to 13,342—to direct election of senators as a referendum during the general election in November 1892. It was followed six years later by Texas. In 1900, the Pennsylvania Legislature took the decisive step of suggesting to the states a coordinated effort to demand a convention; believing that the Senate would not act until two-thirds of the states forced it to do so, it sent to all the states a copy of its convention petition and encouraged them likewise to submit one.[111] Momentum was gained, as, in addition to Pennsylvania, Michigan, Colorado, Oregon, and Tennessee all made application to Congress for a convention in 1901. Kentucky applied in 1902, and Arkansas, Washington, and Illinois followed suit in 1903. Nebraska applied in 1907, as did Indiana, Iowa, Kansas, Louisiana, Missouri, Montana, Nevada, New Jersey, North Carolina, Idaho, Oklahoma, South Dakota, Utah, and Wisconsin in 1908. By 1910, when Maryland applied to Congress for a convention, twenty-seven of the thirty-one state legislatures then required to call a convention had formally petitioned the Congress. Because of its call in 1908 for a convention for another reason (to abolish polygamy), Delaware was widely regarded by the proponents of direct election as constituting a twenty-eighth state; as they pointed out, all that it took to determine that a state's application for a convention was legitimate was a simple majority in both houses of Congress. Arizona and New Mexico were about to become states and were expected to increase the ranks of those supporting such an amendment to thirty. While their admission to the Union would also increase the necessary two-thirds of the states to thirty-two, proponents of direct election noted that Alabama and Wyoming had already submitted resolutions supporting the idea of a convention although without formally calling for one, and that the language of their resolutions could be easily rectified.[112] The fear of a "runaway" constitutional convention, along with the fact that most senators represented states whose legislatures were on record as favoring direct election of the Senate, proved decisive.[113] Thus, on May 12, 1912, the Sixty-second Congress finally approved the Seventeenth Amendment by a vote in the Senate of 64 to 24 (with three not voting) and by a vote in the House of 238 to 39 (with 110 not voting).

The Seventeenth Amendment was quickly ratified by the states in less than eleven months (at the time, the only amendment to have been ratified more quickly was the Twelfth Amendment).[114] Connecticut was the requisite thirty-sixth state to ratify on April 8, 1913. Not only was it ratified quickly, but it was ratified by overwhelming numbers. Two statistics show how overwhelming: In fifty-two of the seventy-six state legislative chambers that voted to ratify the Seventeenth Amendment, the vote was unanimous, and in all thirty-six of the ratifying states, the total number of votes cast in opposition to ratification was only 188, with 152 of these votes coming from just two legislative chambers: seventy-seven came from the Connecticut House and seventy-five from the Vermont House. California played its part in this respect. Governor Hiram Johnson referred the proposed amendment to the legislature early in its 1913 session on January 17; the assembly approved a joint resolution providing for ratification on January 21 by a vote of 73 to 0, and seven days later, the Senate concurred unanimously by a vote of 67 to 0.

CALIFORNIA AND THE
SEVENTEENTH AMENDMENT

The framers incorporated federalism into the Constitution, but without ever defining or even expressly mentioning it. They knew that the federalism they had created was inherently unstable; the precarious balance between its "partly national" and "partly federal" elements would seem inevitably to shift over time, tilting the government toward becoming either more national or more federal. They also worried that, if that shift were to occur, given the widely recognized need for a more powerful national government as well as the actual powers delegated to it in Article I, Section 8, the tilt would necessarily be in the direction of making the government more national. They nonetheless believed that constitutional structure could maintain the balance of national and federal elements they had established. In particular, they believed that the mode they had selected for the election of the U.S. Senate could preserve the original federal design and protect the interests of states as states.

The Seventeenth Amendment fundamentally altered that constitutional structure and upset that federal balance. As the first state to memorialize Congress to adopt an amendment providing for direct election of senators, as the only state that had allowed its people to express support for such an amendment (and overwhelming support it was) through the referendum process, as the first state to seek to bypass opposition to direct election in the Congress by calling for a constitutional convention to consider such an amendment, and as an early state to ratify (and ratify unanimously) the Seventeenth Amendment, California certainly played an important role in bringing about this important structural change to the Constitution. Since the consequence of the Seventeenth Amendment had been to weaken federalism and the interests of states as states, California must be described as having played an important role in rendering itself and the other states less important.

NOTES

1. See Ralph A. Rossum, *Federalism, the Supreme Court, and the Seventeenth Amendment: The Irony of Constitutional Democracy* (Lanham, Md.: Lexington, 2001).

2. The text of the Seventeenth Amendment is as follows:

The Senate of the United States shall be composed of two Senators from each State, elected by the people thereof, for six years; and each Senator shall have one vote. The electors in each State shall have the qualifications requisite for electors of the most numerous branch of the State Legislatures.

When vacancies happen in the representation of any State in the Senate, the executive authority of such State shall issue writs of election to fill such vacancies: Provided, That the Legislature of any State may empower the Executive thereof to make temporary appointments until the people fill the vacancies by election as the Legislature may direct.

This amendment shall not be so construed as to affect the election or term of any Senator chosen before it becomes valid as part of the Constitution. U.S. Const. Amend. XVII.

3. The phrase, "the interests of the states as states," refers to their interests as political rather than merely geographical entities. See Joseph Story, *Commentaries on the Constitution of the United States* (Boston: Hilliard, Gray, and Co., 1833), § 454 (citing James Madison, *Virginia Report* [January 7, 1800], [Richmond, Va.: Thomas Richie]).

4. Not only have these post–Seventeenth Amendment congressional measures increased in number and intrusiveness, they have also become, in Theodore J. Lowi's terms, more abstract, general, novel, discretionary, and prescriptive (in contrast to earlier pre–Seventeenth Amendment legislation that was more concrete, specific, traditional, rule bound, and prospective). Theodore J. Lowi, *The End of Liberalism: Ideology, Policy, and the Crisis of Public Authority* (New York: Norton, 1969), 134–35. This development has led to what Lowi calls "policy without law" (Lowi, *End of Liberalism*, 126) and has weakened not only the states but the Congress itself—after all, with the Senate no longer answerable to state legislatures, it has felt increasingly free to join the House in legislating on every social, economic, or political problem which it perceives as confronting the nation, even if the resulting measures are little more than blank checks of authority to the executive branch and the federal bureaucracy. See Vikram David Amar, "Indirect Effects of Direct Election: A Structural Examination of the Seventeenth Amendment," *Vanderbilt Law Review* 49 (1996): 1360–89.

5. It must be stressed that this is not a "cause and effect" argument; clearly, many factors account for the rapid expansion of the national government, with two world wars and the Cold War, continued industrial growth, and breakthroughs in transportation and electronic communications being chief among them. Moreover, as Bybee acknowledges, it is "a maddeningly difficult proposition to prove" the exact effects of direct election of senators. Jay S. Bybee, "Ulysses at the Mast: Democracy, Federalism, and the Sirens' Song of the Seventeenth Amendment," *Northwestern University Law Review* 91 (1997): 547. Nevertheless, it is clear that the ratification of the Seventeenth Amendment removed a previously existing constitutional brake on these centralizing tendencies, and that federalism, as Zywicki has pointed out, has been reduced to "a pale imitation of its pre-Seventeenth Amendment vigor." Todd J. Zywicki, "Beyond the Shell and Husk of History: The History of the Seventeenth Amendment and Its Implications for Current Reform Proposals," *Cleveland State Law Review* 45 (1997): 212. *See also* Zywicki, "Beyond the Shell," 174–75: Conventional wisdom states that the New Deal commenced a radical shift in the scope of the federal government. In fact, the growth in the federal government began almost immediately after the passage of the Progressive Era amendments. . . . The New Deal simply confirmed the constitutional revolution, which had already transpired.

6. 301 U.S. 1 (1937).

7. 426 U.S. 833 (1976).

8. By composition, I mean, in the words of Oliver Ellsworth, "that in the second branch each state have an equal vote," resulting thereby in a "general government *partly federal and partly national.*" Max Farrand, ed. *Records of the Federal Convention of 1787*, vol. 1 (New Haven, Conn.: Yale University Press 1937), 474 (emphasis in original). This, of course, is the description James Madison will apply to the new federal structure created by the Federal Convention in "The Federalist No. 39" (James Madison). See Zywicki, "Beyond the Shell," 176–79, for an excellent discussion of how bicameralism served to preserve the interests of the states as states. The focus here is not on the composition of the Senate (or on how equal representation of the states and bicameralism advance the interests of federalism) but only on the manner by which the Senate is elected.

9. Farrand, *Records*, 152.

10. Farrand, *Records*, 156.

11. Farrand, *Records*, 150. See also Sherman's argument: "[T]he particular States would thus become interested in supporting the National Government, and . . . a due harmony between the two Governments would be maintained." (*Records*, 150).

12. Farrand, *Records*, 155. In "Yates's Notes" for the same day, Mason is reported as saying: "[T]he second branch of the national legislature should flow from the legislature of each state, to prevent the encroachments on each other, and to harmonize the whole." Farrand, *Records*, 157.

13. Farrand, *Records*, 202. This decision was, of course, subsequently overturned on July 16 when the Convention accepted what is often called either the "Great Compromise" or the "Connecticut Compromise" and agreed that the states would be proportionately represented in the House of Representatives (based on population) and equally represented in the Senate (with each state having two senators). Farrand, *Records*, vol. 2, 15.

14. See Ralph A. Rossum, "James Wilson and the 'Pyramid of Government': The Federal Republic," *Political Science Reviewer* 6 (1976): 113–42.

15. Farrand, *Records,* 343–44.

16. Farrand, *Records,* 406.

17. Roger G. Brooks, "Garcia, the Seventeenth Amendment, and the Role of the Supreme Court in Defending Federalism," *Harvard Journal of Law & Public Policy* 10 (1987): 189, 193.

18. Farrand, *Records*, 407. Roger Sherman had already made much the same argument on June 6: "If it were in view to abolish the State Govts. the elections ought to be by the people. If the State Govts. are to be continued, it is necessary in order to preserve harmony between the National and State Govts. that the elections to the former should be made by the latter" (*Records*, 133).

19. Farrand, *Records*, 407. It must be noted that other "modes" of self-defense were available as well; the three most important were the requirement that the Senate delega-

tion from a state vote as a block, the requirement of rotation in office, and explicit provi
sion for the instruction of senators by state legislatures. See Elaine K. Swift, *The Making of the American Senate: Reconstitutive Change in Congress, 1787–1841* (Ann Arbor: University of Michigan Press, 1996): 39–45; John C. Yoo, "The Judicial Safeguards of Federalism," *Southern California Law Review* 70 (1997): 1369–71. Jay S. Bybee points out the framers had persuasive reasons for rejecting these other "modes" (Bybee, "Ulysses at the Mast," 500). Concerning their rejection of block voting, the framers had learned from experience that caucuses were effectively without representation when their votes were evenly divided. Per capita voting, therefore, ensured that states would be represented, even if they were not represented consistently. It also helped assure that divided delegations would not abstain and frustrate action by the Senate at all. "Moreover, the founders may have assumed that per capita voting would represent the states better, even if a state's senators were divided. Since their elections were staggered, they would "represent different moods or political sentiments. Senators elected by shifting majorities in the state legislature would accurately reflect the shifting political sentiments of the people" (Bybee, "Ulysses at the Mast," 514). Concerning recall, the framers' refusal to embrace this mode "reaffirmed their commitment to the six-year term. Had the Constitution granted states the recall power, then each succeeding legislature might select its own delegate to the Senate, perhaps making the Senate as subject to the winds of political change as the House" ("Ulysses," 530). And concerning instructions, Bybee argues that "the right of instruction was mentioned frequently and was assumed to exist" ("Ulysses," 520). It did not require explicit authorization. As Rufus King declared in the Massachusetts State Ratifying Convention, "state legislatures, if they find their [senators] erring, can and will instruct them," Jonathon Elliot, *Debates in the Several State Conventions on the Adoption of the Federal Constitutions*, vol. 2 (Buffalo, N.Y.: William S. Hein 1996), 47. Likewise, as Alexander Hamilton declared in the New York State Ratifying Convention, the people "have it in their power to instruct their representatives; and the state legislatures, which appoint the senators, may enjoin it also upon them." Elliot, *Debates*, 252.

20. Farrand, *Records*, 408. The importance of having the state legislatures elect the Senate appears, in fact, to have motivated some delegates ultimately to favor equal representation of the states in the Senate. See William Davie's speech of June 30 in Farrand, *Records*, 487.

21. An American Citizen (Tench Coxe), "An Examination of the Constitution of the United States," in *Friends of the Constitution: Writings of the "Other" Federalists: 1787–1788*, ed. Colleen A. Sheehan and Gary L. McDowell (Indianapolis, Ind.: Liberty Fund, 1998), 466.

22. Elliot, *Debates*, 46.

23. Elliot, *Debates*, 47.

24. James Madison, *Federalist* 45, in *The Federalist Papers*, ed. Clinton Rossiter (New York: Mentor, 1961), 291. (Hereafter, the collection will be referred to as *Federalist*.)

25. Madison, *Federalist* 46, 298.

26. Madison, *Federalist* 46, 298.

27. Alexander Hamilton, *Federalist* 59, 364.

28. Hamilton, *Federalist* 59, 364.

29. Madison, *Federalist* 62, 377.

30. Elliot, *Debates,* 306.

31. Elliot, *Debates,* 317–18.

32. Elliot, *Debates,* vol. 4, 40. See also James Iredell, "Answers to Mr. Mason's Objections to the New Constitution, Recommended by the Late Convention," in *Pamphlets on the Constitution of the United States: Published during Its Discussion by the People 1787–1788,* ed. Paul Leicester Ford (Brooklyn, N.Y.: 1888), 340: "They [Senators] have no permanent interest as a body to detach them from the general welfare, since six years is the utmost period of their existence, unless their respective legislatures are sufficiently pleased with their conduct to reelect them. This power of reelection is itself a great check upon abuse, because if they have ambition to continue members of the Senate they can only gratify this ambition by acting agreeably to the opinion of their constituents."

33. Philip B. Kurland and Ralph Lerner, eds. *Founders' Constitution,* vol. 1, (Chicago: University of Chicago Press, 1987), 1232.

34. St. George Tucker, *Blackstone's Commentaries: With Notes of Reference to the Constitution and Laws of the Federal Government of the U.S. and the Commonwealth of Virginia* (Philadelphia: W. Y. Birch and A. Small, 1803), 23–24.

35. Kent, in *Commentaries,* vol. 1, 1826, 211.

36. Story, *Commentaries,* § 704.

37. Farrand, *Records,* 152.

38. Hamilton, *Federalist* 59, 364.

39. Madison, *Federalist* 37, 227.

40. Farrand, *Records,* 53 (emphasis in original).

41. Farrand, *Records,* 53 (emphasis in original).

42. Madison, *Federalist* 51, 320. The mode of electing the Senate was obviously one such constitutional structure that the framers employed to keep the general government in its proper place.

43. Farrand, *Records,* 54.

44. There had been no systematic discussion by the members of the Convention of what powers the new national government was to have when the Committee of Detail was given the task, on July 25, of taking the various resolutions that the Convention had approved to date and converting them into a draft constitution. One of the resolutions was Resolution 6, which then read: "Resolved, That the national legislature ought to possess the legislative rights vested in Congress by the confederation; and moreover, to legislate in all cases for the general interests of the union, and also in those to which the states are separately incompetent, or in which the harmony of the United States may be interrupted by the exercise of individual legislation" (Farrand, *Records,* vol. 2, 27).

45. While both Randolph and Elbridge Gerry eventually mentioned the necessary

and proper clause as one of the reasons for their refusal to sign the Constitution, they never objected to its wording or sought its elimination when the Convention was reviewing the work of the Committee of Detail. See Farrand, *Records*, vol. 2, 563, 632.

46. Beginning with *Scott v. Sandford*, 60 U.S. 393 (1857), and continuing up to *Morrison v. U.S.*, 120 S.Ct. 1740 (2000), the Supreme Court has invalidated twenty-two federal statues on federalism grounds. Included in this number are the statutes invalidated in such highly controversial opinions as *Hammer v. Dagenhart*, 247 U.S. 251 (1918); *Bailey v. Drexel Furniture Co.*, 259 U.S. 20 (1922); *R.R. Retirement Bd. v. Alton Ry.*, 295 U.S. 330 (1935); *Schecter Poultry Corp. v. U.S.*, 295 U.S. 495 (1935); *United States v. Butler*, 297 U.S. 1 (1936); *Carter v. Carter Coal Co.*, 298 U.S. 238 (1936); *Nat'l League of Cities v. Usery*, 426 U.S. 833 (1976); *New York v. United States*, 505 U.S. 144 (1992); *Lopez v. United States*, 514 U.S. 549 (1995); *City of Boerne v. Flores*, 521 U.S. 507 (1997); *Printz v. United States*, 521 U.S. 898 (1997); *Fla. Prepaid Postsecondary Educ. Expense Bd. v. Coll. Sav. Bank*, 527 U.S. 627 (1999); *Coll. Sav. Bank v. Fla. Prepaid Postsecondary Educ. Expense Bd.*, 527 U.S. 666 (1999); *Alden v. Maine*, 527 U.S. 706 (1999); *Kimel v. Fla. Bd. of Regents*, 120 S.Ct. 631 (2000).

47. Herbert J. Storing, ed. "The Essays of Brutus," in *The Complete Anti-Federalist*, vol. 2 (Chicago: University of Chicago Press, 1981), 421.

48. Madison, *Federalist 46*, 295. Compare with (Madison, *Federalist 39*, 245–46) where Madison seems to argue to the contrary. He speaks of a "tribunal" that is to resolve "controversies relating to the boundary between the two jurisdictions." He argues that "the proposed government cannot be deemed a national one; since its jurisdiction extends to certain enumerated objects only, and leaves to the several States a residuary and inviolable sovereignty over all other objects. It is true that in controversies relating to the boundary between the two jurisdictions, the tribunal which is ultimately to decide, is to be established under the general government. But this does not change the principle of the case. The decision is to be impartially made, according to the rules of the Constitution; and all the usual and most effectual precautions are taken to secure this impartiality. Some such tribunal is clearly essential to prevent an appeal to the sword and a dissolution of the compact; and that it ought to be established under the general rather than under the local governments, or, to speak more properly, that it could be safely established under the first alone, is a position not likely to be combated." It is not at all clear, however, that the "tribunal" to which Madison was referring was not the Senate. See George W. Carey, *In Defense of the Constitution* (Indianapolis, Ind.: Liberty Fund 1995), 104–5. ("Madison looked upon the disputes surrounding state-national relations as primarily political issues to be settled through distinctly political, not judicial . . . processes.")

49. See Zywicki, "Beyond the Shell," 174: "[S]tatistical and anecdotal evidence suggests that the Senate played an active role in preserving the sovereignty and independent sphere of action of state governments. Rather than delegating lawmaking authority to Washington, state legislators insisted on keeping authority close to home. . . . As a result, the long-term size of the federal government remained fairly stable and relatively small

during the pre–Seventeenth Amendment era. Although the federal government grew substantially in size in response to particular crises, most notably wars, it returned to its long-term stable pattern following the abatement of the crisis. The 'rachet effect' of federal intervention persisting after the dissipation of the crisis which purportedly spawned it, was absent from American history until 1913."

50. Included among these measures is the passage of the Fourteenth Amendment: While that amendment nationalized citizenship and provided Congress with enormous power under Section 5, so long as the Senate that had to concur in the actual employment of that enormous power was elected by state legislatures, federalism and the interests of the states as states remained secure. Also included are the passage of the Interstate Commerce Act of 1887, 24 Stat. 379 (1887), the Sherman Anti-Trust Act of 1890, 26 Stat. 209 (1890), and the Pure Food and Drug Act of 1906, 34 Stat. 768 (1906). Passage of the Interstate Commerce Act was prompted by Wabash, *St. L. & P. R. v. Ill.*, 118 U.S. 551 (1886), in which the Supreme Court made railroads an interstate issue by declaring that states could not regulate interstate railroad traffic within their own borders, even in the absence of congressional legislation. The Sherman Anti-Trust Act and the Pure Food and Drug Act were appropriate measures for dealing with an emerging national economy, and all three regulatory measures were, as Theodore J. Lowi points out, "traditional," "rule-bound," and "proscriptive." Lowi, *End of Liberalism*, 134.

51. *Scott v. Sandford.* The Court declared unconstitutional Congress's attempt to regulate the spread of slavery in the Missouri Compromise of 1820.

52. During the entire period prior to the ratification of the Seventeenth Amendment, the Supreme Court's invalidations of congressional measures on federalism grounds were few in number and, with the exception of *Scott v. Sandford*, of little consequence. It invalidated only seven congressional measures in the following cases: *Scott v. Sandford, supra* note 46; *United States v. Dewitt*, 76 U.S. 41 (1870); *United States v. Fox,* 95 U.S. 670 (1878); *The Trademark Cases*, 100 U.S. 82 (1879); *The Employers' Liability Cases,* 207 U.S. 463 (1908); *Keller v. U.S.*, 213 U.S. 138 (1909), and *Coyle v. Smith*, 221 U.S. 559 (1911). An eighth statute considered in *In re Heff*, 197 U.S. 488 (1905), could possibly be added here. However, the Court explicitly overturned *In re Heff* in *United States v. Nice*, 241 U.S. 591 (1916), and, consequently, it is not included in these totals.

53. Wallace Worthy Hall, "The History and Effect of the Seventeenth Amendment," Ph.D. diss. (University of California, Berkeley, 1936), 10–11.

54. For a table providing the date, author, title, disposition, and citation for each of these 188 joint resolutions, see Hall, "History and Effect," 443–56 (App. A).

55. The House approved these proposals by a two-thirds voice vote on January 16, 1893; by a vote of 141 to 50 on July 21, 1894; by a vote of 185 to 11 on May 11, 1898; by a vote of 242 to 15 on April 12, 1900; by a two-thirds voice vote on February 13, 1902; and by a vote of 296 to 16 on April 13, 1911. See David E. Kyvig, *Explicit and Authentic Acts: Amending the U.S. Constitution, 1776–1995* (Lawrence: University of Kansas Press,1996), 209; and Hall, "History and Effect," 163–64.

56. The two terms come from Zoeth Skinner Eldredge, *History of California*, vol. 4, (New York: Century History, 1915), 136.

57. A. A. Gray, *History of California: From 1542* (Boston: D. C. Heath, 1934), 526. When the term of Senator Stephan M. White, a Democrat from Los Angeles, expired in 1899, a falling out between Governor Henry T. Gage, a Republican from Los Angeles, and Michael H. de Young, Republican publisher of the *San Francisco Chronicle*, led to deadlock in the Republican-controlled legislature. After 104 ballots, and with the depletion of the legislators' expense allowance for the session, the legislature adjourned on March 19 without electing a senator. The seat remained vacant until Thomas R. Bard, a Republican from Ventura, filled it in 1901. See Ralph J. Roske, *Everyman's Eden: A History of California* (New York: Macmillan, 1968), 447–48; Rockwell D. Hunt, *California and Californians*, vol. 2 (Chicago: Lewis, 1926), 414; Royce D. Delmatier, Clarence F. McIntosh, and Earl G. Waters, *The Rumble of California Politics: 1848–1970* (New York: Wiley, 1970), 133–37.

58. Eldredge, *History of California*, 374–75.

59. Delmatier, *Rumble*, 17.

60. Delmatier, 11.

61. Much of Frémont's time in Washington was spent at the bedside of his wife, Jesse, who took ill on the trip from California to Washington in January of 1850. Arthur Quinn, *The Rivals: William Gwin, David Broderick, and the Birth of California* (New York: Crown, 1994), 80.

62. Hubert Howe Bancroft, *History of California* (San Francisco: The History Company, 1888), 646–47. See also Quinn, *Rivals*, 102–3.

63. Delmatier, *Rumble*, 17.

64. Bancroft, *History*, 681.

65. Eldredge, *History*, 471.

66. Bancroft, *History*, vol. 6, 693. See Quinn, *Rivals*, 160.

67. Bancroft, *History*, vol. 6, 704.

68. The story is wonderfully told in Eldredge, *History*, vol. 3, *supra* note 56, at 502, 504.

69. However, in a letter to Broderick, Gwin wrote: "Provided I am elected, you shall have the exclusive control of this patronage, so far as I am concerned and in its distribution I shall only ask that it may be used with magnanimity, and not to the advantage of those who have been our mutual enemies, and unwearied in their exertions to destroy us. This determination is unalterable; and in making this declaration I do not expect you to support me for that reason, or in any way to be governed by it. But as I have been betrayed by those who should have been my friends, I am powerless myself, and dependent upon your magnanimity." (Bancroft, *History*, vol. 6, 707–8).

70. Eldredge, *History*, vol. 3, 469. See also Bancroft, *History*, 709.

71. Andrew Rolle, *California: A History*, 4th ed. (Arlington Heights, Ill.: Davidson, 1987), 245.

72. For more on Justice Field, see John C. Eastman and Timothy Sandefur, "Justice

Stephen Field: Frontier Justice or Justice on the Natural Rights Frontier?" *Nexus* 5 (2001), 121.

73. Russell Buchanan, *David S. Terry of California: Dueling Judge* (San Marino, Calif.: Huntington Library, 1956), 218–19. On the legal difficulties that befell Neagle for his protection of Field, see *In re Neagle*, 135 U.S. 1 (1890).

74. Story, *Commentaries*, vol. 3, § 703.

75. Kent, *Commentaries*, vol. 1, *211.

76. Kent, *Commentaries*, *211, 225–26.

77. Story, *Commentaries*, § 705.

78. George H. Haynes, *The Election of Senators* (New York: Henry Holt, 1906), 20.

79. The following discussion is based largely on Haynes, *The Election of Senators*, 21–24.

80. Bybee, *Ulysses at the Mast*, 547.

81. 14 Stat. 245 (1866).

82. Haynes, *Election*, 27.

83. Kyvig, *Explicit and Authentic*, 209. See also George H. Haynes, *The Senate of the United States: Its History and Practice*, vol. 2 (New York: Russell and Russell, 1938), 92; and Hall, "History and Effect," 287–301. As Zywicki, "Beyond the Shell," 199, points out, however, despite these problems, Delaware affirmatively voted to reject the Seventeenth Amendment.

84. In the Sixty-second Congress (on April 6, 1911), Senator Root introduced a bill to amend the law of 1866 so that after a legislature had cast ballots for twenty days in an unsuccessful attempt to elect a senator by majority vote, a mere plurality vote would be sufficient. On June 6, the Committee on Privileges and Elections reported the bill favorably, but the Senate took no action on the matter. See S. Rep. No. 62–58 (1911).

85. Zywicki, "Beyond the Shell," 196.

86. Haynes, *The Senate of the United States*, vol. 1, 91.

87. Christopher H. Hoebeke, *The Road to Mass Democracy: Original Intent and the Seventeenth Amendment* (New Brunswick, N.J.: Transaction, 1995), 91.

88. Haynes, *The Election of Senators*, 165.

89. Interestingly, however, Montana returned Senator Clark the following year. Hoebeke, *Mass Democracy*, 92.

90. See Hoebeke, *Mass Democracy*, 96, where Hoebeke argues, contrary to the view that the Senate was aloof and unresponsive to the people, that "the final settlement of the Lorimer case illustrates just how amenable the Senate could be to popular opinion." See also Hall, "History and Effect," 252–74.

91. Zywicki, "Beyond the Shell," 197.

92. Kyvig, *Explicit and Authentic*, 209. See also Hoebeke, *Mass Democracy*, 101.

93. "Election of Senators," H.R. Rep. No. 50–1456 at 2 (1887). See Bybee, *Ulysses at the Mast*, 544.

94. S. Rep. No. 54–530 at 10 (1895).

95. Zywicki, "Beyond the Shell," 185.

96. See Hoebeke, *Mass Democracy*, 18–24.

97. Woodrow Wilson, *The New Freedom: A Call for the Emancipation of the Generous Energies of a People* (New York: Doubleday, 1913), 55.

98. 53 Cong. Rec. 7775 (1894).

99. 54 Cong. Rec. 1519 (1895).

100. Forty-four of the petitions came from various local and state Grange associations; twelve from chapters of the Farmers Mutual Benevolent Association, and thirteen from various labor unions. For a table providing the date and sponsoring group for each of these 238 petitions, see Hall, "History and Effect," 457–81 (App. B).

101. The National Democratic Party Platform of 1900 was the first platform of a major party to contain a plank calling for direct election of the Senate. For a table providing the particulars of these 239 party platforms, see Hall, "History and Effect," 490–505 (App. D).

102. For a table providing the dates of and state legislatures responsible for these 175 state memorials, see Hall, "History and Effect," 512–27 (App. F).

103. Hall, "History and Effect," 319. State direct primary laws fell into three classes:

1. Laws giving to the party state committee the discretion of holding a primary either under state control or party auspices for the purpose of selecting the party senatorial nominee were passed in Georgia (1890–1891), Florida (1901), South Carolina (1902), Alabama (1903), Idaho (1903), Virginia (1904), Arkansas (1905), and Kentucky (1907).

2. Laws making it mandatory upon the parties to select their candidates for senator by means of the direct primary were passed in Mississippi (1902), Oregon (1904), Wisconsin (1904), Louisiana (1906), Iowa (1907), Michigan (1907), Missouri (1907), Nebraska (1907), North Dakota (1907), South Dakota (1907), Texas (1907), Washington (1907), Oklahoma (1907–1908), Kansas (1908), Maryland (1908), New Jersey (1908), Nevada (1909), Tennessee (1909), Colorado (1910), Maine (1911), Minnesota (1911), and Montana (1913).

3. Laws providing that senatorial candidates might submit their names in primary elections but that the vote cast was to be considered by the legislature as an advisory vote only were passed in Illinois (1906), Ohio (1908), and California (1909).

   These laws prompted Zywicki, "Beyond the Shell," 190, to argue that, "by the time the Seventeenth Amendment was adopted, direct election of Senators was already a *fait accomplis.*"

104. Hall, "History and Effect," 335. The twelve states were Oregon (1904), Idaho (1909), Nebraska (1909), Nevada (1909), Colorado (1910), California (1911), Kansas (1911), Minnesota (1911), New Jersey (1911), Ohio (1911), Montana (1912), and Arizona (1912).

105. Sara Brandes Crook, "The Consequences of the Seventeenth Amendment: The Twentieth Century Senate," Ph.D. diss. (Lincoln: University of Nebraska, 1992), 27.

The direct primary was, of course, preceded by the public canvass, in which senatorial candidates would barnstorm the state seeking support for their parties in the state legislature in hopes of securing a governing majority there, which would determine who would be sent to Washington as senator. William H. Riker, "The Senate and American Federalism," *American Political Science Review* 49 (1955), 463. Rev. 453, 463 (1955), contends that the first public canvass occurred in Mississippi in 1834; it did not become widespread, however, until the Lincoln-Douglas debates of 1858. Roger G. Brooks, "Garcia, the Seventeenth Amendment, and the Role of the Supreme Court in Defending Federalism," *Harvard Journal of Law & Public Policy* 10 (1987): 207.

106. Alan P. Grimes, *Democracy and Amendments to the Constitution* (Lexington, Mass.: Lexington Books, 1978), 76.

107. See Allen H. Eaton, *The Oregon System: The Story of Direct Legislation in Oregon* (Chicago: A. C. McClurg, 1912), 92–98. "By 1909, when Oregon's Republican legislature elected a Democratic senator who had won the popular contest, the system's effectiveness was demonstrated." Kyvig, *supra* note 55, at 210.

108. As a consequence, when George Norris, the Republican Party primary nominee for the Senate, defeated his Democratic Party opponent in the 1912 general election, the Democratically controlled Nebraska Legislature duly elected Norris and sent him to the Senate. Crook, "Consequences," 30.

109. But see American Bar Association, Special Constitutional Convention Study Committee, *Amendment of the Constitution by the Convention Method Under Article V* (Chicago: ABA, 1974).

110. Hoebeke, *Mass Democracy*, 149.

111. Kyvig, *Explicit and Authentic*, 210.

112. Hoebeke, *Mass Democracy*, 149–50.

113. "The wake-up call to the Senate was apparently the defeat in 1910 of ten Republican senators who had opposed the proposed amendment." Bybee, *Ulysses at the Mast*, 537–38.

114. The Twenty-sixth Amendment holds the record today for quickest ratification. It was approved by the Congress on March 10, 1971, and ratified by the requisite thirty-eighth state on July 1 of the same year.

Californians and Their Constitution: Progressivism, Direct Democracy, and the Administrative State

Edward J. Erler

> I am persuaded that the good sense of the people will always be found to be the best army. They may be led astray for a moment, but will soon correct themselves. The people are the only censors of their governors: and even their errors will tend to keep these to the true principles of the institution. To punish these errors too severely would be to suppress the only safeguard of the public liberty.
>
> —Thomas Jefferson[1]

> A majority, held in restraint by constitutional checks, and limitations, and always changing easily, with deliberate changes of popular opinions and sentiments, is the only true sovereign of a free people.
>
> —Abraham Lincoln[2]

California's first constitution, adopted in 1849, was praised by a distinguished historian

> as one of the best, if not the very best, of all the thirty-one state constitutions that then existed. Though nearly every provision was copied from some other instrument, there was a rare choice and combination making altogether a compilation of organic principles clearly and tersely expressed and admirable for the wisdom with which they were selected.[3]

One could hardly claim that the current California Constitution, adopted in 1879, is either "clearly and tersely expressed," or a statement of "organic principles." In the sesquicentennial edition of the constitution published by the California legislature, the text runs to more than 250 pages, and addresses so many policy issues that it resembles "the prolixity of a legal code" more than it does organic law.[4] Since 1879, the constitution has been amended nearly five hundred times, often haphazardly and improvidently. Yet, many of these amendments have proved beneficial, while others have simply been trivial. We find, for example, that the salary of public school teachers cannot be less than $2,400[5] and that "[t]he people shall have the right to fish upon and from the public lands of the State,"[6] but not the right to hunt. And there is this helpful rule of construction: "[t]he provisions of this Constitution are mandatory and prohibitory, unless by express words they are declared to be otherwise."[7]

Tax policy, government spending, property assessments, school financing and expenditures, labor relations, usury and an host of other details are provisions that undoubtedly should be in a legal code rather than in California's fundamental law. And in a provision carried over from the constitution of 1849, the people are not only guaranteed the right to pursue happiness, they are also guaranteed the right to obtain it as well.[8] This is no doubt an expression of the optimism of the Gold Rush days, when hopes of success were extravagant. One prominent commentator argues that "California never lost this symbolic connection with an intensified pursuit of human happiness. As a hope in defiance of facts, as a longing which could ennoble and encourage but which could also turn and devour itself, the symbolic value of California endured—a legacy of the Gold Rush."[9] It could also be added that it is this dream—the *guarantee* of human happiness—that fuels California's modern administrative state.

The framers of the 1849 California Constitution followed the model of the Federal Convention for its ratification: they took seriously the social contract origins of constitutional government, and adhered with scrupulous precision to the precept that "[a]ll political power is inherent in the people [and that] Government is instituted for the protection, security, and benefit of the people; and they have the right to alter or reform the same, whenever the public good may require it."[10] The ratification of the constitution was nearly unanimous. Of the 12,875 votes cast on November 13, 1849, 12,064 voted in favor of the new constitution.[11] Admittedly, the pool of voters was small, but the near unanimity of the vote showed something of the common purpose and public spirit that animated Californians in 1849. By 1879, however, that common purpose had dissipated somewhat, as the cacophony of special interests began to displace the voice of the common good. Indeed, government itself had become a special interest and has remained so until the present day. As Theodore Hittell, an astute observer of California politics, remarked in 1897, "[t]here can be no doubt that the constitution of 1879 was framed and adopted at a very unfortunate time and under very unfavorable circumstances. The people were too angry and desperate to make a good constitution. Hittel maintains that "[r]ailroad and labor troubles made genuine deliberation impossible."[12] The main impetus for constitutional change, Hittel argues, was

> occasioned by abuses by Legislatures and officers of their powers, so that it was thought necessary to confine and restrict them within narrow limits. But while some benefits have accrued as results of the new limitations, they have not been unmixed benefits. The difficulty was that they went too far. Almost as much was lost, by preventing, in this too-sweeping indiscriminate manner, action that might have been of benefit, as was gained by preventing action that would have been of injury. For instance, while it cannot be denied that great wrongs were committed under the old Constitution by special legislation, at the same time special acts, which might be of great beneficence, cannot be passed now. The trouble was not so much the old constitution, as the legislators and officers whom the people saw fit to elect and entrust with authority of which they were not worthy.[13]

In contrast to the near unanimous ratification of the constitution of 1849, the constitution of 1879 was ratified by the comparatively small margin of 10,825 votes out of the 145,093 cast.[14] In 1879 the future of the California polity did not seem particularly bright.

Indeed, by the turn of the century it had become painfully evident that the California Constitution, even in its revised form, was inadequate to curb the power of special interests groups that sought to convert California government into the instrument of their special pleadings. The most successful of these special interests was the Southern Pacific Railroad whose far-flung interests dominated the politics of the state. Indeed, one noted commentator expresses what seems to be a consensus among historians when he argues that "[t]o a degree perhaps unparalleled in the nation, the Southern Pacific and a web of associated economic interests ruled the state."[15] The California Progressives were largely successful in eliminating the dominance of the Southern Pacific Railroad by the constitutional reforms that they instituted in 1911. And it is these Progressive reforms—initiative, referendum, and recall—that fuel the most heated contemporary debates about the California Constitution.

These devices of direct democracy were designed to allow the people to take action in the face of government that was either unwilling or unable to serve the public interest. The people could, *sua sponte*, pass laws that the legislature was unwilling or incapable of passing and could defeat by referendum any legislation that was believed to have been improvidently passed. And any public officer who had violated his public trust could be recalled. Furthermore, whenever the people deemed the public good to require an alteration in the fundamental law of the constitution, they could do so by constitutional amendment initiative. The Progressive theory was that all governmental institutions will inevitably be captured by special interests, and thus will be incapable of serving the public good. The people, on the other hand, are incapable of betraying the public good because, by definition, the people can never be a special interest. The people are the natural representatives of the public good, and direct action on the part of the people is a necessary corrective for public corruption. The principal advocate for direct legislation in California, Dr. John Randolph Haynes, argued on the eve of the 1911 election that

> [b]ribery of the people's representatives by special interests is the great demoralizing factor in our unchecked representative system of government. The majority of the electorate are honest, and desire good government. If you wish to have a truly representative government, and an honest and efficient one, give to the honest majority the power to directly legislate and to veto the acts of their representatives. It is much easier to bribe a few representatives than to bribe the majority of the many electors.[16]

Today's heirs of the Progressive tradition, the progressive or liberal constitutionalists, utterly reject this trust in the public spiritedness of the people. As one prominent critic remarks, "[d]irect legislation, the creation of progressives of another era, today poses more danger to social progress than the problems of governmental unresponsiveness."[17] Indeed, we are told that the devices of direct democracy instituted by Progressivism merely allow the public to express its hysteria and latent prejudices in unrestrained majoritarianism. The initiative, which was a Progressive reform to serve Progressive ends, has become a means for self-interested and mean-spirited majorities to promote decidedly non-Progressive ends. In other words, the mechanisms of Progressivism are being used to defeat the ends of Progressivism. We must, therefore, in the spirit of Progressivism itself, reject the means and preserve the ends.

Californians have used initiative and referendum to do battle with their government, mostly to resist Progressive reforms and to thwart what might be called "ideological liberalism." In the early years, these devices of direct democracy were used sparingly, but since the success of Proposition 13 in 1978, the people have learned the efficacy of direct democracy in combating the cutting edge liberalism that has infected California since the 1960s. As one prominent commentator correctly observes, "Proposition 13 prompted a seismic shift in the state's political center. . . ."[18] The radical tax cuts mandated by Proposition 13 signaled the end of California's "communitarian ethos."[19] In the 1950s and 1960s, "California seemed to be a national model of high civic investment and engagement." Proposition 13, however, destroyed this Progressive vision by making California "the lodestar of tax reduction and public disinvestment [in] the 1980s and 1990s."[20] Criticism of Proposition 13 has taken on a frantic quality; ideological liberals are never gracious in defeat. But California voters seem not to have forgotten that the "model of high civic investment" included a tax-funded self-esteem commission—a part of the "communitarian ethos" that sought to promote self-esteem among the elite class of new age liberals who, no doubt, had to learn to overcome any misgivings they might harbor about their privileged status.[21]

A number of prominent legal scholars have criticized the Progressive reforms on constitutional grounds. There is a growing body of scholarship, for example, that maintains that state initiative and referenda procedures are a violation of the Republican Guaranty Clause of the U.S. Constitution. Article IV, Section 4, provides that "[t]he United States shall guarantee to every State in this Union a Republican Form of Government. . . ." The Constitution does not, of course, define "republican government," although any thoughtful observer must be puzzled by the presence in the same article of the fugitive slave clause. Nevertheless, it is clear, say the critics, that the framers rejected direct democracy in favor of republican government, and republican government requires representation rather than the direct intervention of the people. Insofar as initiatives and referenda are devices of direct democracy, they are said to violate the Guaranty Clause. The essential problem, according to these critics, is that republican government requires that all legislation must be the product of *deliberation*, and deliberation can only take place through representation. As one analyst has phrased it: "unlike the legislative process, the initiative is not deliberative. Ordinary citizens simply do not have the time or attention span to focus on complex political issues and their judgment is likely to be erratic and capricious, swayed by momentary passions and prejudices."[22] One particularly acerb critic argues that because deliberation cannot be a part of direct democracy, "it is extremely difficult for policymaking by initiative to actually promote the general welfare. This is especially true if the people are not as well informed as the Progressives believed them to be. It follows that the failings of direct democracy in the end limit the government's ability to pursue the general welfare."[23] Thus, the concept of public deliberation was merely a Progressive delusion: the public is incapable of deliberation. Deliberation can take place only in representative bodies where opposing interests are debated and reconciled. The accommodation of minority interests, which is the hallmark of "legislative deliberation,"[24] is wholly absent from initiative lawmaking. Thus, direct initiatives are always at best only incomplete expressions of the public good, and at worst simply the aggrandizement of majority factions.

The critics of the direct initiative have assiduously cited James Madison as their authority. Madison distinguished between republics and pure democracies and (unlike the Constitution) Madison does give a tolerably clear definition of the republican form of government. In *The Federalist*, Madison wrote that "we may define a republic to be, or at least may bestow that name on, a government which derives all its powers directly or indirectly from the great body of the people, and is administered by persons holding their offices during pleasure for a limited period, or during good behavior."[25] The critics of direct democracy point to this passage as proof that Madison—and by extension the founders generally—argued that the republican form of government contemplated by the Guaranty Clause was predicated upon *the total exclusion of the people in their collective capacity.*"[26] A republic was essentially different from a "pure democracy," which Madison described as "a society consisting of a small number of citizens, who assemble and administer the government in person." A pure democracy, Madison concludes, "can admit of no cure for the mischiefs of faction. A common passion or interest will, in almost every case, be felt by a majority of the whole . . . and there is nothing to check the inducements to sacrifice the weaker party."[27] A republican government, on the other hand, by employing representation—"this great mechanical power in government"[28]—can be extended over a large area and embrace greater diversity. Greater diversity will mitigate the possibility of majority faction and allow representatives "to refine and enlarge the public views." Madison concludes that "it may well happen that the public voice, pronounced by the representatives of the people, will be more consonant to the public good than if pronounced by the people themselves."[29] The whole object of government, according to Madison, is to elevate reason over passion in public discourse: "it is the reason, alone, of the public," Madison wrote, "that ought to controul and regulate the government. The passions ought to be controuled and regulated by government."[30] This seems to be the gravamen of the complaints against the initiative—the public is incapable of deliberation and uses the devices of direct democracy solely to indulge its passions and express its hysterical prejudices.

Madison, of course, did not believe that representation by itself was a sufficient remedy for "the diseases most incident to republican government."[31] Indeed, "experience has taught mankind the necessity of auxiliary precautions."[32] Primary among these precautions was the separation of powers, which was devised not only to prevent tyrannical government, but to promote good government as well. The different branches of government would not only check one another in the service of the public good, but would also exhibit necessary functional expertise. The legislative branch—because it was more numerous and represented a greater variety of interest—would be suited to deliberation; the unitary executive to the execution of the laws, and the insulated Supreme Court to judgment.[33] The Senate in particular was to represent the "cool and deliberate sense of the community" against those "particular moments in public affairs when the people, stimulated by some irregular passion, or some illicit advantage, or misled by the artful misrepresentations of interested men, may call for measures which they themselves will afterwards be the most ready to lament and condemn."[34] Madison does not, however, address the situation where government—the legislative branch in particular—refuses to acquiesce in, or act upon, the "cool and deliberate sense of the community" or where the legislature refuses to act in the public interest. The people can, of course, turn the malefactors out of office in the next election, or they may "alter or abolish" government itself. Direct action may be taken to amend or replace the Constitution by convention; or in the extreme resort, the people may have recourse to the right of revolution. In some sense, the initiative and referendum seems to occupy a kind of middle ground. It allows the people to take direct action without having to resort to more drastic expressions of sovereignty.

Where, then, does the issue of direct democracy stand with regard to the Guaranty Clause? While the Guaranty Clause did not generate significant debate during the Constitutional Convention, the leading scholar on the subject, William Wiecek, concludes that "it was designed to prohibit monarchical or aristocratic institutions in the states."[35] Of course, not all the states had republican governments at the time of the founding, if republicanism is understood as government based on the consent of the governed. According to this definition, and it is surely the one accepted by the founders, *none* of the slave states qualified as republican.[36] The slave states had representative government, but not all representative governments are properly republican governments. It is the ends, not the means, that must decide the question of republicanism. But according to Wiecek, the Guaranty Clause had a prospective element as well, as it

> was not meant to solidify republican government in the mold of existing political institutions. . . . What began simply as a revulsion, grounded in experience and necessity, against rule by kings became transformed into a pledge of popular government. In its positive aspects the clause assured that innovation would be possi-

ble within a republican framework. It was more than the Philadelphia Conventions benediction on the extant state constitutions; it looked to the future, insuring that state governments would remain responsive to popular will.[37]

Thus it is highly unlikely that the framers would have considered the existence of initiative and referendum in state constitutions as evidence of nonrepublicanism, even if (as is likely) they might have believed that such devices of direct democracy were *unwise.*

Madison certainly believed that the danger of majority faction was greater in the states than in an extended republic. In *The Federalist,* Madison reported the widespread complaints "from our most considerate and virtuous citizens that the State governments are too unstable, that the public good is disregarded in the conflicts of rival parties, and that measures are too often decided, not according to the rules of justice and the rights of the minor party, but by the superior force of an interested and overbearing majority."[38] One can readily see that these are almost the precise words used by contemporary critics of initiative and referendum. Madison, of course, believed that an extensive republic would be the primary means of preventing the formation of majority faction. The smaller the society, Madison argued

> the fewer probably will be the distinct parties and interests composing it; the fewer the distinct parties and interests, the more frequently will a majority be found of the same party; and the smaller the number of individuals composing a majority, and the smaller the compass within which they are placed, the more easily will they concert and execute their plans of oppression. Extend the sphere and you take in a greater variety of parties and interests; you make it less probable that a majority of the whole will have a common motive to invade the rights of other citizens; or if such a common motive exists, it will be more difficult for all who feel it to discover their own strength and to act in unison with each other.[39]

Madison apparently believed that the size and population of the United States brought together in a federal republic would supply the requisite diversity to militate against the formation of majority factions. Today, California not only has more than ten times the population the United States had in 1790, but the population represents greater diversity of interests. Surely, the idea that direct democracy can produce only majority factions under these circumstances is hardly credible—but this is the main complaint of the critics of direct democracy.

Several commentators have argued that initiative and referendum establish a plebiscitary rather than a republican form of government. In the eyes of one state supreme court justice, initiatives merely "force a plebiscite on measures of popular passion or self-interest."[40] According to one of California's most astute political observers, after the passage of Proposition 13, "real policy decisions are now being made in the plebiscitary process, and not in the halls of the Legislature or the office of the governor, much less at the school board or the city council."[41] Every reader of Aristotle's *Politics* knows that this great classifier of regimes regarded plebiscitary democracy as one of the worst regimes—if indeed it was a regime at all. As everyone seems to recognize, the initiative in California was originally designed "to provide a check on elected officials. . . . Has it, in fact, replace[d] representative government" altogether?[42]

The initiative in California, of course, exists within a constitutional scheme and is subject to constitutional limits. It is therefore not a plebiscitary system lacking constitutional limits. Although the California Constitution itself may be amended by the initiative process, this procedure cannot be used to revise the constitution, nor can any amendment of the California Constitution violate the Federal Constitution. And all statutory initiatives must conform both to the California Constitution and the Federal Constitution. The U. S. Supreme Court recently invalidated Proposition 198, a statutory initiative passed by the voters in 1996 to establish blanket primaries. The High Court ruled the blanket primary to be a violation of the First Amendment because it represented "a substantial intrusion into the associational freedom" of California's political parties.[43]

California courts have always been deferential in their review of initiatives. In *Amador Valley Joint Union High School District v. State Board of Equalization*,[44] the case that upheld the Proposition 13 constitutional amendment initiative, the court remarked that "[i]t is a fundamental precept of our law that, although the legislative power under our constitutional framework is firmly vested in the Legislature, the people reserve to themselves the powers of initiative and referendum. It follows from this that, [the] power of initiative must be liberally construed . . . to promote the democratic process."[45] This deference, however, has not deterred California courts from invalidating, either wholly or in part, nearly one-half of all initiatives passed.[46] California courts have also not been unwilling to invalidate signature-qualified initiatives on constitutional grounds before they have appeared on the ballot.[47] This high rate of invalidation, coupled with federal constraints, and the fact that only about one-third of initiatives placed on the ballot are successful, hardly indicates a nonrepublican plebiscitary system at work.

The proponents of the Guaranty Clause argument face a massive stumbling block in the U.S. Supreme Court: many years ago the High Court ruled that claims under the Guaranty Clause are nonjusticiable because they are essentially political questions that should be determined by the political branches of government rather than the judiciary.[48] Nevertheless, some opponents of direct democracy take hope in the fact the Supreme Court in its decisions in *Baker v. Carr*[49] and *Reynolds v. Sims*[50] may have evidenced a willingness to narrow the scope of its political questions doctrine.[51] Yet as most observers seem to recognize, the prospects here are uncertain at best. Others, like Oregon Supreme Court Justice Hans Linde, argue that state courts should independently fill the political questions void left by the U.S. Supreme Court. Indeed, Linde argues that it is "beyond dispute" that the U.S. Constitution imposes "the most fundamental duty in American public law" on state courts and other state officials "to maintain republican forms of government."[52] State court judges, Linde points out, are bound, no less than federal judges, to uphold the U.S. Constitution. It is Justice Linde's opinion that "republican government, to the generation that designed and ratified the United States Constitution, meant representative government chosen by, and accountable to, the people."[53] Republican government is thus of the people and for the people, but not by the people. It should not be a government by the people for the simple reason that government by the people is government by collective passion rather than deliberative reasoning.

Justice Linde issues a plea for state constitutional amendments that would force important issues into the "normal legislative process." This will not be an unwelcome change because "voters . . . have had enough of divisive, emotional initiative campaigns driven by ideological, sectarian, or racial passions."[54] Linde has even developed a five-part typology of the kind of initiatives that state courts should disqualify under the Guaranty Clause: (1) any initiative that appeals to "collective passions" by referring to any group in pejorative or stigmatizing terms; (2) initiatives that avoid such terms but are clearly directed against "identifiable racial, ethnic, linguistic, religious, or other social groups;" (3) initiatives that do not name a specific group but in which "the historical and political context" makes it clear to judges and the public that a specific group is nevertheless targeted; (4) "initiatives which appeal to majority emotions to impose values that offend the conscience of other groups in the community without being directed against those groups;" examples here are attempts to restrict the teaching of evolution, to establish moments of silence in schools, enacting the death penalty, antiabortion laws and parental consent laws; (5) initiatives placing affirmative legislation into the constitution weakening the power of legislatures or courts.[55]

This is probably the most massive prescription for state court activism that has ever been proposed—all under the guise of enforcing the Guaranty Clause of the Federal Constitution. With the possible exception of the Equal Protection Clause of the Fourteenth Amendment, no clause of the Constitution has been freighted with greater significance for the cause of ideological liberalism. And no clause, it seems, is less suited to carry such weight. Indeed, Judge Linde's impassioned plea passes the bounds of all reason—it surely reminds Californians of the era of the Bird Court and its ideological activism. Needless to say, Judge Linde is not defending republican government; he has, in fact, written an undisguised brief for judicial oligarchy in which the moving principle of republican government—the consent of the governed—has disappeared completely.

It is probably true that "California puts the fewest restrictions of all states on what can be decided by the initiative, and as a consequence, Californians use the initiative constitutional amendment process often and in many varied ways."[56] At the same time, however, most amendments to the California Constitution originate in the legislature (although there has been an upsurge of initiative constitutional amendments since the 1960s). A legislative constitutional amendment requires a two-thirds majority in both houses of the legislature, and approval by a majority vote of the people. Legislative constitutional amendments have a much greater likelihood of passing than initiative constitutional amendments.[57] The people of California seem quite willing to defer to the "deliberative process" when they have evidence that deliberation has actually taken place. It should be clear even to the meanest observer, however, that the deliberative process doesn't always result in genuine deliberation. What passes for "deliberation" is all too often the result of interest group brokering that ignores the common good.[58] In California, racial, gender, and ethnic preferences in public contracting and university admissions provide a case in point. But this interest group brokering, as we will see, is *praised* by many critics of direct democracy as evidence of deliberation.

It is true, as critics never tire of pointing out, that the initiative process as a whole is unrestrained, and perhaps even provides access to moneyed interests that would otherwise be unavailable. One commentator points to what he calls the "sad irony of California politics. Reforms by the Progressives . . . meant to disenfranchise the corrupt power of the political machines, have been captured, and, in turn, corrupted by the modern political machines. The reason modern economic powers have been able to turn the process of direct democracy against the general welfare" is a direct result of "tragic errors in the reasoning of the Progressives." The principal error

is that the current initiative system allows special interests to set the popular agenda by proposing statutory and constitutional initiatives directly to the people. There is no limit to the power of these agenda-setting interest groups, nor is there a check on the authority of the people to change the constitution.[59]

It is simply hyperbole, of course, to suggest that there is no check on the power of the people to change the constitution. As we have already seen, there are federal constitutional limits as well as restraints in the California Constitution.

It is true that initiatives are often poorly written and deceptive, of dubious constitutionality and many of them impose unreasonable restrictions on policy making. What is more, the grassroots element of the initiative—the core of the Progressive idea—has almost disappeared. Some professional signature gatherers boast that with enough money any proposal can be qualified because "[v]oters frequently sign initiative petitions without knowing anything about the contents." The "signature-collection industry"—so it is alleged—can place virtually any initiative on the ballot.[60] But it is also true that most initiatives are rejected in popular elections and where the voters are uncertain they tend to indulge a healthy skepticism. Two perceptive commentators note that

> [t]he election process itself provides the greatest safeguard against poorly drafted initiatives: through the course of a campaign, debate usually points out and even exaggerates flaws in initiatives, and voters tend to react accordingly. Voters tend to be very cautious and thus are reluctant to approve initiatives at the ballot box. Historically, California's initiatives average a one-third approval rate. This reluctance dramatically increases when voters are uncertain about a measure. When uncertain, the voter generally casts a vote against an initiative in order to maintain the existing public order.[61]

Many of California's most hotly contested initiatives in the last twenty-five years have been attempts to reign in an activist judiciary. Throughout the 1970s and 1980s, the California Supreme Court used the doctrine of independent state grounds as one of the principal weapons in its activist arsenal. This allows state courts to interpret the same or similar language in state constitutions independently of the U.S. Supreme Court's interpretation of the Federal Constitution. The one restriction is that the interpretation of the same or similar language cannot create *lower* standards of protection than is created by the Federal Constitution, but it can create *higher* standards. "Independent state grounds" is something of a misnomer because state courts are not entirely independent in the interpretation of state constitutions—rights can be interpreted only more expansively, and state protections can never fall beneath the federal minimum.

Joseph Grodin, a former member of the California Supreme Court who was turned out of office along with Chief Justice Rose Bird and Justice Cruz Reynoso in the hotly contested judicial confirmation election of 1986, has recently written that "[i]t is, indeed, the rights-protecting provisions of state constitutions that have been the principal focus of the relatively recent revival in state constitutionalism. That this revival occurred at a time when the justices of the Warren Court were being replaced by justices who were more conservative in their approach, and as a consequence protection for individual rights under the Federal Constitution was on the wane, is surely no coincidence."[62] Grodin pointed to Justice William Brennan as the intellectual progenitor of this movement to state constitutions and independent state grounds.

In a 1986 article, Brennan noted that the incorporation of the provisions of the Bill Rights through the Fourteenth Amendment's due process clause "created a Federal floor of protection that allow[s] diversity only above and beyond this Federal constitutional floor."[63] Whenever the U.S. Supreme Court refused to extend the federal floor as far and as fast as Brennan desired, he was quick to advise the states how they might evade the Supreme Court's rulings by invoking independent state grounds. In a dissenting opinion in the 1975 case of *Michigan v. Mosley*,[64] Brennan severely criticized the majority opinion's "erosion of *Miranda* standards as a matter of Federal Constitutional law and pointed out that no State is precluded by the decision from adhering to higher standards under State law." And in a call to arms Brennan urged the states to protect those constitutional rights that were being abandoned by the Supreme Court: "Understandably, State courts and Legislatures are, as matters of State law, increasingly according protections once provided as Federal rights but now increasingly depreciated by decisions of this Court."[65] With the advent of the Burger Court, Justice Brennan feared that liberal judicial activism would have to retreat to state courts and await a more propitious political climate.

One who responded to Brennan's clarion call was the late Justice Stanley Mosk, a longtime member of the California Supreme Court who miraculously survived the 1986 judicial confirmation election that turned his three liberal colleagues out of office. Mosk wrote that state constitutionalism was necessary "to complete the work of the Warren Court . . . on . . . the State level." In Justice Mosk's view, "State courts faced a choice. They could retreat to pre-1953 apathy, or they could employ their State constitutions to maintain decisional consistency with the Warren Court."[66]

Various initiatives have tried to curb the use of independent state grounds. Article I, Section 24, of the California Constitution, added in 1974, supports the use of independent state grounds: "Rights guaranteed by this Constitution are not dependent on those guaranteed by the United States Constitution." Over the years, the California Supreme Court has said that this provision allows but *does not mandate* the use of independent state grounds. Decisions of the U.S. Supreme Court, the California Supreme Court acknowledged, "are entitled to respectful consideration and ought to be followed unless persuasive reasons are presented for taking a different course."[67] The most interesting battles have been fought in the area of criminal procedures and the rights of criminal defendants. One initiative, passed in 1972, added Article I, Section 27, to the California Constitution and required the California Supreme Court to accept federal standards for cruel and unusual punishment in capital cases; another, Proposition 8, the Victims' Bill of Rights, passed in 1980, mandated that the exclusion of evidence proceed on federal grounds rather than independent state grounds. Both of these initiatives were designed to curtail the court's expansion of the rights of criminal defendants under the aegis of independent state grounds, and both of these restrictions on judicial authority were subsequently upheld by the California Supreme Court.

In 1972, in *People v. Anderson*,[68] the California Supreme Court had declared the death penalty unconstitutional on independent state grounds. In a decision that must have pleased Justice Linde, the California Supreme Court declared that the death penalty was "unnecessary to any legitimate goal of the state and incompatible with the dignity of man and the judicial process."[69] A constitutional amendment initiative in 1972 overturned the *Anderson* decision. The initiative itself was subsequently upheld in *People v. Frierson*.[70] As the court tendentiously noted, "[s]ince 1972 the sovereign people of this state twice directly, and through their elected representatives on other occasions, have mounted a continuous, strong, and joint effort to restore the death penalty as a permissible form of punishment."[71] The court—with some reluctance— concluded that "[t]he clear intent of the electorate in adopting Section 27 was to circumvent Anderson by restoring the death penalty *to the extent permitted by the Federal Constitution*."[72] "The decisions of the people . . . may or may not have been wise," the court lamented, "but we think there can be no reasonable doubt as to their intention or purpose."[73] The Victims' Bill of Rights was upheld in *In re Lance W*.[74] Justice Grodin, in what amounted to something of a death-bed conversion a year before he faced reelection, wrote the majority opinion upholding the initiative.

Emboldened by these successes, in 1990 the people of California passed another extensive reform of criminal procedures in Proposition 115. The main purpose of this reform was to withdraw independent state ground powers from the California courts in almost *all* areas touching upon the rights of criminal defendants. The following language was added to Article I, Section 24, of the state constitution, following the Declaration of Rights Initiative:

In criminal cases the rights of a defendant to equal protection of the laws, to due process of law, to the assistance of counsel, to be personally present with counsel, to a speedy and public trial, to compel the attendance of witnesses, to confront the witnesses against him or her, to be free from unreasonable searches and seizures, to privacy, to not be compelled to be a witness against himself or herself, to not be twice placed in jeopardy for the same offense, and to not suffer the imposition of cruel or unusual punishment, shall be construed by the courts of this State in a manner consistent with the Constitution of the United States.

The people had thrown down the gauntlet to the post–Bird Court. The California Supreme Court took up the challenge and promptly declared the most radical provisions of Proposition 115 unconstitutional.[75]

The California Constitution distinguishes between a revision and an amendment. Voters may *amend* the constitution by initiative but a *revision* must take place in a convention called by the legislature. Whenever a putative *amendment* is so far reaching as to amount to a *revision*, the supreme court will declare it unconstitutional. In *Raven v. Deukmejian,* the court noted that as a result of the restrictions imposed on the courts by Proposition 115, "California courts in criminal cases would no longer have authority to interpret the State Constitution in a manner more protective of defendants' rights than extended by the Federal Constitution, as construed by the United States Supreme Court."[76] This, the court noted, "would substantially alter the substance and integrity of the State Constitution as a document of independent force and effect." Thus, Proposition 115 "not only unduly restricts judicial power, but it does so in a way which severely limits the independent force and effect of the California Constitution. . . . [I]t is one thing voluntarily to defer to high court decisions, but quite another to *mandate* the state courts' blind obedience thereto, despite 'cogent reasons,' 'independent state interests,' or 'strong countervailing circumstances' that might lead our courts to construe similar state constitutional language differently from the federal approach."[77] Since, in the court's opinion, Proposition 115 "substantially alters the preexisting constitutional scheme or framework" it clearly amounts to a revision of the California Constitution and is therefore invalid.[78] Curiously enough, however, the opinion reaffirmed its holdings in *Frierson* and *Lance.* Both of these decisions, according to the *Raven* court, involved "only isolated provisions and did not seek far-reaching, fundamental changes in our governmental plan. But neither case involved a broad attack on state court authority to exercise independent judgment in construing a wide spectrum of important rights under the State Constitution."[79]

Less than a year after the decision in *Raven,* the California Supreme Court heard a similar challenge to Proposition 140, the term limits initiative passed in 1990.[80] One commentator has opined that term limits can be "classified as a near-perfect example of populist reform—a change in the governmental process that legislatures are unlikely to impose on themselves."[81] Clearly, Proposition 140 was aimed at Willie Brown, the long-term speaker of the assembly, and his cohorts, who dominated the legislature in a manner that was surely reminiscent (if it did not surpass) the control exercised in previous years by the Southern Pacific Railroad.[82] Yet the court in *Legislature of the State of California v. Eu* refused to countenance the argument that term limits was such a fundamental change in the structure and authority of the California Constitution as to amount to a revision. Petitioners had argued that lifetime term limits would change the "basic governmental plan" in a radical manner with respect to legislative power, and that term limits were an assault upon the legislature as devastating as the assault on judicial power invalidated in *Raven*. The court refused, however, to come to the aid of its coordinate branch of government. Proposition 140, the majority opinion held,

> does not affect either the structure or the foundational powers of the legislature, which remains free to enact whatever laws it deems appropriate. The challenged measure alters neither the content of those laws nor the process by which they are adopted. No legislative power is diminished or delegated to other persons or agencies. The relationships between the three governmental branches, and their respective powers remain untouched. [Any allegations of diminished legislative power] are largely *speculative* ones, dependent on a number of as yet unproved premises.[83]

A large part of the reason Californians undertook the term limits initiative was their perception that the legislature—no less than the judiciary—was utterly recalcitrant on the issue of crime. Willie Brown had almost single-handedly defeated all attempts to enact tough crime measures during a time when crime rates were soaring. The Three Strikes initiative in 1994 brought the debate over direct democracy almost to a crisis point.[84] Three Strikes doubled sentences for second-time felons and imposed mandatory sentences of twenty-five years to life for a third felony. The novelty of this statutory initiative was that, unlike the first and second felony strikes, which had to be serious or violent felonies, the third strike sentence enhancement was triggered by *any* felony. In addition, the initiative did not allow judges discretion in meting out sentences, and allowed the dismissal of a strike-eligible felony indictment only on the motion of the *prosecutor*. The latter provisions were inspired by the public's widespread belief that judges were a major cause of California's escalating crime rate because of their tendencies toward lenient sentences and their willingness to dismiss or reduce charges. Before the initiative was actually voted upon, the legislature also had a deathbed conversion and quickly passed Three Strikes legislation in substantially the same language as the initiative. (The legislature, however, has generally not received credit for passing Three Strikes, because it is conceded in almost all quarters that the pressure of the pending initiative forced it into passing legislation that it would never have otherwise considered.)

Reaction to the initiative from legal commentators and criminologists was intense. The heirs of Progressivism had no qualms about expressing their utter disdain for public support of Three Strikes. Professor Michael Vitiello averred that "Three Strikes passed as a result of public panic, flamed [*sic*] by politicians who spurned rational debate." The inordinate fear of rising crime rates led to an irrational policy choice. Indeed, the passage of the Three Strikes initiative brings into question the very idea of direct democracy itself. "While many tout the initiative process as democracy in action," Vitiello cautions, "politicians' extravagant rhetoric prevented the electorate from making a fully informed decision on three strikes."[85] Franklin Zimring, a law professor at the University of California, is the most vehement critic of Three Strikes.[86] Three Strikes merely expresses a "populist" desire to punish criminals—it is the result of an irrational desire to mete out severe punishment to recidivist criminals. This is a decision, Zimring alleges, that should be left to criminal justice experts, to those who are not motivated solely by what he calls "anti-offender" ire. "It may be," Zimring writes, "that the social authority accorded criminal justice experts provided insulation between populist sentiments (always punitive) and criminal justice policies at the legislative, administrative, and judicial levels. This insulation prevented the direct domination of policy by anti-offender sentiments that are consistently held by most citizens at most times. . . . Three Strikes was an extreme, but by no means isolated, example of the kind of law produced when very little mediates anti-offender sentiments."[87] The public seemed to have the sense that anti-offender sentiments expressed in a law with mandatory sentencing would be the quickest and most efficient way to reduce crime—and they were right. Since it is well known that only a relatively small number of criminals commit a disproportionately large number of crimes, it is obvious that increased incarceration rates will reduce crime. Although Zimring and other criminal justice experts deny any cause and effect relationship, Three Strikes has had a prime role in the precipitous drop in the crime rate since 1994.[88]

The California Supreme Court weighed in on Three Strikes in *People v. Romero* in 1996.[89] Three Strikes allowed the dismissal of a prior felony conviction only on the motion of the prosecuting attorney, but prohibited judges from similarly striking prior felonies. Proponents of the initiative argued that this would limit the discretion of "soft-on-crime judges . . . [who] care more about violent felons than they do victims."[90] In *Romero*, the trial judge, Judge Mudd, on his own initiative, and in clear violation of the plain terms of Three Strikes, struck a prior felony over the objections of the prosecutor. This allowed the defendant to escape a mandatory third-strike sentence. Judge Mudd argued that the basis for his decision was the fact that "judges are the conscience of the community and should be free to evaluate what type of sanction is appropriate."[91]

The court's decision in *Romero* did not reach the level of constitutional analysis, but resolved the issue on statutory grounds. Three Strikes had provided that "[t]he prosecuting attorney may move to dismiss or strike a prior felony conviction allegation in the furtherance of justice pursuant to Section 1385."[92] Section 1385 of the Penal Code had previously provided that "[t]he judge or magistrate may, either of his or her own motion or upon the application of the prosecuting attorney, and in the furtherance of justice, order an action to be dismissed."[93] The question was whether Three Strikes, in its attempt to curtail judicial discretion, had repealed section 1385. The court concluded there was no clear intent on the part of the legislature to do so. And since there was no evident intent to repeal section 1385, requiring that a dismissal in the furtherance of justice can take place only on the motion of the prosecutor is tantamount to conditioning the exercise of a judicial power on the actions of the prosecutor, a member of the executive branch. The court concluded that "the legislature and the electorate may eliminate the courts' power to make certain sentencing choices may be conceded. . . . It does not follow, however, that having given the court the power to dismiss, the legislature may therefore 'condition its exercise upon the approval of the district attorney.' "[94] Thus there are no constitutional barriers to repealing or modifying judicial discretion. Surprisingly, the court held that the power to dismiss in the furtherance of justice is not an inherent or essential judicial power.

When the *Romero* decision was handed down, there was a flurry of activity in the Republican-dominated assembly to overrule the holding by statutory means, but the effort came to naught because the Democrat-controlled Senate would simply have refused to acquiesce. The *Romero* decision, however, has probably helped insulate Three Strikes from attacks on federal due process grounds. Judicial discretion will blunt arguments that allowing any felony to count as a third strike violates the proportionality requirement for punishment under the cruel and unusual punishment clause of the Eighth Amendment. This is surely one unintended consequence of *Romero*.[95]

Peter Schrag expresses what has come to be almost the consensus of those who oppose direct democracy and advocate the rule of experts: "the impulse toward cleaner government and a more perfect democracy in the Progressive movement was always a little hard to separate from the racist and xenophobic." "One essential part of the ethos of direct democracy," Schrag concludes, "almost inevitably reinforces an essentially indifferent, if not hostile attitude toward minority rights."[96] Indeed, one prominent legal scholar argues that majority rule (coupled with a secret ballot) is inherently racist and destructive of minority rights. In a widely cited article, Derrick Bell writes that "[f]ar from being the pure path to democracy . . . direct democracy, carried out in the privacy of the voting booth, has diminished the ability of minority groups to participate in the democratic process. Ironically, because it enables the voters' racial beliefs and fears to be recorded and tabulated in their pure form, the referendum has been a most effective facilitator of that bias, discrimination, and prejudice which has marred American democracy from its earliest day."[97] Almost the same point is made by those who argue that the Progressive movement was a middle-class phenomenon. This is a somewhat more genteel argument than the one put forth by Bell, but the point is essentially the same: "Progressive conceptions of 'the people' apparently excluded large sections of the electorate—workers, immigrants, Catholics, the urban and rural poor. As middle-class moral reformers, Progressives would seem to have fashioned a popular following in their own image."[98] The middle class is widely viewed as the "selfish class" because it seeks to promote its interests at the expense of other classes, and does so with an appeal to populism. The initiative is the perfect vehicle for these middle-class forays against the welfare of minorities and of the poor.

Proposition 209, the constitutional amendment initiative repealing racial and sex preferences, provoked this debate in the most extreme terms. Racial preferences and set-asides represented the epitome of Progressivism for ideological liberals and the attempt to dismantle this government-inspired program was regarded by the minions of the administrative state as utterly reactionary—the use of populism for a retrograde purpose. Although Proposition 209 ultimately survived federal challenges, the Federal District Court opinion initially holding it unconstitutional was revealing for its explication of ideological liberalism.

In *Coalition for Economic Equity v. Wilson*,[99] Judge Thelton Henderson made a familiar argument: the prohibition against discrimination in Proposition 209 is itself discriminatory. By Judge Henderson's irrefragable logic, the Fourteenth Amendment's command that "No State . . . shall deny to any person . . . equal protection of the laws" is unconstitutional. The core of the argument seems to be that the refusal to allow the use of race, sex and ethnicity *is itself an impermissible use of race, ethnicity and sex.* Even though such an unnatural reading of the language of Proposition 209 defies any known principles of logic, Judge Henderson used this precise argument to demonstrate that the initiative was specifically aimed at minorities and women:

> [P]rior to the enactment of Proposition 209, supporters of race- and gender-conscious affirmative action programs were able to petition their state and local officials directly for such programs. After the passage of Proposition 209, however, these same advocates face the considerably more daunting task of mounting a statewide campaign to amend the California Constitution. At the same time, those seeking preferences based on any ground other than race or gender, such as age, disability, or veteran status, continue to enjoy access to the political process of all levels of government.[100]

But Judge Henderson misses the point: disabled minorities and disabled women will have the *same* access as all disabled people; minority veterans and women veterans will have the same access as other veterans; the aged will be made up of all races and both sexes. The equal protection clause disallows—or certainly subjects to strict scrutiny[101]—access based exclusively on race or ethnicity, and mandates that all sex classifications serve important governmental interests. Judge Henderson is mistaken in thinking that the constitution regards racial classes as no different than veterans, the disabled, or the aged.

In overruling Henderson's decision, the Ninth Circuit Court of Appeals, in an opinion by Judge O'Scannlain, argued that

> [p]laintiffs challenge Proposition 209 not as an impediment to protection against unequal treatment but as an impediment to receiving preferential treatment. The controlling words, we must remember, are equal and protection. Impediments to preferential treatment do not deny equal protection. It is one thing to say that individuals have equal protection rights against political obstructions to equal treatment; it is quite another to say that individuals have equal protection rights against political obstructions to preferential treatment. While the Constitution protects against obstructions to equal treatment, it erects obstructions to preferential treatment by its own terms. The alleged equal protection burden that Proposition 209 imposes on those who would seek race and gender preferences is a burden that the Constitution itself imposes.[102]

Perhaps the most tendentious argument made by Judge Henderson involved the locus of decision making. He argued that "[t]he body that enacts an affirmative action measure is free . . . to repeal it."[103] But, Judge Henderson added this inexplicable qualification: if "race and gender-conscious" preferences are to be repealed, they must be repealed by the same level of government that enacted them in the first place. "Once those who support race- and gender-conscious affirmative action prevail at one level of government . . . the equal Protection Clause will not tolerate an effort by the vanquished parties to alter the rules of the game—solely with respect to this single issue—so as to secure a reversal of fortunes."[104] Thus we have something of a constitutional anomaly: an act of the legislature cannot be repealed by a constitutional amendment *nor* by a constitutional amendment initiative. Judge Henderson knows, of course, that special interest pleading is more likely to succeed in the legislature than in the public at large.[105]

This is something that the Progressives understood as well, and Proposition 209 evidenced a better understanding of the public good and constitutional government than those who deliberated on the issue of racial and sex preferences in the legislature. It was the Democrat-dominated legislature under the leadership of Willie Brown that twice passed legislation mandating, not only racial and ethnic preferences for the University of California and California State University systems, but requirements of racial and ethnic *proportionality in graduation rates* as well. Governor Wilson vetoed all attempts to remake California society along the lines of ethnic and racial proportionality.[106] Judge Henderson concluded that much of the campaign rhetoric surrounding the election "had a racial and gender focus," indicating that "the measure was effectively drawn for racial purposes."[107]

Judge Henderson was correct, however, when he observed that "our system of democracy teaches that the will of the people, important as it is, does not reign absolute but must be kept in harmony with our Constitution. Thus, the issue is not whether one judge can thwart the will of the people; rather, the issue is whether the challenged enactment complies with our Constitution and Bill of Rights."[108] Indeed, the framers of the Constitution regarded majority faction as the primary threat to the existence of republican government. James Madison wrote a few months before the opening of the Constitutional Convention that "[t]here is no maxim in my opinion which is more liable to be misapplied, and which therefore more needs elucidation than the current one that the interest of the majority is the political standard of right and wrong."[109] The majority acts legitimately only when it acts in accordance with those constitutional principles that form the organic law of the nation. That is, the majority, as a part, must act in the interest of the whole, not in the interest of a part, whether the part is a majority or a minority. The Constitution, in the famous words of Chief Justice John Marshall, is "the fundamental and paramount law of the nation which was established by the supreme will of the people and the principles . . . so established, are deemed fundamental [and] . . . and designed to be permanent."[110] Any majority formed against the dictates of the fundamental and organic law is illegitimate, and it is the job of the courts to protect the Constitution against such transient majorities.

But can any reasonable person doubt that Proposition 209 more accurately expresses constitutional principles than a regime of racial preferences and set-asides? Racial preferences are incompatible with the principle that all men are created equal and are thereby endowed with equal rights. The Fourteenth Amendment—rightly understood—mandates the equal protection of equal rights.[111] Judge Henderson and the advocates of racial and sex preferences—by and large policy experts one and all—to the contrary notwithstanding, the people of California expressed a superior understanding of the Constitution, the rule of law, and the public good.

Constitutions are designed to facilitate deliberation about the pubic good. In the main, the representative form of government works to promote such deliberation. Of course the real issue is not the form, but the substance, and the test is not the process but the result. A precise adherence to form is necessary to provide stability in government, but on those occasions when the legislature or other government officers refuse to acquiesce in the "cool and deliberate sense of the community," preferring to serve special interests at the expense of the common good, the people of California have the formal constitutional right "to alter or reform [Government] when the public good may require."[112]

The initiative is the constitutional vehicle for altering and reforming government; it occupies a middle ground between reform and revolution. Equal protection of equal rights—which has always been known as equal opportunity—has always been the principle of distributive justice for the United States and for California. The principle has not always been honored in practice, but the goal—the aspiration—has rarely ever been questioned. It has been the cool and deliberate sense of the community since the adoption of the Fourteenth Amendment, indeed since the founding of the nation. Proposition 209 restored that aspiration to its rightful place.[113] And who can doubt that the people of California were far ahead of the policymakers on the issue of bilingual education? Even the much maligned Proposition 187 provoked the Congress to pass a welfare reform bill in 1996, and could have forced the U.S. Supreme Court to reconsider its 1982 decision *Plyler v. Doe*,[114] which had created a right to education for illegal alien children (when, some years earlier, it had refused to recognize a fundamental right to education in the Constitution[115]). It is simply to confuse form with substance to argue that the initiative and referendum violate the Guaranty Clause or that the people are incapable of comprehending anything but appeals to passion and prejudice. The results must be judged by the standard of the public good; and by this standard the people of California have a better record than the partisans of ideological liberalism. Californians seem to have rejected government by the minions of the administrative state—and this is, by all reckoning, a healthy sign for the future of republican government in California.[116]

NOTES

1. Thomas Jefferson, "Letter to Edward Carrington (January 16, 1787)," in *Jefferson: Writings*, ed. Merrill D. Peterson (New York: Library of America, 1984), 880.

2. Abraham Lincoln, "First Inaugural Address," in *Collected Works of Abraham Lincoln*, vol. 4, ed. Roy P. Basler (New Brunswick, N.J.: Rutgers University Press, 1953), 268.

3. Theodore H. Hittell, *History of California*, vol. 2 (San Francisco: Stone, 1897), 783. Cardinal Goodwin, *The Establishment of State Government in California 1846–1850*, at 242 (New York: Macmillan, 1914) reports that "[t]here are, excluding the article on the boundary, one hundred and thirty-six sections in the [1849] California Constitution. Of these about seventy are taken from the constitution of Iowa and about twenty from that of New York. The other state constitutions, whose influence is discernible in the finished product of the Monterey Convention, are those of Louisiana, Wisconsin, Michigan, Texas, and Mississippi."

4. *McCulloch v. Maryland*, 4 Wheat. (17 U.S.) 315, 406 (1819).

5. Cal. Const. of 1879, Art. IX, § 6.

6. Cal. Const., Art. I, § 25.

7. Cal. Const., Art. I, § 26.

8. Cal. Const., Art. I, § 1.

9. Kevin Starr, *Americans and the California Dream 1850–1915* (New York: Oxford University Press, 1973), 68. Starr fails to distinguish between the pursuit of happiness and obtaining happiness. This leads him, quite mistakenly, to refer to the pursuit of happiness as the most compelling of American myths. The pursuit of happiness is one of the natural rights that is an irrefragable conclusion from the fact that—to use the language of the Declaration of Independence—all men are created equal. Thus the right to the pursuit of happiness is not an American myth or any kind of myth. It is simply a principle of human nature which legitimate governments are instituted to secure. The founders of America never confused the pursuit of happiness (which can be guaranteed) with the securing of happiness (which cannot).

10. Cal. Const. of 1849, Art. I, § 2.

11. Hittell, *History*, 784.

12. Hittell, *History*, vol. 4, 639–40.

13. Hittell, *History*, 639–40.

14. Hittell, *History*, 638–39.

15. George Mowry, *The California Progressives* (Berkeley: University of California Press, 1951), 9, 13, 90, 117.

16. "A Debate on Initiative and Referendum: Haynes in Favor; Adams Opposed, a Debate Held on October 11, 1911 at the Commonwealth Club of San Francisco," in *California Controversies*, ed. Leonard Pitt (San Rafael, Calif.: ETRI Pub. Co., 1985), 95.

17. Derrick A. Bell Jr., "The Referendum: Democracy's Barrier to Racial Equality," *Washington Law Review* 54 (1978): 17–18.

18. Peter Schrag, *Paradise Lost* (New York: New Press, 1998), 189.

19. Schrag, *Paradise Lost*, 265, 187.

20. Schrag, *Paradise Lost*, 275.

21. Schrag, *Paradise Lost*, 201.

22. John Ferejohn, "Reforming the Initiative Process," in *Constitutional Reform in California*, ed. Bruce E. Cain and Roger G. Noll (Berkeley, Calif.: Institute of Governmental Studies Press, 1995), 318.

23. Mathew D. McCubbins, "Putting the State Back into State Government: The Constitution and the Budget," in *Constitutional Reform in California: Making State Government More Effective and Responsive*, ed. Bruce E. Cain and Roger G. Noll (Berkeley, Calif.: Institute of Governmental Studies Perss, 1995), 358.

24. Hans A. Linde, "When Initiative Lawmaking Is Not Republican Government: The Campaign against Homosexuality," *Oregon Law Review* 72 (1993): 34.

25. James Madison, "The Federalist No. 39," in *The Federalist Papers*, ed. Clinton Rossiter and Charles Kesler (New York: Mentor, 1999), 209 (hereinafter *Federalist*).

26. Madison, *Federalist* 63, 355 (emphasis in original).

27. Madison, *Federalist* 10, 49.

28. Madison, *Federalist* 14, 68.

29. Madison, *Federalist* 10, 50.

30. Madison, *Federalist* 49, 285.

31. Madison, *Federalist* 10, 52.

32. Madison, *Federalist* 51, 290.

33. See Edward J. Erler, *The American Polity: Essays on the Theory and Practice of Constitutional Government* (New York: Crane and Russak, 1991), 39–57.

34. Madison, *Federalist* 63, 352. Notice also the similar statement by Alexander Hamilton in *Federalist* 71, 400–401.

35. William M. Wiecek, *The Guarantee Clause of the U.S. Constitution* (Ithaca, N.Y.: Cornell University Press, 1972), 62.

36. During the "Petition Crisis" of the late 1830s, many Americans rested their opposition to slavery on precisely this basis. Americans sent hundreds of petitions to Congress demanding, for instance, that Congress refuse to admit Texas into the union, because, as a slave state, it could not be admitted consistent with the Guaranty Clause. See generally William Lee Miller, *Arguing about Slavery* (New York: Knopf, 1996)

37. Wiecek, *Guarantee Clause*, 62–63.

38. Madison, *Federalist* 10, 45.

39. Madison, *Federalist* 51.

40. Hans Linde, "Guaranteeing a Republican Form of Government: Who Is Responsible for Republican Government?" *University of Colorado Law Review* 65 (1994): 710.

41. Schrag, *Paradise Lost*, 195, 177, 224, 254.

42. Bruce E. Cain, Sara Ferejohn, Margarita Najar, and Mary Walther, "Constitutional Change: Is It Too Easy to Amend Our State Constitution?" in *Constitutional Reform in California: Making State Government More Effective and Responsive*, ed. Bruce E. Cain and Roger G. Noll (Berkeley, Calif.: Institute of Governmental Studies Press, 1995), 288–89.

43. *California Democratic Party v. Jones*, 530 U.S. 567, 576 (2000). The classic example of the U.S. Supreme Court invalidating a California constitutional amendment initiative on federal grounds is *Reitman v. Mulkey*, 387 U.S. 369 (1967), which struck down Proposition 14, a property rights initiative, as a violation of equal protection because it put the constitutional authority of the State behind potential racial discrimination.

44. 22 Cal. 3d 208 (1978).

45. *Id.* at 219 (citations omitted).

46. Craig B. Holman and Robert Stern, "Judicial Review of Ballot Initiatives: The Changing Role of State and Federal Courts," *Loyola of Los Angeles Law Review* 31 (1998): 1251.

47. Most recently in Senate of the *California v. Jones*, 21 Cal. 4th 1142 (1999), the California Supreme Court held that Proposition 24 could not appear on the March 2000 ballot because it violated the California Constitution's single-subject rule. The proposition addressed two issues: reapportionment and compensation for state legislators and other state officers. The court ruled that these provisions were not reasonably germane to a single subject as is required by Art. II, 8(d).

48. See *Luther v. Borden*, 7 How. (48 U.S.) 1 (1849). In *Pacific States Tel. & Tel. Co. v. Oregon*, 223 U.S. 118 (1911), the Court specifically applied Luther in the context of initiative and referendum measures.

49. 369 U.S. 186 (1962).

50. 377 U.S. 533 (1964).

51. See Debra F. Salz, Note: Discrimination-Prone Initiatives and the Guarantee Clause: A Role for the Supreme Court, *George Washington University Law Review* 62 (1993).

52. Linde, *Initiative Lawmaking*, 39–40.

53. Linde, *Initiative Lawmaking*, 40.

54. Linde, *Initiative Lawmaking*, 44.

55. Linde, *Initiative Lawmaking*, 41–43.

56. See Cain et al., "Constitutional Change," 265.

57. See Cain et al., "Constitutional Change," 269.

58. See further Clint Bolick, *Grassroots Tyranny* (Washington, D.C.: Cato Institute, 1993).

59. Ferejohn, "Reforming the Initiative Process," 354.

60. Alan Rosenthal, *The Decline of Representative Democracy* (Washington, D.C.: Congressional Quarterly Press, 1998), 34.

61. Holman and Stern, "Judicial Review," 1249.

62. Joseph R. Grodin, "The Role of State Constitutions in a Federal System," in *Constitutional Reform in California: Making State Government More Effective and Responsive*, ed. Bruce E. Cain and Roger G. Noll (Berkeley, Calif.: Institute of Governmental Studies Press, 1995), 32.

63. William J. Brennan, "The Bill of Rights and the States: The Revival of State Constitutions as Guardians of Individual Rights," *New York University Law Review* 61 (1986): 550.

64. 423 U.S. 96 (1975).

65. 423 U.S. 96 (1975), 120–21 (Brennan, J., dissenting).

66. Stanley Mosk, "State Constitutionalism: Both Liberal and Conservative," *Texas Law Review* 63 (1985): 1087–88. The title of this article is misleading. Mosk argues that conservatives should support state constitutionalism because it represents the triumph of federalism. Conservatives would be hard pressed, however, to see such judicial activism—with its disregard for originalism—as an appropriate expression of federalism, however federalism might be understood. See Edward J. Erler, "Independence and Activism: Ratcheting Rights in the State Courts," *Benchmark* 4 (1988): 55–66.

67. *People v. Teresinski*, 30 Cal. 3d 822, 836 (1982).

68. 6 Cal. 3d 628 (1972).

69. 6 Cal. 3d 628 (1972), 656.

70. 25 Cal. 3d 142 (1979).

71. 25 Cal. 3d 142 (1979), 172

72. 25 Cal. 3d 142 (1979), 185 (emphasis in original).

73. 25 Cal. 3d 142 (1979), 186.

74. 37 Cal. 3d 873 (1985).

75. *Raven v. Deukmejian*, 52 Cal. 3d 336 (1990).

76. 52 Cal. 3d 336 (1990), 352.

77. 52 Cal. 3d 336 (1990), 353 (emphasis in original).

78. 52 Cal. 3d 336 (1990), 354.

79. 52 Cal. 3d 336 (1990), 355.

80. Legislature of the State of *California v. Eu*, 54 Cal. 3d 492 (1991).

81. Schrag, *Paradise Lost*, 242. It is a singular—although perfectly intelligible—fact that not one state without the initiative process has adopted term limits.

82. Willie Brown's reputation as an astute Sacramento politician is legendary. One well-known and oft-repeated story has Willie Brown dealing with insurance industry representatives and trial lawyers at a famous Sacramento watering hole. The episode is recounted by Holman and Stern, "Judicial Review," 1248: "In the late 1980s, Assembly Speaker Willie Brown sat down at Frank Fat's restaurant in Sacramento with insurance industry lobbyists and trial lawyers. He negotiated an agreement, written on a cocktail napkin, in which the insurance industry obtained an insurance law with no controls on prices and the trial lawyers were rewarded with no control on lawyers' fees and damage awards. All interests were considered except those of California's consumers, who subsequently revolted and rewrote the state's insurance policy by initiative and placed controls

on insurance costs." The cocktail napkin in question was subsequently framed and currently hangs on the wall at Frank Fat's restaurant.

83. *Eu*, 509 (emphasis in original). Many have argued that term limits was unnecessary because the democratic process allowed the voters to turn any politician out of office. This argument ignores, however, the extent to which reapportionment politics in the legislature allows politicians to select voters and thereby ensure incumbency.

84. Cal. Penal Code, § 667 (West 2001).

85. Michael Vitiello, "Three Strikes and the Romero Case: The Supreme Court Restores Democracy," *Loyola Law Review* 30 (1997): 1652.

86. Franklin E. Zimring, "Populism, Democratic Government, and the Decline of Expert Authority: Some Reflections on Three Strikes in California," *Pacific Law Journal* 28 (1996): 243.

87. Zimring, "Populism," 255.

88. See Brian P. Janiskee and Edward J. Erler, "Crime, Punishment and Romero: An Analysis of the Case against California's Three Strikes Law," *Duquesne Law Review* 39 (Fall 2000): 43–69; where much of the following discussion is developed.

89. *People v. Superior Court ("Romero")*, 13 Cal. 4th 497 (1996).

90. Ballot Pamphlet. Rebuttal to the argument against Proposition 184, as presented to the voters, General Election (Nov. 8, 1994).

91. Vitiello, "Three Strikes," 1649 n. 21.

92. Cal. Penal Code 667(f)(2) (West 2001).

93. Cal. Penal Code 1385(a) (West 2001).

94. *Romero*, 13 Cal. 4th at 528 (quoting *People v. Navarro*, 7 Cal. 3d, 248, 260 [1972]).

95. See Janiskee and Erler, "Crime, Punishment," 64–65.

96. Schrag, *Paradise*, 243, 269. This theme is pervasive in Schrag's account; see *Paradise*, 22, 61, 224, 225.

97. Bell, "Referendum," 14–15.

98. Michael P. Rogin and John Shover, *Political Change in California: Critical Elections and Social Movements 1890–1966* (Westport, Conn.: Greenwood, 1970), 36.

99. 946 F. Supp. 1480 (N.D. Cal. 1996) ("Wilson I").

100. 946 F. Supp 1499. Cf. *Romer v. Evans*, 517 U.S. 620 (1996).

101. See *Adarand Constructors v. Pena*, 515 U.S. 200 (1995).

102. *Coalition for Economic Equity v. Wilson*, 122 F. 3d 692, 708 (9th Cir. 1997) ("Wilson II").

103. Wilson I, 946 F. Supp., 1510.

104. Wilson I, 946 F. Supp., 1510.

105. See further James Buchanan and Gordon Tullock, *The Calculus of Consent* (Ann Arbor: University of Michigan Press, 1962).

106. Schrag, *Paradise*, 235.

107. Wilson I, 946 F. Supp., 1506.

108. Wilson I, 946 F. Supp., 1490.

109. James Madison, "Letter from James Madison to James Monroe (October 5,

1786)," in *Papers of James Madison*, vol. 9, ed. William T. Hutchinson and William M. E. Rachal (Chicago: University of Chicago, 1962), 142.

110. *Marbury v. Madison*, 1 Cranch (5 U.S.) 137, 176 (1803).

111. See Edward J. Erler, "The Future of Civil Rights: Affirmative Action Redivivus," *Notre Dame Journal of Law and Public Policy* 11 (1997): 31; Erler, *American Polity*, 91–122.

112. Ca. Const., Art. II, § 1 (West 2001).

113. A month after the conference at which this paper was delivered, the California Supreme Court held precisely that. By adopting Proposition 209, the Court held, "the electorate desired to restore the force of constitutional law to the principle articulated by President Carter on Law Day 1979: 'Basing present discrimination on past discrimination is obviously not right.' " *Hi-Voltage Wire Works, Inc. v. City of San Jose*, 24 Cal. 4th 537, 562 (2000).

114. 457 U.S. 202 (1982).

115. *San Antonio Independent Sch. Dist. v. Rodriguez*, 411 U.S. 1 (1973). See also Edward J. Erler, "Immigration and Citizenship," in *Loyalty Misplaced: Misdirected Virtue and Social Disintegration*, ed. Gerald Frost (London: Social Affairs Unit, 1997), 83–86.

116. Professor Harry V. Jaffa told me that my analysis of the California Constitution reminded him of Lord Macaulays account of the Toleration Act of 1689. In his magisterial *History of England* Macaulay wrote that "[t]o a jurist, versed in the theory of legislation, but not intimately acquainted with the temper of sects and parties into which the nation was divided at the time of the Revolution, that Act would seem to be a mere chaos of absurdities and contradictions. It will not bear to be tried by sound general principles. Nay, it will not bear to be tried by any principle, sound or unsound. The sound principle undoubtedly is, that mere theological error ought not to be punished by the civil magistrate. This principle the Toleration Act not only does not recognize, but positively disclaims. Not a single one of the cruel laws enacted against nonconformists by the Tudors or the Stuarts is repealed. Persecution continues to be the general rule. Toleration is the exception. . . . But these very faults may perhaps appear to be merits, when we take into consideration the passions and prejudices of those for whom the Toleration Act was framed. This law, abounding with contradictions which every smatterer in political philosophy can detect, did what a law framed by the utmost skill of the greatest masters of political philosophy might have failed to do. That the provisions . . . are cumbrous, puerile, inconsistent with each other, inconsistent with the true theory of religious liberty, must be acknowledged. All that can be said in their defence is this; that they removed a vast mass of evil without shocking a vast mass of prejudice. . . . Such a defence, however weak it may appear to some shallow speculators, will probably be thought complete by statesmen." Lord Macaulay, *History of England*, vol. 2 (New York: Washington Square Press, 1967), 465–66. See Harry V. Jaffa, *A New Birth of Freedom: Abraham Lincoln and the Coming of the Civil War* (Lanham, Md.: Rowman & Littlefield, 2000), 126.

II

INSTITUTIONS

Broken Promise: The Rise and Fall of the California Legislature

Dan Walters

When Ronald Reagan challenged Pat Brown's bid for a third term as California governor in 1966, the two jousted over virtually every facet of political policy, from taxation to urban unrest. There was, however, one issue on which Brown, Reagan, and virtually every California politician of the era agreed: the need to create a full-time, professional legislature.

The two candidates for governor and leaders of both parties promised Californians that if they enacted a measure on the 1966 ballot, the legislature would be transformed into a model of efficiency, independence, and responsiveness. "One of the key arguments in favor of a salary adjustment is that a well-paid legislator is an independent legislator," one newspaper commentator of the era wrote. "Just About Everyone Unites Behind State Constitution Revision Measure," read another headline of the period—a truism underscored by a joint ballot pamphlet statement signed by Brown and Reagan for Proposition 1-A. And, not surprisingly, the voters endorsed the measure, thus giving the era's other domi- nant political figure, Jesse Unruh, a huge personal and political victory.

Unruh, the legendary "Big Daddy" speaker of the state assembly, was a tire- less champion of having a well-paid, full-time legislature with a large staff of consultants. No longer would lawmakers be beholden to lobbyists for informa- tion or personal support, Unruh contended—an argument that resonated with Californians scarcely a decade after the capitol had been rocked by the indict- ment and imprisonment of its most powerful lobbyist, Artie Samish.

Even with a capitol divided between Republican Reagan and the Unruh-led Democrats in the legislature, the full-time legislature seemed to work well in its first years, producing a steady flow of creative, innovative legislation involving consumer and environmental protection and welfare reform during the late 1960s and early 1970s. Journalists and political scientists trekked to Sacramento and in a series of appraisals pronounced the professional legislature to be a brilliant success that should be emulated in other states.

The positive assessments, however, failed to take into account two salient factors that would, when fully activated, turn Unruh's dream into a nightmare, rendering the legislature endemically incapable of making policy for a fast-growing, fast-changing state, spawning new scandals, and inviting voter backlash. The result is a legislature that is demonstrably less effective than the part-time, low-paid body that Unruh said he wanted to reform—and one that shows no signs of getting better anytime soon.

The first of those corrosive factors is that while Unruh may have sincerely believed that a professional legislature would better serve the public, he also saw it as a pathway to personal dominance of the capitol by himself and his successors. Unruh had long resented the commanding role that lobbyists played in both getting politicians elected to the legislature and then influencing them after they were sworn in. Samish had pioneered the system he called "select and elect" and other lobbyists used it to one degree or another. Their goal was to recruit candidates who would be supportive of their clients' interests and then provide enough campaign money and other support, even personal salaries, to make sure those selected were elected.

"I didn't care whether a man was a Republican or a Democrat or a Prohibitionist," Samish wrote about his system. "I didn't care whether he voted against free love or for the boll weevil. All I cared about was how he voted on legislation affecting my clients."

Oddly enough, this very undemocratic approach to governance had its positive side. Since Samish and other lobbyists didn't care what their selectees did on matters not affecting their clients, legislators of the 1940s and 1950s were pretty much free to vote their consciences, and produced a cornucopia of legislation that's still positively affecting Californians. A part-time, ill-paid, semi-corrupt legislature and a series of high-minded governors created world-class colleges, parks, and water and highway systems that put to shame the puny efforts of their ostensibly more honest and better-equipped successors, for reasons that shall become apparent later in this chapter.

For whatever reason, either idealism or ambition or both, Unruh yearned to replace the lobbyists with himself as the central figure in determining the legislature's makeup. And a full-time legislature was the key to reaching that goal. It would allow the speaker and other legislative leaders to take command of the legislative flow, force lobbyists to come to them to pass or kill bills, and thus compel those lobbyists to funnel campaign money through the leadership. Unruh, it became evident, didn't want to replace "select and elect" as a system; he just wanted to control it himself. And centralization worked brilliantly, particularly under Unruh's protégé, the even more famous Willie Brown, who commanded the assembly for fourteen years. It resulted in what one lobbyist termed "an appointed legislature," with assembly speakers and other top-rank legislative leaders designating who would fill seats as they fell vacant. And in choosing political loyalists, those leaders created, consciously or not, a legislature dominated by professional careerists, many of them bred and nurtured on the legislative staff.

The rise of careerism was the second salient factor that the early appraisals of the full-time legislature didn't—in fact, couldn't—include because it took about a decade for it to become apparent. Perhaps the most glaring flaw in those positive assessments of the new system was that their authors simply forgot that the higher salaries, the extra staff, and the longer legislative year were all brought into a capitol that was, at the time, full of lawmakers elected under the old system. Those part-timers had been doing a pretty fair job of taking care of California's needs, and with the new resources, they continued to do a pretty fair job. The big change began to happen when that generation of lawmakers began retiring and was replaced by newcomers handpicked by legislative leaders, as Unruh had planned.

Reagan and Bob Moretti, an Unruh protégé who succeeded him as assembly speaker, deadlocked over redrawing legislative district lines after the 1970 census and the issue wound up before the California Supreme Court, which imposed its own redistricting plan for the 1974 elections. Population shifts during the fast-growing 1960s, the effects of the U.S. Supreme Court's one-man, one-vote decision and the fact that districts weren't being drawn by politicians all contributed to a political map that was very different from its predecessor. Directly and indirectly, the situation persuaded a great many incumbents to retire (a special pension bonus also helped) and the 1974 class of freshman legislators was among the largest in California history, at least until term limits began forcing turnover in the 1990s.

By the dozens, ex-legislative staffers who had been anointed by Moretti and other leaders took their seats and within fifteen years, the ex-staffers had succeeded lawyers as the single most common occupation in the legislature. Indeed, by the 1990s, some seats were in their fourth generation of succession, held by politicians who had been staffers to lawmakers who had been staffers to lawmakers who had been staffers to lawmakers.

This flood of hothouse flowers, bred and reared in the capitol itself, had a huge effect on its culture. It was, in the eyes of many who witnessed the transformation, a kind of implosion. Previously, politics had been the means to the end of policy, but within a few years—especially after Willie Brown took over what became known as the "Imperial Speakership"—policy had become subservient.

Brown's election as speaker in 1980 was, in a sense, the pivotal point of the transformation. Brown had lost his bid to succeed Moretti in 1974—just before the new careerists began appearing in large numbers—and the man who did win, fellow San Franciscan Leo McCarthy, was more oriented toward policy than politics, a throwback of sorts to the pre-Unruh era. But the careerists who had flooded into the capitol didn't like McCarthy's prim-and-proper ways and yearned for a swashbuckling figure. Howard Berman, a Beverly Hills assemblyman who ran a powerful political machine with Congressman Henry Waxman, became the careerists' champion and openly challenged McCarthy in late 1979. A nasty, year-long intraparty duel ensued, one that capitol old-timers still remember with fondness or regret, and in the aftermath of the 1980 elections, with neither McCarthy nor Berman able to win election as speaker, Brown reemerged as the compromise candidate and was elected with Republican help.

Berman's careerists may have lost the battle but they won the war with Brown's elevation. Under the new speaker and a new president pro tem of the Senate, David Roberti, almost everything was aimed at building and holding political power. Professional legislators and staffers engaged in a nonstop process of extracting millions of dollars in campaign funds from special interest groups and then directing that money to the election and reelection of legislators loyal to the leaders. Among insiders, it was called "tithing" and while Brown perfected the system, Republicans practiced it on a smaller scale, as did members of the somewhat less centralized state Senate.

The speakership battle had been an eye-opening exercise on campaign fundraising. Previously, while interest groups provided campaign cash to favored candidates, most legislative office seekers still looked to their districts for most of their money—which was a limiting factor. It wasn't until 1972 that the first $100,000 campaign for the assembly was seen and it was not uncommon, until well into that decade, for someone to win election by spending under $50,000. But McCarthy and Berman needed millions of dollars to finance their duel, particularly when rival candidates did battle in the 1980 Democratic primaries, and both hit the "third house" of lobbyists hard. Much to their amazement, the lobbyists and their clients ponied up, and kept on giving no matter how much was demanded. The lobbyists knew that while the politicians were demanding millions, the stakes for their clients were worth billions.

The expansion of state government's environmental and consumer protection regulatory systems during the 1960s and 1970s, the centralization of budgetary decision making in Sacramento after the passage of Proposition 13 in 1978, and the rise of public employee unions after collective bargaining legislation was enacted in the late 1970s all created dozens, if not hundreds, of new special interest groups. And that, in turn, spawned an expansion of the capitol's lobbying corps to more than one thousand. More interest groups, more lobbyists, and bigger stakes all translated into more opportunity for professional politicians to collect campaign money and they didn't miss it.

As the capitol became increasingly driven by its internal, crassly political dynamics, its connection to the outside world weakened. And, as fate would decree, the outside world was itself changing rapidly and in increasingly desperate need of responsive policy making in Sacramento. After a post–baby boom lull, California's population began to surge again in the 1980s, thanks to a new wave of immigration from other countries and an immigrant-driven spike in baby production. The decade saw a whopping 6 million souls added to California's population—the equivalent of a Virginia or a Massachusetts. Schools and colleges, highways, and parks and water systems all began experiencing new demands. The economy was also changing to a postindustrial mode and because of immigration, the state's culture was beginning its transformation into a melange whose dimensions and effects are yet to be fully felt.

Willie Brown may have proclaimed himself to be the "Ayatollah of the Legislature" and his minions may have been indifferent to what was happening beyond Capitol Park, but outsiders—the media and federal investigators and prosecutors—were not oblivious to what was happening inside the capitol. They began delving into the unseemly relationships between legislation and campaign money, what one lobbyist described in a newspaper article, anonymously of course, as "an abysmally corrupt shakedown." And unbeknownst to anyone inside the capitol (except the governor of the era, Republican George Deukmejian), the FBI set up an undercover sting, trolling for lawmakers who wanted money for their votes.

It was a target-rich environment and FBI agents posing as Southern businessmen seeking special tax breaks for their business venture found no shortage of lawmakers and staffers willing to help them for a price, in the form of either campaign checks or money that went directly into politicians' pockets, often as "honoraria" for speeches never delivered. The agents acquired dozens of hours of secretly videotaped meetings that were to become decisive evidence in later criminal trials. The FBI ran its sting for several years until going public with a series of raids on capitol offices and several years and trials followed, eventually resulting in guilty pleas or convictions of a number of legislators from both parties, some staffers, and Clay Jackson, who had been one of the capitol's most influential lobbyists. And if nothing else, the scandal underscored how the capitol's implosion had created a situation ripe for corruption. It was the darker side of Unruh's idealized legislative body.

Willie Brown was to claim later that he was the specific target of the FBI investigation, but whether that's true or not, the scandal did undermine his speakership and eventually led to his departure from the position for the mayoralty of San Francisco. The vehicle for Brown's departure was a measure placed before voters in 1990, clearly taking advantage of the public's disgust at the sting scandal, which would impose term limits on legislators. Its public sponsor, Los Angeles County Supervisor Pete Schabarum, was a former Republican legislator and longtime Willie Brown foe and he and his backers, proponents of term limits on a national scale, saw in the scandal an opportunity to trim the legislature's wings.

Term limits passed handily, despite united opposition from the capitol's political pros, who predicted that they would destroy the legislature's effectiveness. Lawmakers would be limited to three two-year terms in the assembly and two four-year terms in the Senate, with the calendar beginning to run in 1992. Proponents said term limits, reinforced by abolition of the legislative pension system and legislative spending limits, would get rid of the entrenched scoundrels (implicitly, including Brown) and return control of the legislature to citizen-lawmakers. Opponents, harkening back to the Unruh crusade of the 1960s, said limits would make lobbyists, staffers, and governors more powerful and render the legislature incapable of making effective policy.

Term limits, it is apparent a decade later, have changed the culture of the capitol and altered its dynamics, although it is difficult to separate their effects from those of other factors, such as another court-ordered redistricting plan that also took effect in 1992. It is also apparent, however, that the legislature's product—its policy making for 35 million Californians—has not been radically altered. Simply put, the legislature was ineffective before term limits and still is.

The mandatory turnover of term limits, compounded by the districting plan and elimination of pensions, has meant many fewer ex-legislative staffers seeking seats themselves. It is simply not as attractive a career path as it once was. More lawmakers are coming from private lives and professional careers and from local governments. There also has been an explosion of women and nonwhite politicians in the legislature as term limits forced out the veterans. The limits do not appear to have materially affected the partisan balance. Republicans surged in 1992 and 1994—probably due more to redistricting than limits—but lost seats in the four elections thereafter.

Legislative leadership has been weakened. When Brown left the speakership in 1995 after fourteen years in power, he was succeeded by a series of short-term speakers, including three Republicans (two of them chosen by him). The assembly has settled into a pattern of leadership. A second-term Democrat accedes to the speakership every other year and then serves until the halfway point of his third term before turning the position over to his successor. But speakers can no longer dictate legislation and serve more as coordinators and negotiators than bosses. Indeed, the Senate has replaced the assembly as the more dominant legislative house, with virtually all senators moving up from the assembly.

One of the greatest impacts has been on the lobbying corps, which must contend with constantly changing legislative memberships—a third new assembly members every two years—and leaders. They have learned, some of them the hard way, that leaders cannot deliver the votes by snapping their fingers and lobbyists have been forced to line up support for or opposition to bills one vote at a time. They have also learned that campaign contributions have relatively less impact and that grassroots organization is a powerful tool among lawmakers who come from local communities and, for the most part, will return to them. Some lobbyists have retired rather than change tactics. Others have adapted with gusto, partially resurrecting the old "select and elect" system by recruiting and financing their own friendly candidates in primary elections, thus replacing legislative leaders' formerly dominant role. The primaries have become all-important because a 2001 redistricting plan designated, in effect, the partisan ownership of every legislative district. Special interest groups concentrate money and other resources on the Democratic primaries in districts that are vacant due to term limits. The 2002 primaries were dominated by contests between liberal candidates backed by environmentalists, trial lawyers, and others on the left side of the Democratic Party and business-backed moderates.

In general, the liberals won, thus validating another theory about the redistricting agreement: that it would tend to drive both legislative parties toward their extremes and thin the ranks of centrists, because it includes very few, if any, "swing" districts that could be won by either party. And since the Democrats are guaranteed to dominate the legislature for at least a decade, it means that the legislative body as a whole will be moving to the left. The tilt to the port was very apparent in 2002 as dozens of bills backed by labor unions, consumer groups, personal injury lawyers, and environmentalists, many of which had been bottled up for years, went to Governor Gray Davis, mostly to be signed. And the legislature shifted even further to the left as the first post-redistricting class of lawmakers took office in late 2002—a syndrome that's likely to hold even if California as a whole continues to be a relatively moderate state.

Critics, professional politicians and lobbyists especially, bemoan the changes. But California voters rejected one legislatively sponsored effort to modify term limits and seem satisfied that the system is superior to returning to the old professional era. An objective appraisal would be more mixed, however. Term limits did nothing about the full-time legislature itself, nor did they demonstrably improve its product. Those coming to Sacramento may have better attitudes, in the main, about doing the public's business but they also know less about how to do it, and get little guidance from inexperienced, short-term leaders. There is more chaos and churning but, as an energy crisis and a budget crisis demonstrated, no greater ability to come to grips with real issues arising out of California's fast-growing and fast-changing cultural and economic climate.

Would other systemic changes be in order? Should California experiment with parliamentary-style government to make officeholders more accountable for outcomes, should the legislature be expanded to make districts smaller and lawmakers closer to their constituents, should California have a variety of parties to represent its diversity, or should California simply return to the old part-time legislature? Finally, is it possible, just possible, that when a society becomes as complex as California, no system can really work well? Perhaps the answer to California's crisis of governance lies outside the capitol, in creating civic and social consensus that the politicians would be willing to ratify.

Whatever the answer may be, it's evident that nearly four decades of tinkering with the structure has not found it.

No Allegiance but to the State: California Governors Hiram Johnson and Gray Davis

Brian T. Kennedy

In the rich political history of California many names come to mind: Leland Stanford, Hiram Johnson, Earl Warren, Goodwin Knight, Pat Brown, Richard Nixon, Ronald Reagan, Jerry Brown, S. I. Hayakawa, Willie Brown, and Pete Wilson.[1] It is clear that the current governor, Gray Davis, will wander into this band of notables. If Davis is remarkable it shall not be because he oversaw and mostly caused the state's infamous electricity crisis or that during his reelection campaign he grossly misstated the state's fiscal condition such that Californians were clamoring for his recall in the early months of 2003. If Davis will be remembered it will be because his governorship marked a period in California political history where the Progressive reforms of the administration of Governor Hiram Johnson had reached their ridiculous conclusion and had made constitutional government in California all but impossible.

To understand Gray Davis then one must first understand his most influential predecessor, Hiram Johnson.

HIRAM JOHNSON, TWENTY-THIRD GOVERNOR (REPUBLICAN 1911–1914, PROGRESSIVE 1914–1917)

Born in Sacramento in 1866, Hiram Johnson was Sacramento City attorney and later San Francisco assistant district attorney who came to political fame battling the corrupt union boss Abraham Ruef. Johnson, a Republican, was a product of the Progressive ideas that were sweeping the nation at the turn of the century. In 1910 he was elected on the promise he would eliminate the influence of the Southern Pacific Railroad from California politics. Although a reluctant candidate for office, he campaigned throughout the state giving speech after speech where he would not only imitate fellow Republican and Progressive Theodore Roosevelt's famous "Bully!" but would declare, "The Southern Pacific must keep its dirty hands out of politics."[2]

It was indeed an age where the Southern Pacific Railroad exerted enormous influence in the politics of the Golden State. Johnson and his political followers were eager to limit the influence of not only the railroads, however, but of any so-called private interest from California politics.

Hard-driving and humorless in public, Johnson's first inaugural address set the tone of his administration and forever altered California's political landscape:

The electorate has rendered its decision, a decision conclusive upon all its representatives; but while we know the sort of government demanded and decreed by the people, it may not be amiss to suggest the means by which that kind of *administration* may be attained and continued. (emphasis mine)

He would go on to say:

In some form or other nearly every governmental problem that involves the health, the happiness, or the prosperity of the state has arisen, because some private interest has intervened or has sought for its own gain to exploit either the resources or the politics of the state. I take it, therefore, that the first duty that is mine to perform is to eliminate every private interest from the government, and to make the public service of the state responsive solely to the people. The state is entitled to the highest efficiency in our public service, and that efficiency I shall endeavor at all times to give. It is obvious that the requisite degree of efficiency can not be attained where any public servant divides his allegiance between the public service and a private interest.[3]

It would be in this first inaugural that Johnson would call for the establishment of a civil service system to create a new class of public employee. In addition, so that government would be more responsive to the people, he would call for constitutional amendments to enact the referendum, the initiative, and the recall. Although Johnson states that these would not be a panacea, they would be a first step in creating a new "popular" government. Whether Johnson understood such reforms as being antirepublican is unclear. What is clear is that Johnson believed in "trusting the people" to decide essential questions of public policy versus their elected representatives who may or may not be "corrupted" by private interests. What became evident at the time, however, was the extent to which the governor, state officials, and public employees became corrupted by a narrow conception of the "public" interest that was itself private in nature.

Consider first the establishment of the civil service system. In seeking to remove any so-called private interest, Johnson sought first the removal of any political opponents from the government or state commissions on the grounds that anyone not on his side politically must obviously be on the other side. And although Johnson's political machine came into office running against the practice of fund-raising from public employees, such a practice was easily justified when it became clear that this was an easy way of maintaining their political power. As George Mowry has pointed out, there was not any discernible corruption in the Johnson administration and whatever else was true such actions were done in the service of the "people."[4] Of course this view of corruption is only possible if one rejects the commonsense notion that it is quasi extortion for a governor's political machine to be seeking contributions from public employees. No doubt many public employees donated because they saw their own interest melded to the political fortunes of a governor and legislature. Today, however, donations by public employees are in the form of mandatory union dues that are very difficult to avoid and have tended to go overwhelmingly to pro-big government candidates as represented by the Democratic Party and Democratic candidates.[5]

Consider also the referendum, initiative, and recall. Although elected representatives could pass laws that regulated the safety of the people, the people would have a new voice in California politics whether they used it or not. In Johnson's words, the threat of a recall would be an essential "precautionary measure" against any "recalcitrant" official. The precaution of course was that the will of the people would somehow not be carried out and that the recall would be a healthy reminder of how an elected official ought to behave.

Taken together, the referendum, the initiative, and the recall, were the perfect populist method of undermining representative and republican government. For the first time in California history direct power would be given to the people at the expense of elected officials. Instead of having a government of "reflection and choice" as had been argued for in *The Federalist Papers*, California would have a government by accident and force—or in the Progressive spirit, based on the will or passions of the people. That California today addresses the most serious matters of public policy with the initiative should not be seen as a vindication of the Progressive reforms of Johnson but rather as the ultimate failure of constitutional government. Proposition 13, which limited property taxes, Proposition 187, which sought to deal with state payments for illegal immigrants, Proposition 209, which eliminated quotas and preferences in state admissions and contracting, Proposition 227, which sought to end bilingual education—as well as other initiatives—all should have been debated and voted on by legislatures and signed or vetoed by governors.

It should have been so not because the people were not wise in their decision-making in these instances, ironically, but because these were intended to be a function of the state legislature. Rather than building political organizations to pass such initiatives, political efforts would have been made to build political majorities around principled policy positions. Politicians would then have to defend their views in public rather than simply watch from the sidelines. It is not certain whether Johnson and the Progressives in California saw initiatives as an outlet for the passions, or in the case of the propositions listed above the righteous anger, of the voters. In any event it has come to pass in California that it is not necessary to organize and build a political majority to advance a political issue but rather simply to organize to gather enough signatures and to campaign in a seemingly nonpartisan fashion.

Johnson and the Progressives did understand that they had created a "new philosophy of government" and that "a state has been freed politically, its public servants yielding now no allegiance but to the state."[6] It is in this light—after eighty years of this type of government—that Gray Davis serves as governor of California.

GRAY DAVIS, THIRTY-SEVENTH GOVERNOR
(DEMOCRAT 1999–)

The charge leveled by opponents against Gray Davis during the 2002 gubernatorial election campaign was that he was a mere tool of moneyed interests—those "private" interests that Hiram Johnson decried. Having raised $30 million before election year and a total of $60 million the year of the election, Davis broke all records for fund-raising. It was charged that to seek an audience with the governor you had to be a donor. It went so far as the famous incident where students at UC Berkeley were encouraged to attend one of the governor's less expensive fund-raising events in order to meet him and discuss student concerns. It was from this that the "pay to play" chorus was heard throughout the campaign between Davis and businessman/philanthropist Bill Simon. The latter even charged Davis, erroneously, with accepting contributions on state property in violation of state law. Unfortunately for Simon it turned out that voters did not care that much about a politician raising money and rather expected that they would do such things. Never did the voters learn about the many principled differences the two men possessed or why Gray Davis should be returned to the office he had longed for his adult life.

Davis was once described by the *San Jose Mercury News* as "perhaps the best-trained governor-in-waiting California has ever produced." Davis graduated from Stanford University and Columbia Law School before serving in Vietnam in 1968–1969. He would return to California and enter politics first working on campaigns and then as chief of staff to Governor Jerry Brown. From there he would serve in the legislature, as state controller, and then as lieutenant governor during the term of Governor Pete Wilson.

On two of the more divisive policy issues, Davis is pro-choice and pro-death penalty. Rarely does he take a stance that is not well measured in public opinion. Members of the outwardly moderate Democratic Leadership Council, Davis's rhetorical models are Bill Clinton and Al Gore who manage mostly to appear to be all things to all people. Very much like Clinton, Davis is moderated by his ambition for higher office. Because he would like to be president, and because of his demonstrated fund-raising abilities, he never quite takes any stand that would alienate liberal and moderate Democrats or would otherwise scare off liberal Republican business interests. He does not have to by virtue of the initiative process given California by Hiram Johnson. Any really controversial subject is left to citizens' groups to organize initiatives against.

Consider his stand on Proposition 209, which ended quotas and preferences. Lieutenant Governor Davis was publicly in Bill Clinton's "mend it don't end it" camp. This means that he is, of course, against quotas and preferences but is also against "the politics of division and exclusion." He can be, as it were, openly against quotas and preferences but see Proposition 209 as not the right avenue for solving the problem. As governor he administers the government and influences the Board of Regents in ways that allow for quotas and preferences so long as they are not called quotas and preferences but are masked in other names and practices.

So fine an ear has Davis for politics that even he, a lifelong Democratic partisan, would not let slip an opportunity to reach across the aisle when former governor Ronald Reagan had commemorative license plates made in his honor. Governor Davis would say at the public ceremony, "He took this country to new frontiers of human freedom. In the early 1980s, when the country was wracked with self-doubt after Vietnam and Watergate, he taught us to believe in ourselves again. And more than anything else he restored confidence in America and reasserted patriotism as a true American value."

It was with political acumen such as this that Davis garnered the endorsement of California's other gifted politician, Willie Brown, former speaker of the California assembly and mayor of San Francisco, when Davis first ran for governor. Although Brown and Davis had known each other for many years, many were surprised when Brown, never one to risk his own political capital, endorsed Davis early over two wealthy and viable candidates in businessman Al Checchi and popular Congresswoman Jane Harman. Never a very exciting speaker, Davis ran on the theme, "Experience Money Can't Buy." It turned out that indeed Davis had experience money could not buy and that Democratic voters appreciated it.

In the general campaign he ran against Attorney General Dan Lungren who believed in the age of Bill Clinton that good character had to amount for something. Unfortunately for Lungren it was not obvious that just because you say you have good character the voters will believe you or that it was obvious that Gray Davis, whose picture in military uniform was featured in almost every advertisement, had bad character. Davis became governor with a 58 percent to 38 percent landslide vote.

So far two episodes have marked Davis administration: his handling of the electricity crisis and the budget disaster of 2003.

The electricity crisis emerges very much out of the Progressive movement's attempt to regulate public utilities such as railroads and the electricity companies. For most of the twentieth century electric utilities were heavily regulated for a reason. In return for building power plants—and attracting the necessary capital to do so—the investor-owned utilities were granted monopoly status over a certain geographic territory. They in turn promised to serve all in the territory. Because they had monopoly power, a government body, the California Public Utilities Commission (CPUC), set their rates based on a formula that granted them a reasonable rate of return. That system worked reasonably well until government mandates forced the use of higher-cost and environmentally-fashionable renewable sources, and no-growth policies imposed restrictions on the construction of new power plants.

It was believed that the inefficiencies and high costs of the government-regulated monopoly system could be fixed by the restructuring that took place in 1996 with AB 1890. The idea of that law was to develop a competitive marketplace for electric generation, a service that previously was the exclusive obligation of the regional investor-owned utilities and publicly-owned municipalities and power agencies. The investor-owned utilities would sell off their generators to new and existing private power companies. These companies would in turn sell the power into a new "generation market" run through two new state agencies, the Power Exchange and the Independent System Operator. By this means it was thought that competition would drive down prices and ensure consumers a sufficient supply of electricity.

Two serious miscalculations were made. First, the legislature failed to take into account that a competitive free market of electricity requires the ability of new generators to enter the market at a fairly rapid rate. Today it takes three years, under the best circumstances, to complete the permitting process before a new power plant can go online. As a result the monopoly power once held by the investor-owned utilities was transferred to the new and existing power generators. But whereas utility company rates were regulated by the CPUC, private generators are regulated only by market forces and the selective imposition of price caps. Thus began the controversial blackouts and high cost of electricity in the summers of 1999, 2000, and 2001. Generators of electricity tried to make as much money as they could—a natural instinct in a market economy—and sometimes would not sell power if they believed they would not get paid. Governor Davis publicly charged the generators, many of them from Texas, with manipulating the market and it is still the subject of litigation whether the generators engaged in any wrongdoing.

The failure of Governor Davis was in not seeing the newly created monopoly power of the generators and trying to find free markets solutions such that were being employed in other parts of the country. It is widely believed now that if the governor and his appointed CPUC would have allowed the generators and the utilities to enter into long-term contracts in 1999—contracts that would have locked down lower prices—the crisis would have been averted. Only when the situation had gotten out of hand did the governor engage in such long-term contracting and even then threatened to not honor the contracts if it was believed that a bad deal had been made.

Although the restructuring of the electricity system was not of Davis's making, the crisis that ensued was almost entirely caused because Davis would not act. It was in this circumstance that the solution required statesmanship, or at a minimum, leadership. The people could not be turned to for answers because they were most complex. Lacking an understanding of the will of the people to guide him, Davis merely did nothing and caused the electricity market to be manipulated to the disadvantage of Californians and the California economy.

The budget disaster is of a different sort. Here Davis was merely responding to the needs of his constituents: the public employees of the state of California. There are approximately 800,000 state and local government employees in California. Almost all belong to public employee unions from those who work in state agencies, to county and local governments, policemen, firemen, prison guards, service workers, and the most powerful, the state's teachers.[7] Together these groups contributed millions to Gray Davis's election and reelection campaigns. It was not to be inconceivable that in the governor's budgets that the size and scope of the state agencies would grow. How much they would grow would begin the problem.

In 2001 there were federal tax changes that would mean a one time rise in California's state tax revenues. This was widely acknowledged and warnings were put out by Republican budget experts and even the nonpartisan Legislative Counsel not to spend the excess money in new ongoing programs. That of course is what immediately happened in a budget passed by the Democratically controlled legislature and signed by Governor Davis. When in 2002 the economy continued to turn down and when the one time revenues were no longer available, a projection was made by the governor's Department of Finance that 2003 revenue would be $14 billion less than budgeted. After Davis reelection these deficit figures were revised upwards to $20 and then $38 billion. The gap was closed by a blend of deficit bonds, an increase in the car tax, and spending cuts. The anger over the deficit helped incite a recall campaign against Davis, one that raged even as this edition went to press.

What does this suggest about Gray Davis as governor? Certainly he does not intentionally mean the state of California harm. But he is guided by no more than the interests of the state. And here is not meant the state of California but the state as the apparatus of governing California. It is to the state and its public employees that Davis owes his allegiance. It is their interest that he seeks to serve. This does not make him an evil man by any stretch but rather merely a product of the "new philosophy" of government given California by Hiram Johnson. Whether this has led to more corruption or less corruption is for citizens to decide for themselves.

NOTES

1. The author would like to thank Melanie Marlowe for her research assistance on this essay.

2. George E. Mowry, *The California Progressives* (Berkeley: University of California Press, 1951), 119.

3. Inaugural Address, Hiram Johnson, Presented January 3, 1911, at www.governor .ca.gov/govsite/govsgallery/t/documents/inaugural_text_23.html.

4. Mowry, *California Progressives*, 138–39.

5. The Beck Decision allows that a union member, including members of public employee unions, can have returned the part of their dues that go to politics. As a practical matter this is a tedious exercise since it requires constant written requests to the unions who then are allowed to define what portion, usually negligible, actually goes to "politics."

6. Second Inaugural Address, Hiram Johnson, Presented January 5, 1915, at www .governor.ca.gov/govsite/govsgallery/t/documents/inaugural_text_23b.html

7. United States Census Bureau, *The Statistical Abstract of the United States* (Washington, D.C.: U.S. Government Printing Office, 2002), 269.

The Progressive Court

Harold Johnson

California's reputation as a trendsetter, the place "where the future happens first," was certainly borne out in the legal arena during the decades following World War II. From the 1940s through the mid-1980s, California's Supreme Court pioneered the nationwide movement to give judges expansive new powers as agents of progress.

Some have argued that in carving out a dynamic governing role for itself, the court was following the school of "legal realism," which sees judges not merely as custodians of received law but as architects who apply and shape the law to accommodate, and even direct, social change.[1] But it could also be said that the Progressive movement, decades after the textbooks mark its close, found an echo at the Golden State's Supreme Court. Efficiency in government, after all, had been a rallying cry for Progressives who were impatient with the change-resistant constitutional structures, the cumbersome checks and balances, bequeathed by the founders. What could be more efficient and expeditious than policy making by stroke of the judicial pen?

The Progressives had also advocated professionalization of government, ceding more power to the credentialed specialists in the courts. More regulatory supervision of the private marketplace was another goal of Progressivism. Facilitating lawsuits against business excesses, as California's high court would do from the 1940s onward, harmonizes with this agenda.

There were risks, of course, in courts becoming drivers of political and social reform. When unelected jurists take on powers that have traditionally been the province of the representative branches, they expose themselves to the slings and arrows of politics. Under California's provisions for what one might call "people power," judges who flout the popular will can be voted out—something that happened with a vengeance to a trio of Supreme Court liberals in 1986. In other words, headstrong pursuit of a Progressive mission can be tempered—even punished—by direct-democracy tools that are, ironically a legacy of the Progressives.

The post war California Supreme Court is identified above all with one name: Roger J. Traynor. Appointed to the court in 1940, Traynor was elevated to chief justice by Gov. Edmund G. (Pat) Brown twenty-four years later. A former law professor at UC Berkeley, his judicial opinions were striking not merely for their scholarly depth but because they reached beyond legal precedent, to arguments from reason, experience, and commonsense.

Asserting that the judiciary must be more than a conduit of established legal principles, Traynor declared that "[c]ourts have a creative job to do when they find that a rule has lost its touch with reality and should be abandoned or reformulated to meet new conditions and new moral values."[2] To be sure, he wasn't the first to make this case. "What made Traynor unique," wrote legal commentator Preble Stolz, "was his success during his thirty years on the California Supreme Court in persuading a majority of his colleagues and the bar to widen their vision of what was appropriate grist for argument and decision."[3]

The court's signature achievement during the Traynor era was to open the door—critics would say floodgates—to new categories of tort liability for businesses, particularly manufacturers. The concept of fault was at the center of the transformation. Traditional tort law looked for evidence on which to assign culpability—usually, negligence on the manufacturer's part, an absence of ordinary prudence. The Traynor Court considered this "blame game" an obstruction to justice. Merely being the maker of a problem product should be enough to warrant liability, under the new view that the court came to champion. In the 1963 case of *Greenman v. Yuba Power Products, Inc.*, involving an injury caused by a power woodworking tool, Traynor wrote for a unanimous court that a manufacturer would be held "strictly liable" for a defect in a product—with no need to show specific negligence. Traynor was building on a concurring opinion he had authored eighteen years earlier, when the Supreme Court found manufacturer liability in the case of an exploding soft-drink bottle. Traynor had stepped out in front of his colleagues in that case, *Escola v. Coca Cola Bottling Co.*, by arguing for strict liability in such situations because manufacturers could spread the risk of injury.

The triumph of Traynor's liability theory "was a great leap," as Peter Huber, a skeptic of the loosening of the old tort rules, puts it. "The need to find negligence had been [a] troublesome barrier to tort theories of liability. Now, at one bound, the courts could leap directly to the desired goal. . . ." It wasn't long before other courts would pick up Traynor's arguments and run far with them (not always in directions the California jurist explicitly had intended). Strict liability eventually would be applied not just to defects in the *manufacturing* of a product, but also to *design*; this would invite juries to speculate on the best blueprint for a lawnmower, electric switch, or ladder—decisions the old tort law would have considered beyond their competence.[4]

Old principles of contract also went by the boards. No longer could a manufacturer delineate in advance the extent of its responsibility for a product's safety, with the customer implicitly agreeing by purchasing the product. In the 1963 case of *Vandermark v. Ford Motor Co.*, the California Supreme Court refused to recognize any company disclaimer relating to safety, calling the contract "immaterial." Liability, the argument in such cases went, could not be cordoned off by restrictions over which the buyer inherently had no leverage. Legal scholar Grant Gilmore famously labeled as "the death of contract," this interment by the courts of traditional relations between maker and purchaser.[5]

Businesses faced additional vulnerability to lawsuits with the California Supreme Court's unveiling of the "alternative liability" theory, whereby a plaintiff could go after any one of several parties who *might* have been the cause of an injury, even though only one of them actually was at fault. *Summer v. Tice* (1948), which announced this rule, arose out of the accidental shooting of a hunter by one of his two companions—but it wasn't clear which one, because both had been firing indiscriminately. The precedent foreshadowed later cases where plaintiffs would be allowed to target the potential defendants who had the biggest bankroll—the "deepest pockets"—even if their degree of fault was slight.

In addition to fostering a system of "business regulation by litigation," the court in the Traynor years, and beyond, did not shrink from fashioning broad social policy. In 1971, the year after Traynor's retirement, the ruling in *Serrano v. Priest* upended the state's financing system for public schools. The court argued that uneven funding among school districts violated state equal protection guarantees. Legislators were plunged into fights over how to divvy up education dollars so as to protect parochial political interests and still meet judicial approval.

The next year, the public reacted with furor to *People v. Anderson*, which declared that the death penalty violated the state constitution's ban on "cruel or unusual" punishment. By the end of the decade, two ballot initiatives and two statutes had been enacted, all in an effort to undo this decision. The turmoil showed that the state's high court had become a political player—and a force that set political upheavals in play.

The Progressives were not champions of property rights. Far from it. They demanded that private property must give way to assertions of the public good, as if secure rights in property are in tension with other freedoms, rather than supportive of them (as the founders believed). Theodore Roosevelt articulated this new notion in 1910:

> We are face to face with new conceptions of the relations of property to human welfare, chiefly because certain advocates of the rights of property as against the rights of men have been pushing their claims too far. The man who wrongly holds that every human right is secondary to his profit must now give way to the advocate of human welfare, who rightly maintains that every man holds his property subject to the general right of the community to regulate its use to whatever degree the public welfare may require.[6]

From at least the 1960s to the present day, the California Supreme Court has been a spear carrier for the philosophy that denigrates property rights. The court shocked landowners up and down the state in 1971 with its ruling in *Gion v. City of Santa Cruz*, declaring that some coastal property owners had made an "implied dedication" allowing public access to their property merely because people had been trespassing in large numbers for some time without being confronted and explicitly told to leave. It did not matter to the court that signs had been posted saying the land was private. The legislature responded almost immediately with an effort to limit the "loss of rights" for property owners; henceforth, the new statute stated, courts could not decree that an owner had given the public a right of access, unless he had *actually done so*—that is, unless he had issued an "express written irrevocable offer of dedication."[7]

The California Supreme Court continued to push back the boundaries of private property with a 1980 decision stating that the public's free speech rights superseded the rights of shopping-mall owners. *PruneYard Shopping Center v. Robins* defined privately owned shopping malls as modern equivalents of town squares, so signature-gatherers and petitioners could claim a right of access to spread their message, regardless of the wishes of the owners.

Daunting obstacles have been erected for California property owners who try to challenge government land-use decisions as oppressive or unconstitutional. Through rulings such as *Hensler v. City of Glendale* (1994) and *Kavanau v. Santa Monica* (1997), the state Supreme Court has decreed that a plaintiff "pursue five or six separate administrative and judicial proceedings to receive the relief that the Constitution supposedly guarantees" from overzealous property regulations, as Gideon Kanner, an authority on land-use law, describes the dizzying legal maze. "This is an obviously contrived process that consumes years and hundreds of thousands of dollars in litigation expenses and is evidently intended to discourage California landowners. . . . Its burdens have simply shut out small landowners from the judicial process."[8]

Judicial hostility to property rights in California is bipartisan. *Hensler* and *Kavanau* were decisions of a court largely appointed by Republican governors; but they displayed a continuity with decisions of the 1960s and 1970s, when Democratic appointees were in the majority. Because of the court's consistency in these matters, it was not surprising a decade ago when a survey of property law specialists found California "a near unanimous choice as the state least likely to protect landowner rights. [California public officials and land-use regulators] are accustomed to meeting little resistance in the courts."[9]

The trademark innovations of the Progressive era in California were the initiative, the referendum, and the recall process, allowing voters to write or repeal laws, and remove errant elected officials. The system for review of high court justices, dating in its current form from the early 1930s, exhibits the same deference to the authority of a popular majority. Justices are nominated by the governor and must receive approval by a three-person Commission on Judicial Appointments. Afterwards, they go before the electorate for retention every twelve years. These are not contested elections, but up or down votes on whether a jurist should get another term.

For half a century California Supreme Court elections were a formality, with all justices routinely returned to office. This tradition ended with a thunderclap in the mid-1980s. The aggressively liberal chief justice, Rose Elizabeth Bird, along with two associate justices who had also been appointed by Gov. Jerry Brown and shared Bird's ideological inclinations, became targets of a heavily funded political campaign led by Republican politicians and business leaders. It culminated in their ouster by landslide margins in the 1986 general election.

Conventional tellings of the saga attribute their defeat to the Court's obstinacy on the death penalty. From the late 1970s to the date of the 1986 election, more than two hundred death sentences were imposed in murder trials around California. None was carried out. In every one of the more than sixty death penalty cases that came before her, Bird voted for reversal. The Court crafted an "intent"-to-kill requirement so metaphysically subtle that even when a thug fired five shots at point-blank range into the chest area of a Brinks guard, the chief justice said it could not be assumed that he intended for the guard to die, without specific evidence on the killer's state of mind.[10]

In *People v. Alcala* (1984), a 5–1 majority ordered a new trial for the accused kidnapper-killer of a teenage girl, on the grounds that discussion of his abuse of other young women had been improperly admitted at trial. The ruling's result, complained Kern County's district attorney, was that "It practically has to be an identically committed crime before you can get it in" as evidence.[11] "My little daughter Robin never got to her ballet lesson," the victim's mother recounted in a TV commercial for the dump-Bird campaign. "But the man who kidnapped and killed her is still alive."[12]

Yet if the death penalty was the campaign's cutting edge, the Court's overreaching in the *civil* realm also stirred a powerful, if less populist, backlash. Thus, more than half the contributions to the multimillion-dollar campaign against three targeted justices came from banks, insurance companies, and real estate developers; the largest single contributor during one reporting period was the Independent Oil Producers Agency.[13]

These opponents charged the Bird Court with a reckless eagerness to subject corporate defendants to tort liability. Arguably, the justices were merely working out the implications of the Traynor Court's precedents. But given the conventional wisdom's veneration for the Traynor era, it was safer for business interests and conservative legal commentators to argue that Bird and her two targeted colleagues were following new paths, to ludicrous extremes. A favorite example of critics was 1983's *Bigbee v. Pacific Telephone & Telegraph Company*. The plaintiff had been in a phone booth when a drunk driver veered off the road and crashed into it. The Court found the phone company liable for defective design, location, and installation of the booth. Such rulings, as one analyst put it, turned tort law into a form of social welfare, "an off-budget program for compensating the needy, administered by judges and juries without the constraints of the legislative process."[14]

Critics identified a haughty, cavalier attitude toward lawmakers and their statutes in *Isbister v. Boys Club of Santa Cruz* (1985), where the court ordered the Boys Clubs to admit girls. This was an act of legislation, not legal interpretation, responded UC Berkeley Law Professor Phillip Johnson. "[T]he California Legislature made a decision to restrict the application of the Unruh Act [the state's antidiscrimination law] to only a certain kind of institution—business establishments," he wrote in a pamphlet widely circulated during the 1986 campaign. It "[robbed] this term of all meaning" to apply the Unruh Act to a nonprofit, voluntary, community service organization.[15]

Supporters of the imperiled justices hoisted the banner of "judicial independence."[16] Former state Bar president Anthony Murray declared that voters should consider only the matter of "competence"—i.e., whether justice decided cases "based on a reasonable exercise of discretion and legal analysis," even if the decisions themselves might be unpopular.[17] Former Justice Otto Kaus used a colorful analogy to warn against judges being subjected to potential removal for controversial rulings. It was like "having a crocodile in your bathtub," he said. "You keep wondering whether you're letting yourself be influenced, and you do not know. You do not know yourself that well."[18]

But these objections did not square with the text of the state constitution. Nothing in the provisions for judicial retention elections dictates any "right" or "wrong" reasons for voting justice up or down. The freedom—the responsibility—to sift good reasons from bad is left with the people.

In fact, Justice Kaus's son found irony in the concerns of Bird's defenders. "It is certainly a bit late for California's liberals to start complaining of politics polluting the judiciary," journalist Mickey Kaus wrote in the *New Republic* as the anti-Bird effort gained momentum.

> Like their counterparts elsewhere, [California's liberals] have long championed the role of judges as bold social reformers. One California justice, the late Matthew Tobriner (a colleague of Traynor's), used to give speeches on the Court's obligation to react to 'the economic imbalance in our society' and 'the plight of the economically downtrodden.' If judges are going to claim such a broad right to respond to 'society's demands,' (as Tobriner put it), then it's hard to deny society, at election time, its right to demand something else.[19]

From the vantage point of nearly two decades later, it is hard to argue that the 1986 election had no effect on jurists' behavior in the Golden State. Certainly the California Supreme Court in succeeding years has not been the engine of innovation that it once was. The fact that six of the seven current justices are centrists or moderate conservatives appointed by the Republican governors of the 1980s and 1990s is a primary reason. But it would be remiss also not to give some credit (or blame, depending on one's perspective) to the voter revolt of 1986, and its enhancement of what Justice Kaus might have called the "crocodile effect."

Would the Progressives have been troubled by all this? No, answered *Los Angeles Times* editorial writer Ernest Conine immediately after Bird's defeat. "Hiram Johnson, God rest his soul, must be grinning from ear to ear as he contemplates the results of the . . . elections in California," Conine speculated. It was no surprise, he wrote, that voters perceived Bird's record as one of "judicial arrogance, and reacted by using the processes provided by the California Constitution to retire her from office."

For better or worse, California's constitutional framework rests on the tenet that direct governing power ultimately rests with the people, who may pull rank on any mediating institutions, as well as on legislators and even judges. "Individual Americans," Conine wrote in his rhapsody on the Progressive creed, "range from stupid to brilliant, from good to bad and from generous to unconscionably greedy," but "collectively, we are a pretty sensible bunch."[20] For judges who wish to test the limits of that Progressive proposition by ignoring or opposing a firmly held popular consensus, the election of 1986 stands as a warning that they risk a righteous retribution.

NOTES

1. Preble Stolz, *Judging Judges: The Investigation of Rose Bird and the California Supreme Court* (New York Free Press, 1981), 76.

2. Roger J. Traynor, "Law and Social Change in a Democratic Society," *University of Illinois Law Forum* (1956), 232.

3. Preble Stolz, *Judging Judges*, 77.

4. Peter Huber, *Liability: The Legal Revolution and Its Consequences* (New York: Basic, 1988), 37, 38, 39.

5. Grant Gilmore, *The Death of Contract* (Columbus: Ohio State University Press, 1974).

6. Theodore Roosevelt, *The New Nationalism* (Englewood Cliffs, N.J.: Prentice-Hall, 1961), 322; quoted in Tom Bethel, *The Noblest Triumph: Property and Prosperity through the Ages* (New York: St. Martin's, 1998), 174.

7. California Civil Code, Section 1009.

8. Gideon Kanner, "California Judges' War on Property Rights, Camarillo, CA," *California Political Review* 9 (1998): 27.

9. Kanner, "California Judges' War," 25, quoting from Dennis Coyle, *Property Rights and the Constitution* (Albany: State University of New York Press, 1993).

10. *People v. Fuentes*, 1985.

11. Mary Ann Galante, "California Justices Face Own 'Executions': Bitter Campaign Focuses on Death Penalty," *National Law Journal* 3 (November 1986): 1.

12. Galante, "California Justices," 1.

13. Gerald Uelman, "Shopping for Judges, California Style," *Los Angeles Times*, September 30, 1986, Metro, pt. II, 5.

14. Richard K. Willard, "Wheel of Fortune: Stopping Outrageous and Arbitrary Liability Verdicts," *Heritage Foundation: Policy Review* 36 (1986): 40.

15. Phillip E. Johnson, *The Court on Trial* (Santa Monica, Calif.: The Supreme Court Project, 1985).

16. Uelman, "Shopping for Judges," 5.

17. Anthony Murray, "Understanding Retention Elections," *California Lawyer* (September 1985), quoted in Phillip Johnson, *Court on Trial.*

18. Dan Morain, "Kaus to Retire from State Supreme Court; Deplores Strident Attacks on Justices in Anti-Bird Effort," *Los Angeles Times*, July 2, 1985, pt. 1, 1.

19. Mickey Kaus, "Flipping the Bird," *New Republic*, April 15, 1985, 21.

20. Ernest Conine, "Hiram Johnson Had It Right; '86 California Vote Supports His Faith in Grass-Roots Wisdom." *Los Angeles Times*, November 10, 1986, Metro, pt. 2, 5.

The Elections of 2002: Clear-Cut or Ambiguous?

Richard H. Reeb Jr.

California's statewide election of 2002 contained few surprises but, as usual, provided plenty of food for thought for students of politics. The Democrats continued their domination of the state legislature and congressional delegation, and made a clean sweep of the executive constitutional offices. But Republicans, though clearly the minority party, made a few inroads in the legislature and, under California's constitutional requirement of a two-thirds vote for budget passage, exerted considerable influence on the 2003 budget.

Only days after the November 5 election was over, Governor Gray Davis began to make it clear that the huge $20 plus billion budget deficit (later estimated at nearly $38 billion) his opponent Bill Simon failed to turn to his and his party's advantage was not only a real problem, but that the Republicans's favored solution—budget cuts—might well prevail over the Democrats's favorite—tax increases. Indeed, the next shoe to drop was the announcement that the first round of budget cuts would come in midyear, not postponed until the next fiscal year.

In other words, the state's budget crisis is dire and will not be overcome merely with tax increases, even though enough of the voters showed, by their election of the Democrats to the vast majority of the public offices, not to mention by their approval of four multibillion bond measures, their preference for the Democrats's solution. Each and every time a bond measure is proposed, including in 2002 Propositions 46 (housing), 47 (schools), 49 (after-school programs), and 50 (water quality), its supporters recite the mantra of "no new taxes," meaning merely a long-term debt (that can be paid off by mostly younger taxpayers who may never know what their forebears imposed on them). Davis's own preferred public posture is "centrist," which means he is more willing (at least publicly) than unabashed liberal Democrats to work with Republicans to get the state through its budget crisis. However, the recall campaign has forced Davis to lurch left to protect his office.

As *Sacramento Bee* political commentator Dan Walters has repeatedly observed, Davis is risk averse and prefers at least the appearance of moderation. But massive problems that only begin with the budget and threaten to make it worse, namely, the neglect of the state's infrastructure, including water, power and transportation, and heavy taxation and regulation of California business, were deliberately ignored to ensure Davis's reelection.

California government and politics have long been in great contradiction between its Jacksonian origins in the mid-nineteenth century and its Progressive overlay at the beginning of the twentieth. The state has multiple elective offices at the state, county, district, and city level, which were manageable as long as there were strong political parties that could ensure voter loyalty. But the introduction of direct democracy, nonpartisanship, and professional expertise has engendered growing risk aversion by politicians and cynicism and indifference by voters. Add to this mix the computerized gerrymandering that guarantees legislative incumbents of both major parties extremely safe seats, and one gets political drift.

Let us descend into particulars. The Democrats's sweep of the numerous executive offices was characterized by the governor falling behind three of the other candidates of his own party. Davis, who carried 47 percent of the vote (compared to Simon's 42 percent), was outpolled by Attorney General Bill Lockyer with 51 percent, and Lieutenant Governor Cruz Bustamante and newly elected Treasurer Philip Angelides, each with 49 percent. The closest and most interesting races were those for secretary of state and controller, where Republicans Keith Ohlberg and Tom McClintock fell to Kevin Shelley and Steve Westley, respectively. Meanwhile, John Garamendi returned to the Insurance Commissioner's office with a close win over Gary Mendoza. Undoubtedly, the more successful Democratic candidates are looking four years hence to a possible gubernatorial bid, while Davis's hopes for the presidency or the vice presidency are all but dashed by the recall election.

How, then, did Davis win in 2002? He announced immediately after Simon's defeat of White House-favored Richard Riordan in the state's earliest-ever March primary election that he would go on the attack. Simon, Davis charged, was anti-choice on abortion, antigun control, antigay, and antienvironmental. Thus, Davis was reassuring the left wing of the Democratic Party and the "moderates" in the Republican Party (Is this a distinction without a difference?) that he was their man. He abandoned the usual incumbent posture of "pointing with pride" (How could he defend his handling of the energy and budget crises?) and urged his fellow Californians to "view with alarm" the purportedly repulsive characteristics of his conservative challenger.

Most assuredly, Simon viewed Davis with alarm but his own lack of political and governmental experience cost him dearly. Davis's attack ads repeatedly portrayed Simon as a corporate fat cat who cheated his associates out of millions of dollars—and those ads continued to run even though an appeals court judge overturned a mistaken jury verdict against Simon. Simon's attempt to capitalize on Davis's reputation as a governor whose public policy decisions are for sale to a host of bidders foundered on a mistaken location for the then-lieutenant governor's acceptance of a large campaign contribution, which turned out not to be in his office but in a private home.

It would not be an unreasonable inference that, for a plurality of California's voters, neither Davis's energy-crisis fumbling nor his budgetary difficulties nor his alleged corruption mattered as much as the "social issues," as issues of morality are called these days. (That term was once applied to the campaign for civil rights, which was also a moral issue.) And here the great divide of California politics becomes clear. Like the nation, this state has red and blue counties, a distinction popularized in the 2000 presidential campaign. In both cases, the red or conservatives counties vastly outnumbered the blue or liberal counties.

But while Davis carried only eighteen of California's fifty-eight counties, most on or near the Pacific coast (and most heavily populated), Simon's impressive multicounty appeal mattered little. Besides the historic tendency of urban areas with large numbers of blue-collar workers, ethnic minorities and liberals to vote Democratic, one must remember the left-wing revolution effected on university and college campuses in the 1960s which converted those institutions into additional party bastions. Finally, the state's inland-coastal split is reflected in the fact that only Los Angeles and Imperial counties joined their Democratic brethren from Monterey County to Humboldt County and those in or adjoining the San Francisco-Oakland-San Jose metropolitan complex, who supported Davis by large margins.

These counties (and others that managed to slip out of the Democratic camp this time, such as Ventura, Santa Barbara, and San Luis Obispo) were part of the intellectual source and provided many of the foot soldiers for the radicalization of the Democratic Party, beginning with George McGovern's ill-fated presidential nomination in 1972 and Jerry Brown's successful race for governor of California two years later. (Brown was soon dubbed "Moonbeam" by the late Michael Royko, *Chicago Sun Times* political writer, for his apparent rejection of the industrial revolution and his embrace of "small is beautiful" as a governing principle.) As much of the nation appears for the moment (judging from the remarkable results of the 2002 elections outside of California) to be willing to give Republicans a chance to govern in all three elective branches of the federal government and in many of the states, Davis could count upon the California liberal left to provide his margin of victory. Unless the Republicans find a way to cut into this built-in liberal advantage or turn out more of their own base, they will continue to lose elections in California.

For years, Republican hopes depended upon success in statewide races. Brown and his father, Edmund, before him, and his protégé Davis after him, have been the only Democratic governors since Culbert Olson in 1943. But, beginning with the Democratic sweep which Edmund G. (Pat) Brown led in 1958, the state legislature has been largely in Democratic hands. The Republicans failed to capitalize on a judge-made redistricting plan in 1980 that put two assembly districts in each state Senate district and respected county lines and geographical differences. So in 1990 and again in 2000 they have had to swallow Democratic majorities in both houses of the state legislature and California's (now) fifty-three-person House delegation.

Of course, Republican legislators were paid in the solid coin of incumbency protection. Only a handful of seats were in contention and—surprisingly—Republicans actually made small gains in both state houses. Now although the safe incumbency pattern is repeated across the country, one should note its comical and ironical aspects in California. Of the twenty (one half of the total of forty) Senate seats in contention, fourteen were won by Democrats and six by Republicans. Only one race was won by less than 50 percent, only two between 50 and 60 percent, fourteen between 61 and 80 percent, and five with 100 percent! This is reminiscent of the famous Bell Curve, which in both intelligence and classroom tests supposedly reveals the normal mental spread in the population. In a state that officially values professional expertise in government, this could be a sign of many high achievers or the usual large contingent of average people.

The same sort of pattern appeared in all eighty assembly races. Forty-eight Democrats and thirty-two Republicans were elected. With four times as many members to be elected, three persons won with less than 50 percent of the vote, thirteen between 50 and 60 percent, fifty with 61 to 80 percent, nine with 81 to 90 percent, and only three with 100 percent.

Finally, U.S. House races in the state were won by the Democrats by thirty-two to twenty-one over the Republicans. No races were won with less than 50 percent of the vote, four between 50 and 60 percent, forty-four with 61 to 80 percent, and three over 80 percent. There were no candidates elected unopposed. The most publicized race for the seat of the disgraced Gary Condit was held by the Democrats. Do, then, elections mean anything in California? It is a question at least worth exploring, even if one must ultimately decide that they do. The reason for doubt is as follows: all officeholders are nominated by voters who have no responsibility for their choices; laws are made by legislators and signed by governors who share lawmaking authority with the people, to whom they refer all bond issues and many policy choices; and local officials are ostensibly nonpartisan or professional managers who, willy-nilly must practice politics but deny it. In California, the buck passing goes on unabated.

The major element of the Progressive heritage is the evisceration of the parties and even of the idea of party government. California's voters have absorbed the lesson that parties do not matter, and since the election of Moonbeam, or for the last generation, they truly haven't because the Deukmejian and Wilson Republicans avoided being party leaders. Thus, the voters are convinced that it probably does not matter who gets elected; and until a Republican gubernatorial candidate campaigns as the leader of his party and as the advocate of a party reform agenda that impresses the voters as superior to the left-wing Democrats agenda of income redistribution and interest group liberalism or buying everybody off by giving them everything they want—politics and government "out of control," fiscally and programmatically—the state will continue to have the same regime it has had for the last generation.

Term limits and primaries have contributed to the voting public's inability to hold its public officials accountable to any sense of a governing agenda. In fact, couldn't we describe California government since 1975 as government by hidden agendas? More than once California voters (and 2002 was no exception) cast their ballots one way and got something else. For example, voters in 1978 approved Proposition 13, the property tax rate-cutting measure, by a solid 2–1 margin, in an obvious protest against high taxation. But they also reelected Democratic Governor Jerry Brown and a Democratic legislature, which proceeded to bail out cash-strapped local governments by diverting inflation-swollen income tax revenues back to them. A *Los Angeles Times* exit poll that year found that the greatest single reason voters approved the famous proposition was to "cut welfare." They failed to realize that welfare was state-mandated (not to mention politically favored), so social welfare was virtually unaffected.

In 1986, voters approved Proposition 105 to cut automobile insurance rates but elected Republican Governor George Deukmejian, whose handpicked Insurance Commissioner systematically undermined the measure. This led to the establishment of the elective insurance commissioner, designed by Democrats to prevent a repeat of that experience. How much they succeeded is another question. In 2002 voters both elected a heavy majority of Democrats and approved expensive state programs but their "centrist" Governor Gray Davis by virtue of the two-thirds majority budget requirement needs the votes of minority Republicans in both houses of the legislature to get his budget passed.

But that is not the whole story. The social (sexual?) revolution having long since become more dear to the heart of liberal Democrats than economic matters (after all, millions of dollars were made by Democrats in the stock market during the bubbly 1990s boom), the Democratic legislature will continue to pass laws protecting abortion, legitimizing homosexuality (including "civil unions") and limiting gun ownership. It is not clear that the majority of California's voters approve of that agenda, but at least a large plurality of them have more confidence in Democrats than in Republicans, and it is Democrats who will therefore make policy in the state. It is left to Republicans only to slow the process down. The latter's best hope was to have a Republican governor who could veto parts of the now-$100 billion budget, not to mention legislation favored by the defenders—and active practitioners—of sexual freedom and alternative lifestyles. The hard hats and minorities may or may not turn out for election day, and many of them did not in 2002. But the far left wing of the Democratic Party votes in large numbers because it has much at stake.

III

LOCAL GOVERNMENT

The Problem of Local Government in California

Brian P. Janiskee

> A very civilized society finds it hard to tolerate attempts at freedom in a local community; it is disgusted by its numerous blunders, and is apt to despair of success before the experiment is finished. . . . Hence, until communal freedom has come to form part of mores, it can easily be destroyed, and it cannot enter into mores without a long-recognized legal existence.
>
> —Alexis de Tocqueville[1]

In his classic 1835 work *Democracy in America*, Alexis de Tocqueville argued that a strong system of local government would educate its citizens as to the importance of political life. A patchwork system of small autonomous communities would establish a level of government in which the average citizen would have an opportunity to participate directly in public affairs. As a result of this participation, a patriotic transformation would take place within the souls of the citizenry. Among the many fruits of this transformation would be a strong attachment to one's community. This natural loyalty would in turn provide a vital bulwark against the centralizing tendencies of state and national administration.

However, the tangled nature of California local government does not provide the proper ground upon which this patriotic transformation can take place. If Alexis de Tocqueville were to examine the present condition of local government in California he would find a cacophony of counties, cities, school districts, and special districts. California has 58 counties, 471 cities, 991 school districts, and 4,780 special districts.

This analysis is unique in its criticism of the tangled web of California local government, especially the proliferation of special districts. The attack upon special districts is usually made by liberal policy advocates who see such entities as a hindrance to the creation of a more efficient, centralized administration. The criticism of special districts offered in this analysis is derived from an entirely different point of view. It is the conclusion of this study that the existence of special districts, albeit unwittingly, fosters the enhancement of the administrative state's power.

INTRODUCTION

Alexis de Tocqueville believed that he had discovered the essence of democracy in America. The ghost in the American machine was the principle of equality. It was everywhere and nowhere, moving through a myriad of political institutions: "The laws vary; their form changes; but the same spirit gives them all life."[2] This spirit had no less a goal than the establishment of a spirit-numbing uniformity. This desire for the leveling of all differences would lead to the creation of a centralized administration that would implement a soft despotism in the United States.[3]

One of the vital bulwarks against the rising tide soft despotism was local self-government. From his observations of New England town meetings, Tocqueville argued that a certain degree of local autonomy helped foster a spirit of civic duty. Citizens could then see how their immediate welfare was tied to the welfare of the community; visceral self-interest is transformed into self-interest rightly understood. If the Americans could acculturate their citizens with this spirit, then they might have a chance to avoid the creation of a centralized administration. If Tocqueville were to examine the condition of local government in California today, he would find that local government in California was a maze of counties, cities, school districts, and special districts.

OVERVIEW OF CALIFORNIA
LOCAL GOVERNMENT

Counties

There are fifty-eight counties in California.[4] Counties are legal subdivisions of the state.[5] The governing body of each county consists of a legislative entity, usually known as a Board of Supervisors, which must have at least five members.[6] Most of the counties select their supervisors by means of a single-member district system as opposed to an at-large method. In addition, a county must have a sheriff, district attorney, and assessor. These positions are required to be filled through a direct election.[7] A county may provide other elected offices if called for in the county's charter.[8] Any county may adopt a charter upon majority support of a ballot measure.[9]

The primary areas of policy responsibility for counties are law enforcement, public health, public records, sanitation, tax collection, and welfare. Most of a county's policy responsibilities are mandated by the state or federal government. The costs of running the court system are included in this. Counties provide approximately 60 percent of the funding for the state's court system. In addition, some counties have contracts with local governments within their jurisdiction to share the costs for certain services. This is called the "Lakewood Plan," after the California city that initially adopted this method of providing services. The most common policy areas that fall under the Lakewood Plan are fire and police services.[10]

Most counties in California belong to regional associations. These organizations are quasi-governmental units devoted to cooperation and discussion on issues of regional concern, with mass transit being a prominent example. Counties within a regional association send representatives to serve on a board of directors, share research data, conduct studies, and resolve intercountry disputes. The two largest associations are the Southern California Association of Governments and the Association of Bay Area Governments. The Southern California association is comprised of representatives from Imperial, Los Angeles, Orange, Riverside, San Bernardino, and Ventura counties. The Bay Area group is comprised of representatives from Alameda, Contra Costa, Marin, Napa, San Francisco, San Mateo, Santa Clara, and Solano counties.

Cities

There are 471 cities in California.[11] These cities belong to two categories: charter and general law. There are 384 general law cities and 87 charter cities. General law cities are operated according to specific provisions in the California code. A charter city, on the other hand, has more flexibility in the management of administrative and fiscal affairs. Any city may adopt a charter pursuant to the state constitution in the manner prescribed by statute.[12]

The council is the basic institution of government for California cities. City councils consist of at least five members, elected to staggered four-year terms.[13] City council elections can be based on either the ward system or the at-large system. The ward system operates much like elections to the California legislature, with council members being elected from single-member districts—

wards—within the city. On the other hand, council members in an at-large system do not represent a specific district within the city. Instead, the entire council is selected in a single citywide election. For example, if a city council were to have five members, the top five candidates in a citywide election would serve on the city council, regardless of the neighborhood from which they hailed.[14]

Mayors can be directly elected by the city at-large or selected by the city council from among its members. A mayoral position can be either weak or strong. Strong mayors have extensive powers to hire and fire city officials. Weak mayors are without these powers, and fulfill a more ceremonial role. All but the largest of cities, which include Los Angeles and San Francisco, employ a city manager as the chief municipal administrative officer. The job of the city manager— sometimes called a city administrator—is to run day-to-day operations. Since the city manager serves at the pleasure of the city council, the level of flexibility given to a city manager is a barometer of the balance of power between a mayor and a city council. In the political science literature, weak-mayor cities are often called "council/manager governments" and strong-mayor cities are referred to as "mayor/council governments."[15]

LAFCOs

Should the city incorporate adjacent areas? What should be the long-run relationship between the services provided by a city and adjacent unincorporated areas? How can urban sprawl be prevented or successfully managed? These questions are addressed by a Local Agency Formation Committee (LAFCO).[16] There is a LAFCO in each California county. Most LAFCOs consist of two representatives from county government, two from city governments, and one representative from the public at-large.[17]

The most challenging issue faced by LAFCOs is secession, a process whereby a portion of one city seeks to separate and form a new city. The City of Los Angeles was confronted with several secession movements in 2002. The most notable was in the San Fernando Valley. The Los Angeles County LAFCO determined that the San Fernando Valley, as an independent city, could provide the basic level of city services without significant financial damage to the rest of Los Angeles.[18] Therefore, the secession measure was approved for placement on the ballot where it eventually failed.

School Districts

There are 991 school districts in California—574 elementary, 93 high school, 318 unified, and 6 common administration.[19] The local government body of a school district is the school board. The chief executive officer of a school district is the superintendent. The relationship of the superintendent to the school board is much like that of the city manager to the city council. The superintendent of a school district serves at the pleasure of the school board. As is the case in most states, school districts are major political battlegrounds in California. Bilingual education, school prayer, and vouchers are among the most controversial issues in state politics. In the 2000 general election, California voters faced two ballot proposals—Propositions 38 and 39—that could have had profound and lasting effects on education in the state.

Proposition 38 was soundly defeated, 71 to 29 percent. Had it been approved, it would have instituted a public school voucher system. At the discretion of parents, the state would have provided $4,000[20] per student for private or parochial school tuition.[21] Proponents argued that "[c]ontrol over the education and destiny of California's children must be taken from bureaucrats and given to parents."[22] However, opponents of the measure contended that "not every child will have access to this new system of voucher schools," because "voucher schools will be able to reject students who apply based on their gender, their ability to pay and their academic and physical abilities."[23] On the other hand, proponents of the measure pointed to the successful implementation of a pilot voucher program in Milwaukee, Wisconsin. Milwaukee mayor John Norquist argued that "[a]ll of the things that the critics pointed to as problems haven't happened." Norquist stated further that *public schools* have improved because of the voucher system. They are forced to concentrate on achieving "higher quality" education "that can attract positive attention from parents."[24] The defeat of Proposition 38 could be the death knell for school choice efforts in California. However, the home school movement poses a serious and growing challenge to the status quo.

Proposition 39, which passed by a vote of 53 to 47 percent, offers a departure from the previous means of local school capital finance. Before Proposition 39, school bond projects required a two-thirds level of support from voters. Furthermore, a similar two-thirds vote was required to exceed the level of taxation allowed under Proposition 13. Under the terms of Proposition 39, the voting requirement for both of these will be changed from two-thirds to fifty-five percent. Supporters of the measure all but conceded that the measure will increase taxes. On the other hand, they stressed additional measures in the proposal that would, so the argument goes, increase accountability and reduce wasteful bureaucracy. Opponents of the measure argued that Proposition 39 could have the potential to become a significant financial burden to homeowners in that "there is no limit on how much property taxes can eventually increase with passage of 55 percent bonds."[25]

Proposition 13

The debate over Proposition 39 can be traced back to what is perhaps the most controversial ballot initiative in California history, Proposition 13. During the early 1970s, housing values in California were skyrocketing, resulting in a dramatic increase in property taxes. The successful passage of Proposition 13 in 1978 rolled back property taxes to 1975 levels, set a rate ceiling at 1 percent of assessed valuation, and limited any potential increase in the tax rate to 2 percent per year. Furthermore, any special new local taxes beyond the property tax restrictions in Proposition 13 could only be passed by a two-thirds vote.

Critics of Proposition 13 argue that before the measure went into effect, local public services in California were the envy of the nation.[26] After the measure's enactment, opponents argue, California's public services deteriorated to the point where they are now among the worst. In addition, opponents argue that the limit on property tax revenue encourages cities to favor retail development instead of residential development, because the cities will be able to harvest sales tax dollars, which are not under the strict limits of Proposition 13. This drives up property costs, so the argument goes.

Finally, the opponents decry the loss of local autonomy in financial matters. The loss of revenue control has left local governments more dependent on Sacramento than ever. At first glance, this line of reasoning has a conservative cast to it: a repeal of Proposition 13 would give cities greater flexibility to deal with unique local problems. One might be convinced of this logic if one were to see these opponents call for a reduction in statewide taxes in exchange for increased local control over raising revenues.

According to many supporters of Proposition 13, the most fundamental lesson to be learned from the controversy is not the level of taxation alone but also the very nature of the property tax itself.[27] First of all, the property tax is one of the most regressive taxes. It is not tied to a person's ability to pay. The homeowner must pay the same amount, or even a higher amount, whether or not the person has received a raise, a pay cut, or lost a job. Second, the property tax is difficult to administer. In California, counties are largely responsible for property assessment. As part of this responsibility, counties must provide an assessment appeals process, in the likely event of disputes over assessed value. Lastly, the property tax provides homeowners a perverse incentive not to improve their property, for fear of an increased assessment.

In addition to Proposition 13, there have been other successful ballot initiatives affecting local government finance. Among the most significant are Propositions 62 and 218. Proposition 62 was passed in 1986 and mandated that, in addition to an increase in special taxes, any increase in general taxes must be approved by the voters in that jurisdiction. Proposition 218, which was approved in 1996, extended the provisions of Proposition 62 to charter cities.

Special Districts

There are 4,780 special district governments in California.[28] Special district governments are distinguished from general purpose governments—counties and cities—in that they are devoted to narrow policy concerns. A special district is "any agency of the state for the local performance of governmental function within limited boundaries."[29] A special district government creates conditions whereby the costs and benefits of public services are limited to a particular area. They allow "local citizens to obtain the services they want, at a price they are willing to pay."[30] Special districts are governments in the sense that they can collect revenue and own property. However, they do not have the full scope of regulatory powers that a general government possesses. That is to say, special districts have, on the whole, *corporate* powers but not *police* powers.[31]

California ranks second only to Illinois in the number of special districts.[32] Special districts are created to find additional sources of revenue that may not be available from a general purpose government. Most districts have been formed to provide the following: (1) services to rural areas; (2) services on a regional basis; and (3) services that were beyond the ability of existing local governments.[33] The first special district in California was created over a hundred years ago in the San Joaquin Valley. The Turlock Irrigation District in Stanislaus County was created under the Wright Act of 1887.[34] Subsequently, over fifty irrigation districts were created in the next twenty years to deal with the problems of financing such projects.[35] Most of the districts were in northern and central California and were devoted to agricultural concerns. However, after the 1950s, water districts began to appear in Southern California as well, with their main purpose being to aid urban development. The passage of the Utility District Act of 1921[36] allowed for the creation of special districts for needs other than water.[37] Since then, the number of varieties of special districts has grown considerably.

It is a matter of controversy whether or not tax and expenditure limitations (TELS), like Proposition 13, are a significant factor in the creation of special districts. Nancy Burns points out that "[t]raditional scholarship on the creation of special districts suggests that these districts are largely a technical financing maneuver by existing local governments that have hit taxing and spending limits and yet want to continue providing services."[38] However, the findings of a blue-ribbon panel charged with conducting an analysis of California special districts cast some doubt on the claims of traditional scholarship.[39] California had 9.96 special districts per 100,000 people in 1977, one year prior to the passage of Proposition 13. In 1992, the same figure was 9.05.[40]

A general purpose government may call for the creation of a special district within its boundaries. The creation of a special district has two distinct phases, the proposal period and the ballot campaign. During the proposal period, governing bodies are required to hold public hearings as to whether or not a ballot measure should be offered. In addition, approval by the county LAFCO is required in many cases. If a measure survives the proposal period, then the special district will be created upon majority approval by voters within the boundaries of the proposed district.

Districts can be broken down into various categories depending upon the following criteria: (1) whether or not they provide more than one type of public service; (2) whether or not they have the ability to charge fees for their services; and (3) whether or not they have their own governing board, as opposed to being governed by an already existing general purpose government.[41] Special districts that provide only one type of public service are known as single-function districts, while those that provide more than one are known as multifunction districts. Most special districts are in the multifunction category.[42]

Enterprise or Nonenterprise [43]

Special districts that have the ability to charge fees for their services are known as enterprise districts. Since the 1980s, most new districts have been in the enterprise category.[44] Those that must rely upon general revenues alone—property taxes in most cases—are known as nonenterprise districts.[45] Nonenterprise special districts found their source of property tax revenues significantly depleted after Proposition 13. In response to this, the state created the Special District Augmentation Fund (SDAF) to provide a supplemental source of revenue for nonenterprise special districts. The state distributes SDAF funds to counties according to a predetermined formula. It is then up to the county legislative body to distribute the funds.[46]

However, in addition to their fee-based revenue, enterprise districts can also receive appropriations from the general revenue fund of counties or cities. This double dipping, as it were, has allowed some enterprise districts to amass considerable reserve funds. As of the 1996–1997 fiscal year, 592 special districts reported having reserves in excess of 300 percent of their annual operating costs. For example, the Metropolitan Water District of Southern California has an annual operating cost of $708,881,000. Yet its reported reserve fund as of June 30, 1999, was an astounding $4,046,288,932. This is 571 percent of its annual operating costs.[47] Of the $19.4 billion in fund balances for all special districts, enterprise districts held $18.2 billion.[48]

Independent or Dependent

Special districts that have their own governing boards are known as independent districts, while those that are governed by an existing general purpose government are known as dependent districts. During the proposal period, the general purpose governing body makes a determination as to whether or not a district will be dependent or independent. Most special districts are independent.[49] Whether independent or not, the initiative, referendum, and recall provisions of California government apply to all special districts.[50] Furthermore, special districts must adhere to the government accountability measures in the Public Records Act[51] and the Brown Act.[52]

Dissolution

Special districts may be dissolved by means of a petition by the requisite number of registered voters or landowners, depending upon the specifics of the district's statutory authorization. Once a petition is qualified, the LAFCO of the county in which the district lies holds a hearing on the proposed ballot measure.[53] If the LAFCO approves the proposal, it is then sent to the general purpose governing body—County Board of Supervisors or City Council—in which the district lies. The governing body holds a similar hearing. If the dissolution measure receives a favorable decision, it is placed on the ballot. The district would then be dissolved upon majority approval of the ballot measure.

In addition, proposals to dissolve a special district may be initiated by the LAFCO itself. This is a result of the Gotch Amendment (AB 1335) to the Cortese-Knox Local Government Reorganization Act of 1985.[54] The purpose of this act is to consolidate overlapping districts into a more coherent system of local government or dissolve districts that have outlived their purpose. However, since the passage of the Gotch Amendment, only one LAFCO-initiated proposal has led to the dissolution of a special district.[55]

The two main reasons for the failure of LAFCOs to reduce the number of special districts are (1) the nearly prohibitive cost of financing a dissolution study, and (2) the reluctance of LAFCO officials to eliminate the positions of their counterparts in special districts.[56] Therefore, "districts formed in a different time to meet different needs survive today—even if they are no longer the most effective service provider or the reason for their formation has ceased to exist."[57]

Perhaps the most illustrative examples of this phenomenon are California's health care districts. As of 1999, twenty-four of the seventy-four health care districts no longer operated hospitals. Of these twenty-four, a majority continued to collect property tax revenues.[58] Why do they continue to exist? Some officials in these districts argue that, while they no longer operate hospitals, they continue to be active in policy decisions and provide vital funding to hospitals. Furthermore, there is no financial incentive to eliminate a health care district due to the fact that the property tax revenue would simply be returned to the state.[59]

Advantages and Disadvantages

Special districts can provide public services according to the unique characteristics of local demand. In addition, the costs of public services are directly linked to the benefits. Thus, the argument goes, because they are specific entities, devoted to particular concerns, they are responsive to their constituents. On the other hand, it can be argued that special districts are inefficient. "In urban areas, districts often provide the same services provided by cities and counties and overlap one another, occasionally creating conflicts and competition."[60] They hinder regional planning and, due to the sheer number of governmental units, lessen accountability.[61] "Special districts often escape wide public attention because their functions are narrow and technical."[62] This is especially true when one considers the massive reserves that have been accumulated by many special districts. These large pools of funds are "largely unknown and unexamined by the public or policy makers, and are often not considered in statewide or regional infrastructure planning and financing."[63] In addition, "[m]any Californians do not know what a special district is—let alone which one serves them."[64]

The sheer amount and variety of California local governments is breathtaking. A California citizen would achieve no small feat by simply locating all of the different units of local government that exercise authority in a particular local area. One study found that every citizen in the state is a resident of a dozen or more units of local government.[65] According to Nancy Burns, "two neighbors might be in the same transit district but in different water districts, housing districts, and economic development districts."[66] As opposed to city or county limits that are marked by road signs, the boundaries of special districts are not obvious to passersby. Locating and charting the special districts that have jurisdiction over one's life and property could be a daunting task, as Don Bowen laments, "without the benefit of [a] surveying or cartography background."[67] And even if one did have a professional background in political geography, and were able to identify and draw the boundaries for all of the governments in one's area, there is no guarantee that the results of one's labors would provide a clearer picture. It is not uncommon for the boundaries of local governments to "have irregular and uneven boundaries and take on a 'Swiss Cheese' design."[68]

CONCLUSION

Tocqueville contends that the properly functioning local government is so constituted as to "form the nucleus of strong attachments," without "attract[ing] the hot hearts of ambitious men."[69] It is safe to say that such attachments are sorely lacking today. A selection from the minority report of the California Constitution Revision Commission provides an excellent analysis of our present predicament:

> One of the hallmarks of successful government in America has been the primacy and preponderance of local institutions. This success was built upon local discretion in all matters administrative, and upon local responsibility for funding local matters. No state mandates encouraged local spending and taxing. Restraint and economy, built upon voluntary labor and local responsibility, were the rule. This gave rise to a wonderfully various and adaptable system. It was a marvel. We have lost it.[70]

Special districts lie beyond the common sense experience of most citizens; their very purpose is to divorce a narrow element of policy from the consideration of those charged with the maintenance of the common interest. Clear lines of political accountability must be created if local government is to be strengthened. And this might involve the dissolution of special districts. As outlined above, such procedures are currently available in California law.

The chaotic local government structure in California is a fertile field for the onrushing flood of the administrative state, whose edicts wash inexorably from Washington, D.C., to Sacramento, and down into the backwash of California's municipalities. Such chaos does not create an environment in which local government can foster a spirit of liberty-loving civic responsibility that will resist the seductive charms of soft despotism. In assessing the damage done to the republican spirit by the overwhelming force of centralized administration, we should consider the full meaning of Tocqueville's understanding of the genesis of local government: "man creates kingdoms and republics, but townships seem to spring directly from the hand of God."[71]

NOTES

1. Alexis de Tocqueville, *Democracy in America*, ed. J. P. Mayer, trans. George Lawrence (Garden City, N.Y.: Doubleday, 1969[1835]), 62.

2. Tocqueville, *Democracy*, 82.

3. This is a recurring theme in Tocqueville's writing. See, for example, *Democracy*, 57 (contrasting "manly and legitimate passion for equality," with "debased taste for equality."); 255 (noting effect of leveling principle on thought in America: "I know of no country in which, speaking generally, there is less independence of mind and true freedom of discussion than in America"); 692 (warning of regulatory state which "covers the whole of social life with a network of petty, complicated rules . . . [which] does not destroy anything, but prevents much from being born").

4. San Francisco is a special case, being that it is both a city and a county. For the purposes of this study, it is included in both totals.

5. Cal. Const., Art. XI, § 1; Cal. Government Code, § 23002 (West 1998).

6. Cal. Government Code, § 25000 (West 1998).

7. Cal. Const., Art. XI, § 1.

8. Cal. Const., Art. XI, § 4.

9. Cal. Const., Art XI, § 3. Charters may be proposed by the county's legislative body or by an appointed charter commission. The proposal would then be placed before the voters for approval or rejection.

10. The Lakewood Plan is attractive to many cities because it provides a cost-effective means by which they can provide public services. This is in addition to a county's general ability to lend money to a city pursuant to California Government Code, § 23010.2 (West 1998).

11. Controller of the State of California, *State of California Cities Annual Report, Fiscal Year 1997–1998*, (Sacramento, Calif.: State of California, 2000), iii.

12. Cal. Const., Art. XI, § 3; Cal. Government Code, § 34450 (West 1998). The manner of charter adoption is similar to that for a county. A charter city is given wide power to legislate on any matter of "municipal concern," but not on matters of "statewide concern." See generally *California Fed. Sav. & Loan Ass'n v. City of Los Angeles*, 54 Cal. 3d 1 (1991). Whether something is a statewide or a municipal concern is a judicial question. See *California Fed. Sav. & Loan Ass'n v. City of Los Angeles*, 16.

13. Councils in larger cities, like Los Angeles for example, can have as many as fifteen members.

14. The nature of the relationship between an elected official and their constituents has been broken down by political scholars into two major categories: trustee and delegate. A trustee is someone who sees the role of the representative as one who is expected

to take into account the views of the constituency but who, in the end, will see it as his duty to exercise independent judgment on policy matters. A delegate is a representative who views his role as one who implements the will of their constituents. See Edmund Burke, *The Works of the Right Honourable Edmund Burke*, vol. 2 (Boston: Little, Brown, 1866), 95–96; Walter Lippman, *Essays in the Public Philosophy* (Boston: Little, Brown, 1955); John C. Wahlke, Heinz Eulau, William Buchanan, and LeRoy C. Ferguson, *The Legislative System* (New York: Wiley, 1962); Roger H. Davidson, *The Role of the Congressman* (New York: Pegasus, 1969); Charles G. Bell and Charles M. Price, "Pre-Legislative Sources of Representational Roles," *Midwest Journal of Political Science* 13 (1969): 254. Traditionally, city council members were likely to behave as trustees. However, there has been a recent trend toward the delegate model. There is evidence to believe that this trend is the result of the increased "professional" nature of a city council seat and the increased frequency of such a position as a stepping-stone for higher office. Previously, city council seats were held by "amateurs" who looked upon the role of a city council member as community service rather than a means by which to advance one's political career. See James H. Savra, "Conflict and Cooperation in Electoral-Administrative Relations in Large Council-Manager Cities," *State and Local Government Review* 31 (1999): 173; John Nalbandian, *Professionalism in Local Government* (San Francisco: Jossey-Bass, 1991).

15. Robert L. Linberry and Edmund P. Fowler, "Reformism and Public Policies in American Cities," *American Political Science Review* 61 (1967): 701; Roy Green, *The Profession of Local Government Management* (New York: Praeger, 1989); John J. Harrigan, *Politics and Policy in States and Communities* (New York: HarperCollins, 1994).

16. LAFCOs were created as a result of the Knox-Nisbet Act of 1963. See Cal. Government Code, § 56300 (West 1998).

17. The counties of Los Angeles, Sacramento, Santa Clara, and San Diego are allowed to deviate from this formula. See Cal. Government Code, § 56325 (West 1998).

18. The technical term used by the LAFCO is whether or not the secession will be "revenue neutral."

19. Controller of the State of California, *State of California School District Annual Report* (Sacramento, Calif.: State of California, 2000), iv.

20. The $4,000 per pupil figure is valid for the first year. In succeeding years, per pupil funding would have been the greater of the following three amounts: 1) $4,000; 2) 50 percent of the U.S. mean level of per pupil spending; and 3) 50 percent of the California mean level of per pupil spending. See Secretary of State, State of California, *Official Voter Information Guide, General Election, November 7, 2000* (Sacramento, Calif.: State of California), 33.

21. There are two types of initiatives, statute initiatives and constitutional initiatives. In order for a statute initiative to be placed on the ballot, supporters must collect petition signatures equivalent to 5 percent of the total votes cast in the most recent gubernatorial election. The signature requirement for a constitution initiative is eight percent. If successfully placed on the ballot, a majority vote is needed to approve the measure. A suc-

cessful statute initiative becomes part of the California Code. A successful constitution initiative becomes part of the California Constitution. Propositions 38 and 39 are constitutional initiatives.

22. *Voter Information Guide*, 36.

23. *Voter Information Guide*, 37.

24. *Voter Information Guide*, 37.

25. *Voter Information Guide*, 41.

26. Jean Ross, "Perspectives on Proposition 13: Flawed Reform," *California Journal* 28 (1997): 26.

27. John J. Harrigan, *Politics and Policy*, 72.

28. Controller of the State of California, *Special Districts Annual Report, Fiscal Year 1997–1998* (Sacramento, Calif.: State of California, 2000), 4. Special districts must provide an annual report to the Controller pursuant to Cal. Government Code, § 12463.1. However, the Controller does not have oversight or audit powers with respect to special districts. See Little Hoover Commission, *Special Districts: Relics of the Past or Resources for the Future?* (Sacramento, Calif.: Little Hoover Commission, 2000), 9. For specific definitions of special district governments see Cal. Government Code, § 54775, 56000, 61000 (West 1998).

29. California Senate, Local Government Committee, *What's So Special about Special Districts: A Citizen's Guide to Special Districts in California* (Sacramento, Calif.: State of California, 1991), 2.

30. California Senate, *Special Districts*, 2.

31. California Senate, *Special Districts*, 2. Mello-Roos districts are weaker still. They do not directly provide services. They are financing mechanisms.

32. The U.S. Census Bureau defines a special district according to the following three criteria: 1) existence of an organized entity; 2) governmental character; and 3) substantial autonomy. See U.S. Bureau of the Census, "Government Finances, No. 2," *1982 Census of Governments*, vol. 4 (Washington, D.C.: Government Printing Office, 1982), vi.

33. Little Hoover Commission, *Special Districts*, 1.

34. California Senate, *Special Districts*, 4.

35. League of Women Voters of California, *Guide to California Government* (Sacramento, Calif.: League of Women Voters of California, 1992), 149.

36. Cal. Public Utilities Code, § 12801 (West 1998).

37. California Senate, *Special Districts*, 4.

38. Nancy Burns, *The Formation of American Local Governments* (New York: Oxford University Press, 1994), 16.

39. Little Hoover Commission, *Special Districts*, 11–12.

40. Little Hoover Commission, *Special Districts*, 11–12. The authors rely on a prior study for these numbers. See Paul G. Lewis, *Local Government Structure in California* (San Francisco: Public Policy Institute, 1998).

41. Little Hoover Commission, *Special Districts*, 11–12.

42. Little Hoover Commission, *Special Districts*, 6.

43. Both enterprise and nonenterprise districts may issue bonds.

44. California Senate, *Special Districts*, 15.

45. California Senate, *Special Districts*, 7.

46. California Senate, *Special Districts*, 8.

47. Little Hoover Commission, *Special Districts*, 55.

48. Little Hoover Commission, *Special Districts*, 56.

49. Little Hoover Commission, *Special Districts*, 56.

50. Cal. Elections Code, §5150, 27320 (West 1998).

51. Cal. Government Code, § 6258 (West 1998).

52. Cal. Government Code, § 54959 (West 1998).

53. Cal. Government Code, § 56375 (West 1998).

54. Cal. Government Code, § 56000 (West 1998).

55. Little Hoover Commission, *Special Districts*, 51.

56. Little Hoover Commission, *Special Districts*, 33–34.

57. Little Hoover Commission, *Special Districts*, 29.

58. Little Hoover Commission, *Special Districts*, 48.

59. Little Hoover Commission, *Special Districts*, 50.

60. Little Hoover Commission, *Special Districts*, 12.

61. California Senate, *Special Districts*, 10.

62. California Senate, *Special Districts*, 13.

63. Little Hoover Commission, *Special Districts*, 53.

64. Little Hoover Commission, *Special Districts*, 1.

65. A. G. Block and Charles M. Price, eds. Local Government," *California Government and Politics Annual, 1999* (Sacramento, Calif.: StateNet, 2000), 68.

66. Burns, *Formation*, 11.

67. Don L. Bowen, "Reshaping Special District Government in Arizona," *Arizona Review* 32 (1984): 12.

68. Douglas R. Porter, Ben C. Lin, and Richard B. Peiser, *Special Districts: A Useful Technique for Financing Infrastructure* (Washington, D.C.: Urban Land Institute, 1992), 30.

69. Tocqueville, *Democracy*, 69.

70. Larry Arnn, et al., "A Difference of Principle: The Minority Report of the California Constitution Revision Commission, California Constitution Revision Commission, Final Report and Recommendations to the Governor and the Legislature," *Final Report and Recommendations to the Governor and Legislature* (Sacramento, Calif.: Forum on Government Reform, 1996), 93.

71. Tocqueville, *Democracy*, 62.

Local Government Finance in California

Steven B. Frates

Local government finance in California is a complex and interwoven tapestry of fiscal relationships between the state and the various local governments. There are more than 480 cities in California, nearly 1,000 school districts, and well over 4,500 special districts. Each of these subordinate local governments, cities, counties, school districts, and special districts is impacted by the state's regulatory powers and financially affected by the state's budget allocation priorities. In addition, many of these local governments, especially school districts and counties, receive a major portion of their financing directly from the state. While cities and special districts tend to receive less money directly from the state, their financial operations are nonetheless hugely impacted by state legislative and policy decisions.

It is useful to keep these factors in mind when examining local government finances in California. It is also important to understand that the state's legislation and policies can and do have substantially different impacts on individual cities, special districts, school districts, and counties. In addition, the state's policies regarding each category of these local governments has changed over the past quarter century, and this phenomenon continues.

Of course, a major factor in any discussion of local government finance in California must involve Proposition 13, the precedent-setting Howard Jarvis Property Tax Limitation Initiative, and subsequent legislative repercussions. In the mid-1970s, property values in California exploded upwards, and property taxes increased in lock step. Many people, especially elderly people on fixed incomes, faced the prospect of being forced out of their homes because they could not afford property tax increases. As the crisis became more acute, the

179

state legislature and the governor took very little substantial action to provide property tax relief for homeowners. The temperature in the resulting political cauldron was increased by the fact that the state was sitting on a then quite large, multibillion-dollar surplus. The combination of legislative lethargy and voter frustration resulted in a landslide victory for Proposition 13, which functionally cut property taxes and greatly moderated the annual increase that could be levied.

The legislative establishment in Sacramento was at first stunned by the passage of Proposition 13, and then furious with voters who had overwhelmingly supported it. As a result, the legislation enacted to implement the provisions of Proposition 13, the infamous Assembly Bill 8 (AB 8), was crafted in a very convoluted and confusing way. AB 8 was designed, in part, to punish cities and counties that had been fiscally prudent and kept property taxes low, and reward cities and counties that had high property tax rates.

Subsequent legislation has exacerbated many of the distortions created by AB 8 and hence, the local government fiscal situation in California is quite complex. For example, during the recession of the early 1990s the state legislature changed the allocation formula for local property taxes, giving more local property tax money to schools and reducing the amount of property tax revenue available to cities and counties. This legislation, euphemistically referred to as ERAF (Educational Revenue Augmentation Fund), has had a substantial impact on municipal and county finances in California. In essence, ERAF has also meant that the state legislature now has virtually total control over public school funding in California, and local school districts have very little fiscal flexibility. Ironically, the political and philosophical nature of this arrangement clearly suited the majority of the then sitting legislature and the then incumbent Republican governor.

A brief overview of municipal finances will serve to reinforce an appreciation of the complexity of local government fiscal matters in the state of California. In general terms, the primary revenue source for cities is charges for services. Statewide, about 40 percent of total municipal revenues are derived from these charges. Most such charges are for municipally provided utilities, such as water, waste, and electric systems. Many cities, however, do not operate such utilities and in these cities, sales and property taxes tend to constitute a much greater percentage of municipal revenues. However, there has been a clear trend in the last ten years toward charging for many other services. Examples of such charges are building inspection fees, recreation program fees, and fees charged to groups using community facilities.

While charges for current services constitute about 40 percent of municipal revenues, taxes represent, on average, a little over 30 percent of revenues. Interestingly enough, of the municipal tax revenue in California, sales taxes comprise almost 32 percent, by far the largest category. Property tax revenues constitute about 22 percent of the total municipal tax revenue in the state, with utility user taxes, business license taxes, and other locally levied taxes making up the balance of municipal tax revenue.

Other sources of municipal revenue in California include funding from the state and federal government, which constitute about 13 percent of total municipal revenue and special benefit assessments, licenses, permits, fines, rents, and interest income. While the above-mentioned percentages provide an overall picture, the reader should be aware that there is tremendous variability in revenue sources among the 480-plus cities in California. Some cities generate a very large percentage of their total revenues from property taxes, while others get a much greater percentage of their tax revenue from sales taxes. Individual cities have taken very different approaches to raising revenue, depending upon local political preferences and economic circumstances.

One of the more interesting examples of the impact of tax revenue generation on municipal land use policies is the so-called fiscalization of land use. This term refers to the tendency of many municipalities to make land use zoning decisions based on projected revenues generated and costs incurred. Many cities have gone out of their way to encourage big-box retailers, automobile dealers, and shopping malls in an attempt to bolster their sales tax revenue. In California, the state receives 5 percent of the sales tax, but cities can receive 1 percent. A string of successful car dealerships might generate as much as $20 to $30 million a year for the municipal coffers. Even more appealing to municipal decision makers is the fact that such sales tax revenues are virtually unrestricted and may be used for any purpose.

By way of comparison, property taxes may not generate as much revenue for any particular municipality. As previously mentioned, in the early 1990s this legislature stripped substantial amounts of municipal and county property tax revenues away from cities and counties and directed those property tax monies to finance school districts. The result has been that many cities are very wary of encouraging housing, manufacturing, office space, or other related land uses, because these land uses do not generate as much revenue as a retail sales operation. In addition, many municipal decision makers have concluded that zoning for housing is a net loss proposition in terms of revenues generated versus costs incurred. In other words, the comparatively meager property tax revenue generated from such development does not offset the cost of providing police, fire, recreation, and other services to new housing developments.

This "fiscalization of land use" is a major public policy issue in California that is having wide-ranging implications for the entire state. With a large and growing population, California needs something over 250,000 new housing units every year. Over the past ten years, only about 150,000 new housing units have been produced annually in the state. Of course, there are winners and losers from this situation. The obvious losers are predominantly low-income and younger families looking to buy their first house. Many of these people are simply priced out of the housing market and can only afford to rent increasingly scarce apartment units. The winners include families that already own houses, as the increased demand for housing drives up the market value of their existing homes.

The "fiscalization of land use" is an excellent example of the complexity of local government finance in California having a major impact on public policy in the state. It has given rise to some perhaps contradictory messages from the state legislature. On the one hand, the state legislature is forever admonishing cities and counties to encourage more housing (in part by trying to mandate low-cost housing in redevelopment areas.) On the other hand, the state's property tax policies clearly discourage cities and counties from zoning developable land for housing.

Municipal expenditures consist primarily of public safety (approximately 27 percent), community development and health services (approximately 21 percent), public utilities (approximately 20 percent), transportation (approximately 15 percent), cultural and leisure activities (approximately 8 percent), and the euphemistically referred to category of "general government" (a little over 8 percent). Funding police services accounts for two-thirds of the public safety expenditures, while fire protection accounts for another 26 percent of such expenditures. Emergency medical services and street lighting account for the majority of remaining expenses for public safety. For public utilities, electricity accounts for almost 59 percent of the expenditures, water for slightly less than 40 percent, and natural gas accounts for the balance.

The 480-plus municipalities in California provide basic public services to the vast majority of the state's population. Various actions by the state legislature, especially since the recession of the early 1990s, have steadily eroded the municipal property tax base in the state. Cities have adapted by encouraging sales tax generating development, and by increasing fees charged for services.

The situation with counties is somewhat more complex. More so than municipal governments, counties are agencies of the state and are charged with carrying out various state functions, especially regarding public health and welfare. The revenue structure of counties in California reflects this reality. More than

63 percent of county revenues come primarily from the state and, to a lesser extent, from the federal government. Overall, the state contributes about twice as much to county revenues as does the federal government. Taxes in general constitute an ever-decreasing amount of county revenue in California. In fiscal year (FY) 1988–1989 taxes of all sorts constituted about 28 percent of county revenues, dropping to around 15 percent just nine years later in FY 1997–1998. Like the cities, counties have turned to fees for services to increase revenues, although such fees only constitute about 11 percent of county revenues. Other sources of county revenue are fines, forfeitures, penalties, licenses, permits, rents, and interest, which, taken together account for less than 10 percent of the total county revenue.

Counties, like cities, have tried to increase sales tax revenue. While there has been a slight increase in sales tax revenue over the past decade and a half, it is unlikely that sales tax will ever become a substantial revenue source for counties. This is in part due to the fact that cities are always very anxious to encourage sales tax revenue-producing businesses within their boundaries, which obviously tend to be closer to the shopping consumer.

Some counties do run enterprise activities that generate revenue, such as airports, hospitals, or sanitation operations. Hospitals, which have high costs and are often a losing business proposition, constitute the bulk of these activities. Many counties are getting out of the hospital service delivery business by selling their hospitals to universities or private operators.

Overall, the largest single component of county expenditures is public assistance, which is primarily welfare, social services, and child protection services. Statewide, over 35 percent of county expenditures in FY 1997–1998 were for public assistance. Public safety (sheriff, jails, courts, probation, flood control, and fire protection) accounted for close to 30 percent of county expenditure in the same fiscal years. Health and sanitation expenditures were about 17 percent of the total, with general government overhead, debt service, and roads and public facilities making up the balance.

An interesting trend in county government finances has been the sharp increase in lease purchase obligations. Under these arrangements, counties sign long-term lease agreements with somewhat artificially created public facilities agencies to lease government buildings and other infrastructure over a given period of years. At the termination of such leases, the title to the public facility reverts to the county. This fiscal artifice, facilitated by Certificates of Participation (COPS), is undertaken because the public facilities agencies and the counties can get together to create a legal entity called a Joint Powers Authority (JPA).

These JPAs can issue debt (in other words sell bonds to finance the facilities) without a public vote.

This latter point is particularly important because it illustrates another complicating factor in local government finance in California. In California, local governments can only issue general bonded debt with a two-thirds affirmative vote from the public. JPAs allow counties and other local governments to get around this requirement for a public vote to issue debt. For many years, the state legislature and other advocates of increased government spending unsuccessfully tried to get California voters to reduce the requirement for a two-thirds affirmative vote before any local government could issue property tax financed debt. Recently, however, a successful initiative persuaded the voters to reduce the requirement for school bond debt to only a 55 percent positive vote. In any case, counties have clearly turned to the convoluted JPA/COPS financing mechanism to finance public infrastructure.

As mentioned earlier, the state legislature has directed increasing amounts of property tax revenue to the public school districts. In just the five-year period since the ERAF was instituted in the early 1990s, revenues for public schools increased by almost a third. During the same period, from FY 1993–1994 to FY 1997–1998, the student population increased less than 3 percent. Schools were clearly the winner in the legislative shootouts precipitated by the recession of the early 1990s. General obligation school bond debt more than doubled over the same five-year period from FY 1993–1994 to FY 1997–1998. The increase in school bond debt will probably continue its upward trend, in part because of the lower threshold (55 percent) of votes needed to incur such debt.

In general terms, the state accounts for almost 54 percent of public school revenues in California. Local sources, noted above, are essentially defined by the state and account for about 31 percent of school revenue. The federal government contributes approximately 8 percent, and other financing sources account for the balance.

Teacher salaries constitute the largest percentage of expenditures statewide (over 35 percent). Research by the Rose Institute of State and Local Government has revealed wide variations among school districts in the percentage of total district expenditures going to teacher salaries. In some districts, typically smaller elementary school districts, well over 50 percent of district expenditures may go directly to classroom teachers. In other districts allocations for classroom teachers are under 40 percent of district expenditures.

Over the past fifteen years, the state legislature and the citizens have decided to allocate a greater proportion of local government resources to public education. It should also be noted that Proposition 98, a statewide initiative, mandated that 40 percent of the state budget go to elementary and secondary public education. Here again, what has traditionally been a local government function, in this case elementary and secondary public education, is increasingly impacted by state legislative decisions.

Special districts, as noted earlier, are the largest category of local governments in California. Of the more than forty-seven hundred special districts in California at the end of the 1990s, almost sixteen hundred were governed by a county board of supervisors. The vast majority were governed by either elected or appointed independent governing boards. Special district revenues are quite substantial, approaching $8 billion by the end of FY 1996–1997. The bulk of the special district revenues in California, well over two-thirds, are garnered by enterprise special districts. Far and away the largest revenue recipients are water districts, followed at some distance by sanitation districts, electric utility districts, transit districts, and hospital districts. Airport districts and harbor and port districts make up a significant, but much smaller proportion, of the enterprise special district picture.

Unlike most other local governments in California, special district revenues have in most cases comfortably exceeded expenditures over the past ten years. This is particularly true for water districts. In fact, a report by the Little Hoover Commission (a state-appointed government oversight board) revealed that at the turn of the century, water districts in California were sitting on close to $13 billion in financial assets. These special districts, particularly the water districts, tend to have a lower public and political profile, and clearly many are very successful and solvent enterprises.

Part of the solvency of water districts is of course due to the fact that if consumers do not pay, the water can be turned off. But selling water is not the only revenue source for many water districts. Many water districts, established in then rural areas over a century ago, are recipients of property tax revenue. As the state has grown in population and the urban/suburban areas have greatly expanded, many of these formally rural water districts have found themselves in the enviable position of having substantial property tax revenue from the newly developed land within their borders.

For whatever constellation of political reasons, the state legislature, which has aggressively gone after the property tax revenue of cities and counties, has not yet made similar raids on water district property tax revenues or the cash balances of water districts.

The last significant group of local governments is redevelopment agencies. Redevelopment agencies are entities created under the auspices of the state legislature for the purported purpose of refurbishing rundown areas. They have since metastasized into development arms for many cities and some counties. For local government officials, the appeal of redevelopment areas revolves around the fact that when a redevelopment area is established, existing property tax revenues are capped and their allocations to various local governments are frozen. Any increase in property taxes generated by the newly refurbished properties is dedicated directly to the redevelopment agency itself (although this has recently changed somewhat.) Redevelopment agencies can also use the power of eminent domain to assemble substantial tracts of property within their boundaries. This attribute is particularly appealing to developers who like cities to use the power of eminent domain to assemble large parcels, which are often offered to developers at very attractive rates. In addition, redevelopment agencies can often be persuaded to provide much of the infrastructure, including streets, intersections, water and sewer connections, and landscaping amenities, that developers find so helpful to the economic success of their projects.

One of the rationales for redevelopment agencies is that the new development will generate economic activity, particularly sales tax revenue, which will benefit the local municipal coffers. In addition, some cities have been very aggressive in charging off staff expenditures to redevelopment agency budgets, and it is not unknown for new city halls to be located within redevelopment agency boundaries. There is considerable political controversy about the appropriateness of such arrangements. That, coupled with the fact that redevelopment agencies can generate cash, has caught the attention of the legislature. At this writing, it remains to be seen if the legislature will modify redevelopment agency finances.

In sum, local government finance in California is not a strictly local matter. Every aspect of local government finance in California is directly affected by state legislative action, and it is likely that there will continue to be substantial changes in the financial ground rules under which local governments operate in the future.

The California Tax Revolt

Jon Coupal

When Massachusetts patriots dressed up as Mohawk Indians and dumped British tea into Boston Harbor, they had no way of predicting that the same spirit of outrage over excessive taxes would once again rise up two hundred years later. Indeed, the epicenter of the latter revolt would be at the exact opposite end of a country yet to be formed in a faraway place called Los Angeles, California.

While the anger and outrage were the same, the means were much different. In 1773, engaging in a tax revolt could very well earn one a date with a tall tree and a short piece of rope. In the 1970s, the tax revolt would be executed through the legal means of initiative.

THE INITIATIVE

The initiative process is the means by which citizens, rather than the legislative body, "initiates" the enactment of a statute or constitutional amendment. The scope of the initiative power varies from state to state with some providing for a very limited power while others, such as California, provide for the expansive use of initiatives.[1]

Considering that the creation of the initiative power had to begin with the legislature (which, by its nature, is loath to surrender political power) one would rightly conclude that it took a nearly cataclysmic set of circumstances for the initiative power to come to life. Indeed, that is precisely what occurred in the late 1800s and early 1900s. While "town meetings" were common in New England, direct democracy at the state level was uncommon until the rise of the Progressive movement. That movement was a reaction against powerful moneyed interests including, in California, the Southern Pacific Railroad. It is little secret that the California Legislature in the late 1800s was no more than a puppet of the railroads and the citizenry had had enough.

Leading the Progressive movement was Hiram Johnson, who would later become governor of California from 1911 to 1917. By 1907, several major cities in California had adopted both initiative and referendum powers. The power was enshrined in the state constitution in 1911 making California the tenth state to provide for initiatives.[2]

Getting an initiative passed, particularly in modern times, is both difficult and expensive. While it is very easy to file a proposal ($200 gets you a title and summary from the attorney general), obtaining the signatures can be a grueling process, even if the measure has major financial backing. As the text in the endnote reveals, the number of *valid* signatures to qualify a constitutional amendment is 8 percent of the votes for all gubernatorial candidates in the most recent election. Because many signatures obtained "on the street" are invalid, the rule of thumb has been that between 1 million and 1.2 million signatures are needed to qualify a measure. Fewer signatures are needed for a statutory initiative.[3]

Early initiative proposals included everything from abolishing the death penalty to creating a racing commission. But it is no accident that one of the earliest successful uses of the initiative power was to secure tax relief. In 1914, Proposition 10 repealed the state's poll tax that had been in existence since 1850. Thus began the long relationship between the power of initiative and the goal of tax relief. Despite its use for other myriad purposes, the initiative power in California has been used to limit the power to tax more than other purposes.[4]

THE MODERN TAX REVOLT

After World War II, California saw a rapid influx of population from other states. Attracted by the warm climate, plenty of jobs, and a relaxed lifestyle, California's newest citizens enjoyed, during the fifties and early sixties, California's Golden Age.

Unlike today, real estate in California was reasonably priced in the postwar period. Moreover, demand for public services, other than infrastructure needs, was reasonable as well. Higher than average affluence kept welfare rolls limited. All in all, only a few Californians during this period considered themselves overtaxed. Nonetheless, a tax protest of about six thousand people was held at the Los Angeles Coliseum in the late 1950s.

Beginning in the 1960s, things began to heat up. A newspaperman from Utah by the name of Howard Jarvis was a leading champion of tax relief for home-owners. Helped by a number of radio personalities, he attempted to pass his first property tax measure in 1968, a full decade before the passage of Proposition 13. This measure failed to qualify with Jarvis obtaining only one hundred thousand of the signatures he needed. However, the Los Angeles County Assessor, Phil Watson, did qualify a tax relief measure (as mostly a politically defensive measure) but this proposal failed at the polls badly. (That an elected tax official proposes a tax reduction is a good example of covering your assessor.)

Watson proposed another tax cut proposal in 1972 as Proposition 14. However, it was opposed by then-Governor Ronald Reagan who had his own ideas about tax relief. Indeed, it was the promise of a Reagan-backed tax relief measure that undoubtedly led to Proposition 14's defeat.

Reagan's measure, Proposition 1 appeared on the ballot the next year in 1973. Jarvis was a spokesman for the campaign and made several appearances urging its passage. Although it failed at the polls, the margin of defeat was much smaller than the Watson initiatives.

There is an old saying: "That which does not kill you makes you stronger." These early defeats were instrumental in laying the foundation for Proposition 13. Not only did they steel Howard Jarvis's resolve, but he further refined his proposals with every campaign.

In the meantime, homeowners were being taxed very heavily and, for many, it became a crisis. The problem was not that the property system was being misapplied, it was that it was being applied *as it was* designed. For example, the traditional method of taxing property is to tax it at its "highest and best use." Therefore, even if a vacant lot had a low value, assessors would value the property higher if it were surrounded by business properties. One retired couple in the City of Newhall was suddenly assessed $1,800 in 1966 because their modest home was near some apartment complexes. This couple's entire annual retirement income was $1,900.[5]

The property tax crisis grew during the 1970s. The average tax rate throughout California was about 2.6 percent of market value, and there were no limits on either the tax *rates* or the annual increases in *taxable value*. Indeed, in a single year, some property owners saw their tax bills triple.

The problem was particularly acute in southern California. In one year in Los Angeles County alone, four hundred thousand people had not paid their property tax because they didn't have the money, running the risk of being forced out of their homes. Elderly people were among the hardest hit. Many had paid off their mortgages yet faced losing their homes because they couldn't afford property taxes.

By 1976, Howard Jarvis had paired with Paul Gann, a taxpayer activist from Sacramento, in an effort to pass a new measure. Combining a property tax rate limit of 1 percent with a 2 percent limit on annual increases in taxable value, they drafted what eventually became Proposition 13.

Proposition 13 appeared on the ballot on June 6, 1978. Virtually every major newspaper and interest group in the state opposed it. Contrary to urban legend, it was opposed by the business community, which had placed a competing measure on the ballot at the same time. The campaign was heated and, at times, emotional, but Howard Jarvis did not back down. Spending less that $30,000, he qualified Proposition 13 with 1.2 million signatures.

An overwhelming majority of Californians—more than 4 million—voted for Proposition 13 because they knew that the initiative would finally take power away from the tax collectors and give it back to the taxpayers. Despite the predictions that the passage of Proposition 13 would lead to the end of Western civilization, the pass rate was an amazing 66.4 percent. And with its passage, property taxes in California became predictable, manageable, and fair.[6]

THE POLICIES OF PROPOSITION 13

Under Proposition 13, property tax valuation was set at the 1976 assessed value, and property tax increases were limited to no more than 2 percent a year as long as the property was not sold. Once a property is sold, the property is reassessed to current value against which the 1 percent rate applies. However, purchasers of property get the same 2 percent limit on annual increases in taxable value.

Indeed, one of the common misunderstandings of Proposition 13 relates to its benefits to new homebuyers. Many detractors of Proposition 13 claim that it is "just for old folks" and, as soon as the original benefactors of Proposition 13 die off, there will be a revolt *against* Proposition 13. The facts refute this and, indeed, political support for Proposition 13 continues to be very high.

Proposition 13 is fair to new homebuyers because it treats equally property owners who purchase property of similar value *at the same time*. Unlike any other tax system in the country, it provides absolute certainty to homeowners as to what their tax bills will be in future years. It prevents a homeowner's taxes from skyrocketing as a result of the vagaries of the real estate market—something over which they have no control. Instead, the amount of property tax liability will depend almost exclusively on the *voluntary* act of purchase.

The California Supreme Court recognized Proposition 13's inherent fairness shortly after its adoption by the voters. Justice Richardson, speaking for a nearly unanimous court, concluded that "an acquisition value system . . . may operate on a *fairer* basis than a current value approach."[7]

The fairness of Proposition 13 becomes apparent when one looks beyond the concept that property taxes should always be based on current value. Admittedly, Proposition 13 is unique. However, as a matter of law and policy, there is nothing that requires property taxes to be confined to a system that arguably has more inherent unfairness to it than does Proposition 13.

Once preconceived notions are discarded, Proposition 13 starts making a great deal of sense. Property taxation based on a trended acquisition value is a hybrid between a property tax and a sales tax. After all, if sales taxes can be based on acquisition value, there is no policy reason why property taxes should not reflect some of the same indicia. Even Justice Richardson noted that Proposition 13 introduced a tax system "roughly comparable" to a sales tax.[8]

Critics might concede that Proposition 13 provides absolute tax certainty and yet still assert that the system is flawed because owners of similar property may be paying different tax amounts. The response to this is that it should be no concern whatsoever to a new resident what his neighbor's tax is as long as his or her own tax is reasonable. The absolute cap of 1 percent imposed by Proposition 13 makes *everyone's* tax reasonable.

Critics also complain that owners of similar properties are paying different amounts for the same public services. However, this is no more unfair that the traditional method of taxation under which owners of more valuable property pays more for the same services. This entire argument ignores the nature of taxes. If we were that concerned with proportionality between the amount of tax and the level of service, we would resort to a system of nothing but user fees. Because proportionality between tax liability and services has *never* been an attribute of property taxes, it is unfair to level this charge against Proposition 13 alone.

Proposition 13 is fair. It is fair to existing property owners because it bases tax liability on acquisition value, not on the mercurial real estate market. It is fair to local governments because it allows for periodic reassessment of property when it changes ownership and under circumstances as well. Few people realize that total property tax revenues to local governments in California have increased at a rate exceeding inflation and virtually all other economic indicators.

Finally, Proposition 13 is fair to new property owners because it gives them two things they otherwise would not have: the benefit of a reasonable maximum property tax of 1 percent, and the absolute certainty as to what their tax bills will be in future years. In light of skyrocketing property values, this is not a minor consideration.

POST–PROPOSITION 13 INITIATIVES

There is no doubt that the passage of Proposition 13 was the initial shot in the modern tax revolt. Even politicians who opposed the measure started jumping on the bandwagon. Then-Governor Jerry Brown characterized himself as "a born-again tax cutter."

The immediate impact was the introduction of a statewide spending limit to complement the tax cuts. Paul Gann introduced the Gann Spending Limit (Proposition 4), which, unlike tax reductions, sought to reduce the growth in the size of state and local governments. The measure passed in 1979 and worked well until its efficacy was diminished into oblivion by subsequent propositions sponsored by public employee unions.

Many of the subsequent measures—by necessity—were sponsored by Howard Jarvis to close loopholes in Proposition 13. Most related to the circumventions of Section 4, dealing with voter approval for new taxes.

In order to prevent the savings to taxpayers from being circumvented, Proposition 13 imposed a two-thirds vote requirement for "special taxes." The intent of this provision was simply to provide some degree of protection for taxpayers—via a supermajority vote—as a condition for the imposition of new local taxes of any kind. These taxes could typically include the local element of the sales tax (referred to as the Bradley-Burns tax), utility user taxes, hotel taxes, real estate transfer taxes, and business license taxes.

The text of Proposition 13 was, as initiatives go, fairly sparse. The plain language has proven to be both a blessing and a curse. One downside has been the proclivity of the Legislature and the courts to provide definitions and "clarifications" of the initiative in a manner—not surprisingly—contrary to the interests of taxpayers.

Two rulings from the California Supreme court in the early 1980s ripped two holes in Proposition 13. The first, the *Farrell* decision, held that the phrase "special taxes" meant taxes intended for a special purpose. Therefore, a local utility users tax going into a general fund was not subject to the two-thirds vote requirement. As a direct result of the *Farrell* decision, California taxpayers saw an explosion in unvoted utility user taxes as well as other general fund taxes including hotel and business license taxes.

In the *Richmond* decision, the Supreme Court defined the term "special district" in a bizarre manner to permit the imposition of a sales tax for transportation purposes without a two-thirds vote. This, too, led to an epidemic of increased sales taxes, mostly by counties.

The *Farrell* and *Richmond* decisions, in combination with Legislative chicanery, made it clear that Howard Jarvis's work was not done. Government, by its nature, has an insatiable appetite for more tax revenue. Therefore, additional initiatives would be required to close the loopholes being punched into pro-taxpayer measures. The first of these was Proposition 62 adopted in 1986 to close the *Farrell* and *Richmond* loopholes. Although it was not the original intent of Proposition 13 to distinguish between "general" and "special" taxes at the local level, it was imperative that all local taxes be subjected to *some* degree of voter approval. Therefore, Proposition 62 required that these "general" taxes receive a minimum of a simple majority vote. It also closed the loophole in the definition of "special district" and, as a result, special county sales taxes for transportation purposes once again required a two-thirds vote.

Howard Jarvis passed away shortly after Proposition 62's passage. However, by this time he had formed an organization, now known as the Howard Jarvis Taxpayers Association, to carry on his work.

Also in the 1980s and early 1990s, another Proposition 13 loophole was widening. Benefit assessments are a unique form of property levy usually imposed in small areas to finance streets, sidewalks, water mains, and other capital improvements that directly abut property. The amount of the assessment is determined by a licensed engineer who apportions the cost among the benefited properties according to the benefits conferred. After Proposition 13 was enacted, local governments began to abuse this financing technique by using it to finance general governmental services such as police, fire, and schools on a citywide, or even countywide, basis. In short, rather than true benefit assessments for capital improvements that had a *direct* benefit to property in a neighborhood, local governments were imposing de facto flat rate parcel taxes. The sole purpose for this abuse was to avoid voter approval.

Thus, in 1996 the Howard Jarvis Taxpayers Association sponsored Proposition 218, which the voters approved by a 57 percent margin. It took the earlier provisions of Proposition 62—which was a statutory initiative—and put them in the constitution. It limited the financing technique of benefit assessments to its original purposes and it guaranteed new protections for local taxpayers wishing to use the *local* initiative power to reduce or eliminate any fee, charge assessment, or tax.

THE FUTURE

In a perfect world, elected officials would be sensitive to the needs of the taxpaying public. But California enters the new millennium in a far less than perfect state. As Hiram Johnson understood, only through the initiative process could ordinary people match the power of well-funded special interests. That is even more true today. The number of lobbyists and the amount of campaign cash advocating more government spending is overwhelming. The people can only protect themselves, and their pocketbooks, through the initiative process.

In addition to ongoing efforts to close loopholes in Proposition 13, likely initiatives include a proposal to reinvigorate the state's spending limitation and proposals to increase the homeowners' exemption that has been stuck at $7,000 since 1972. The possibilities are endless and creative efforts to protect taxpayers will be matched only by equally creative efforts to extract more money from the taxpaying public.

NOTES

1. For example, California is one of the few states that permit amendments to the state constitution (Article II, Section 8). Other states place such burdensome requirements on the initiative process that it is almost never used. Other restrictions come from the courts. In Florida, the Florida Supreme Court has applied the "single-subject rule" in such a restrictive manner so as to prevent several tax relief measures from appearing on the ballot.

2. The initiative power derives both from a general provision recognizing that all political power resides in the people and a specific provision relating to the process. The former is set forth in Article II, Section 1, of the California Constitution, which provides: "All political power is inherent in the people. Government is instituted for their protection, security, and benefit, and they have the right to alter or reform it when the public good may require."

The specific provisions are set forth in Article II, Section 8:

SEC. 8. (a) The initiative is the power of the electors to propose statutes and amendments to the Constitution and to adopt or reject them.

(b) An initiative measure may be proposed by presenting to the Secretary of State a petition that sets forth the text of the proposed statute or amendment to the Constitution and is certified to have been signed by electors equal in number to 5 percent in the case of a statute, and 8 percent in the case of an amendment to the Constitution, of the votes for all candidates for governor at the last gubernatorial election.

(c) The Secretary of State shall then submit the measure at the next general election held at least 131 days after it qualifies or at any special statewide election held prior to that general election. The governor may call a special statewide election for the measure.

(d) An initiative measure embracing more than one subject may not be submitted to the electors or have any effect.

(e) An initiative measure shall not include or exclude any political subdivision of the state from the application or effect of its provisions based upon approval or disapproval of the initiative measure, or based upon the casting of a specified percentage of votes in favor of the measure, by the electors of that political subdivision.

(f) An initiative measure shall not contain alternative or cumulative provisions wherein one or more of those provisions would become law depending upon the casting of a specified percentage of votes for or against the measure.

3. Of the 910 submissions that were titled and summarized by the attorney general between 1912 and 1995, only 250 qualified for the ballot—and far fewer—seventy-eight—were actually adopted by the voters. See Bill Jones, *History of the Initiative Process* (Sacramento, Calif.: California Secretary of State, 1995), 8.

4. From 1912 to 1995, forty-one measures dealing with taxation qualified for the ballot. The next closest in subject area is health/medicine/science with twenty-seven. See Jones, *History*.

5. The tax revolt was further fueled by gross corruption in many assessors' offices. Traditional methods of taxing property provided an incentive for corruption in that assessors could cut deals with the owners of business properties. For a lower assigned value, the assessors were taking kickbacks. The Legislature began to conduct hearings and ultimately passed laws requiring that assessments be "equalized" and brought up to current value on a more frequent basis. In the meantime, the assessors for San Francisco and Alameda Counties went to prison and the San Diego assessor committed suicide.

6. The fact that Proposition 13 provides a more equitable system of taxing property should not preclude debate as to whether *any* property tax system is fair. The truth is that the taxation of property is an obsolete vestige of feudal England. It is one of the few taxes that has as its "incidence" the mere position of property for a given period of time—usually one year. In this respect, it is different from income or sales taxes which impose a levy on the incidence of an *economic transaction*. The shift from property taxes to user fees for property-related services is not an unhealthy trend assuming such fees replace the outdated *ad valorem* levies and are not merely piled on to existing tax bills.

7. *Amador Valley Joint Union High School Dist. v. State Board of Equalization*, 22 Cal. 3d 208, 235 (1978).

8. *Amador*, 236.

IV

STATESMANSHIP

Armageddon in the West:
California's Hiram Johnson

Scot J. Zentner

It is no exaggeration to describe Hiram Johnson as the father of the modern state of California.[1] More than any other figure, he brought about the Progressive transformation of the state in the early years of the twentieth century. Elected governor in 1910, he was the principal force behind dozens of sweeping reforms, including the adoption of the initiative, referendum, and recall, the outlawing of partisanship in local elections, the implementation of civil service reform, and the creation of farm and labor regulations. Indeed, the legislative activity that Johnson engineered as governor was undoubtedly the most dramatic in the state's political history and served to render California, for better or worse, a model for the welfare state that emerged nationally in later generations.[2]

Johnson is important not only because of his legislative achievements in California,[3] but because he is a model for the Progressive idea of leadership. Like other leaders in the movement, he was motivated by a passionate desire to rid government of what he considered to be corrupt special interests, especially the large corporations and trusts that had emerged in the late 1800s. The Southern Pacific Railroad, in particular, which was very influential in the state at the time, was the principal target of Johnson's first campaign for governor. He believed that the railroad had used its monopoly power to set shipping rates unfairly high, which benefited its owners at the expense of others in the state that directly or indirectly relied on its services. Corporations like the Southern Pacific often insulated themselves politically by co-opting party leaders and government officials. Hence, the Progressives concentrated their efforts on direct democracy reforms like the initiative and the recall in order to undercut the party machines and the bosses that controlled them. Indeed, Johnson himself initially came to prominence as the lead prosecutor in the dramatic San Francisco graft trials of 1908, which invigorated the movement toward Progressive reform.[4] So aggressive was he in his 1910 gubernatorial campaign that Johnson described the railroad's political influence as something of an open conspiracy against the people. Calling it "the system," he conceived of this "unholy alliance between big business and politics" as the "gravest menace" to the republic.[5]

This harsh, polarizing approach to popular leadership was the hallmark of Johnson's leadership. In fact, his natural rhetorical skills, as much as anything, eventually made him a preeminent figure in the national Progressive movement.[6] As a speaker, he was more than a rival to other leaders such as Theodore Roosevelt and Robert LaFollette. Indeed, in every election from 1912 until his death in 1945, presidential candidates specifically sought him out to campaign for them on the stump.[7] Moreover, it has been suggested that Johnson's political "success depended upon his rhetorical abilities," particularly his talent for convincing people of his "honesty and integrity."[8] This was especially important, of course, since the thrust of the movement was to criticize the corruption of the reigning parties and interests. His first political campaign (the 1910 run for governor) provides especially clear evidence of his success in this regard. There was little substantive difference between himself and his general election opponent, Democrat Theodore Bell, since both candidates had campaigned for reform and against the railroad. Johnson's speaking ability, it seems, was a major factor in the campaign. In fact, to a great extent, the "campaign came down to differences of personality rather than of issues," with Johnson's superior abilities as a kind of political "entertainer" going a long way to secure him the victory.[9]

But Johnson's entertainment was presented as a form of high drama, not mere comedy. There was a moralizing tendency in Progressive leaders like Johnson, who especially portrayed his cause as something of a religious struggle. Consider his appraisal of his performance in the 1912 campaign for the vice-presidency on the Progressive party ticket with Teddy Roosevelt:

> I really think that I was responsible for transmitting the struggle into a real fight in behalf of humanity and the preaching that we did and that finally was done by every Progressive talker in the Nation in behalf of human rights, and women and children will be of lasting benefit. This I considered my great contribution.[10]

That is, Johnson understood his contribution to be the leadership of a kind of moral or religious awakening in the country. He thought of himself as a preacher who would not revolutionize the political system, but would cause within it a great awakening. "His unswerving determination was typical of the Progressives," according to Michael Weatherson and Hal Bochin. "Self-righteous and intolerant of opposing views, they saw themselves as crusaders against injustice and corruption. Compromise was out of the question because it required a sacrifice of their moral and political values. They feared it might eventually lead to their own corruption."[11] A principal concern of Johnson and his Progressive cohorts, then, was to impress upon the people the sincerity of their conviction to rid the government of corruption. But they did so with a kind of puritanical fervor not always seen in American politics.

This concern to present himself as a kind of progressive puritan is a major reason for Johnson's combative speaking style. His impassioned performance on the stump at the 1912 Republican Convention, for example, apparently dwarfed TR's. One journal noted of Johnson's speech: "We can't imagine anyone's listening to Johnson for five minutes without wanting to fight—either to fight with or to fight against him. . . . He gives you the impression of a man carried away entirely on the flood of his own feelings."[12] Johnson's peculiar brand of invective is seen in his 1910 description of conservative *Los Angeles Times* publisher Harrison Gray Otis: "He sits in senile dementia, with gangrened heart and rotting brain, grimacing at every reform, chattering impotently at all things that are decent, frothing, fuming, violently gibbering, going down to his grave in snarling infamy."[13] Johnson's speeches, especially at the height of the Progressive era, go on and on like this. Richard Lower describes the visual sense of Johnson's oratorical style:

> Indeed it was on the political stump that he was most effective. A rapid speaker, he crisply enunciated each word while outdistancing reporters who attempted verbatim notes. His somewhat high-pitched and occasionally rasping voice had a power that gripped his audience. On the stage he stood his ground, rarely bending or swaying his body, while emphasizing his points with emphatic gestures. His most characteristic move was a downward drive with his right arm and upraised fist.[14]

Johnson consciously portrayed himself as a fighter. "When posing for newspaper photographers," Lower notes, "he often assumed the stance of the boxer, a stocky scrapper, his fists clenched in readiness, his feet planted for the knockout blow." Earlier in his career as a lawyer this verbal pugilism at times descended into the real thing; he twice was embroiled in actual physical brawls in the courtroom, on one occasion being fined for minor assault.[15] In general, he followed Roosevelt's lead as a campaigner, playing the part of the fiery and manly defender of the public interest against the corporations and the trusts.

Yet, Johnson was more than merely a charismatic speaker. In order to understand his greater significance, we must understand the relationship between his rhetorical style and his conception of state and society. His hostility toward "the system" was not that of the radical, of either the socialist or the communist variety. In fact, it has been suggested that Progressives in general actually were more hostile to labor interests than they were to business interests.[16] While this was not really the case with Johnson, who as governor signed into law many measures supported by organized labor, he did oppose the notion that politics is necessarily defined by conflict between classes or interests, including that between capital and labor.[17] "Although well-educated," George Mowry has written, "[the California Progressive] was all but excluded from politics unless he accepted either corporate or labor domination, a thing he was exceedingly loathe to do. His church, his personal morality, and his concept of law, he felt, were demeaned by the crude power struggle between capital and labor."[18] Johnson and his followers did not view themselves as part of a proletarian movement against the capitalists; their position was subtler.

This nuance was seen most clearly in Johnson's hostility toward Franklin Roosevelt's New Deal. As Senator from California, Johnson initially supported FDR's program, going so far as to campaign and vote for him for president in both 1932 and 1936. However, he rebelled against FDR in 1937 and afterward, the first point of conflict between them being the dispute over the latter's "court packing" plan. Johnson also attacked Roosevelt's proposed executive reorganization bill, which he believed would cede too much power to the president. Moreover, like a number of other holdovers in the Senate from the Progressive era, he began to balk at the seeming aimlessness of the New Deal, especially its inability finally to solve the worsening economic conditions of the late 1930s.[19] The old Progressives began to see the aggrandizement of FDR's power as the only real result of the continuing reforms. Yet, they did not see their opposition to the New Deal as a retreat from their earlier Progressivism. As Otis Graham notes: "One can see their reasoning; the objective was a certain sort of America, and if for a time the chief threat to it was the corporation, they were alert enough to respond when the threat came from welfare state liberals or from international communism."[20] The key to understanding Progressives like Johnson, of course, is to identify just what that "certain sort of America" is. But it is clear that they were not statists in the conventional, socialist sense, though they clearly were proponents of dramatically increased government power. Johnson opposed the kind of regimented government regulation that FDR offered because it was, in effect, the wrong kind of statism. For example, in 1938 Johnson opposed the second Agricultural Adjustment Act as too restrictive on the freedom of farmers, noting that he would not "take the farmers of this land by the scruff of the neck and tell them what they must do and how they shall do it."[21] Given this antipathy to government regimentation, Mowry goes so far as to say that Johnson and other Progressives were a "class of supreme individualists,"[22] men dedicated to maintaining something like the original American idea of individual freedom.

Whether Mowry is correct remains to be seen, especially with respect to Johnson. For it is difficult, on the surface, to locate exactly what his view is. After all, the Progressive plan to battle corporations like the Southern Pacific necessitated substantial expansion of government power to control the economy. It is hard to deny that the creation of the centralized "administrative state"[23] during the New Deal and afterward was not, in principle, consistent with Johnson's view; it is, after all, the principal reason why he initially supported FDR.[24] According to Johnson's theory of government, the primary task of the state was, in fact, to provide, through its expanded regulatory and redistributive powers, a much fuller reconciliation of private and public interests than had been thought possible before the Progressive era. In his second inaugural speech as governor, he provided a gloss on the meaning of the new government that he had introduced to California:

> [The] social program which gave to women who toil shorter hours and more happiness, and to men something of the justice that had been denied them has now covered with the mantle of care and tenderness of the state the injured and maimed members of society, and has planted the beacon light of social justice and humanity far beyond the point to which the most ambitious commonwealth has yet gone.[25]

The government, traditionally thought of as an artificial creation of the people, the result of a social contract dedicated to protecting the natural rights of the people, now would provide "care and tenderness" to those harmed by society or otherwise unable to find success within it. That is, through a new kind of paternalism, the state itself, according to Johnson, would be personified as a feeling and compassionate being. But by 1937, Lower explains, Johnson came to see the New Deal state as a vehicle for merely "whetting Roosevelt's imperial ambitions." "The caring government Johnson had always championed," Lower continues, "had given way to a manipulative government; the progressive society he had hoped to see flourish was rent by anger and social division. A free society, he concluded, was giving way to social regimentation."[26] However stark his naïveté may have been, Johnson apparently seemed to think that a government, like an actual person and unlike the mature New Deal state, really could care for people, that it could be something other than the cold monster of administrative centralization.

Johnson, then, was neither a classical liberal nor an abject socialist, but one who thought of himself as holding on to some kind of individualism, albeit an individualism regulated by the tender and caring state. The key to his view was the quality or character of the leaders who would manage that state. He was, in this sense, part of a wider "protest by some peculiarly individualistic social and economic groups"[27] that made up the Progressive movement, leaders who understood themselves as part of a special kind of elite. This protest was more than a new form of populism. For example, unlike the rural roots of populism, almost all of the Progressive leaders were "city men of the upper middle class," especially "professional men, a large number of whom attended graduate schools."[28] A lawyer himself, Johnson believed that the existing capitalist system needed only to be subsumed under a more rational and sympathetic state, presumably with learned and inspired men such as himself in positions of power. More liberal scholars often criticize Progressives like Johnson for this point of view, suggesting that it does not take into account sufficiently what they take to be the thoroughly economic basis of social and political conflict.[29] Mowry, for example, recalls the observation of one Johnson supporter that, "The people . . . elected Governor Johnson to get moral and political reform."[30] He disapprovingly notes that the word "economic" was "significantly absent" from this statement. "From today's vantage point," he suggests, "the Progressive's aim of a capitalist commonwealth may seem incredibly naive."[31] Mowry implies that even a regulated capitalist order would necessarily serve the interests of the few at the expense of the interests of the whole. But Johnson and the Progressives took a different approach. For reasons of either cynicism or goodwill, viewed from either the left or the right, they understood that significant change could come about only if something like the traditional "individualistic" view of society at least appeared to remain. In order to understand Johnson's politics, one must understand that view, particularly its implications for the relationship between society and its political leaders.

The Progressive conception of the individual's relationship to state and society was presented in its most popular form in Theodore Roosevelt's "New Nationalism,"[32] which he articulated in a series of speeches in 1910, the year of Johnson's first campaign for governor. TR, it should be noted, was the most important political influence on Johnson and the California Progressives generally. The "League of Lincoln-Roosevelt Clubs," the principal vehicle for Johnson's Progressive insurgency within the California Republican Party, considered TR almost the equal of Lincoln in moral stature. The league followed Roosevelt's criticism of President Taft and the "Old Guard" within the party, who largely opposed Progressive reforms. As Mowry notes, TR's "name and doctrines were grafted into the very origins of the movement," and those "doctrines struck close to the California progressive ideal."[33] Johnson followed Roosevelt's example not only rhetorically, but programmatically as well. At the outset of his gubernatorial campaign, he explicitly stated that he was "making the fight as a Progressive Republican on the Roosevelt lines."[34] He continued to follow those lines after his victory. His legislative agenda as governor was, in reality, a "practical application of New Nationalism's demand for government control over large, efficient, corporate enterprise."[35] "A sort of western Theodore Roosevelt," one writer notes, "Hiram Johnson invested the cause of political reform in California with a similar brand of dynamic righteousness."[36] Indeed, two years later he would be the logical choice as TR's running mate in the "Bull Moose" campaign for the White House, the two men remaining friends and political partners until Roosevelt's death in 1919. Johnson's embrace of the New Nationalism was about as strong as that of anyone other than TR himself.

Indeed, the New Nationalism may be seen as the clearest expression of Progressive sentiments in America at the height of the Progressive era. It was closely related to, if not exactly based upon, Herbert Croly's *The Promise of American Life*,[37] perhaps the most important work in Progressive literature. Just a few months before his New Nationalism speaking tour, Roosevelt read Croly's book and wrote to the author, remarking that, "I do not know when I have read a book which I felt profited me as much as your book on American life." Indeed, Roosevelt informed Croly that, "I shall use your ideas freely in speeches I intend to make."[38] The importance of Croly's work is obvious. In it, William Leuchtenberg has written, "we can find a more systematic statement of Roosevelt's New Nationalism than Roosevelt himself ever found time to set down, and for this reason it commands our attention."[39] In particular, Croly defends the thesis that TR's New Nationalism was an extension of the American founders' "individualist" view of state and society, much as Lincoln was thought by Progressives to have updated the same view for his time.[40] In this sense, then, the New Nationalism was defended as an extension or evolution of the founders' political principles; the principles of Roosevelt and Johnson presumably would make good on the "promise" of America set forth at its origins.

Yet, Croly's conception of America's promise is quite different from that of the founders. In brief, he advocates a mixing of what he understands to be Hamiltonian nationalism and Jeffersonian democracy. He suggests that both Hamilton and Jefferson "were individualist in spirit, and they were chiefly interested in the great American task of improving their own condition in this world. They both wanted a government which would secure them freedom of action for this purpose." What is now required, Croly believes, is to pursue the shared "individualist" goal of Hamilton and Jefferson, but with an adequate understanding of the strengths and weaknesses of each. Hamiltonians, he argues, rightly emphasized the need for a strong national government, but wrongly aimed to secure the interests of the few. Jeffersonians, on the other hand, rightly aimed to benefit all of society, but wrongly emphasized the need for limited government to achieve that end. The New Nationalism, on the other hand, would take the best from each approach and avoid the worst. That is, the centralized state would assume greater power, but for the benefit of all, not just the few.[41]

Croly notes that his "own preferences are on the side of Hamilton rather than of Jefferson." Jeffersonians sacrificed "a desirable liberty to an undesirable equality," too concerned as they were with protecting a merely formal equality of rights. "In Jefferson's mind," he concludes, "democracy was tantamount to extreme individualism." Jeffersonians, Croly argues, ignored the reality of the growing limitations placed upon the common man's actual liberty. The modern economy has shown "that the automatic harmony of the individual and the public interest, which is the essence of the Jeffersonian democratic creed, has proved to be an illusion."[42] In other words, equality and liberty are in tension with one another, with the protection of the former leading to the destruction of the latter. As Leuchtenburg notes, in Croly's eyes, Jefferson himself merely "prattled about the equality of all men."[43] The doctrine of human equality and natural rights enshrined in his Declaration of Independence was, in fact, only a "seductive example of triumphant intellectual dishonesty, and of the sacrifice of theory to practice, whenever such a sacrifice was convenient."[44] For Croly, the doctrine was nothing but an instrument of expediency.

Oddly enough, Lincoln, who was the chief moral exemplar of Croly, Roosevelt, and Johnson,[45] proclaimed the principle of equality to be the "standard maxim of free society, which should be familiar to all, and revered by all." Indeed, the claim of equality was anything but expedient to Lincoln, who suggested that "the assertion that 'all men are created equal' was of no practical use in effecting our separation from Great Britain."[46] As a statement of supreme moral authority, the principles of the Declaration were thought to be anything but contradictory.[47] Liberty could not be threatened by equality because both were expressions of man's nature as a rational being; we have liberty *because* we are equal. Equality and liberty are unchanging human qualities, not historical or social conditions. Jefferson explained this, noting the "palpable truth . . . that the mass of mankind has not been born with saddles on their backs, nor a favored few booted and spurred, ready to ride them legitimately, by the grace of God." It is an objective and eternal truth, Jefferson argues, that no man stands in relation to any other man as any man stands in relation to a horse; no man is naturally a slave. In this sense, the principle of equality is nothing more than an expression of natural morality or natural right. In marked contrast to the Progressives, Jefferson understood the widening acceptance of this principle to be the basis of a different kind of progress, brought to the world through the "general spread of the light of science." These principles, he thought, "are grounds of hope for others." Rather than reject the equal rights of man, Jefferson suggested that we should "forever refresh our recollections of these rights, and an undiminished devotion to them. . . ."[48] Lincoln, of course, did just that.

Despite Croly's attempt to portray it as a combination of Jeffersonian and Hamiltonian ideas, the New Nationalism rejected the core principles of the founders. However "peculiarly individualistic" Progressives might have been, their view differed markedly from the "individualist" principles of the founders and Lincoln. This was especially so regarding Jeffersonianism. Croly admitted that, while Hamilton's "nationalism can be adapted to democracy without an essential injury to itself," Jefferson's "democracy cannot be nationalized without being transformed." "It must," he insisted, "cease to be a democracy of indiscriminate individualism. . . ."[49] But individualism as such seemed to be an intractable problem for Croly. Unlike the founders, he did not distinguish between individual rights and individual interests. In fact, his turn to Hamiltonianism really had less to do with Hamilton's ideas than it did with finding a rhetorically effective way to speak of common or "national" interests against "individual" interests. In reality, what was necessary, Croly thought, was the very transformation of the idea of individuality itself.

In a revealing statement, Croly suggests that, "Jeffersonian individualism must be abandoned for the benefit of a genuinely individual and social consummation." This "consummation" is to come about through the kind of caring and tender state described by Johnson, through "a democracy devoted to the welfare of the whole people by means of a conscious labor of individual and social improvement."[50] Society and the individual are to come together in a new, more complete fashion. Croly suggests reforms, especially in education, that will bring about "in some way" this individual and social consummation.[51] He follows the lead of most other Progressives, who, as Wilson Carey McWilliams notes, "saw science, commerce, and education enlarging and extending human sympathy and altruism in a gradual march toward a kind of 'species being.'" The Progressive view, however, is less Marxist or even socialist than this depiction makes it seem. Socialism as commonly understood did not, according to the Progressives, fundamentally alter the problem of Jeffersonian individualism, its tendency toward greed and selfishness. As McWilliams explains:

European socialism was bound to fail because its doctrine was materialistic, not a new synthesis or transformation, but the mirror image of the theory of economic man—individualism constrained into an outward equality. The true socialist goal—and the end of history—was a kind of inwardness, an equality of spirit.[52]

What is necessary, according to the Progressives, is a transformation of the very souls of the people, not just the material conditions of their existence. Indeed, Croly explicitly rejects socialist revolution as a threat to the "Christian civilization" that forms the basis of social and political life. The Progressive attack on business interests, he suggests, is necessary merely to combat the "licensed selfishness" that has evolved out of Jeffersonian individualism.[53] In the Progressive idea of equality, each individual soul will instead enter into, as it were, a communion with all of the other souls of society. The founders' idea of equality, however, does not allow this "genuinely individual" life because it insists upon a clear distinction between state and society, which distinction is a logical consequence of the idea of limited, constitutional government. The state, Croly believes, must be expanded to take on the task of educating the people in the new faith. Hence his preference for Hamiltonian Progressivism, through which the "central government is to be used, not merely to maintain the Constitution, but to promote the national interest and to consolidate the national organization."[54] That is, the state will do more than protect the rights of the people; it will aim to save their souls.

The necessity to go beyond the law for the sake of souls is indicated most forcefully in Croly's 1914 book, *Progressive Democracy*,[55] a central theme of which is the replacement of the old law with the new faith, the faith in the democratic spirit of America. Croly metaphorically compares America's Progressive advance to the Christian movement beyond the original Jewish law. "Faith in things unseen and unknown," he writes, "is as indispensable to a progressive democracy as it is to an individual Christian." After the advent of Christianity, he notes, "the highroad to salvation was traced by an uncompromising faith, the constructive effect of which was incomparably greater than was conformity to any Law or the study of its learned commentaries." Similarly, Americans today would be mistaken to put their trust in any "abstract system of natural law."[56] Not loyalty or obedience to an unalterable law, but a "faith in human values," a "faith in the power of faith," should be the guiding purpose of the new Progressive democracy. Croly describes a kind of secular, millennial religion, but one that accepts not Christianity's Holy Spirit, but the "social will" as the "primary creative agency of social improvement."[57] Consider Eldon Eisenach's description of this phenomenon:

In many other Progressive writings the sociological and economic proofs of the progress of this faith seem to overwhelm and even displace their religious causes. In its stead, democracy itself becomes a faith in the American Way of Life, which includes, but now transcends, its earlier regional, denominational, and even biblical formulations.[58]

Indeed, as Mowry describes it, "Under the influence of Darwinism, the rising social sciences, and a seemingly benign world, the Progressive had traded some of his old mystical religion for a new social faith."[59] In keeping with this evolutionary theme, Croly's ever-changing social will necessarily "give to any specific formulations of the social law a merely temporary and instrumental value."[60] The Progressive faith, then, is truly a faith in faith because it does not rest in any fixed or determinate order of things, in any idea of nature, law or god.

In order to make good on this faith in faith, a new kind of leadership is required. Croly claims that most "men cannot be made disinterested for life by exhortation, by religious services, by any expenditure of subsidized words, or even by a grave and manifest public." Yet, since all laws are of "merely temporary and instrumental value," reforms in education and elsewhere can only come into being and be sustained through repeated appeals to the Progressive faith. Not surprisingly, and despite his disclaimers, Croly's language, like Johnson's, naturally tends precisely toward religious exhortation. He suggests that the "redemption of the national Promise has become a cause for which the good American must fight." Indeed, as is seen in the example of Johnson, righteousness and combativeness are central to Progressive rhetoric. One suspects that this is inevitable when faith, the conviction in one's heart, displaces self-evident truths as the ground of political life. "Like all sacred causes," Croly insists, the "American idea," the faith in faith, "must be propagated by the Word and by the right arm of the Word, which is the Sword."[61] Indeed, the Progressive leader must become the instrument of such a crusade, the voice of the social will. The essence of the New Nationalism, then, was not class warfare or individualism or even statism as such, but rather the leader as the embodiment of the secular, Progressive faith. Theodore Roosevelt, in perhaps his most memorable speech, exemplified this role in his heated performances before the Republican and Progressive national conventions in 1912. "We fight in an honorable fashion for the good of mankind," he proclaimed, "fearless of the future; unheeding of our individual fates; with unflinching hearts and undimmed eyes; we stand at Armageddon, and we battle for the Lord."[62]

Here we return to the most significant aspect of Johnson's role as a Progressive leader. His aggressive and spirited campaign style captured the peculiar evangelism of the Progressive movement in a way not often matched by other leaders, including TR. Consider the following summary of his rhetorical exploits in his first run for the governorship in 1910:

> Johnson's campaign for governor may be better described as a religious crusade than as a political campaign. The Riverside *Press* reported that his speeches sounded more "like the inspiring appeals of some prophet or crusader of the delivered truth" than a politician seeking office. Edmond Norton, writer for *La Follette's Magazine*, noted that he saw in some of Johnson's audiences a "moral fervor fusing the assemblies into almost a spiritual frenzy for a few seconds; a mass phenomenon . . . rarely or never witnessed outside of religious meetings." A writer for *McClure's* characterized Johnson as a "political revivalist."[63]

Johnson expressed on the stump the kind of religious passion implied in Croly's Progressive, religious warrior. In the Bull Moose campaign he called himself a "crusader for a new cause," that he was "carrying a Bible in one hand and a claymore in the other."[64] As Mowry notes, in that campaign, at the peak of the Progressive movement, Johnson "appeared . . . as an evangelical pleader for righteousness and social justice."[65] Such "spiritual frenzy" of the evangelical kind is necessary to embolden the people to move beyond the laws, the constitutions that Madison once called the "political scriptures" of the people, "the most sacred part of their property."[66] In this respect, Johnson was a premier Progressive evangelist.

Johnson's role as a preacher of the new Progressive faith went beyond his performances on the stump. For example, in lamenting the fortunes of the losing Bull Moose campaign of 1912, he engaged in what was, for him, typical hyperbole: "Somebody, in a movement of this sort, has to pioneer the way, and if the sacrifices are made with the sort of contest we are about to commence, the harvest will be gathered four years hence. I have the feeling this year that 'The Blood of the Martyr will be the seed of the church.' "[67] Such language was an integral part of Johnson's self-understanding. Not only was his Progressivism a kind of secular Christianity, but he also saw himself as a priest of this new faith. And like a priest, his goal was to save individual souls. Lower notes that

> it was precisely on the spiritual intensity he unleashed that Johnson built his hopes for the good society, for at the root of his Progressivism was his conviction that if the bulk of his audience understood the plight of others they could be led to transcend their immediate self-interests and would, as he did, sympathize and respond. On the most fundamental of levels, Johnson sought the conversion of a people.[68]

Such conversion of individual souls is manifested socially and politically in a renunciation of the old law for the new faith. This is the heart of the Progressive consummation of society and the individual, a conversion that occurs in the heart, not just in the state. This is why an excessive, regimented, socialist order would be contrary to Johnson's views. The consummation, rather, would come about through a combination of progressive, religious exhortation and progressive, statist education. The leader takes upon himself the role of priest, one above corruption and reproach, who can serve as the honest carrier of the faith into the offices of government. The warrior posture of the leader is, in fact, only the face of the otherwise humble servant who, by his example, serves as a model for the conversion of others. Johnson's tender and caring state exists by virtue of the humble souls that lead it. This is why, for example, Progressives praise Lincoln so highly: not simply for his statism, but for his martyrdom. Lincoln's humility, according to Croly, allowed him to enter into "the most fruitful and the most universal of all religious ideas."[69] Not "political religion" or fidelity to the law, as Lincoln suggested in his Lyceum speech of 1838,[70] but sacrifice for the faith is the essence of the new progressive religion.[71]

This religiosity was quite pronounced among progressives of all stripes. Indeed, as Eisenach puts it, "No matter what the context . . . Progressive writings on American nationality are filiopietistic to the core."[72] But this is piety of a peculiarly secular and puritan kind. For example, even Woodrow Wilson, who was a principal opponent of Johnson and TR on numerous occasions, wrote of the "ideality" of "political salvation" toward which America was marching. Like other Progressives, he drew heavily upon New Testament imagery, proclaiming that "there is a law greater than [the Constitution] that cannot be changed." That law, according to Wilson, is the "law written on our hearts which makes us conscious of our oneness as a single personality in the great company of nations."[73] Like other Progressives, Wilson believed that the new faith would lead America beyond the old law and to a higher consummation.

But Johnson did not see Wilson as a sincere member of the flock, and such sincerity was central for Johnson. Latter-day observers may see little real difference between, say, Wilson's New Freedom and TR's New Nationalism; each seems to be a Progressive reflection of the other. But for Johnson, the question went beyond party policies and platforms. One might argue that, from his point of view, the purity of the leader was more important than the progressivism of the program. His goal was the religious conversion of the people. For this conversion to take place, the leader must have the people's trust; and he can only arrive at this trust, Johnson seems to think, by keeping himself above reproach, by being incapable of compromise, in some sense apolitical. In other words, the people can only have faith in "human values" if they have faith in their all-too-human leaders, which, as a practical matter, amounts to the same thing. Eisenach, for example, argues that progressivism "lost" its promise precisely because the creation of the administrative state has not resulted in a new national community of faith. Johnson seemed to have understood this problem early on. This accounts, perhaps, for his tendency to draw severe distinctions of character not only between himself and his opponents, but also between himself and his ostensible allies. In this sense Johnson was, as Lower notes, "a bloc of one," who continually questioned not only the policies, but more importantly, the sincerity or convictions or faith of those around him.

Johnson's pride and ambition, of course, played a part in his decisions and actions, as they do for any politician. But he consistently took a puritanical approach to policy questions. For example, his isolationist foreign policy stance, which dominated his Senate career and led to a break between himself and many other Progressives, was largely driven by his deep skepticism about international corporate and banking interests. That is, he was not a sunny optimist, like many more "internationalist" Progressives, because he was more skeptical about human nature altogether. "In his quest for political isolation," Lower notes, "Johnson often discovered dire threats in the most innocent circumstances. Those who disagreed with his prescription, he charged, were either wicked or naive." The wicked were those business interests who would entangle America in foreign adventures against its own interests. The naive, especially many in the Progressive movement, were victims of a "misplaced idealism and too often blinded by the propaganda" of those same wicked interests.[74] In other words, his "America First" stance was as much a matter of Progressive distrust of the rich as it was a kind of cultural nationalism, although it certainly was the latter as well.[75] He had no faith in the ideals or habits of foreign leaders any more than he did in the leaders of the corporations and trusts.

Johnson's eventual break with FDR was similarly related to a distrustful, even inquisitorial streak in his personality. "Fundamentally," Lower notes, "Johnson's early ties to the White House had been based on his trust in Roosevelt and his faith that the New Deal was a lineal descendant of progressivism. The president's manner, the warmth of his fireside chats, his very willingness to act, had seemed to demonstrate that kinship."[76] But as the New Deal wore on, Johnson began to doubt Roosevelt; that is, he lost "faith" in FDR, and so lost faith in the New Deal. Graham wonders how it is that Progressives like Johnson "could reject a reform movement apparently so akin to their own, and do so largely in terms of familiar Progressive principles."[77] But this rejection of the New Deal likely came about, in part, because the old Progressives like Johnson looked to a new faith as the binding social force of the nation, a substitute for the political religion of Lincoln and the founders, which religion they no longer thought efficacious in the modern industrial world. The interest group politics that emerged out of the New Deal simply had no room for such faith, to say nothing of the founders' political religion. Hence, Johnson believed that he had not forsaken his Progressive views, but that FDR had. "In all my political life," he maintained, "I have pursued one course, and at my present age I could not if I would, and I would not if I could alter that course."[78]

The one course of Johnson's career was reform in the service of a Progressive political faith. In this, he was actually something of a conservative insofar as he aimed to revive moral order through something like a religious awakening. Like most Progressives, he was motivated, in part, by a desire to hold on to the past, to keep something of the older way of life in America.[79] "Progressives," Sidney Milkis has written, "sought to sustain a sense of national identity in the face of the profound changes brought by the rise of the corporation and the expansion of immigration."[80] Morton Keller likewise argues that "the Progressive movement was the last gasp of a polity seeking to preserve what it could of a (rapidly receding) American past."[81] It is perhaps not surprising that leaders like Johnson and TR found so appealing Croly's attempt to link Progressivism with the founding principles. It is also not surprising that Johnson would eventually oppose the New Deal. Yet, as he makes clear in his claim of consistency, he did not turn from Progressivism when he began to see its statist fruits in the New Deal. For that would require that he give up his faith, the defining element of his self-understanding. He believed that, despite all evidence to the contrary, the regimentation of the new order, with its threat to individual freedom, was not the logical end of the changes that he and other leaders had initiated a generation earlier. Instead of returning to America's founding principles as Lincoln did, he evangelized for a conversion of souls.

NOTES

1. The principal biography of Johnson is Richard Coke Lower's *A Bloc of One: The Political Career of Hiram W. Johnson* (Stanford, Calif.: Stanford University Press, 1993). See also Michael A. Weatherson and Hal W. Bochin, *Hiram Johnson: Political Revivalist* (Lanham, Md.: University Press of America, 1995). For a general account of the Progressive movement in California, see George E. Mowry, *The California Progressives* (Berkeley: University of California Press, 1951) and Spencer C. Olin, *California's Prodigal Sons: Hiram Johnson and the Progressives, 1911–1917* (Berkeley: University of California Press, 1968).

2. See Olin, *Prodigal Sons*, chapter 3.

3. More generally, Johnson was among the most influential of politicians ever to emerge from California. Reelected governor in 1914, he was selected in 1916 to represent the state in the U.S. Senate, where he remained until his death in 1945. He was the vice-presidential candidate on the Progressive party ticket with Theodore Roosevelt in the historic 1912 election. He twice sought the presidency, in 1920 and 1924, failing both times to secure the Republican nomination. He was a major figure in the Senate almost from the moment he arrived there, and became renowned for taking presidents to task on the great issues of the day, especially Woodrow Wilson's diplomacy during and after World War I and Herbert Hoover's handling of the economic crisis of the Great Depression.

4. Lower, *Bloc of One*, 16–17.

5. A widely circulated address at Blanchard Hall, Los Angeles, June 3, 1910, Hiram W. Johnson Papers, The Bancroft Library, University of California, Berkeley, cited in Weatherson and Bochin, *Political Revivalist*, 30.

6. Johnson first gained a wider reputation as a brilliant orator through his courtroom speeches as a lawyer. Much earlier, at the age of thirteen, he was selected to recite a poem on the occasion of Ulysses S. Grant's 1879 visit to Johnson's hometown of Sacramento. Even at that age he apparently possessed the ability to connect with his audience. "The world's greatest military chieftain," according to one newspaper report of the event, "displayed much difficulty in suppressing his emotion during the young Hiram Johnson's spirited recital of 'Sheridan's Last Ride' and how his voice trembled as he openly complimented the lad on his forensic ability." Unidentified newspaper clipping, Johnson Papers, cited in Weatherson and Bochin, *Hiram Johnson*, 4.

7. Weatherson and Bochin, *Hiram Johnson*, 63.

8. Weatherson and Bochin, *Hiram Johnson*, 29.

9. Weatherson and Bochin, *Hiram Johnson*, 33.

10. Johnson to Fremont Older, November 15, 1912, Johnson Papers. Quoted in Weatherson and Bochin, *Hiram Johnson*, 64.

11. Weatherson and Bochin, *Hiram Johnson*, 64.

12. Anonymous, "Johnson of California: A Progressive in a Hurry," *Current Literature*, August 1912, 156. Quoted in Weatherson and Bochin, *Hiram Johnson*, 53, 54.

13. Lower, *Bloc of One*, 21.

14. Lower, *Bloc of One*, 44–45.

15. Lower, *Bloc of One*, 6, 14, 22.

16. Mowry, *California Progressives*, 92–93.

17. Lower, *Bloc of One*, 34–35.

18. Mowry, *California Progressives*, 96.

19. Lower, *Bloc of One*, 291–301.

20. Otis L. Graham, *An Encore for Reform: The Old Progressives and the New Deal* (London: Oxford University Press, 1968), 44 n. 32.

21. Lower, *Bloc of One*, 303.

22. Mowry, *California Progressives*, 96.

23. On the use of this term, see John A. Rohr, *To Run a Constitution: The Legitimacy of the Administrative State* (Lawrence: University Press of Kansas, 1986). See also John Marini, *The Politics of Budget Control: Congress, the Presidency, and the Growth of the Administrative State* (Washington, D.C.: Crane Russak, 1992).

24. Lower, *Bloc of One*, 262–65.

25. Quoted in Weatherson and Bochin, *Hiram Johnson*, 72.

26. Lower, *Bloc of One*, 302.

27. Mowry, *California Progressives*, 89.

28. Alfred D. Chandler Jr., "The Origins of Progressive Leadership," in *The Letters of Theodore Roosevelt*, vol. 8, ed. Elting E. Morison (Cambridge, Mass.: Harvard University Press, 1954), 1462. See also Mowry, *California Progressives*, 92.

29. See John Chamberlain, *Farewell to Reform: The Rise, Life and Decay of the Progressive Mind in America* (Gloucester, Mass.: Peter Smith, 1958).

30. Chester Rowell, quoted in Mowry, *California Progressives*, 102.

31. Mowry, *California Progressives*, 102–3.

32. These speeches are collected in Roosevelt's *The New Nationalism*, ed. William Leuchtenburg (Englewood Cliffs, N.J.: Prentice-Hall, 1961).

33. Mowry, *California Progressives*, 90.

34. Johnson's 1910 Republican gubernatorial nomination acceptance speech, quoted in Howard R. Melendy and Benjamin F. Gilbert, *The Governors of California* (Georgetown, Calif.: Talisman, 1965), 308.

35. Olin, *Prodigal Sons*, 67–68.

36. Olin, *Prodigal Sons*, 23.

37. Herbert Croley, *The Promise of the American Life* (Archon Books, 1963 [1909]).

38. Quoted in Leuchtenburg, "Introduction," in Roosevelt, *New Nationalism*, 11.

39. Leuchtenburg, "Introduction," *New Nationalism*, 13.

40. See TR's discussion of Lincoln as a direct model for the Progressives in the initial New Nationalism speech at Osawatomie, Kansas, August 31, 1910. Roosevelt, *New Nationalism*, 22–27.

41. Croly, *Promise*, 32, 27–51, 168–70.

42. Croly, *Promise*, 29, 43–44, 152.

43. Leuchtenburg, Introduction, *New Nationalism*, 13.

44. Croly, *Promise*, 419.

45. Croly, *Promise*, 87–99.

46. Abraham Lincoln, *The Collected Works of Abraham Lincoln*, ed. Roy P. Basler, vol. 2 (New Brunswick, N.J.: Rutgers University Press, 1953), 406.

47. See Harry V. Jaffa, *A New Birth of Freedom: Abraham Lincoln and the Coming of the Civil War* (Lanham, Md.: Rowman & Littlefield, 2000).

48. Thomas Jefferson, *The Portable Thomas Jefferson*, ed. Merrill D. Peterson (New York: Penguin, 1986), 585.

49. Croly, *Promise*, 214.

50. Croly, *Promise*, 153, 214.

51. Croly, *Promise*, 418ff.

52. Wilson Carey McWilliams, "Standing at Armageddon: Morality and Religion in Progressive Thought," in *Progressivism and the New Democracy*, eds. Sidney Milkis and Jerome Mileur (Amherst: University of Massachusetts Press, 1999), 112.

53. Croly, *Promise*, 210–11, 49.

54. Croly, *Promise*, 39.

55. Herbert Croley, *Progressive Democracy,* (New Brunswick, N.J.: Transactions, 1998 [1914]).

56. Croly, *Progressive Democracy*, 168–69, 174.

57. Croly, *Progressive Democracy*, 170, 168, 177.

58. Eldon J. Eisenach, *The Lost Promise of Progressivism* (Lawrence: University Press of Kansas, 1994), 61–62. Eisenach examines the New England Puritan roots of Progressivism stretching back to the nineteenth century. The branches of this development, however, easily extended to the Pacific. As Mowry notes, "The long religious hand of New England rested heavily upon California progressivism, as it has on so many American movements." *California Progressives*, 87.

59. Mowry, *California Progressives*, 98. Consider the following contemporary sociological account, cited by Eisenach, *Lost Promise*, 60 n. 22:

> The relative truth [religious creeds] once had . . . are now, for most of us, not creeds at all, since they are incredible; but creeds of some sort we must have . . . we need to believe, and we shall believe what we can. . . . The perennial truth of what Christ taught comes precisely from the fact that it was not a system, but an intuition and expression of higher sentiments. . . . All finality in religious formulas is discredited philosophically by the idea of evolution.

Charles Horton Cooley, *Social Organization: A Study of the Larger Mind* (Glencoe, Ill.: Free Press, 1956 [1909]), 375–78.

60. Croly, *Progressive Democracy*, 177.

61. Croly, *Promise*, 418, 21.

62. TR at the 1912 Republican National Convention, quoted in John Allen Gable, *The Bull Moose Years* (Port Washington, N.Y.: Kennikat Press, 1978), 17.

63. Weatherson and Bochin, *Hiram Johnson*, 31–32.

64. *San Francisco Bulletin*, August 31, 1912, quoted in Mowry, *California Progressives*, 187.

65. Mowry, *California Progressives*, 187.

66. James Madison, *The Papers of James Madison*, ed. William T. Hutchinson, William M. E. Rachal, Robert A. Rutland, et al., vol. 14 (Chicago and Charlottesville, Va.: University of Chicago Press and University Press of Virginia, 1962), 192, 218.

67. Johnson to W. F. Chandler, August 21, 1912, quoted in Weatherson and Bochin, *Hiram Johnson*, 59.

68. Lower, *Bloc of One*, 45.

69. Croly, *Promise*, 97.

70. Lincoln, *Collected Works*, 1: 112. See Harry V. Jaffa, *Crisis of the House Divided: An Interpretation of the Issues in the Lincoln-Douglas Debates* (Chicago: University of Chicago Press, 1982), chapters 9–10, and Lucas Morel, *Lincoln's Sacred Effort: Defining Religion's Role in American Self-Government* (Lanham, Md.: Lexington, 2000).

71. As Eisenach notes, "the chief connecting link of Puritanism to Progressive conceptions of American nationality and Puritanism is Abraham Lincoln—'father Abraham'—and the Civil War." *Lost Promise*, 65.

72. Eisenach, *Lost Promise*, 63.

73. Woodrow Wilson, *The Papers of Woodrow Wilson*, ed. Arthur Link, vol. 5 (Princeton, N.J.: Princeton University Press, 1966), 61–62.

74. Lower, *Bloc of One*, 163.

75. Like many other Progressives, Johnson generally held to certain racist and anti-Semitic views. These views were generally consistent with the Progressive notion of a national community sharing a single cultural identity and political faith. See Lower, *Bloc of One*, 37, 333.

76. Lower, *Bloc of One*, 302.

77. Graham, *Encore for Reform*, 45.

78. Johnson to H. L. Baggerly, September 24, 1937, quoted in Graham, *Encore for Reform*, 45.

79. See Robert H. Wiebe, *The Search for Order: 1977–1920* (Westport, Conn.: Greenwood, 1980).

80. Milkis, Sidney M. and Jerome M. Mileur, eds. "Introduction: Progressive, Then and Now," in *Progressivism and the New Democracy* (Amherst: University of Massachusetts Press), 5.

81. Morton Keller, "The New Deal and Progressivism: A Fresh Look," in *The New Deal and the Triumph of Liberalism*, eds. Sidney M. Milkis and Jerome M. Mileur (Amherst: University of Massachusetts Press, 2002).

Nixon, California, and American Politics

John J. Pitney Jr.

In 1936, during the Christmas break of his third year at Duke Law School, Richard Nixon and two classmates made the rounds of major law firms in New York. Nixon got only an "iffy" response from one firm, and no offer from Sullivan and Cromwell, his top choice and home of GOP foreign policy mandarin John Foster Dulles. "If they had given me a job," Nixon said in 1958, I'm sure I would have been there today, a corporation lawyer instead of vice president."[1]

A few months later, he applied to be a special agent of the Federal Bureau of Investigation. The official FBI report on his application was generally positive, saying that he "perhaps" had executive ability and that he was "above average in intelligence and mental alertness" and "manly appearing, possessing a good physique."[2] But again, no offer came. (Years later, J. Edgar Hoover told Nixon that the Bureau had accepted his application but could not hire him because of budget cuts.) H. Claude Horack, dean of the Duke Law School, knew that the student had vague political aspirations, so he told him: "Dick, if you're going to go into politics, go back to your hometown and establish yourself in a law firm."[3] Nixon did just that, joining Wingert and Bewley, in Whittier, California.

Those of us who counsel young people on their careers should note this story, for Dean Horack's advice changed history. Had Nixon gone anywhere but California, the course of his political life would have been radically different, and he might not have had one at all. As it turned out, he happened to be in the right state at the right moment for a dramatically quick ascent. California also shaped his career—and the nation's political life—by teaching him a tough, individualistic style of campaigning and endowing his public philosophy with a distinctly

219

progressive bouquet. Had he hailed from another state, he probably would have learned other ways to win votes and adopted a more orthodox brand of Republican conservatism. A Nixon from New York or Ohio would not have been the Nixon we know.

WHEN CALIFORNIA MATTERED

In the summer of 2000, Fred Barnes wrote a *Weekly Standard* article titled "California Doesn't Matter." Barnes argued that the state's leftward political trends had deprived it of bellwether status, and that its decaying quality of life had undercut its standing as a role model for other states.[4] Barnes may well be right today, but it was quite another story in Nixon's day.

For much of American history, one state or another has held a preeminent position in national politics. In the early days of the Republic, that state was Virginia, the home of Washington, Jefferson, Madison, and Monroe. Then the title passed to the powerhouse of population and commerce, the State of New York. Except for 1896, every presidential election between 1864 and 1948 included at least one major-party presidential or vice-presidential nominee from New York. On three occasions (1904, 1940, and 1944), *both* major-party presidential nominees were New Yorkers.

California became a state in 1850, and at first seemed an unlikely rival. But by the early twentieth century, it had grown to a respectable size. Fittingly, the first presidential election of Richard Nixon's lifetime was also the first in which California decided the outcome. In 1916, when Nixon was three years old, Woodrow Wilson carried the state by a mere 3,420 votes. The national election was so close that if Republican Charles Evans Hughes (a New Yorker) had won California's thirteen electoral votes, he would have defeated Wilson by a tally of 267 to 264. The state could make that difference because of the three House seats (and thus three electoral votes) that it had gained after the 1910 census.

Herbert Hoover won the presidency in 1928, becoming the first Californian in the White House and only the second to gain a major-party nomination. (Republican John C. Frémont was the first, in 1856.) Hoover's California residency had much less to do with his nomination than his service as commerce secretary and his world fame for his leadership of relief efforts following World War I. After his presidency, however, he kept an interest in California politics, quietly offering counsel and financial patronage to promising young GOP politicians—especially his fellow Quaker, Richard Nixon.

By the 1940s, California had become a major political prize. Population growth had already put it into the top tier of the Electoral College, and the economic boom of World War II was accelerating the process. Furthermore, California was highly competitive, backing Republicans and Democrats alike. In 1949, Carey McWilliams wrote: "California is a state that lacks a political gyroscope, a state that swings and sways, spins and turns in accordance with its own peculiar dynamics."[5] Accordingly, it made more and more sense for party leaders to consider Californians for their national tickets. In 1944, New York governor Thomas Dewey twice asked California's popular Republican governor Earl Warren to be his running mate. Warren declined the offer, doubting that even he could carry the state for Dewey against FDR, who had handily won it three times.[6] Four years later, Warren accepted Dewey's offer. Though he undoubtedly helped, he could not quite overcome Dewey's bungling and Truman's last minute surge: the Dewey-Warren ticket lost the state by half a percentage point.

So whether or not Dean Horack knew it when he advised young Nixon, this setting was just about the best possible launching pad for a national political career. As soon as he returned from law school in 1937, Nixon started making the most of his opportunity, building a name as a dynamic speaker for local organizations, laying the foundation for a future race for office.[7] These early efforts paid off in 1946, when he won a seat in the House of Representatives, but this victory also required two additional pieces of luck.

First, Nixon had the good fortune to live in the district of a potentially vulnerable Democrat, Jerry Voorhis. Had he settled in a place with a GOP incumbent, he would have had to wait for his big break. With his intelligence and political instinct, he would have eventually made it, but if he had won his seat even two years later, he would have come too late to expose Alger Hiss. Republicans lost their majority in the election of 1948, and as a freshman member of the minority party, he would not have had the chance to oversee a major investigation.

Second, fate also kept him from running too *early*. Service in the Office of Price Administration and then the navy took him out of the local political scene for several years. In the meantime, Voorhis easily dispatched his GOP opponents in 1942 and 1944—and he probably would have defeated Nixon, too. When Nixon left the service, leading local Republicans asked him to run, and by this time the seat was ripe for the taking. The national political winds were at long last favoring the GOP, mainly because of frustration with the postwar economic transition and the growing threat of communism abroad. And in this particular case, the Twelfth Congressional District was rapidly filling up with new voters who tended to vote Republican and who had little knowledge of the incumbent.[8] In those days before jet travel and large congressional staffs, California's members of Congress found it hard to visit their districts frequently and keep in touch with local developments. During the 1946 campaign, Voorhis took too long to grasp the seriousness of the GOP challenge.[9] In the fall, Nixon stunned him.

After his initial election to the House, Nixon found that California had political advantages beyond its sheer size. A burgeoning state economy meant new sources of campaign financing, though as Irwin Gellman has documented, many writers have exaggerated how much money Nixon raised and spent during his early races.[10] Just as important, the rest of the country had a growing fascination with this state of mountains, palm trees, swimming pools, and movie stars. All other things being equal, a politician from California could pique more national interest than a colleague from Illinois or Pennsylvania.

Nixon benefited from California glamour by fighting one of its leading symbols. In 1950, he ran for the U.S. Senate against Representative Helen Gahagan Douglas, a former actress (star of the first movie version of *She*) and wife of the distinguished actor Melvyn Douglas. As we shall see shortly, the contest became notorious for tough campaign tactics. It also provided Nixon with the chance to cast himself as the champion of ordinary hard-working Americans against the left-wing cultural elites. The *Los Angeles Times*, at the time a very conservative paper, echoed Nixon's attacks, calling Douglas "the darling of the Hollywood parlor Pinks and Reds."[11]

His smashing victory over Douglas, following his successful effort to bring Alger Hiss's espionage to light, confirmed his status as a Republican star. When Eisenhower clinched the GOP presidential nomination in 1952, Nixon was a logical choice for the second slot. A Californian could help bring the state—now with thirty-two electoral votes—into the Republican column for the first time since Hoover in 1928.) In hindsight, Eisenhower probably would have won the election, along with California, even without Nixon. But victory did not seem so inevitable at the time: Republicans had not gained the White House in nearly a quarter century, and as of August 1952, the Gallup Poll showed Stevenson only six points behind.[12] In any case, Nixon was the best available Californian. He was more acceptable to the conservative Taft wing than Governor Warren, and so could help unify the party. He was also younger and brighter than the state's senior senator, William Knowland. ("In his case," Eisenhower later wrote of Knowland, "there seems to be no final answer to the question, 'How stupid can you get?' "[13])

The Eisenhower-Nixon ticket carried California in 1952 and 1956. In 1960, while losing the presidency, Nixon edged out Kennedy in the state because of the customary GOP advantage in absentee ballots. These showings led many Republicans to think that Nixon could stage his comeback in the 1962 gubernatorial race against incumbent Democrat Pat Brown. The governor's chair had its attractions for Nixon. It would allow him to sit out an expected Kennedy reelection victory in 1964, while building a base for 1968 and keeping his distance from inept congressional Republicans. It would also give him a chance to build a concrete record of accomplishment, which had eluded him as vice president. In the early 1960s, the postwar economic boom still enabled California state government to carry out new programs in transportation and education that were as popular as they were massive.

Unfortunately for Nixon, that is exactly why Brown proved so tough to beat. Moreover, as Nixon candidly admitted in his memoirs, "The real problem was that I had no great desire to be governor of California."[14] His cherished international concerns had little relevance to the issues of Sacramento, or to the criteria by which Californians judged candidates for state office.[15] The editor of the *Sacramento Bee* said: "One of his aides was griping to me. He said, 'You know, we come to some of these towns and they ask him how many black swans should be on the lake?' That is what the local paper wanted to know; that's the only thing they had. He was very impatient about that. First, he didn't know; and second, he didn't think it was important, and he let them know he didn't think it was important."[16] After a bumpy campaign, Nixon lost badly and gave his "last press conference."

Soon afterward, he joined a New York law firm. He did not seek a political base in the state; rather, such a position offered a big salary along with free time and international travel, which would enable him to stay in the public eye.[17] For the next several years, he carefully worked toward his political resurrection and in 1968 he won the Republican presidential nomination. His closest competition was Nelson Rockefeller, the last New York governor so far to be a serious presidential contender. Nixon won in November, and his narrow margin in California was crucial. Had the state's forty electoral votes gone instead to Hubert Humphrey, Nixon would only have had 261—nine short of a majority—and the election would have gone to the House of Representatives.

As president, Nixon reestablished his residency in California, symbolically completing the state's ascendancy over New York. Since then, the only New Yorker on a national ticket has been Representative Geraldine Ferraro of Queens, Democratic vice presidential candidate in 1984. Jack Kemp, the GOP's 1996 vice presidential candidate, did represent the Buffalo suburbs in the House, but he grew up in Los Angeles and lived in Maryland at the time of his nomination.

INDIVIDUALISM AND POLITICAL CULTURE

In 1972, Nixon put his bid for a second term in the hands of the Committee to Re-elect the President, known forevermore as CREEP. The organization would become notorious as the sponsor of the Watergate break-in, but even apart from the scandal, CREEP marked a turning point in presidential campaigns. As the liberal Ripon Society put it in a critical 1974 analysis: "For the first time in American politics, a completely centralized national political machine was created, with direct lines of command coming from Washington that did not rely at all on local political parties or on local power centers for its operational efficiency."[18] Not only did Nixon bypass the Republican Party and its efforts to win offices other than the presidency, he tacitly backed Democratic lawmakers who had sided with him on key votes.[19] In part, Nixon's approach was just rational strategy. In 1972, the Democrats had a huge lead over Republicans in party identification, so a close embrace of the GOP label might have done him more harm than good. And since Democrats were sure to keep control of Congress no matter what he did, it would have seemed risky to antagonize them by fighting to elect Republicans.

At the same time, CREEP also represented an extension and refinement of California's brand of electoral politics. And in an ironic but rather direct way, it was an outgrowth of the state's Progressive heritage.

Through Nixon's time, California politics revolved around political leaders and their own personal camps instead of parties and blocs. Many of the people who came to California throughout the twentieth century were intentionally escaping past social attachments and were reluctant to form new ones. James Q. Wilson wrote in 1967 that the migrants brought with them an "individualistic orientation" that downplayed group identities in favor of "a cult of personality that dominated every aspect of life."[20] And when they reached California, they did not settle into the socially connected neighborhoods that had spawned traditional local party organizations in the East. As a Los Angeles Republican leader told Theodore H. White in 1964: "There's a transitory quality about this electorate. Our turnover of homes is 20 percent a year. . . . Fundamentally, Californians aren't in touch with their neighbors. So the impact media have a flamboyant effect."[21] Facing an electorate without firm party commitments, California politicians learned early in the century they would rise or fall on their personal appeal—a lesson that politicians throughout the country would later have to apply as well.

More concretely, state laws weakened political parties. Reacting to the perceived corruption of party organizations, California Progressives systematically set out to undercut them through a series of institutional measures: a ban on pre-primary endorsements of political candidates by party committees; a system of nonpartisan local elections, elimination of patronage through civil service, direct legislation through the initiative and referendum, and the cross-filing system by which members of one party could run in the primary of the other party.

This environment fostered intraparty feuds, since personal ambition overrode party loyalty and no one had the power to mediate disputes. As Nixon rose, he came into conflict first with Governor Earl Warren, then with Warren's successor Goodwin Knight, and still later with his onetime friend, Senator William Knowland. In 1959, journalist Philip Potter observed: "None of the state's leading Republicans of the past decade bear him goodwill."[22] Seeking the governorship in 1962, he got an unwelcome surprise when conservative Republicans turned against him in the primary, instead supporting State Assembly GOP leader Joe Shell. And when he ran for the Republican presidential nomination in 1968, the state's convention delegates ditched him for their new favorite son, Governor Ronald Reagan. In this way, Nixon learned that he could never count on "the party." He had to stand alone.

As a corollary, he learned how to reach beyond the GOP. In his races for the House and Senate, Nixon took advantage of cross-filing, a procedure that stayed on the books until 1959. During his 1946 race against Jerry Voorhis, he won a respectable 16 percent of the Democratic primary vote, which should have been an early warning for the much better known incumbent. Two years later, cross-filing enabled him to avoid a November contest altogether by winning both parties' nominations. And in 1950, he had no major opposition for the GOP Senate nomination, so he put some effort into scoring high in the Democratic primary. His effort forced Helen Douglas to divert even more resources from the fall campaign, though she already had to contend with an internal challenge from R. Manchester Boddy, editor, and publisher of the *Los Angeles Daily News*. (It was Boddy, not Nixon, who dubbed her "the pink lady."[23]) In the primary, the Nixon campaign downplayed his partisan affiliation—even to the point of issuing a mailing to registered Democrats titled "As One Democrat to Another." With "Democrats for Nixon" as the sponsor, the pamphlet nowhere mentioned his party affiliation.[24] In a manual for Nixon campaign workers, campaign consultant Murray Chotiner explained the approach: "We must appeal to Democrats to help win the election. Therefore, do not make a blanket attack on Democrats. Refer to the opposition as a supporter of the socialistic program running on the Democratic ticket."[25] Douglas won the Democratic primary and got some votes in the Republican primary, but Nixon's total in both primaries topped her's by 169,349—a margin that foreshadowed his victory in the fall.

As vice president, Nixon often had to play the Republican partisan so that Eisenhower could stay above the battle. In his presidential campaigns, however, he returned to the cross-party tactics that he had learned so well in California. In 1960, he relied not on state party organizations but on groups such as "Nixon-Lodge Volunteer Clubs" and "Democrats for Nixon-Lodge." Similarly, his 1968 campaign was long on personal appeal and short on overt partisanship. And in 1972, Nixon did not just deemphasize the GOP: he tried to transcend it completely with a "New Majority" of Republicans, Democrats and Independents who sided with his centrist domestic policies and his pragmatic foreign policies. William Safire reports that Nixon wrote a note to himself in October 1972: "Generally support Republican candidates, no blanket endorsement of all candidates—where a Dem supports policy, I shall not campaign against him."[26] Just as he had used a "Democrats for Nixon" organization to criticize Helen Douglas for being outside the mainstream in 1950, he now made the 1972 "Democrats for Nixon" group the official sponsor of anti-McGovern ads. Campaign consultant Peter Dailey said of the spots: "[W]hen Democrats for Nixon was formed, we changed the signature to Democrats for Nixon and found in testing that the same commercials were far more effective with that signature than Committee for the Re-election of the President. What the material did was to reinforce the attitudes of Democrats who were defecting."[27]

By 1972, the use of professional consultants such as Dailey was commonplace in national campaigns, but California had been decades ahead. In 1933, two Bay Area public relations experts founded Campaigns, Inc., the first political management firm in the United States. Its subsequent success inspired others to enter the California political arena, including advertising agencies, public relations firms, and an ever-increasing number of political consulting specialists. This trend grew out of two features of state politics, both the product of Progressive-era reforms. First, the demise of strong party organizations had left candidates without a dependable source of advice and technical support, which the new firms could provide. Second, the ballot initiative process gave interest groups a way to pass laws they wanted in case they could not sway state legislators. Interest groups on the other side had a stake in blocking their foes' initiatives. Therefore, campaigns both for and against ballot initiatives could supply the consultant corps with a great deal of business.

Nixon used a consultant in his 1946 race for the House. Murray Chotiner later gained a reputation as an evil Yoda, whose teachings on attack politics brought Nixon to the Dark Side. Actually, Chotiner had only a marginal role in Nixon's 1946 race, but he did run the 1950 campaign against Douglas.[28] In that race, Chotiner's strategy was to link Douglas with Vito Marcantonio, a New

York congressman sympathetic to the Communist Party. A "pink sheet" listed House votes on which she and Marcantonio had taken the same position, suggesting that a vote for Nixon was a vote against "the Douglas-Marcantonio axis." These attacks were harsh, but contrary to myth, Douglas was no innocent victim. In her speeches, she said she despised "Communism, Nazism, and Nixonism" and called his supporters "a backwash of young men in dark shirts"—an allusion to Mussolini's fascists.[29]

In 1956, a young advertising executive named H. R. Haldeman served as an advance man for Nixon as he campaigned for a second term with Eisenhower. Over the years, Nixon increasingly relied on Haldeman, who became his chief advance man in 1960 and manager of the ill-fated 1962 gubernatorial campaign. With the advice of Leone Baxter, one of the founders of Campaigns, Inc., Haldeman and the Nixon campaign concocted "The Committee for the Preservation of the Democratic Party in California," which sent out circulars denouncing Governor Pat Brown as an extremist.[30] The Democrats got a court order to stop the circulars on the grounds that they violated state disclosure requirements. The Democrats's consultants, in turn, invented a group called "Independent Voters of California," which published leaflets attacking Nixon for once owning a home with a restrictive covenant.[31]

Earl Mazo and Stephen Hess observed in 1968 that such tactics "have given the state a well-earned reputation for having the dirtiest politics in the country."[32] California hardly invented negative campaigning—Jefferson and Lincoln were targets of nasty personal attacks—but the state's political consultants brought it to a new level of sophistication. And in Nixon's case, the candidate's ideological moderation made negativism all the more tempting. As Larry Sabato explains: "A candidate near the extreme ends of the spectrum can be himself in direct mail, but for more centrist candidates, emotion must be manufactured, either by selective and exaggerated emphasis on a couple of issues or by sharp, personal contrast with the opponent."[33]

When Haldeman became chief of staff in the Nixon White House, he brought his California political habits with him, thereby reinforcing Nixon's more aggressive tendencies.

Memories of the Democratic assaults made things even worse. During the 1972 campaign, Nixon operatives vowed to have a "Dick Tuck capability," after a notorious California Democratic dirty trickster. During the Senate Watergate hearings, Haldeman reportedly said to Tuck: "You S.O.B., you started this."[34] Neither Tuck nor Haldeman really "started it," for they were both products of California's professionalized style of individual political combat, which itself was an unintended offspring of Progressivism.

PROGRESSIVISM AND POLICY

Progressivism not only gave rise to the California institutions and political practices that shaped Nixon's career, it also affected the way he thought about leadership and governance.

Nixon sprouted from Progressive soil. In 1912, the year before Nixon's birth, Theodore Roosevelt narrowly carried California as the candidate of the Progressive Party. (He undoubtedly got a boost from running mate Hiram Johnson, the state's governor.) As the candidate of the party's 1924 incarnation, Robert LaFollette had one of his best showings in the state, winning a third of the vote and outpolling Democratic candidate John W. Davis. Both times, one Progressive vote came from Nixon's father, Francis Anthony Nixon.[35] In 1916, his mother Hannah voted for the champion of another version of Progressivism, Woodrow Wilson.[36] As he recalled in his memoirs, his studies at Whittier College left their mark as well:

> Dr. Paul Smith was probably the greatest intellectual inspiration of my early years. . . . His doctorate was from the University of Wisconsin, where he had studied under the great Progressive historian Glenn Frank. Dr. Smith's approach to history and politics was strongly influenced by the Progressive outlook, and it came as a revelation to me that history could be more than a chronicle of past events—it could be a tool of analysis and criticism.[37]

In his addresses and writings, Nixon frequently mentioned the Progressives: his last two speeches as president included lengthy quotations from Theodore Roosevelt. In 1968, Nixon told Garry Wills that Woodrow Wilson was "our greatest president of this century."[38] In fact, he probably quoted more from Wilson than from any other American statesman.[39]

So what did Nixon learn from the Progressives? In her memoir of his postpresidential years, Nixon aide Monica Crowley quotes him as recommending Wilson's famous speech, "Leaders of Men."[40] In his speech, Wilson defined leadership as the interpretation of public opinion:

> The general sense of the community may wait to be aroused, and the statesman must arouse it; may be inchoate and vague, and the statesman must formulate and make it explicit. But he cannot and he should not do more. The forces of the public may be blind: he must lend them sight; they may blunder: he must set them right. He can do something, indeed to create such forces of opinion; but it is a creation of forms, not of substance:—and without such forces at his back he can do nothing effective.[41]

Nixon, like Wilson, saw himself as a tribune of the people. According to speechwriter William Safire, one can find "the basic approach of Richard Nixon to the business and the art of governing" in a little-noticed radio address from October 21, 1972.[42] One may also hear echoes of Wilson in Nixon's description of public opinion, and his own leadership of "the silent majority."

> On November 3, 1969, I came before my fellow Americans on radio and television to review our responsibilities and to summon up the strength of our national character. The great silent majority of Americans—good people with good judgment who stand ready to do what they believe to be right—immediately responded. The response was powerful, nonpartisan, and unmistakable. The majority gave its consent, and the expressed will of the people made it possible for the Government to govern successfully. I have seen the will of the majority in action, responding to a call to responsibility, to honor, and to sacrifice. . . . That is also why I speak with pride of the "new majority" that is forming not around a man or a party, but around a set of principles that is deep in the American spirit.[43]

Woodrow Wilson introduced the word "vision" into American politics. Whereas Old Testament prophets would get their "visions" from God, politicians in the Progressive tradition get their "vision" from "the future." As Charles Kesler reminds us: "The leader becomes a kind of prophet, a secular prophet, predicting where history is going to take the country and trying to marshal the people so that they will get there more efficiently and sooner than they otherwise would."[44] That is exactly how Nixon thought.

In a toast to one of his heroes, Charles de Gaulle, he said: "And then there is one other quality we have found always in our visits with you and which we seek now and are finding now, and that is the quality of wisdom and vision—the vision that sees beyond the crisis of the moment, that sees the great forces that are at play in the world and, therefore, is able to have the perspective that leaders need to make the right decisions, the decisions that will stand well in history and not just in the headlines of tomorrow."[45] In his 1970 State of the Union Address, he put it this way: "As a people, we had too many visions—and too little vision." Listing all the goals he could foresee for the country, he concluded:

> I see an America in which we have made great strides in stopping the pollution of our air, cleaning up our water, opening up our parks, continuing to explore in space. Most important, I see an America at peace with all the nations of the world. This is not an impossible dream. These goals are all within our reach. In times past, our forefathers had the vision but not the means to achieve such goals. Let it

not be recorded that we were the first American generation that had the means but not the vision to make this dream come true.[46]

Nixon's adherence to the Wilson model had more specific aspects. According to Daniel Patrick Moynihan, who served as Nixon's domestic adviser: "In his first two years of office Nixon adopted a legislative and administrative program that was not so much liberal as progressive, similar in ways to that of Woodrow Wilson, whom he admired most of twentieth-century presidents."[47] Progressives had a fascination with government reorganization, particularly reforms that would strengthen the executive. In April 1969, Nixon named corporate executive Roy Ash to head the President's Council on Executive Organization, whose key recommendation was to replace the Bureau of the Budget with the Office of Management and Budget, giving the White House more direct control over administrative planning and regulation. A. James Reichley explained: "Behind Nixon's drive to gain mastery over the bureaucracy, as well as behind his offensive to cut programs and costs in the 1974 budget, lay a view of the presidency as a tribune for the 'general interest' of the national public against the 'special interests' championed by Congress, the bureaucracy, and the lobbies. . . ."[48]

Though Nixon often spoke of reducing the federal bureaucracy and returning power to the states and localities, his policies had the practical effect of strengthening the national administrative state.[49] In the environmental tradition of Theodore Roosevelt, he signed the Endangered Species Acts of 1969 and 1973, the National Environmental Policy Act of 1970, the 1970 Clean Air Act Amendments, and the Safe Drinking Water Act of 1974. In the broader Progressive tradition, he increased federal regulation of business by signing such measures as the Coal Mine Safety and Health Act and the Occupational Health and Safety Administration Act.

Some caveats are in order. First, Nixon's policies were a product not just of a philosophy that he absorbed in California, but of the political conditions he faced in office. Throughout his tenure, Democrats controlled Congress, which meant that proposals for increasing the power of the executive branch promised to make his life much easier. And to some extent, his acceptance of "Progressive" measures was a bow to political reality. Most of these initiatives were popular at the time, and Congress would have passed much more liberal versions had he not cooperated on more moderate ones.

Second, Progressivism had different strands. Whereas some Progressives wanted to move away from party politics, Wilson wanted to strengthen the party system.[50] In this respect, Nixon departed from Wilson and followed the California tradition. Furthermore, one could also note a number of differences between

Theodore Roosevelt's New Nationalism and Woodrow Wilson's New Freedom, and ponder how each may have influenced Nixon. Such an analysis, however, is beyond the scope of this chapter.

Third, one cannot assume that all California political leaders are steeped in Progressive traditions. Nevertheless, we have recently witnessed a revival of the Wilson-Nixon "vision thing." In a 1999 interview with the *San Francisco Chronicle*, Governor Gray Davis compared his perspective to that of state lawmakers. "They have a totally different view of the world than I do, totally different. It was my vision that commanded a 20-point victory, the largest victory in forty years. People expect government to reflect the vision that I suggested. Nobody else in the legislature ran statewide. Their job is to implement my vision. That is their job."[51]

NIXON, CALIFORNIA, AND AMERICA TODAY

Michael Barone wrote in 1999: "To an extent few people appreciate, we still live in Richard Nixon's America."[52] His perspective on leadership, his style of campaigning, his administrative method, and his domestic policy philosophy— all are part of national politics today, and all have roots in Nixon's California background. As Governor Pete Wilson said at Nixon's funeral: "He moved on the world stage. He voiced bold ideas, and he left global footprints. But for all his world grasp and mastery of global strategy, it was right here in this small house, in this little town in Orange County, that Richard Nixon learned and never forgot the values that shaped him and helped him shape our world."[53]

Wilson himself was part of the Nixon legacy. He gained some of his earliest experiences working in Nixon campaigns, and drove Nixon home from his 1962 "last press conference." His combination of combative campaign politics and centrist policies was a reflection of this influence. "Pete and the president are very much the same," said Ken Khachigian, a speechwriter for Nixon and Reagan who helped Wilson write the eulogy.[54]

Wilson, however, was not able to follow Nixon onto the national stage: his race for president in 1996 met an early and ignoble end. And by the time he left Sacramento, he had become highly unpopular in much of the state, and "radioactive" in Republican circles. This reversal of fortune stemmed less from any misstep on Wilson's part than from larger changes that would have thwarted any Nixonian politician. In many ways, we do live in Nixon's America, but in other ways, we are entering an America that Nixon would not have recognized.

In his 1967 essay on Southern California, James Q. Wilson recalled: "I never heard the phrase 'ethnic group' until I was in graduate school."[55] Even at the time he wrote the essay, many Californians could still make a similar claim. In the 1970 census, 78 percent of Californians were non-Hispanic whites and only 12 percent were Hispanic. In his California campaigns, then, Nixon could forgo "identity politics" and talk about broad issues that appealed to the working and middle classes.

In the years after Nixon left office, the state Hispanic population increased sharply, rising to 26 percent in 1990. And according to the most recent census estimate, that figure stands at 32 percent, with non-Hispanic whites constituting just fewer than 50 percent.[56] This trend points to a new politics, in which Nixon might not have fared as well. In 1998, the Republican candidate for governor was Attorney General Dan Lungren, whose father was Nixon's physician. Like Nixon in 1968, he ran on a tough anticrime platform. Though the white vote split nearly down the middle, the Latino vote went to Gray Davis 78 to 17 percent, thereby handing Lungren a humiliating defeat overall.[57] Looking at national demographic trends, journalist John O'Sullivan sees a similar fate for Republican presidential candidates: "An America with the ethnic composition forecast for 2050 would have voted for the Democratic presidential candidate in every election since 1968, with the sole exception of 1972."[58]

At the state and national levels, Republican politicians may well figure out a response to this challenge. But because the battlefield has changed, they cannot look to Nixon's career for a complete guide to strategy and tactics.

NOTES

1. Quoted in Earl Mazo and Stephen Hess, *Nixon: A Political Portrait* (New York: Popular Library, 1968), 22.

2. J. H. Hanson, Federal Bureau of Investigation report on Richard M. Nixon, July 17, 1937, at www.thesmokinggun.com/archive/nixonfbi7.shtml (Accessed April 12, 2003).

3. Quoted in Stephen E. Ambrose, *Nixon: The Education of a Politician 1913–1962* (New York: Simon & Schuster, 1987), 82–83.

4. Fred Barnes, "California Doesn't Matter," *The Weekly Standard*, July 31, 2000, 22–25.

5. Carey McWilliams, *California: The Great Exception* (New York: Current, 1949), 192.

6. Richard Norton Smith, *Thomas E. Dewey and His Times* (New York: Simon & Schuster, 1984), 396.

7. Roger Morris, *Richard Milhous Nixon: The Rise of an American Politician* (New York: Henry Holt, 1990), 200–203.

8. Tom Wicker, *One of Us: Richard Nixon and the American Dream* (New York: Random House, 1991), 42.

9. Irwin F. Gellman, *The Contender: Richard Nixon: The Congress Years 1946–1952* (New York: Free Press, 1999), 57–58.

10. Gellman, *Contender*, 456.

11. Quoted in Ronald Brownstein, *The Power and the Glitter: The Hollywood-Washington Connection* (New York: Vintage, 1992), 121.

12. The August 10, 1952, Gallup poll showed Eisenhower with 47 percent, Stevenson with 41 percent. John H. Runyon, Jennifer Verdini, and Sally Runyon, eds., *Source Book of American Presidential Campaign and Election Statistics 1948–1968*, (New York: Frederick Ungar, 1971), 270.

13. Quoted in Stephen E. Ambrose, *Eisenhower the President* (New York: Simon & Schuster, Touchstone, 1985), 118.

14. Richard M. Nixon, *RN: The Memoirs of Richard Nixon*, vol. 1 (New York: Warner, 1979), 295.

15. James Gimpel, *National Elections and the Autonomy of American State Party Systems* (Pittsburgh: University of Pittsburgh Press, 1996), 144–45.

16. James Wrightson, quoted in Gerald S. Strober and Deborah Hart Strober, *Nixon: An Oral History of His Presidency* (New York: HarperCollins, 1994), 12.

17. Stephen E. Ambrose, *Nixon: The Triumph of a Politician 1962–1972* (New York: Simon & Schuster, 1989), 17.

18. The Ripon Society and Clifford W. Brown Jr., *Jaws of Victory* (Boston: Little, Brown, 1974), 68.

19. Ripon Society and Brown, *Jaws of Victory*, 71–73.

20. James Q. Wilson, "A Guide to Reagan Country: The Political Culture of Southern California," *Commentary*, May 1967, 39.

21. Julius A. Leetham, quoted in Theodore H. White, *The Making of the President 1964* (New York: Signet, 1966), 156.

22. Philip Potter, "Political Pitchman: Richard M. Nixon," in *Candidates 1960*, ed. Eric Sevareid (New York: Basic, 1959), 76.

23. Gellman, *Contender*, 299.

24. Mazo and Hess, *Nixon: A Political Portrait*, 69–70.

25. Quoted in Ambrose, *Nixon: The Education of a Politician*, 211.

26. William Safire, *Before the Fall: An Inside View of the Pre-Watergate White House* (New York: Ballantine, 1977), 713.

27. Quoted in Ernest R. May and Janet Fraser, *Campaign '72: The Managers Speak* (Cambridge, Mass.: Harvard University Press, 1973), 198–99.

28. Gellman, *Contender*, 286.

29. Jonathan Aitken, *Nixon: A Life* (Washington, D.C.: Regnery, 1993), 188.

30. Aitken, *Nixon*, 301.

31. Ambrose, *Nixon: The Education of a Politician*, 661.

32. Mazo and Hess, *Nixon: A Political Portrait*, 271.

33. Larry J. Sabato, *The Rise of Political Consultants: New Ways of Winning Elections* (New York: Basic, 1981), 241.

34. Quoted in Larry J. Sabato and Glenn R. Simpson, *Dirty Little Secrets: The Persistence of Corruption in American Politics* (New York: Times Books, 1996), 186.

35. Herbert S. Parmet, *Richard Nixon and His America* (Boston: Little, Brown, 1990), 57.

36. Ambrose, *Nixon: The Education of a Politician*, 28–29.

37. Nixon, *RN*, 18.

38. Garry Wills, *Nixon Agonistes* (New York: Mentor, 1970), 30–31.

39. Parmet, *Richard Nixon and His America*, 71.

40. Monica Crowley, *Nixon Off the Record* (New York: Random House, 1996), 10.

41. Woodrow Wilson, "Leaders of Men," in *The Papers of Woodrow Wilson*, vol. 6, ed. Arthur S. Link (Princeton, N.J.: Princeton University Press, 1969), 661.

42. Safire, *Before the Fall*, 838.

43. Richard M. Nixon, radio address to the nation, October 21, 1972, in *The Public Papers of the Presidents, Richard Nixon 1972* (Washington, D.C.: Government Printing Office, 1973), 999.

44. Charles R. Kesler, "Statesmanship for America's Future," remarks delivered at The Claremont Institute's President's Club Meeting, Laguna Beach, California, May 28–30, 1998, at www.claremont.org/kesler8.cfm (Accessed September 26, 2000).

45. Toasts of the President and President de Gaulle at a Dinner at the Elysee Palace in Paris, February 28, 1969, *The Public Papers of the Presidents, Richard Nixon 1969* (Washington, D.C.: Government Printing Office, 1970), 168.

46. Richard M. Nixon, Annual Message to the Congress on the State of the Union, January 22, 1970, *The Public Papers of the Presidents, Richard Nixon 1970* (Washington, D.C.: Government Printing Office, 1971), 10, 15.

47. Daniel Patrick Moynihan, *The Politics of a Guaranteed Income: The Nixon Administration and the Family Assistance Plan* (New York: Vintage, 1973), 447.

48. A. James Reichley, *Conservatives in an Age of Change: The Nixon and Ford Administrations* (Washington, D.C.: Brookings, 1981), 247.

49. For overviews of Nixon's domestic policies, see Joan Hoff, *Nixon Reconsidered* (New York: Basic, 1994); and Melvin Small, *The Presidency of Richard Nixon* (Lawrence, Kans.: University Press of Kansas, 1999).

50. Sidney M. Milkis, *Political Parties and Constitutional Government* (Baltimore: Johns Hopkins University Press, 1999), 74–75.

51. Robert B. Gunnison, "Davis Says He Calls All the Shots; Legislature's Job Is to 'Implement My Vision,'" *San Francisco Chronicle*, July 21, 1999, A1.

52. Michael Barone, "Nixon's America," U.S. News and World Report, September 20, 1999, 21.

53. Pete Wilson, Remarks at Funeral of Former President Richard Nixon, April 27, 1994, at www.ibiblio.org/pub/archives/whitehouse-papers/1994/Apr/1994–04–27-Remarks-by-President-and-Others-at-Nixon-Funeral (Accessed April 12, 2003).

54. Quoted in Richard L. Berke, "Bland but Tough, Gov. Wilson Uses Lessons of Nixon," *New York Times*, July 2, 1994, 1.

55. Wilson, "A Guide to Reagan Country," 39.

56. James S. Fay, ed., *California Almanac*, 6th ed. (Santa Barbara, Calif.: Pacific Data Resources, 1993), 3; U.S. Department of Commerce, Bureau of the Census, "Population Estimates for States by Race and Hispanic Origin: July 1, 1999," at www.census.gov/population/estimates/state/srh/srh99.txt (Accessed April 12, 2003).

57. Exit poll data from Everett Carll Ladd, ed., *America at the Polls 1998* (Storrs, Conn.: Roper Center, 1999), 98.

58. John O'Sullivan, "As Goes California," *National Review*, September 25, 2000, 42.

Ronald Reagan and the Transformation of Modern California

Steven F. Hayward

> Twentieth-century American conservatism has been something of an
> orphan in historical scholarship. . . . [I]t would be hard to argue that the
> American right has received anything like the amount of attention from
> historians that its role in twentieth-century politics and culture suggests it
> should. Given the history of the last twenty years, this is coming to seem
> an ever more curious omission.
>
> —Alan Brinkley[1]

Ronald Reagan remains a misunderstood figure, even by most of his ideological
friends, but especially by his many critics. Reagan's popularity over two terms as
governor of California did little to prepare the Establishment for his eventual
accession to the White House. John P. Roche, a former head of Americans for
Democratic Action, wrote in 1984 that "Reagan's election was thus an 8-plus
earthquake on the political Richter scale, and it sent a number of eminent statesmen—Republican and Democratic—into shock."[2] Most contemporary histories
still treat the conservative movement and its greatest champion as an alien force
in American life. The presumptive right of liberals and liberalism to rule
America lurks beneath the surface of most historical and political writing in our
time. Even authors who affect sympathy and admiration for Reagan, such as
Lou Cannon, nonetheless cannot seem to avoid heavy notes of condescension in
their writing about Reagan and conservatism. This has left a gap in our historical
understanding, which Columbia University historian Alan Brinkley, perhaps the
foremost liberal historian of our time and arguably the heir to Richard Hofs-
tadter, has candidly acknowledged.

   With the arrival of Matthew Dallek's *The Right Moment: Ronald Reagan's First*

Victory and the Decisive Turning Point in American Politics,[3] the gaps in the historical spectrum that Brinkley noted are beginning to be filled. Dallek, a student of Brinkley's at Columbia, writes with considerably more sympathy and respect for Ronald Reagan than did his father, the UCLA historian Robert Dallek, and hence suggests a measure of progress and maturity on the part of liberal scholarship that should be appreciated and praised. It is a welcome sign that liberalism is starting honestly to come to grips with its own failures over the last two generations, and coming to acknowledge the legitimacy of conservatism in the modern American political tradition. Conservative writers, on the other hand, must also reflect deeply and critically on the trajectory of the Reagan phenomenon, and beware the same temptation of triumphalism that led to the undoing of liberalism.

For all of its virtues and fairness, however, Dallek's fine-grained account of Reagan's initial foray into elective politics still occasionally betrays a lingering incomprehension and incredulity that Reagan succeeded. This is exhibited in small and subtle phrases that seem to be the irrepressible nervous tics of the ideological Tourette's syndrome that afflicts liberal writers when they treat conservatives. There is the pervasive use of "right-wing" and "far right," which would be unobjectionable if stylistic symmetry were practiced (i.e., if "left-wing" and "far left" were employed for the coordinate positions on the other end of the ideological spectrum).

This stylistic nervous tic is belied by the understanding Dallek conveys that Reagan, almost single-handedly, transformed political conservatism from a fringe movement into a significant mainstream movement that redefined the political center.[4] At the time of Reagan's arrival on the political scene, conservatism, James Q. Wilson summarized, was "widely regarded as expressing the deviant sentiments of an unimportant minority."[5] (Even many Republicans agreed with this assessment. California's Republican senator Thomas Kuchel in 1965 attacked conservatives as "a fanatical, neo-fascist political cult, overcome by a strange mixture of corrosive hatred and sickening fear."[6])

Still smarting from the disastrous excesses of Joseph McCarthy, the undeserved prominence of the John Birch Society, and the stinging electoral rebuke of Barry Goldwater in 1964, it is understandable why liberals dismissed Reagan as a joke. "We thought the notion was absurd and rubbed our hands in gleeful anticipation of beating this politically inexperienced, right-wing extremist and aging actor," Governor Pat Brown reminisced later. "Like Barry Goldwater," Brown said after Reagan's victory in the June 1966 Republican primary, "he is the spokesman for a harsh philosophy of doom and darkness." *The New Repub-*

lic's TRB column described Reagan as "anti-labor, anti-Negro, anti-intellectual, anti-planning, anti-twentieth century."

The first and most important achievement of Reagan in California is that he served as a "dekooking agent," in the words of *Washington Post* columnist Joseph Kraft, for the conservative wing of the Republican Party.[7] He deliberately kept his distance from the John Birch Society and other groups who would today be regarded as the "black helicopter crowd." In doing so he began to rehabilitate conservative anticommunism from the dark night of the McCarthy backlash. He was able to do this because of the comprehensive breakdown of liberalism that began in the mid-1960s.

Irving Kristol famously remarked that while the American people knew that Joseph McCarthy was against communism, of American liberals they knew no such thing. As liberals responded weakly to the rise in crime, campus disruptions, and racial strife of the 1960s, voters extended their doubts about whether liberals "get it" with regard to social issues as well. It was not simply the failure of established liberalism, and leading liberal politicians such as President Johnson and Governor Brown, to respond vigorously to this turmoil that destroyed their popularity, but the sense that liberalism had brought on these troubles. Liberalism in its Great Society form represented its explicit transition from Progressivism to utopianism (*explicit* because utopianism was always implied in liberalism's Progressive premises). The Great Society didn't just promise to ameliorate poverty and racism; it promised to end them, and quickly. Liberals were surprised and disoriented when things began to go wrong. The result of these events was that, as Pat Moynihan wrote in 1975, "Most liberals had ended the 1960s rather ashamed of the beliefs they had held at the beginning of the decade."[8]

Matthew Dallek finds an early harbinger of the liberal travail to come in the success of Proposition 14 in 1964, a ballot initiative that repealed the Rumford Fair Housing Act, which was very much in the main current of civil rights legislation of the time and the prototype for the federal Fair Housing Act that would pass in Congress a few years later. Liberals were incredulous that California voters would reject such an obviously goodhearted civil rights measure by a 2 million-vote margin, especially as they were simultaneously rejecting the candidacy of Barry Goldwater by a similarly huge margin. The incongruity between these conflicting results generated considerable cognitive dissonance among liberals. California was not Mississippi; although patterns of racial discrimination could be observed in California, the Golden State had experienced neither Jim Crow nor anyone like Bull Connor. The National Urban League had even named Los Angeles as one of the best cities in the nation for blacks to live. When the California Supreme Court overturned Proposition 14 and reinstated the Rumford Act, liberals breathed a sigh of relief, not perceiving that this judicial remedy would be resented as a usurpation of democracy.

What were voters mad about in voting against the Rumford Act? While racial resentment was not insignificant, a larger cause is simply a reasonable fear about the pace of social change. Public resistance to seemingly overreaching laws such as the Rumford Fair Housing Act at the same time the public expressed, to pollsters at least, substantial support for civil rights reflected the public view that liberalism had lost its sense of moderation. Californians were worried about character of their neighborhoods in the face of rapid change—not unlike the public sentiment today against urban sprawl, which, while having unfortunate racial and distributional effects, is not chiefly motivated by race or class resentment. James Q. Wilson wrote of this controversy in 1967: "There have been, I would guess, fewer attacks on Negro families seeking homes in white neighborhoods in Southern California than in, say, Pennsylvania, Ohio, or Illinois. The housing issue was fought out at a more general level—not over whether one was for or against Negroes, but over alternative conceptions of what freedom requires."[9]

As has been observed by numerous writers, the turmoil and resistance to civil rights might have subsided had not urban rioting taken place on such a spectacular scale throughout the nation, starting really with Watts in 1965. The riot stunned liberals, President Johnson and Governor Brown included. President Johnson took it personally, to the point of being distraught. White House aides had trouble reaching Johnson on the phone; the usually prompt Johnson ignored repeated phone calls, and he refused to look at the cables from Los Angeles. "How is it possible, after all we've accomplished?" he asked, doubtless thinking of the Civil Rights and Voting Rights Acts.[10] Yet who can blame young, passionate black leaders, their righteous indignation justly aroused by the civil rights movement, who saw the grandiose promises of the Great Society as a cruel hoax by self-serving white politicians?

Matthew Dallek's book focuses on Governor Brown's confused response to Watts, and therefore misses the broader point. The civil rights movement lost its innocence and moral authority after Watts, and liberalism overreacted by deriving the wrong lessons and indulging in its own guilt. Brown appointed a commission to investigate the riot (Warren Christopher was vice chairman), which concluded that only about 2 percent of people in the Watts area participated in the riot (no more than ten thousand), although social scientists who swarmed to Watts estimated the proportion much higher, perhaps as many as 10 to 15 percent, or well over thirty thousand.[11] Whichever estimate is correct means that it was a small minority participating in the rioting. While no one would suggest that conditions in Watts were good, the severity of the riot came as a surprise in the city that had been regarded as one of the best for blacks in America. A survey of over a thousand arrestees added to the seeming anomaly of the riot: 73 percent of this sample had full-time jobs; half earned between $200 to $400 a month—a near middle-class wage at that time.[12] And the *New York Times* reported a 1966 poll of blacks in Watts that found they were more concerned about "police protection" than "police brutality."[13]

More shocking and consequential than the riot itself was the reaction to the riot. Though riots have been a feature of urban life since the dawn of civilization and had not been rare in America's history, the Watts riot took on an unprecedented political character. Black voices began referring to the riot as a "rebellion," "insurrection," or even "manifesto." A poll of blacks in Watts found 27 percent held a favorable view of the riot, 38 percent thought it helped the Negro cause, and 58 percent expected a favorable outcome. The pollsters concluded that "a riot 'ideology' is developing in the Negro community, an ideology in which riots assume the position of a legitimate and justifiable form of protest."[14] "Riot ideology," urban affairs critic Fred Siegel later observed, became "a racial version of collective bargaining."[15] Burn your neighborhood; get a federal grant. (Indeed, the federal government rushed $18 million to Watts in the first six months after the riot; the Hispanic community in Los Angeles promptly complained that they weren't getting their fair share.) The *right* to riot was born. It would not be long after Watts that the civil rights movement endorsed a $100 billion "Marshall Plan" for American cities. (This, at a time when the total federal budget was still less than $200 billion.) Mainstream reform liberals failed to see how their own words had paved the way for the legitimization of the right to riot. Even President Kennedy had remarked in 1963 that "In too many parts of the country, wrongs are inflicted on Negro citizens for which there are no remedies at law. Unless the Congress acts, their only remedy is in the streets." Bobby Kennedy went further: "There is no point in telling Negroes to obey the law. To many Negroes the law is the enemy."[16]

As had been foreshadowed in the much smaller Harlem riot in the summer of 1964, Watts widened the fissure within the civil rights movement between moderate leaders such as Martin Luther King, who urged nonviolent protest as a means of generating change through the democratic process, and more militant radicals who embraced a violent racial overlay to garden-variety class struggle ideology. Martin Luther King was very coolly received in Watts when he visited a few days after the riot ended. One meeting of more than five hundred people jeered him. "All over America," King exhorted, "the Negroes must join hands."

"And burn!" yelled a heckler. His plea that the crowd treat Los Angeles Mayor Sam Yorty and Police Chief William Parker "with courtesy" brought a roar of laughter.[17] King and other civil rights leaders who flocked to the scene were stunned at the triumphalism that was evident among many rioters. "We won," a young unemployed black man told Bayard Rustin. How? Rustin asked. Homes and businesses have been destroyed, and people were killed. "We won because we made the whole world pay attention to us," the youth replied. (Two years later, a survey found that 92 percent of the small businesses burned during the riot had not reopened.[18])

At the same time that black opinion was facing the pressure of radicalization, liberal guilt among whites began to kick in. Thus began a polarization among white liberals that was nearly as severe as the polarization among blacks. Los Angeles Mayor Sam Yorty, a Democrat, blamed the unrest on the Great Society rhetoric that he thought was unreasonably raising expectations. (Yorty had been one of the prime movers behind a U.S. Conference of Mayors resolution attacking LBJ's ill-considered Community Action Program for fomenting "class struggle."[19]) "It's politicians running around making promises to the people in the ghettoes they can't keep that have created an intolerable situation for the police," Yorty said a year later in a heated exchange with Bobby Kennedy. Even Governor Brown's official commission investigating the riot suggested that a major contributing cause was the failure of the war on poverty "to live up to press notices." Police Chief Parker was more direct, blaming the violence on liberals who "keep telling people they are unfairly treated." President Johnson, who spoke cautiously in the days after the riot, let slip a few days later that more rioting might be expected anywhere "people feel they don't get a fair shake . . . that justice is not open to them."[20] It was just the first in a long line of expressions of liberal sympathy for rioters, the worst being Vice President Hubert Humphrey's incautious comment that if he had been born in a ghetto, he might riot too.

It didn't take long for intellectuals to pick up the cue and begin assigning metaphysical meaning to riots. The approval of the ideology of riot-as-legitimate-protest would eventually start to meld with the growing protest against the Vietnam War, and both were reducible to the razor of "the system." The system that made the Vietnam War possible was also the system responsible for poverty and racism. (The apotheosis of this sentiment was the infamous cover of the *New York Review of Books* in 1967 featuring a diagram of how to make a Molotov cocktail.)

At the remove of thirty-five years it is easy to forget that the Watts riot occurred within a few days of the release of infamous "Moynihan report" on black poverty. In fact, it was Watts that had more to do with the firestorm that enveloped the report than the contents of the report itself. After Watts the media spin on the Moynihan report was that it was the government's explanation of Watts. This infuriated the Left, which saw any attempt to shift the focus from society's injustice as "blaming the victim." *The Nation* magazine, in a widely reprinted article by William Ryan that grossly distorted the report, attacked the Moynihan report as a "smug document" filled with "irresponsible nonsense."

What might have been a manageable debate about a chicken-and-egg style misunderstanding spun out of control. Was black family instability the *cause* of poverty or the *effect* of poverty and racism? The Left emphatically thought the latter, and though Pat Moynihan did not fundamentally disagree (the report had declared, "white America must accept responsibility; it [black poverty and family decay] flows from centuries of oppression and persecution of the Negro man"), the differing emphasis of the two sides in the volatile atmosphere after Watts made calm debate impossible. The irony of the reaction to the Moynihan report is that Moynihan was trying to discredit "color-blind" policy, and hoped to establish policy directed specifically to the problems of black Americans— exactly what his leftist critics would soon demand themselves. But the Left's moral fervor for the wholesale transformation of society ("justice now!") trumps calm discussion of real policies for real problems.

Yet it was not enough for the Left to charge that Moynihan was "blaming the victim." Soon critics began asking: What's wrong with single-parent families anyway? Andrew Young, whom Martin Luther King tapped as his representative to the White House conference on the issue, said that "there probably isn't anything wrong with the Negro family as it exists."[21] The concern with family stability, critics said in a now-familiar refrain, was an attempt to "impose middle-class values" on the poor. In fact, it was asserted, the black female-headed household is "a cultural pattern superior in its vitality to middle-class mores." "College professors," Moynihan observed, "waxed lyrical on the subject of the female-headed household. . . . This is the scholarship of Che Guevara."[22]

A White House conference on black poverty would soon confirm Moynihan's complaint. A planning panel reported out the sense of the delegates that "All families should have the right to evolve in directions of their own choosing . . . and should have the supports—economic and noneconomic—to exercise that right."[23] The conference planners demanded that "the question of 'family stability' be stricken entirely from that agenda." The White House—and liberals— beat a hasty retreat; it would be twenty years before the subject of black family stability could be discussed again, and even then only with great difficulty.

The short span of these few weeks in the summer of 1965 transformed the national debate about poverty and race, and doomed the Great Society. It was only a short step from the just-grievance mentality given fresh life by the riots to the view that government aid is a just entitlement for the oppressed. Henceforth, historian Gareth Davies has written, "references to self-help, equality of opportunity, and reciprocal obligation were conspicuous by their absence."[24] Only the government had any responsibility or obligation—to give money and power to the dispossessed.

Meanwhile, the escalation of rioting and the rhetoric of riot ideology delivered a grievous blow to the civil rights movement. "Until then," Moynihan noted, "theirs had been the aggrieved, the just, the righteous cause." The civil rights movement had prospered because they understood the rule that the first side to resort to violence lost. Every televised beating of a peaceful marcher by a southern sheriff was good for another five points of public approval in the polls. Watts reversed this presumption. The civil rights movement, associated in the public mind, however unfairly, with rioting, began hemorrhaging public support. Martin Luther King and other civil rights moderates were compelled to begin equivocating their views about civil unrest in a desperate attempt to maintain their leadership position among blacks. It didn't work.

This "preposterous and fruitless controversy," as Moynihan called it, left him despondent about the prospect for meaningful social reform. Moynihan came to see that "the liberal Left can be as rigid and destructive as any force in America." A window of opportunity had slammed shut: "The era of white initiatives on behalf of Negroes is over. . . . An era of bad manners is almost certainly begun." Sure enough, public opinion surveys showed that between 1964 and 1966, the number of people who thought that integration efforts were being pushed too fast rose from 28 percent to 52 percent; the numbers first started jumping right after the Watts riot.[25] Moynihan also wrote, with a prescience that would not be vindicated for more than a decade, that "The nation is turning conservative at a time when its serious internal problems may well be more amenable to conservative solutions than to liberal ones."[26] Liberals couldn't see this; Edward Shils once remarked that during the 1960s "Liberals would sooner see their society ruined than learn something valuable to its preservation from conservatism."[27] Historian Ronald Radosh derived an even more discouraging lesson: "Few realized that a new habit within the Left had been born, and would recur, that of willing subordination by white liberals and radicals to the demands and programmatic initiatives of radical blacks."[28]

If the large problems of race and poverty were not damaging enough for liberalism, the simultaneous problem of what may be summarized in a phrase as "the youth movement" represented the other source of liberalism's agony. Just as

Watts presaged the wave of riots that would spread over the nation in the late 1960s, the Free Speech Movement at Berkeley in 1964 presaged the broader currents of student unrest and antiwar protest that disfigured higher education throughout the nation. Just as liberals tended to excuse if not sympathize with black radicals, so too they tended to excuse if not sympathize with all the various manifestations of student protest. In January 1966 *Time* magazine, for example, selected the "under-25 generation" as its "Man of the Year" instead of a single individual. "This is not just a new generation," *Time* wrote, "but a new kind of generation." The youthful penchant for self-indulgence was receiving sanction from a pillar of the Establishment itself: "With his skeptical yet humanistic outlook, his disdain for fanaticism and his scorn for the spurious, the Man of the Year suggests that he will infuse the future with a new sense of morality, a transcendent and contemporary ethic that could infinitely enrich the 'empty society.'"[29] "Indeed it could be argued," *Time* concluded, "that in their independence of material possessions and their emphasis on peacefulness and honesty, hippies lead considerably more virtuous lives than the great majority of their fellow citizens."[30] This is the sort of pretentious nonsense that led Joan Didion to remark caustically that the half-comprehending media "continued to report 'the hippie phenomenon' as an extended panty raid," and constituted "the most remarkable if unwitting, extant evidence that the signals between the generations are irrevocably jammed."[31]

In California, the weak and confused liberal reaction to the initial upheavals of the Free Speech Movement and the Watts riot made liberalism come to resemble Leo Strauss's famous description of Weimar: "the sorry spectacle of justice without the sword or of justice unable to use the sword."[32] It was a simple matter, therefore, for Ronald Reagan to embrace the "law and order" theme more than two full years before Nixon did. "Obey the rules or get out" became Reagan's law and order corollary for campus disorders.

Reagan proved to have more staying power than Nixon on these issues for reasons that are easier to grasp when one examines his reaction to the student movement. Nixon once famously described student protestors as "bums," for which he was widely criticized. Reagan was able to get away with equally blunt language—"cowardly little fascist bands" he called protestors at one point—because of his legendary demeanor and the way he leavened his attacks with his quips. "I had a nightmare last night," Reagan said in his standard after-dinner speech in the late 1960s, "I dreamed I owned a Laundromat in Berkeley." Reagan's public approval ratings with California voters soared to 78 percent at one point in 1969, up sharply from the year before. This was the New Left's gift to Reagan. "Every time he shakes his finger at one of those mobs," a supporter remarked to *Newsweek*, "it gets him 10,000 votes." A Reagan campaign aide told the *New York Times*: "Campus unrest is an issue between Reagan and the people with nobody in between. They understand what he's saying. Reagan is a polarizing politician, much more than Nixon. With Nixon, there are all shades of gray, but that's not the way Reagan operates—he lays it out there."

Lately we have seen the nostalgia for the World War II generation, in such works as *Saving Private Ryan* or Tom Brokaw's *The Greatest Generation*. Neither work would have been conceivable in the hothouse atmosphere of the late 1960s or the desiccated 1970s. Once again Reagan was ahead of his time in displaying a core understanding of the American character that Nixon probably shared in equal measure, but was unable to articulate as fully as Reagan. The simultaneous popular success of Sam Hayakawa in forcefully resisting student protest at San Francisco State is further evidence of the deep strain of public sentiment that Reagan understood and liberals didn't.

Reagan refused to be swayed by the elite approbation of youth culture, or concede any blame for his generation. "The leaders of today's so-called establishment did not have to listen in a classroom lecture or make a field trip to the ghetto to learn about poverty. We lived it in the depths of the Great Depression. The horrors of war are not just a subject for a term paper to a generation that sent it finest young men to fight at Omaha Beach. . . ." Most significantly, Reagan refused to indulge the moral earnestness of the protest Left and its moderate liberal sympathizers. In testimony about campus unrest to the House Committee on Education and Labor in 1969, Reagan attacked the "mythologies" of the

> well-meaning apologists for anti-social behavior . . . who seek to make their excuses acceptable through sheer repetition. . . . To rationalize their permissiveness and appeasement, administrators themselves often promote myths which confuse those both on campus and off. They speak disparagingly of a "generation gap" at a time when too many parents are in awe of, and tend to imitate, their own children. They speak of a "new breed with wisdom and conscience" at a time when research has clearly indicated a social and emotional immaturity of youth to a degree previously unknown.[33]

If there was a "generation gap," it was entirely the fault of the younger generation. To the contrary, Reagan asserted:

> We have been picked at, sworn at, rioted against and downgraded until we have a built-in guilt complex, and this has been compounded by the accusations of our sons and daughters who pride themselves on "telling it like it is." Well, I have news

for them—in a thousand social science courses they have been informed "the way it is not." . . . As for our generation I will make no apology. No people in all history paid a higher price for freedom. And no people have done so much to advance the dignity of man. . . . We are called materialistic. Maybe so. . . . But our materialism has made our children the biggest, tallest, most handsome and intelligent generation of Americans yet. They will live longer with fewer illnesses, learn more, see more of the world, and have more successes and realizing their personal dreams and ambitions than any other people in any other period of our history—because of our "materialism."

"Those who want to get an education, those who want to teach," Reagan said in a 1969 press conference, "should be protected in that at the point of a bayonet if necessary." So it was not surprising that when the "People's Park" protest broke out at Berkeley in 1969, Reagan not only called out the National Guard immediately, but also sanctioned the first-ever air raid on a college campus; three helicopters were dispatched to drop tear gas.

Reagan naturally attracted fierce criticism for his blunt rhetoric and stern action. The *Los Angeles Times* called him "anti-intellectual," and the cochairman of the California Democratic Party said that Reagan's response "has been so oppressive and so indiscriminate in its application that he has done enormous damage to the colleges and universities of this state." Reagan arguably went too far on one occasion. Answering a question about New Left campus tactics before a meeting of the California Council of Growers in Yosemite in April 1970, Reagan said: "If it takes a bloodbath, let's get it over with. No more appeasement." Liberals howled with indignation. Assembly speaker Jesse Unruh, Reagan's opponent for reelection that fall, said that Reagan "had forfeited any right to hold public office." Others complained that Reagan was actually inciting violence on campus. Even Reagan's stalwart friends at *National Review* worried that "the potential for political disaster here is huge." But Reagan backed and filled and clarified as only he could do, and the storm blew over.

Two closely related questions remained to be answered: Why was Reagan so far ahead of his time, and why did the conservative political renaissance begin in California?

What happened to Reagan ideologically in the 1950s would happen to countless liberal intellectuals in the 1970s. Reagan could be considered the first "neoconservative," which Irving Kristol, the ex-Trotskyite, famously defined as "a liberal mugged by reality." Reagan's detractors assumed that someone—his second wife Nancy, perhaps—had talked him out of his liberalism. Reagan himself explained it in 1976: "Eventually what happened to me was, because I did my own speeches and did the research for them, I just woke up to the realization one day that I had been going out and helping to elect the people who had been causing the things I had been criticizing. So it wasn't any case of some mentor coming in and talking me out of it. I did it in my own speeches."[34] This was much the same formula for the wave of conversions to conservatism in the 1970s and 1980s. But how did Reagan come to see all by himself so much earlier than anyone else that liberalism's lack of a limiting principle would be its undoing, especially since the most severe derelictions of liberalism lay in the future?

Most people, including Reagan's own partisans, are content to leave this among the mysteries and complexities of the man. Yet the unfashionable case must be made that Reagan had a deeper intellect than anyone, even his admirers, have been willing to perceive or admit. Reagan was the first national political figure since Calvin Coolidge to make a frontal assault on the esoteric premises of the administrative state. Reagan anticipated the public distrust of the federal government years before it became obvious, and he understood instinctively the reasons why it would happen. In 1968, Reagan observed in a speech in New York:

> At the moment there appears to be a panic fear afloat in the air, partly due to a feeling that government is now a separate force beyond the people's control, that their voices echo unheeded in the vast and multitudinous halls of government. I do not remember a time when so many Americans, regardless of their economic and social standing, have been so suspicious and apprehensive of the aims, the credibility, and the competence of the Federal establishment.

At the time Reagan said this, it was not widely true. Polls at that time still showed that while public trust in government was rapidly eroding, a majority of people still expressed confidence in government. (Today the number of people expressing confidence in the federal government is 20 percent or less, down from about 70 percent in the early 1960s.) To Reagan it was "obvious" that "the sophisticated approach of seeking complicated answers by government to complicated problems isn't necessarily the best approach." Reagan saw the thread of administrative expertise running through foreign policy as well. The prosecution of the Vietnam War offered an important object lesson for Reagan: "The fetish of complexity, the trick of making hard decisions harder to make—the art, finally, of rationalizing the nondecision, have made a ruin of American foreign policy." "For many years now," Reagan said in his first inaugural address as governor, "you and I have been shushed like children and told there are no simple answers to complex problems which are beyond our comprehension.

Well, the truth is, there are simple answers—but there are no easy ones." In a subsequent speech in mid-1967, Reagan adumbrated the point even more directly: "I think we have had enough of nineteenth-century rule of the many by the few, even if the few are supposed to be some kind of intellectual elite, who are more gifted than the rest of us." This attack on the premises of the Progressive administrative state is what made Reagan's particular brand of conservatism so significant.

Just as Reagan was ahead of his time, trends in California presaged the political trajectory of the country over the coming decade, making it nearly inevitable that the same social and political trends that brought Reagan to the governor's mansion in Sacramento would take him to the White House. The best analysis of this remains James Q. Wilson's 1967 *Commentary* magazine article, "A Guide to Reagan Country: The Political Culture of Southern California." More than ten years ago, after Wilson had returned to California after more than three decades in the east, I asked him about the genesis of the article, and he said he proposed to Norman Podhoretz to write an article explaining how it was that California, where Democrats outnumbered Republicans by more than a million voters at the time, could possibly have elected Ronald Reagan as its governor by nearly a million votes. "You're not going to endorse Reagan," Podhoretz asked Wilson with some alarm. Surely not, Wilson reassured him. Wilson hastened to reassure *Commentary*'s readers as well: "I left [California] a long time ago to acquire some expensive Eastern postgraduate degrees and a political outlook that would now make me vote against Reagan if I had the chance. I do not intend here to write an apology for Reagan; even if I thought like that, which I don't, I would never write it down where my colleagues at Harvard might read it."

Southern California was different from the rest of the country, Wilson observed, because of the kind of people who settled there in large numbers in the middle part of the twentieth century, and the kind of business and political culture they established. Southern California was the political center of gravity in the state because migrants to southern California outnumbered migrants to northern California by nearly 10 to 1. Many of these migrants were from the Midwest and the border states, and they were the advance guard for the wave of suburbanization that swept the nation in the postwar years. "They brought an essential ingredient of Southern California life," Wilson observed, "fundamentalist Protestant individualism." This individualism manifested itself several ways. The Western lifestyle, Wilson observed, "produced a feeling of *property*" (whereas the eastern lifestyle produced a feeling of *territory*). Economically individualism expressed itself in an efflorescence of small business entrepreneurialism. This condition would come to characterize the national economy over the next twenty years, but in the mid-1960s this represented yet another liberal mis-perception of reality. Orthodox liberal political economy of the Kennedy-Johnson years depreciated entrepreneurialism, going so far as to regard the entre-preneur as an obsolete or anachronistic figure in American life, and therefore the small business entrepreneurial sector of the economy as insignificant. Economic growth would henceforth come from a combination of Keynesian fiscal policy and the efforts of giant corporations in the basic large industries.

Prior to the mid-1960s liberal governance in California accommodated the social and economic manifestations of individualism. "The purpose of [Califor-nia] government," Wilson wrote, "was to facilitate this kind of growth—open up new land, bring in water, make credit easy, keep the defense plants rolling." In his early years Governor Pat Brown was the epitome of this kind of govern-ment, spending nearly 20 percent of the state budget for massive public works such as roads, water projects, and university campuses. California has not built on such a scale since then, even though its population has nearly tripled.

"Why, then," Wilson asked, "are [southern Californians] so discontent? It is not with their lot that they are discontent, it is with the lot of the nation. *The very virtues they have and practice are, in their eyes, conspicuously absent from society as a whole*" (emphasis in original). In this Wilson discerned the rise of "social issues" as the central axis of American politics over the succeeding generation. In a passage that reads ironically today from the same author who would go on to write *The Moral Sense*, Wilson observed:

> Surveys I have taken, and others I have read, indicate that the single most wide-spread concern of middle-class Americans is over the "decline of values"—evidenced by "crime in the streets," juvenile delinquency, public lewdness, and the like, but going much beyond these manifestations to include everything that sug-gests that people no longer act in accordance with decent values and right reason. In many places, especially the Northeast, our political institutions (happily) do not allow such views to play much part in elections. Parties, led by professionals, instinctively shun such issues, feeling somehow that public debate over virtue is irrelevant (what can government do about it?) and dangerous (nobody can agree on what virtue is or that your party has more of it).[35]

That same year Wilson wrote this, Moynihan concurred that "Family is not a subject Americans tend to consider appropriate as an area of public policy."[36] "Our system of government cannot handle matters of that sort," Wilson ended his essay, "and it may be torn apart by the process."

Wilson concluded that "the political culture of Southern California will never be *the* political culture of our society." But it arguably was the dominant political culture of the nation in the 1980s, for reasons that Wilson recognized in the middle of his essay:

> Is Southern California's political culture unique? Not really—it is but the earliest, most publicized, and most heavily populated example of a pattern now found throughout much of the Southwest. It appeared first in Southern California because more people went there and because California's political institutions gave almost immediate expression to it. . . . The Southern California political style is spreading; it seems to be, at least in the Western part of the United States, the concomitant of the American success story.[37]

In other words, Wilson had foreseen the suburban "sunbelt" phenomenon, but had underestimated its full potential. Everyone thinks Kevin Phillips came up with the idea in *The Emerging Republican Majority* in 1969, but Wilson was here first.

What now are we to make of the Wilson thesis and the initial Reagan phenomenon nearly thirty-five years later? Wilson offered the clue in his essay: "If I had to cite only one way in which Southwestern politics differ from Northeastern politics, it would be this: the former region is developmental, future-oriented, and growth-conscious; the latter is conserving [as distinct from conservative], past- or present-oriented, and security conscious. . . . A conserver . . . needs *more* government in order to protect present stakes from change, from threats posed by other groups, and from competition."

Today I venture to say California has become, largely on account of its economic success (it may pass Great Britain before the end of the year to become the world's fifth largest economy), more "northeastern" in its outlook. We no longer demand that government "open up new land" and facilitate rapid growth, as can be seen not simply by the deep antisprawl sentiment but by the wider salience of "quality of life" issues that generally incline toward preserving the status quo rather than promoting change and expanding opportunity. In 1909 Lord James Bryce gave a speech at Berkeley in which he posed the challenge:

> What will happen when California is filled by fifty millions of people, and its valuation is five times what it is now, and the wealth will be so great that you will find it difficult to know what to do with it? The day will, after all, have only twenty-four hours. Each man will have only one mouth, one pair of ears, and one pair of eyes. There will be more people—as many perhaps as the country can support—

and the real question will be not about making more wealth or having more people, but whether the people will then be happier or better.

The day of 50 million Californians is in sight, which is one reason why the "quality of life" issue Bryce raised has now come to center stage in California.[38]

Today it is Texas, and not California, that most closely embodies the political culture of 1960s California, which gives the 2000 presidential contest a dimension that has been largely unappreciated in the media analysis of the campaign. Texas remains hell-bent for growth (outside of Austin, there is little controversy over sprawl, in the state with the second-fastest growing population in the nation), and the political culture there keeps state government well in check. In 1966, Ronald Reagan and California represented the leading edge of the way America was going. The question in the election of 2000 is whether President George W. Bush and Texas still represent the future, or the last remnant of what Ronald Reagan began in 1966.

NOTES

1. Alan Brinkley, *Liberalism and Its Discontents* (Cambridge, Mass.: Harvard University Press, 1998), 277.
2. John P. Roche, "The Passing of the Class of 1941," *National Review*, October 19, 1984, 26.
3. Matthew Dallek, *The Right Moment: Ronald Reagan's First Victory and the Decisive Turning Point in American Politics* (New York: Free Press, 2000).
4. William F. Buckley Jr.'s *National Review* was reforming *intellectual* conservatism, a necessary prelude to rehabilitating *political* conservatism, but the latter could not take place without an actual political figure leading an electoral movement.
5. James Q. Wilson, "Reagan and the Republican Revival," *Commentary*, October 1980, 25.
6. *National Review*, October 5, 1965, 892.
7. *National Review*, December 26, 1967, 1415.
8. *A Dangerous Place*, 24.
9. James Q. Wilson, "A Guide to Reagan County," *Commentary*, May 1967, 44.
10. Robert Dallek, *Flawed Giant: Lyndon Johnson and his Times, 1961–1973* (New York: Oxford University Press, 1998). 223.
11. David O. Sears and John B. McConahay, "Riot Participation," in *The Los Angeles Riots: A Socio-Psychological Study*, ed. Nathan Cohen (New York: Praeger, 1970), 259–60.
12. *National Review*, November 29, 1966, 1199.
13. Tom Bray, "Reading America the Riot Act," *Policy Review*, Winter 1988, 34.

14. T. M. Tomlinson and David O. Sears, "Negro Attitudes toward the Riot," in *The Los Angeles Riots: A Socio-Psychological Study*, ed. Nathan Cohen (New York: Praeger, 1970), 288–96.

15. *The Future Once Happened Here.*

16. *National Review*, April 23, 1968, 379.

17. Gerald Horne, *Fire This Time: The Watts Uprising and the 1960s* (Charlottesville: University of Virginia Press, 1995), 183.

18. *National Review*, August 8, 1967, 874.

19. *National Review*, September 6, 1966.

20. Gareth Davies, *From Opportunity to Entitlement: The Transformation and Decline of Great Society Liberalism* (Lawrence: University Press of Kansas, 1996), 79.

21. Davies, *From Opportunity to Entitlement*, 96.

22. Moynihan, "The President & the Negro," 40, 42.

23. Davies, *From Opportunity to Entitlement*, 96.

24. Davies, *From Opportunity to Entitlement*, 97.

25. Thernstroms, 175.

26. Moynihan, "The President & the Negro," 44.

27. Edward Shills, "Totalitarians and Antinomians," in *Political Passages*, ed. John Bunzell (New York: Free Press, 1988), 31.

28. Ronald Radosh, *Divided They Fell*, 48–49.

29. *Time*, January 6, 1996, 23.

30. *Time*, July 7, 1967, 22.

31. Joan Didion, *Slouching toward Bethlehem*, 121–122.

32. Leo Strauss, *Spinoza's Critique of Religion* (New York: Schocken,1965), 1.

33. Testimony before Subcommittee on Education of the Committee on Education and Labor of the U.S. House of Representatives, Washington, D.C., March 19, 1969.

34. Witcover and Cohen, "Where's the Rest of Ronald Reagan?" *Esquire*, March 1976, 92.

35. James Q. Wilson, "A Guide to Reagan Country: The Political Culture of Southern California," *Commentary*, May 1967, 45.

36. Moynihan, "The President & the Negro," 35.

37. Page 44.

38. Large numbers like "50 million people" sound daunting, but need to be kept in perspective. While California is already the most populous state, only about 5 percent of the state's total land area is urbanized. This means that *95 percent of California's land is open space of some kind*. Even at 50 million people in the year 2030, California is still likely to be less developed than most Atlantic seaboard states today. New Jersey, for example, is 32 percent urbanized; if California had the same net population density as New Jersey, California would have a current population of 170 million.

V

POLICIES AND PERSPECTIVES

Affirmative Action and Proposition 209

Ward Connerly

> The state shall not discriminate against or grant preferential treatment to any individual or group on the basis of race, sex, color, ethnicity or national background in the operation of public education, public employment or public contracting.

IN THE BEGINNING . . .

When I arrived to serve as a member of the University of California Board of Regents in March 1993, affirmative action and using race, gender, and ethnicity to build diversity were concepts that went unchallenged in the hallowed halls of the academy. Although most Americans clearly understood that the application of different standards to different individuals on the basis of their race, color, gender, ethnicity, or national ancestry constituted acts of discrimination, in the world of higher education such was not the case.

In the world in which the academic resided, in 1993, differential standards were not only tolerated, they were expected—to ensure that underrepresented minorities were adequately represented in the student body, the faculty, the administration and the supply of vendors used by the university. In short, diversity was a legitimate excuse to discriminate with the blessings and protection of the university and the quiet acquiescence of the public. That all changed on July 20, 1995, when the Regents approved resolutions that I had drafted and sponsored to end the consideration of race and related characteristics in all activities of the University of California (UC).

While I was engaged in what I viewed as a fiduciary duty to end what I had begun to call "race preferences" at the UC, a similar effort was being mobilized by Glynn Custred and Tom Wood—two individuals associated with the California Association of Scholars—to prohibit discrimination and preferential treatment on a statewide basis. Although on a somewhat parallel track, the efforts of Custred and Wood and mine were totally independent of each other. Nonetheless, it did not require an act of great insight for them and Larry Arnn, chairman of the California Civil Rights Initiative (CCRI), to conclude that because I had succeeded in banning preferences at UC, perhaps my services could be enlisted to aid in their mission as well. Thus, an all-out blitz was initiated to procure my involvement in the campaign to qualify CCRI for the ballot and to bring about its passage.

If there was one thing I had learned during my eight-month tour of duty to end preferences in the foxholes of diversity at UC, it was that the intersection of race and politics is a very treacherous one and should be avoided lest one become road kill at that intersection. This was one of the reasons why I rejected several entreaties to assume a role in the CCRI campaign. The second reason was that I suspected that the color of my skin was not an inconsequential factor in the desire to bring me onboard the noble ship of equality whose occupants were almost exclusively white males. Obviously, it would be decidedly more difficult to assign motives of racism to an initiative headed by a "minority" than one being steered by three white guys. Such is the crass calculation that some had to make: to increase the chances of getting an initiative passed that would take California a major step forward toward a "color-blind" government, color consciousness in the selection of the public face of the initiative was a factor. No amount of denials of this reality would be persuasive to me.

Although no one ever even hinted to me that such a factor was part of the equation—probably because they knew that it would guarantee my outright and unequivocal rejection—I consider myself a reasonably savvy student of politics and the knowledge that I would give CCRI a powerful shot of inoculation against charges of racism did not escape me.

DECIDING TO DO THE RIGHT THING

My reticence to get involved in a campaign that had such moral clarity at its core is suggestive of the reason why race preferences have survived for as long as they have. "Whites" do not want to be perceived as racists and "minorities," especially "blacks," do not want to be subjected to charges of race treason, "sell-out," "Uncle Tom," and similar terms of indictment of one's character. Thus, bad public policy flourishes from the nutrients of political correctness, fear, and intimidation. Based on my experience with the issue to that point, I thought that Arnn, Custred, and Wood either had to be some of the most naive individuals on the planet, or some of the most courageous. The latter came to be my sentiment.

As a college student, I was involved in a project that I considered important but which did not enjoy the support of the college administration. When I consulted one of my favorite professors with the question of whether I should abandon the project or proceed despite the objection of the college administration, Dr. Robert Thompson urged me to consult my "knower" for guidance.

"What's that," I asked?

"Your heart, your conscience, your gut, your *knower*," he responded. He said that there are times in life when logic and our power of analytical reasoning fail us and we are left to rely upon our "knower" to give us direction.

Without knowing it, Larry Arnn, with his charming Southern drawl, guided me to my knower when he came to visit me in the summer of 1996. Arnn was president of the Claremont Institute and Chairman of CCRI. During lunch at a popular watering hole in Sacramento, Arnn made the case that the Declaration of Independence represented a vision of our nation's founders that could only be made real if people of conviction accepted the challenge to breathe life into that Declaration.

With moral clarity seeping out of every pore of his body and every word that he uttered, Arnn brought back the ghosts of Lincoln, Jefferson, Madison, King—and God knows who else—but all heroes mine, to make the case for my involvement. Although I maintained my decision not to get involved, my "knower" was now fully engaged and it was telling me that Arnn was right. More importantly, it was reassuring me that Arnn, Custred, Wood, Arnie Steinberg, Richard Ferrier, Gail Heriot, Manny Klausner, Ken Masugi, and others whose names had been mentioned to me in connection with CCRI, were motivated by principle.

This collection of ideologues had no personal stake in "affirmative action." They simply saw a policy that had morphed into something that was very wrong and they wanted to change it. Every CCRI representative that I met seemed to be guided by a powerful sense of wanting to do what was right for the country. Virtually all of them had read the *Federalist Papers* and could quote figures of history to make the case against preferences based on race, gender, and ethnicity. As one who had spent months in the trenches at UC doing battle with those who often seemed unaware that the United States even had a Constitution, let alone any sense of obligation to honor it, I found Arnn and these other individuals to be refreshingly principled. They gave me a powerful sense of comfort that what I had accomplished as a Regent was widely approved by a large segment of California.

After my meeting with Arnn, I was haunted by his words. They caused me to question my own character. How could I know that something was wrong, such as race preferences, and decline the opportunity to contribute to end them for fear of what might happen to my business, my reputation, or even my life? What if those who came before me—King, Rosa Parks, Lincoln—had been guided by the same factor of cowardice that threatened to immobilize my own sense of right and wrong? If they had yielded to fear, America would be a far different place than it is, and my life would be infinitely worse. Arnn summoned the "better angels" of my nature—my knower—and in the end I answered the call.

The personal decision-making process that led to my decision to chair CCRI (which had become Proposition 209 by the time I accepted that responsibility) is one that President John F. Kennedy asked every American citizen to ask of himself or herself: "Ask not what your country can do for you; ask what you can do for your country."

America is an idea that only becomes real when the ideals that define it are given life. Ideals like freedom and equality are hollow, empty rhetoric unless ordinary citizens are prepared to accept extraordinary burdens to make these ideals real. It was this thought, triggered by my "knower," that compelled me to become involved with Proposition 209.

Once I decided to get involved, the question that remained was, at what level? Because I was convinced that win or lose, 209 would forever change my life— even more radically than had been the case as a result of my actions at UC—I made being the chairman of 209 a nonnegotiable prerequisite. If I was going to suffer insults (and possibly even worse), then let it be under conditions over which I had control. Thus, when I became chair of 209, I became the undisputed face of the initiative, its primary spokesperson, its chief fund-raiser, and the person responsible for every detail that I thought to be of sufficient importance to warrant my attention.

TAKING THE SKELETON OUT
OF THE CLOSET

The path that I traveled in arriving at the decision to chair the CCRI 209 campaign is a valuable lesson about race in America and why, despite our enormous national progress in improving what we call race relations in our nation, so many problems with racial implications remain unsolved. Americans are reluctant to talk openly and honestly about race, afraid to place their convictions on the table for the public to digest, afraid to be thought of as racists or sellouts, afraid of not being liked, afraid to contest those with whom they disagree. Fear of change allows the status quo to prevail in nearly all areas of public policy. But, with regard to race, fear and its many manifestations are overwhelming and ultimately destructive of any desire to seriously explore issues relating to this topic.

In a democratic society, it is not supposed to be this way. Free people should not be afraid to bring their ideas to the marketplace and subject them to vigorous scrutiny—and let the best idea win. This is how national consensus is supposed to be reached on any policy issue. While there are many public policy issues where this expectation is the theory, but far from the rule, in no other arena has democracy failed so miserably than in the arena where race is the topic.

Affirmative action, initially intended to be temporary, has consistently received a renewal of its lease on life by being clothed in misleading language, false characterizations of its benefits and liabilities, and the smothering fear that its proponents will politically crush anyone who dares to challenge it.

More than anything else, the significance of Proposition 209 is that it represented the first time in America that the public would be provided with a forum to discuss affirmative action, and at the end of the discussion they would be allowed to vote yes or no in the privacy of the voting booth. Until 209, affirmative action was a policy that affected every American citizen, was opposed by a substantial number of them, but was beyond the reach of those who opposed it. Presidential executive orders and court decisions had created a Frankenstein for which there was no political prescription for discussing it, let alone killing it.

THE IMPORTANCE OF LANGUAGE

Although I am often referred to as the "father of 209" or the "author of 209," I always try to correct the record by making it clear that 209 was the brainchild of Custred and Wood. When I accepted the chairmanship, I accepted what many thought was a lose-lose situation. My very good and longtime friend, Bob White, chief of staff to then-Governor Pete Wilson, urged me to stay out of the campaign. "If it loses, you and the governor (because you are so closely aligned with him) will be blamed. If it wins, you will be despised by the forces of political correctness. You can't win."

Indeed, although the 209 campaign had a lot of baggage, not the least of which was an organization that was in financial ruins, there *was* one thing that Custred and Wood bequeathed to me that represented bulletproof armor against attack and a silver bullet for our offense: the wording of 209. The thirty-seven words of 209 were powerful in their simplicity and articulated a value already universally accepted in American life: fairness.

The centerpiece of our strategy for securing the passage of 209 was a page from the playbook of Dr. Martin Luther King Jr. Dr. King did not set out to convince America that to change its behavior toward black people required new ground to be plowed and a new policy to be forged. Instead, he often invoked the Declaration of Independence and, in doing so, he essentially said to America: You say that equality is what you believe in, "now live out the true meaning of your creed." I decided that our task was similar to that of the original civil rights movement and that a similar strategy ought to be employed. In our case, the Civil Rights Act of 1964 guaranteed that all Americans would be treated equally by their government *without regard* to race, color, or creed. Our task was to remind the people of California of that fact and to demonstrate that "affirmative action" had become something that violated the 1964 Civil Rights Act and our dedication to fairness.

So, we took the compelling language that we had inherited from the founders of 209—Custred and Wood—and we charted a course, using that language, to explain how current policies and practices betrayed America's creed of equality and fairness. To succeed, we had to remove the moral fig leaf behind which affirmative action hid. Thus, affirmative action had to be repackaged as what it had truly become: a regime of "race preferences." In the minds of the public, the two had to become synonymous, although they need not be. Our opposition cooperated fully with our strategy. By resorting to extreme representations of what would happen with the passage of 209, its critics, including Colin Powell, contended that "all affirmative action would end" if 209 passed. They reinforced our message that 209 was, indeed, about race preferences, often masquerading as affirmative action.

To be certain, 209 passed because of its brilliantly conceived language and our success in putting a new label on the container of affirmative action to honestly disclose that its contents had become a blatant system of race preferences. In real estate, they say that the three most important considerations are "location, location, location." For 209—as it is with all debates about affirmative action, diversity, inclusion, and equal opportunity—the three most important considerations are "language, language, language."

THE POLITICS OF RACE

No return to the campaign of 209 would be a complete journey without appropriate attention being given to its opponents. For them, no tactic was too dirty, no lie too big, no claim too preposterous. Opponents of 209 used images of burning crosses and the Ku Klux Klan in their television ads; recruited David Duke, a former (and possibly current) white supremacist, to argue the pro-209 position in a university-sponsored debate; claimed that 209 would return women to the days before they had the right to vote; asserted that the passage of 209 would "resegregate" the university (and this statement was made by former President William Clinton); and resorted to personal attacks as a standard operating procedure.

Two facts became clear to me at the outset. First, those who defended race preferences were not doing so because of any moral imperative. They were guided by politics and saw the issue as a battle between "people of color," with women thrown in for good measure, and white males. In their narrow world, this was a classic case of good versus evil, equal opportunity and equity versus white privilege and leveling the playing field and no amount of logic or facts or appeal to reason and constitutional principles would influence them. They simply had to be defeated by the power of the electorate, not converted by futile appeals to their sense of right and wrong.

Second, no matter what the outcome of the vote, the issue of affirmative action was not going to die with the 209 election. Like the odor of a dead skunk on the side of the road, affirmative action would waffle through the air for many miles after the carcass had passed. Such is the nature of race in our beloved country. Proposition 209 represented yet another, but highly significant, milestone in America's quest to achieve a society in which the color of one's skin, the origin of one's grandparents, and other such traits would have no currency in American life.

The very personal lesson of 209, for me, is that when one is confronted with what appears to be an unpopular moral mission, one must put his faith in the hands of history and never cease to believe that in the fullness of time history will be kind and vindicating. This is a fundamental lesson of leadership that applies in every area of human endeavor. Those who seek to influence public policy must always be guided by the view that we live not for ourselves but for history. Our constituents and those who will judge the wisdom of what we have wrought are not yet born.

If I had not adopted such an attitude, I would have been constantly overwhelmed by self-doubt as to whether the possible benefits of my efforts were worth all of the negatives that were coming my way. Few public policy issues require such introspection more than race. Throughout American history, the full effects of the sacrifices made to accomplish progress with respect to issues relating to race are not realized until long after the activists promoting various changes have passed. Proposition 209 will be judged by the same yardstick of time.

Western Justice: John Ford and Sam Peckinpah on the Defense of the Heroic

John Marini

The motion picture has become the most influential and compelling form of mass entertainment ever created. It combines art and technology in a way that appears to defy the laws of nature as well as commonsense. In the movies, the apparent seem to be real. Once under its spell, the real, itself, can become the apparent. California gave birth to the American cinema, and for more than a half century, it was home of the most distinctive form of American entertainment: the Hollywood Western. Perhaps no American art form attained greater worldwide popularity than the Western.

Like California itself, the movies have become the progenitor of myth and illusion. The hold they exert over public perceptions of reality has made it increasingly difficult to distinguish reality from the celluloid version of it. California was the real home of the make-believe Western, though it was not, strictly speaking, a part of the Old West. The great Western novelist, Wallace Stegner, was right when he noted that "California is west of the West."[1] California was only a dream, especially, for those who lived in the West. The cowboy was always *going to* California, but he never seemed to make it there.

The Old West, celebrated in the movies, existed somewhere between the civilized East, and the oasis, the garden, of California. It was situated in the godforsaken wilds of the desert or the wilderness—without community, without law, without civilization. It was a place where simple survival was difficult, a place where nature was uncompromising, just as society had been uncompromising in the places they had left. The West offered the possibility of a new beginning, of refounding, of establishing governments from reflection and choice, rather than mishaps of birth and tradition. In the West, it was thought, they had it in their power to make the world over again. But the Western movie showed that even in a new land, the law was not easily established on principles of justice and the common good. More often, as Alexander Hamilton had lamented, government was a product of accident and force.[2]

Even so, in the process of showing the coming into being of community—the establishment of civil society—the Western confronted the fundamental questions of politics. It attempted to examine the distinction between nature and convention, law and justice, the individual and the community. It sought to establish the meaning of genuine freedom, and the obligations of equality. In raising those questions, the Western movie brought to light the moral virtues necessary in every kind of political association. It probed the deepest tension in modern political thought: that expressed in the disagreement between John Locke and Jean Jacques Rousseau on the nature of the just society. The differences between Locke and Rousseau are made apparent in conflicting conceptions of the virtues of civil society, with its emphasis on rights and property, as opposed to the natural state, where man is born free, uncorrupted, and without private property. It is law and society, or civilization itself, according to Rousseau, which deprived man of his natural liberty and robbed him of his individual goodness. The coming into being of social man required the imposition of law and morality as the condition of freedom within community. Nonetheless, for Rousseau, every civil society is itself a kind of bondage.

The Western movie provided the opportunity to participate in the establishment, or foundation, of the political order. In re-creating the conditions of man in his origins, civilized man is once again confronted with a natural environment. In the attempt to create a political community, it was necessary to raise the question of the importance of the establishment of private property, and law, as that which provided the ground of freedom. But the state of nature also presented the beguiling possibility, given a philosophic defense by Rousseau, that freedom is the absence of all restraint, including that of law itself. The Western could portray the struggle between those human beings who retained the closest connection to the condition of man in the state of nature, and those who had come to understand the meaning of private property and law. It pitted the Indian (who was born free and had not put himself in chains) against the enslaving forces of society and civilization. The result was the portrayal of a noble savage, engaged in a confrontation with civilization and its technology, who would become the defender of a kind of presocial state of natural freedom.

The Western, therefore, could raise the question concerning the supposed virtues of progress, and the forces—perhaps more virtuous—opposed to it. It did not take the superiority of civilization for granted. The law, and civilization, too, had to justify itself in an almost philosophic way. It is for this reason that the appeal of the Western was a universal, not just an American, phenomenon. When the Western movies grappled with universal questions, it attained a level of influence and popularity, worldwide, which no other American artistic form, excepting perhaps music, could rival. Only when the Western lost sight of the universal problems, and the dilemmas posed by them, and attempted to understand the past in light of contemporary prejudices, as it did after the 1970s, did it lose its appeal.

THE WESTERN AS POETRY

The American Western was an artistic response to the intellectual triumph of Progressivism. By the time film arrived, the historian had ceased to celebrate the past in a way that was socially meaningful. The Western movie was intended to fill a gap created by the abandonment of the heroic understanding of the past, by those who interpreted it.[3] The professional interpreters of the past, historians, social scientists, were increasingly technicians who were incapable of understanding the fullness of the past. More important, they could not appreciate its greatness. Their method required the abandonment of passion, enthusiasm, or love for the past. It was not surprising, therefore, that professionals began to denigrate the past, and to celebrate the future, or the promise of the future. The historians, the civics teachers, had become devotees of a new scientific method that promised mastery of nature, and control of man as well. It sought to tame man, and reshape his environment by subordinating man and nature to the technical rationality of science. It did so in a manner reminiscent of the great political thinkers, like Hegel, who had purportedly understood, and therefore rationalized, the past. At the point at which man came to understand the rationality of history, he had become fully knowledgeable. Therefore he had nothing of significance to learn from the past.

The professional observer of society attempted to rationalize the present by constantly reinterpreting the past. But understanding of the past was made intelligible only with reference to the *future*, or the idea of *progress*. In the view of the historian or the social scientist, the virtues of the founders and the fathers were understood to be simply their values, or myths—prejudices of a less enlightened time. Consequently, these professionals could no longer speak simply of virtue or of vice. Rather, they spoke of *socially acceptable* behavior in the context of its time. And political scientists lost sight of the meaning of *justice*, which became simply a subjective value—the preferences of a given community. The new social scientists spoke meaningfully only about the empirical world, of facts beyond dispute, which are understood within the methodology of science. The dominance of Progressivism, and the growing authority of the social sciences in interpreting man and society, made it nearly impossible to understand human virtue and vice. And as a consequence, the notion of human greatness fell from sight.

The Western sought to address this problem of human greatness, and necessarily, of human depravity, by reexamining the old virtues. The Western looked at individual human beings in terms of such things as courage, nobility, moderation, and honor. Of course, the vices associated with them—cowardice, ignobility, intemperance, and dishonor—had to be elucidated as well. Progressivism looked to a glorious future, but the implicit premise of the Western was that our fathers were better than we are.[4] The Western attempted to recreate the heroic virtues of the founders; our ancestors. The historian and the civics teacher could no longer do this, but unlike the social scientist, the artist was able to understand the past, because the artist could not sever his own connection with it. The greatest directors of Western movies incorporated the experiences of the past in a way that recognized the necessity of confronting the heights and depths of human behavior. In the process, they exposed the virtues and vices associated with the human experience. It became possible, perhaps even necessary, in the Western movie, to celebrate human greatness, and to confront its opposite.

John Ford and Sam Peckinpah grew up in a time and place in which the heroic past still lived. Ford's father had planned to leave Ireland and join his four brothers, who came to fight in the American Civil War. He arrived too late to fight, but two of Ford's uncles fought on the side of the North, one for the South, and the other apparently collected pensions from both sides. In Ford's movies, although he typically sides with the North, he treats the Southern soldier, as he did the Indian, with great respect. He celebrated the heroic actions of the fighting man. In the hands of John Ford, the virtues of the father, turned out to be the virtues of the common man. In most cases, it was the right kind of *virtue*, in the right kind of *society*, which enabled ordinary men to achieve extraordinary things.[5] It is not surprising, therefore, that in the case of both Ford and Peckinpah, the man who most embodied the virtues of the common man, was a most uncommon man, Abraham Lincoln.[6]

THE DEFENSE OF THE HEROIC

John Ford had a lifelong fascination with Abraham Lincoln. He admired Lincoln's deeds, but he was most interested in the growth of the Lincoln legend.

When he made *Young Mr. Lincoln*[7] in 1939, he wanted to show the *potential* greatness in the young Lincoln, before his deeds had transformed him into the legendary figure. At the time the movie was made, Lincoln was still a revered figure in America. In fact, Henry Fonda refused to play him when first approached to do the film. Many years later, he told Lindsay Anderson that when he was given the script, he read it and said, "Fellas, it's a beautiful script, beautiful, but I can't play Lincoln. To me it was like playing Jesus Christ or God. Lincoln is a god to me."[8] Ford had to convince Fonda that he would not be playing Lincoln the god. Rather, he wanted to portray Lincoln as the young man who had, early on, displayed the qualities of virtue that gave rise to the legend. The film, Ford insisted, would only attempt to show his potential greatness. Nonetheless, in the final scene, the man and legend are brought together, when Lincoln is shown climbing a hill in a thunderstorm. At the top of the hill, the sun unexpectedly breaks through the dark clouds as Lincoln walks away, seemingly into the future. Ford, seeing the possibility inherent in the circumstance, told Peter Bogdanivich later, "Let's have him walk away, and then we'll dissolve into the statue at the Lincoln Memorial."[9] In Ford's portrayal, the greatness of the young Lincoln had been transformed into the heroic legend.

In looking back to his family's past, Peckinpah, too, had learned to appreciate the sturdy, often heroic, qualities of those who had tamed the Western Frontier. His family was among the first settlers in the foothills of the Sierra Nevada Mountains, east of Fresno. He spent his summers in the shadow of Peckinpah Mountain, which was located near his grandfather's ranch. He was made fully aware of his family's history, beginning with their arrival in Pennsylvania in the 1750s. Like the country itself, they moved steadily west, settling first in Indiana, moving eventually to California by the end of the nineteenth century. Peckinpah came to admire the pioneer spirit of his ancestors, by observing the toughness, integrity, and honesty of the cowboys who worked on his grandfather's ranch. Most of all, he had come to revere his father and grandfather, both lawyers and judges. His grandfather had been a Congressman before World War I. He said that his father, whose hero was Abraham Lincoln, "believed in the Bible as literature, and in the law."[10] His first great movie, *Ride the High Country*,[11] was made shortly after his father's death, and it is clearly a tribute to his father. Indeed, his sister was so deeply moved by the similarity of the main character to her father, that she could hardly bear to watch the film.

In the hands of the best directors, like Ford and Peckinpah, the Western allowed us to go back to school again, by understanding not only the full range of the past—the facts—but also the things that created the legend, and give enduring meaning to the facts. The standard by which to judge the difference between fact and legend was not to be found in an objective science or contemporary social theory. Rather, it required knowledge of the whole. That knowledge could be gained only by reflecting on the greatest thinkers and writers of the past. It is not an accident that both Ford and Peckinpah were deeply influenced by the language and the themes of the Bible and Shakespeare, and their movies are full of the influence of both. They also incorporated elements of the sacred and the religious, frequently using the old hymns and music of the churches. They were well versed in history, literature, and even the philosophic tradition. Indeed, many of Peckinpah's friends and associates commented on his reading of the classics, especially the Greeks. More than one noted that Peckinpah had read Aristotle's *Poetics* so many times that he had it down cold. Consequently, in their movies, Ford and Peckinpah sought to recreate the whole, with reference to a standard of the whole, of truth, and in politics, justice, as the means by which to know the whole.

In *The Man Who Shot Liberty Valance*,[12] Ford attempted to re-create the necessary conditions for the emergence of a democratic regime. He does so by showing those forces which permanently menace the regime of civil liberty, governed by the rule of law. In the film, Ransom Stoddard (James Stewart) represents the word and the law. Both are necessary for civilization and a political order. He is confronted by several characters, in what can only be called a state of nature, the town of Shinbone, which is located in the territory. The cattlemen and others who oppose law and private property, also oppose statehood. There are two dominant figures in Shinbone: Liberty Valance (Lee Marvin), an outlaw, who understands freedom as the indulgence of his desires in the absence of any restraint—he has no home or family—and Tom Doniphon (John Wayne), a kind of naturally superior individual, who wants only a private existence, and because of his superiority, can ensure it. Apparently, he owns a slave: his boy Pompey. His only desire is to marry Hallie. Everyone in town knows that Hallie was his girl, until Ransom Stoddard, the law, and education, come to town.

When Stoddard, an Eastern lawyer, approaches the town of Shinbone, he is beaten and left for dead; Liberty Valance rips his law books to shreds. Doniphon rescues Stoddard, and brings him to the house of his girl, Hallie, who subsequently nurses him back to health. When he is sufficiently strong, Stoddard makes it clear that his assailant should be brought to justice, through the law, not through the vengeance of a handgun. But, as Doniphon notes, "Out here a man settles his own accounts." Stoddard cannot believe his ears: "You're saying what he said! What kind of community have I come to?" But in Shinbone, there *is* no community; there is no law; there is no necessity for the written word: Hallie cannot read or write. The other residents in town, many of whom are illiterate immigrants, know little of the obligations citizenship entails. So Ford literally takes us into the classroom, and provides a lesson on the principles of democratic government. He shows how it is that private individuals are transformed into a *public*: how passion is subordinated to reason, and how the rule of law replaces the deeds of those outside law. Before the rule of law can emerge, both the benevolent, noble character, Tom Doniphon, and the malevolent tyrant, Liberty Valance, must be banished.[13]

Stoddard's classroom is the office of the newspaper editor, Dutton Peabody (Edmond O'Brien). It is Peabody who allows Stoddard to put up his lawyer's shingle; the law and the word belong together. On the blackboard of the classroom, Stoddard writes, "Education is the basis of law and order." In the classroom are the Spanish-speaking children of the Sheriff, Hallie, Peter and Nora Erickson, who want to become citizens, and Pompey, Doniphon's slave. First, Stoddard insists that the children recite the alphabet in order to show that they have learned the importance of a common language—in this case, English. Then, he asks the class what is distinctive about the United States. The immigrant, Nora replies, "Here the people are the boss." Finally, he asks what the fundamental law of the country is, and hints that it is something that is sometimes amended. Clearly, he means the Constitution, but Pompey replies, "It was writ by Mr. Thomas Jefferson: 'We hold these truths to be self-evident—'" but he forgets the rest. Stoddard does not attempt to correct him, by noting that Pompey is not describing the Constitution; he merely says "Yes." But, then he corrects him by noting that he is reciting The Declaration of Independence. By making the two purposely ambiguous, Ford shows the dependence of the Constitution upon the Declaration.

Another student subsequently completes Pompey's statement. He is anxious to show that he knows what it is that Pompey had forgotten, namely, "that all men are created equal." Stoddard replies, emphatically, that "a lot of people forget that part." Indeed, no one in Shinbone seems to understand the meaning of the Declaration of Independence, or the importance of a constitution. Indeed, both Doniphon and Valance have denied its truth. They believe that the legitimacy of rule rests on force alone. Ford makes it clear in this scene that it is only because men are equal, that the people *can* be the boss. It is clear the law offers no protection to Pompey. Perhaps it is because he doesn't understand the meaning of equality, and therefore, he can't know what "We the people" means. In short, he doesn't know *why* the people should be the boss. Thus, he cannot know that government is based upon consent. He thinks of himself, as does everyone else in town, as nothing more than Doniphon's boy. As a result, as soon as Doniphon returns from his trip, he comes into the class and orders Pompey out of school; the lesson on the rights of man is over. Doniphon does not want him to become educated. He insists that Pompey must go back to work. The school is shut down when it is learned that Liberty Valance is coming back to town.[14]

Liberty Valance is a strange Western. The hero, Tom Doniphon, does not become wealthy or famous. He is without any kind of conventional honor. He does not even win the girl's hand. He dies a pauper's death, without his boots or gun. And only the man who has profited from his heroism knows the truth about him, and the importance of his deeds. Tom Doniphon makes the right choice at every crucial juncture. But he does so, always, for personal or private reasons. In his most important decision, at the behest of his girl, he murders Liberty Valance in cold blood—but he makes it appear that Valance was shot by Ransom Stoddard.

Even Stoddard himself is not aware of the truth at the time when it happens, but at the next crucial juncture, he comes forward to reveal himself as the Man Who Shot Liberty Valance. He does so in order to persuade Stoddard to accept the nomination as the delegate for statehood from the territory. Stoddard had become a hero because of his reputation as the Man Who Shot Liberty Valance. When the opposition tries to paint him as a man whose only qualification is the blood on his hands, he rushes from the hall, conscience stricken, with every intent of returning to the East. Doniphon stops him, though, and informs him of the fact that Stoddard had not killed Liberty Valance. Instead Doniphon, lurking in the shadows, murdered him with a rifle. "I can live with that," he tells Stoddard, who taught Hallie to read. "Now give her something to read about." Doniphon then disappears from the movie. The man of superior virtue, truly the superior man by nature, has made it possible to bring about a regime of civil liberty, but cannot be a part of it.

The Western recreated the historic past in a poetic manner, to make clear how the past could not be understood with reference to the facts alone. Nor could contemporary theories born of the idea of progress and science be of much help. Rather, the Western sought to understand history in the light of a standard outside of history. It looked to the permanent truths by which it becomes possible to determine how the facts are made worthy of becoming legend. This is best shown in the famous ending of *The Man Who Shot Liberty Valance*. When the editor of the newspaper gets the story of his life—the truth about the Liberty Valance's death—he refuses to print it. He said, "This is the West, sir. When the legend becomes fact, print the legend."

Ford's movie, as a whole, presents the facts and the legend, in light of the standard of truth. Only by understanding the whole, do we learn why the legend, properly understood, more closely approximates what is demanded by both truth and justice, not to mention prudence, than is possible by any comprehension of the facts alone. In short, the Western makes it clear that the right kind of poetry is better able to comprehend the *truth* of the past than is history. The Western movie, at its best, provided a kind of poetry of the old order, which could be of value for the present, if only its lessons could be learned. Although Ford and Peckinpah admired those virtues, their movies make us aware of the great difficulty implicit in living up to them, when the theoretical ground of the virtues has been undermined.

THE DEFENSE OF NOBILITY

Sam Peckinpah's first major film, *Ride the High Country*, came out the same year as *Liberty Valance*, one of John Ford's last. In this film, he paid tribute to his father. It is about two old lawmen whose time is past, and the ways in which changing society puts their old virtues to the test. The old men are hired by a bank to bring some gold from a mining camp back to town. Steven Judd (Joel McCrea) remains true to his principles, but Gil Westrum (Randolph Scott) is tempted to abandon the old morality in exchange for the pleasures of wealth. He is aware of the fact that the old deeds are no longer celebrated, and their virtues scorned. He tries to entice Judd to abandon his integrity, tempting him with the lure of gold. "What's on the back of a poor man when he dies? The clothes of pride. And they're not any warmer to him than when he was alive. Is that all you want, Steve?" Judd replies, "All I want is to enter my house justified."

Subsequently, we learn that Judd, too, had once been on the road to perdition, but was saved by an old sheriff. After one of his lawless escapades, the sheriff "dried me out in jail and then we went out back and he proceeded to kick the bitter hell right out of me." Westrum, knowing how tough Judd was, says "That took some doing." "Not much," Judd replies. "See, he was right and I was wrong. That makes the difference." Although the law still embodies many of the old virtues, it has become more difficult to defend them theoretically. When Gil asks Judd who is to say what makes the difference between right and wrong, Judd replies, "Nobody. That's something you just know." Judd still lives by the old virtues, but he cannot say why.[15]

By the end of the 1960s, Peckinpah had lost faith in the law. He began to search for some kind of virtue *outside* of the law, and even society itself, for he had come to see only corruption in society. He believed that the law had become the tool of the powerful and wealthy. In *The Wild Bunch*,[16] he attempted to discover some kind of nobility in portraying of a gang of outlaws. The Wild Bunch is a collection of old misfits, still living by the gun in a time when law is just being established in the West. But as Peckinpah had lost faith in the legitimacy of the law, he could no longer portray the virtues in the service of the law. In one scene in *The Wild Bunch*, Dutch Engstrom (Ernest Borgnine) is cursing a former member, now working as a railroad detective, in pursuit of the gang. Pike Bishop (William Holden), the leader of the Wild Bunch, defends him by saying, "He gave his word." "To a *railroad*," Dutch replies. "It's his *word*," says Bishop. But, Dutch responds, "It's not your word that counts, but who you give it to." Can integrity, or honor, be maintained if there is no legitimate authority to give your word to? If the law could no longer be the source of legitimacy, was honor possible—in *any* kind of society? Perhaps, Peckinpah came to believe, every kind of political society—perhaps civilization itself—had only served to undermine the virtues of the individual.[17]

Peckinpah was doubtful that law, or society as it had evolved, had brought about real progress in the human condition, particularly as regards morality, which provides the ground of community and happiness.[18] He was therefore led to seek justice, or the good society, in the state of nature, or in some kind of prepolitical band. The Wild Bunch is like a family or a tribe, where friendship and loyalty are paramount; it is the absence of any regime. At one point, when the gang members begin to quarrel among themselves, Pike intervenes and insists that, "When you side with a man you stay with him, and if you can't do that, you're like some animal. You're finished. We're finished; all of us."

In his rejection of law, society, not to mention science and technology, Peckinpah attempted to recreate the original ground of romanticism. He tries to recover what Rousseau called the sweetness of life, that joy of existence which natural man had before he entered, and was corrupted by, civil society.[19] In one of the most telling scenes of *The Wild Bunch*, Peckinpah takes us into the Mexican village where one of the members, Angel (Jaime Sánchez), was born. It is a kind of idyllic Eden, where innocence seemed to be possible once more. Pike Bishop sits talking to the village chief, and they both observe, and comment upon, the behavior of the gang members, who, before arriving in the village, appeared to be little more than a bunch of barbarians. Here they seem to be reborn: they laugh and play games with the young women, without any apparent lust or overt vulgarity, in what seems to be a state of pure innocence. Before entering the village, not a woman—mother or grandmother—was safe from their desires, made obvious in the most vulgar way. Now Pike watches in astonishment, and tells the village chief he cannot believe his eyes. The village elder replies, "We all wish to be a child again, even the worst of us, perhaps the worst most of all."

The film ends in an epic confrontation between the gang and the corrupt Mexican Army. The battle grows out of an attempt to save Angel, who is being tortured by the Army for stealing a case of rifles. In the encounter, all the members of the gang, and much of the Mexican Army, are killed. In their willingness to die in a hopeless attempt to save their friend, they have come to understand the importance of loyalty, and honor, as the basis of society. Although they have plenty of money, and are, for a time, seduced by the pleasures of wine and women, they abandon all of this. Subsequently, their sense of integrity and duty overcomes their desire for even the most comfortable self-preservation. At once, almost without a thought or word, they know instinctively what Pike Bishop means when he says "let's go." They move forward as one in the face of the enemy and death. They have come to understand that, in his behavior during his prolonged ordeal, Angel had shown his loyalty and his sense of honor. He would not implicate the gang in the theft of the rifles. As Dutch notes, "He played his string right out to the end." In their final decision to rejoin Angel, the members of the Wild Bunch has come to realize that you can give your word only to those who know the importance of keeping their word. Peckinpah seems to have come to the conclusion that there is little likelihood of living nobly in an increasingly mechanized society, without a moral foundation. But there remains the possibility of dying nobly.

Peckinpah's hostility to the idea of progress, and his denial of the beneficence of technology, led him to seek a way back to nature—to skepticism toward the assumption that the progress of civilization had improved the condition of man. Rather, it had undermined morality, and made it nearly impossible to achieve happiness and greatness. The progress of science and technology had only served to weaken human character. Peckinpah said once, "I detest machines. The problem started when they discovered the wheel." Ironically, Peckinpah refused to believe that the camera was a machine. "You're not going to tell me the camera is a machine," he said. "It is the most marvelous piece of divinity ever created."[20] And perhaps he was right about the divinity of the camera. The motion picture really has had the power to create and destroy, both myth and illusion. It has the capacity to represent truth, but also to undermine it—to show reality, and misrepresent it. It could ennoble or degrade those who came under its spell.

In its early days the Western became the first and most popular genre in the medium of television, as it had been in the movie decades before. The television Western was a morality play in which good and evil jousted, and the good, defended by the virtuous, always prevailed. But it was not long, in television and the movies, before moral clarity vanished. By then it had become clear to the sophisticated that contemporary man could not, and should not, live up to a standard that was without foundation. When the motion picture abandoned every objective moral standard, and attempted to portray "reality as it is," it became far more tolerant of vice. Before long, only the portrayal of virtues became intolerable.

By the end of the twentieth century, it had become clear that the divinity of the camera of which Peckinpah spoke was no longer in the hands of a John Ford, or a Sam Peckinpah. Their poetic art was used to elucidate the virtues celebrated in the Western movie, and in Western civilization. Perhaps their art can be understood only as a kind of piety which, in some way, makes up for the loss of those virtues. To Peckinpah, it might have been a substitute for his failure to live up to those virtues in the manner of the men he most admired. One thing is certain, however: there was no doubt in Peckinpah's mind, or Ford's, that the place to look for the most important things is to the fathers, and not the future. Unfortunately, the so-called divinity of the camera is now more commonly in the hands of those without appreciation of the virtues of the past. Thus the greatness or nobility of the past is rarely celebrated in film today. Perhaps it is because the new directors, unlike Ford and Peckinpah, do not have the kind of education, upbringing, the capacity, or the artistic integrity to understand those virtues which make human greatness possible. As a result, the new gods of the screen have gone a long way toward undercutting the authority of the God of religion, of nature, and reason itself: precisely those things that made the past worth preserving.

NOTES

1. Wallace Stegner and Richard W. Etulain, *Stegner: Conversations on History and Literature* (Reno: University of Nevada Press, 1996).

2. Alexander Hamilton, "The Federalist No. 1," *The Federalist Papers*, ed. Clinton Rossiter (New York: Mentor), 33.

3. No one understood this transformation better than Woodrow Wilson, nor gave clearer expression to the Progressive view. In his essay "What Is Progress," he indicates that his role as educator was "to make the young gentlemen of the rising generation as unlike their fathers as possible." The reason for this is that the older generation had "lost touch with the processes of life . . . and therefore they were out of sympathy with the creative, formative and progressive forces of society." The problem was that in a traditional education, greatness was thought to be in the past. Wilson noted the change. "Progress! Did you ever reflect that that word is almost a new one? No word comes more

often or more naturally to the lips of modern man, as if the thing it stands for were almost synonymous with life itself, and yet men through many thousand years never talked or thought of progress. They thought in the other direction. Their stories of heroism and glory were tales of the past. The ancestor wore the heavier armor and carried the larger spear. 'There were giants in those days.' Now all that has altered. We think of the future, not the past, as the more glorious time *in comparison with which the present is nothing*." Woodrow Wilson, "What Is Progress?" (visited September 17, 2001) www .hax0r.org/~dragon/nf/progress.html (emphasis added).

4. It is difficult to be utopian, if it is believed that the fathers are better than we are.

5. Note here the similarity to Aristotle, for whom "the form of government is best in which every man, whoever he is, can act best and live happily." Aristotle, *The Politics*, in *Basic Works of Aristotle*, ed. Richard McKeon (New York: Random House, 1984), 1127, 1279.

6. The biographical material on Ford and Peckinpah is derived from Scott Eyman, *Print the Legend: The Life and Times of John Ford* (New York: Simon & Schuster, 1999) and David Weddle, *If They Move, Kill 'Em!: The Life and Times of Sam Peckinpah* (New York: Grove Press, 1994).

7. Twentieth-Century Fox, 1939.

8. Lindsay Anderson, *About John Ford* (London: Plexus, 1981), 221.

9. Peter Bogdanovich, *John Ford* (Berkeley: University of California Press, 1978), 74.

10. Paul Seydor, *Peckinpah: The Western Films, A Reconsideration* (Urbana: University of Illinois Press, 1980), 116.

11. MGM, 1962.

12. Paramount, 1962.

13. Aristotle suggests that "he who by nature and not by mere accident is without a state, is either a bad man, or above humanity." Aristotle, *Politics*, 1129.

14. Nearly all of the quotations from the movies are found in William Darby, *John Ford's Westerns: A Thematic Analysis, with a Filmography* (Jefferson, N.C.: McFarland, 1996), 147–84.

15. Much of the dialogue I have quoted from this film is found in Michael Bliss, *Justified Lives: Morality & Narrative in the Films of Sam Peckinpah* (Carbondale: Southern Illinois University Press, 1993), 32–57.

16. Warner Bros., 1969.

17. The dialogue for this film is found in Seydor, *Peckinpah*, 137–212.

18. Although *The Wild Bunch* shows the influence of Rousseau, Peckinpah is also aware of that other powerful influence on the American mind, that represented in the thought of John Locke. Peckinpah's view of progress, wealth, and property, is presented most clearly in the movie, *The Ballad of Cable Hogue*. In that movie, progress is presented as a bittersweet phenomenon, and happiness is not simply a matter of wealth. In it, Peckinpah shows the coming into being of the entrepreneur. Cable Hogue stepped right out of the pages of John Locke. He is a man who appreciates the value of private prop-

erty. Hogue is left in the desert, by two of his so-called friends. In his attempt to survive, he asks God for help in bringing him to water. But, his dependence upon God is not sufficient, no water is forthcoming. When he is about to expire, he digs frantically in the earth, and lo and behold, water comes forth. He quickly rejects any dependence upon God, and asserts, "This is my water." Thereafter, no one drinks who has not paid. The first person who tries to do so, Hogue kills. Subsequently, he files a claim which establishes ownership. He creates a lucrative business, which catered to the stagecoach line. In the end of this tragic-comedy, Hogue is killed by an automobile, that new invention which would have made his business obsolete. On his tombstone, he wanted the inscription, "he found water where there was none." If turning water into wine was considered a miracle, there is certainly something miraculous about finding water where there is none. There is no question that the discovery or production of wealth is a kind of miracle. But capitalism requires recognition of the fact that man cannot depend, completely, upon God for his subsistence. When he learns the value of his own labor, he creates something like a miracle, for he creates the useful out of nothing, or out of something that was useless before.

19. Peckinpah's view is much like that of Rousseau. In Paul Seydor's book, he uses a quote from Perry Miller as an epigraph. The epigraph is quite appropriate as a description of American artists in general, and of Peckinpah, in particular. In it, Miller observed that the American artist, "cherishes in his innermost being the impulse to reject completely the gospel of civilization, in order to guard with resolution the savagery of his heart."

20. Seydor, *Peckinpah*, 330.

California Farming in a Classical Context

Victor Davis Hanson

Less than one percent of America now produces food. Even fewer are family farmers, who are vanishing nationwide, purportedly over the past two decades at rates of two thousand a week—although figures from both farm activists and the Department of Agriculture are always somewhat suspect, inasmuch as it is difficult to define what constitutes the "end" of a farm (does the family farm end when it is rented out, when the owners are forced to seek off-farm employment, when one family member buys out others, etc?). Yet by whichever standard one uses to define the nature of land tenure, we are in the midst of a momentous shift in the way our nation grows food. Nowhere is this agricultural revolution more radical than in California, ground zero in the transformation from small family holdings to large vertically integrated concerns.

The Jeffersonian idea that a man and his family might live on their inherited ground, stay rooted as citizens of their local community, and pass on their land to the next generation may well be gone for good. Yet how could this catastrophe arise when the world's population is skyrocketing, and the earth's resources are finite? Just as California seems short of power, petroleum, and housing space, why has not its skyrocketing population driven up food prices, and thereby enriched the state's farmers? State agencies, after all, warn us that each year 140 acres *a day* of farmland are lost to suburban sprawl each year, a rate of farm annihilation that will more likely accelerate than cease. Surely at the millennium food should be ever more precious, its growers the most prosperous of our citizens, as ever fewer acres in California are asked to feed ever more people.

Yet just the opposite is true. The year 2000 was one of the worst years in the history of the California farming—tree fruit and grape prices in real dollars were at all-time lows in the one hundred fifty-year history of the state. Cotton, almonds, and milk returns were equally depressed. And 2001 may see the greatest agricultural fallout in the last half century, as thousand of California farmers fail to meet past mortgage and production loan payments, and so find themselves cut off from lending agencies. High power prices, diesel fuel spikes, increases in the minimum wage, continually more sophisticated and costly labor and environmental regulations, and skyrocketing insurance premiums could not come at a worse time, as the California farmer receives ever less for the harvests he produces.

Yet the bitter truth is that the world is awash in food as never before. Output per acre worldwide continues to rise. Genetic and chemical engineering promises even more productive species of fruits, vegetables, grains, and animals to come—and an ever-wider array of herbicides, pesticides, fungicides, and hormones. Millions of new irrigated acres are coming into production for export in Asia, Africa, Australia, Mexico, and South America—many with climates and crops similar to California's. Westernized agribusiness the world over is replacing traditional subsistence farming, grazing, and pristine forests. Globalization has created a universal food market, in which produce flows across national boundaries with increasing rapidity, oblivious to local supplies, tariffs, and sanctions. Visit a supermarket in California during any January and you will find that most of the fresh produce on the shelf comes from thousands of miles away, harvested under labor, environmental, and chemical protocols far different from those mandated in our state.

California farmers now compete with peanut growers in Africa, raisin producers in Turkey, wineries in Spain, row crop conglomerates in Mexico, and grain operatives in Russia—all of which export with little environmental oversight, far cheaper labor, and ample government subsidies. The result is that commodity prices across the board for the California farmer—grains, cotton, fresh and dried fruits, vegetables, beef, and milk—are at historic lows, and they show little sign of rising in the near future. Again, we in California are in an agricultural depression unmatched since that of the 1930s.

Two consequences arise from this continuing dilemma of depression-era prices—and both bode ill for the traditional family farm in California. When wheat, grapes, or plums crash, many of the smaller farmers go to town to teach, change tires, or weld—and then return home in the evening to lose some of the money that they made hours earlier. Persevering with their hearts rather than their heads, they keep their smaller acreage in production, their land in the family—and so with their off-farm income subsidize cheap food for the rest of us.

Today in California there are literally thousands of acres of farmland that habitually lose money, but are kept in production by their owners' other jobs. I plead guilty to just such an irrational practice; I commute to Fresno each morning to subsidize the losses of my vineyard in Selma.

On the other end of the agricultural spectrum, vertical integration continues unabated. There is no money anymore in growing, but astronomical gains are made in packing, processing, shipping, and distributing food. Farmers get six dollars a box for peaches, but those boxes sell in the grocery stores for ten times that and more. Corn loses the farmer money, but Corn Flakes are ever more expensive on the shelf. Those with vast plants, fleets of trucks, and brokers make fortunes bringing food from the farm to consumer, and so they also subsidize what they lose farming through shipping and selling. Their ample off-farm profits are then plowed back into the countryside as they buy more land from families who fall by the wayside. Tax laws, depreciation, and investment speculation also lead to ever more consolidation of former family farms, as rural America is now largely a culture of corporations not yeomen. Today on California's westside, from the Grapevine to the Delta along the Coast Range Mountains, it is almost impossible to find small or medium-sized family farms—or any operations smaller than one thousand acres. Even on the eastside of the Central Valley, between the 99 freeway and the Sierra—the historical birthplace of the California homesteader and hardscrabble yeomen—we are beginning to see tree-fruit conglomerates of ten thousand acres and more, quite bizarre super-farms that encompass over a million peach, nectarine, and plum trees, or farm 5 million vines.

The state's age-old remedies for disastrous farm prices—collective bargaining agreements, granges, and cooperatives—have proven to be relics. In California in the past two decades alone, some of the largest and most hallowed of farm cooperatives and brokerage associations—Tri-Valley Growers, Blue Anchor, and California Canners and Growers—have either gone broke, declared bankruptcy, recouped their losses by confiscating their own growers' capital retains, or quietly disbanded. Their reason to be—to recoup the profits of marketing and distribute it among their struggling farming membership—has often become forgotten or proved impossible. Indeed, their own processing and selling costs sometimes exceed those of private companies. Many cooperatives in the 1980s and 1990s also entrusted their management to outside corporate teams, whose salary, culture, and sympathies were often at odds with their very membership. Neither cooperatives nor national farmers' unions have ever been able to restrict harvests to increase prices. Most feel it is impossible now in a world economy, or that American farmers are simply too diverse, independent, and cantankerous ever to unite in curtailing their production of food.

Although farmer's markets and other direct sales to consumers make up 10 percent of Californians's daily consumption of fresh produce, and have therein been a great salvation to a number of agrarians, such outlets still represent sales of less than 20 percent of most family farms' production. And farmers markets are increasingly corrupted themselves—the haunt of peddlers, not farmers, or arenas in which the full-time employees of corporate farms unload their culls or unneeded harvests in company vans at fifty and more markets a week.

The beleaguered family farmer of forty to three hundred acres in the middle between the commuter and vertically integrated concern is too busy to work in town and too small and poor to become a packer and processor. So he lives and dies on what he does alone—simply grow food. And that now means agricultural Armageddon. The tragedy is that he actually farms more cheaply and efficiently than either the part-time grower or the agribusinessman, but has access to the capital of neither. Government offers little hope: most of the $40 million budgeted for agricultural assistance this year will go to the largest who need it the least. In California, less than sixteen thousand farmers received nearly a billion dollars in federal payouts; yet no support goes to the small peach grower of sixty acres or the vineyardist who farms forty acres. But such small growers alone turn out to be California's true rural conservatives, rare individualists who succeed or fail on their accord, who rarely chat with visiting politicians, and who are a world apart from the world of agribusiness that so often professes to share their pain.

Most Californians, who consume the least expensive food in the world, care little about the demise of the family farmer. Why, they reason, is family farming any more privileged than the defense or electronics industries that have seen millions in California thrown out of work and entire towns desolated by recession? Why should consumers in Los Angeles or San Jose complain that their food is the cheapest at any time in history, especially when produce alone of daily necessities still seems affordable? And are not labor and land in California increasingly too valuable anyway to devote for farming when both can be found far more abundantly and cheaply overseas? University researchers tell us that we could pave over the entire San Joaquin Valley and thereby obtain a net water surplus, since an acre of five to seven houses uses less water than its counterpart of some six hundred vines.

Are there other concerns to the consumer from this inevitable transformation in the manner in which we in California obtain our food? For now, the alarmist cries of a poisoned food supply and a toxic farm remain largely that—alarmist.

Throughout this radical shift in land tenure, the California shopper has nevertheless found produce cheaper, not more expensive—indeed, more plentiful than ever and available at almost anytime of the year. The fruit of agribusiness is hard and tasteless, but not, as environmentalists and radical farm activists allege, deadly—at least not yet. Fruit Tarts and Sugar Pops may not be whole bran, but they are not toxic either. Hard tomatoes may bounce, but that does not mean that pizza toppings or spaghetti sauce will kill you. Still, how can we continue to know that our food is safe when we will soon be ignorant of the conditions under which it is produced in distant corporate farms? The problem is not the safety of our present but rather our future food supply.

We mostly forget that for generations California family farmers have always been the canaries in the mine of the state's food supply. After all, they, not agribusinessmen, put pesticides in their spray tanks right next to their children's swing set, and they, not absentee owners, shank in fertilizer a few feet above the aquifer from which our kids drink. Those who live where they farm are more informed of, and skeptical about, cloning and new-age chemicals than those who are agribusiness managers on salary or owners distant in the city. When they eat and drink, they have to be where they farm. Should we simply assume that harvests shall continue to be cheap when only a few conglomerates grow, process, ship, and sell them? More likely food will become as costly as gasoline, electricity, or prescription drugs when its production and sale are entirely in the hands of a few.

But let us cease the alarmism for a moment, and, for the sake of argument, accept that to meet the insatiable appetite of the California consumer for food that is pretty, cheap, attractive, and mostly safe, agribusiness—not family farming—possesses the requisite capital, production facilities, transport, and infrastructure to supply our tables from around the world in an instant. Then, is there any other reason—perhaps cultural, political, or social—why we should lament the demise of our state's historic family farming class? If history is any guide for the future, the answer is, unfortunately, yes. The land, as the Greeks taught us, grows people as well as food. California should have concerns about the countryside besides the safety of its produce. Our citizens are increasingly suburban, divorced from nature, and dependent on someone else for their food, wages—and lives. Timidity and conformity, not individualism and eccentricity, keep most of us afloat at the school, office, and plant. Conservatives should worry about these trends most of all, since we are creating in the state a vast population of suburbanites who look to government for employment, entitlement, and security—and feel comfortable with just those leaders who assure them that they shall be taken care of; that every appetite is not only possible but necessary; that the purpose of the state is not to protect freedom and promote liberty, but to ensure equality of result rather than of opportunity.

Rooted farmers remind us of another, older way in which public shame, not private guilt, holds us honest. When the grape crop is lost to rain a few hours before harvest, we learn that life is sometimes without remedy or therapy, a tragedy in which there are not always easy answers or solutions. When there are at least some Californians who have learned that nature can destroy their orange harvest in a second, they are not so romantic about the wild, or confident that there will always be an agency to repair hurt and give recompense to loss. Farmers are therefore confused over California's citizens who demand ever more electric power for ever more comforts, even as they are ever more reluctant to build plants to satiate just that insatiable desire; and then fall into despair, panic, even hysteria, when their electricity begins to fail. After all, farming teaches us that the age-old enemies of man—cold, illness, hunger—are more dangerous than man himself and that we are in a constant struggle to save ourselves from the cruel and age-old threats to humankind. Farmers who graft wild rootstocks to weak, tame cultivars to produce productive strong fruit trees, know that neither nature let go, nor man himself in his excess, is the answer, but rather a proper mix of the two is needed to produce something better than both. Balance—what the Greeks called *to meson*—is the lesson of farming, and one vanishing among our population at large.

Family farms also offer us beauty, so rare in this age of rampant development and sprawl. Driveways of shady trees, ancestral barns, and clapboard houses do not necessarily make strict economic sense; farms, after all, are homes, not mere factories. Yet we Americans need something besides both the crowded mall and the empty wilderness, something in between that is near and beautiful, and not just an assembly plant of food. Family farms are a creation of neither man nor the wild, but an aesthetic combination of both. We can see the ancient divide between family farming and *latifundia* clearly in our own great Central Valley. The western side is mostly a treeless expanse of corporate farms, whose owners in large part live in either Los Angeles or Fresno; towns like Five Points, Huron, Tranquility, or San Joaquin are mostly monolithic communities of farm workers, in which local hospitals, Rotary Clubs, and Little Leagues are rare—far different towns from their rural counterparts to the east, which were the offspring of thousands of small farmers of trees and vines. A Reedley, Selma, or Kingsburg was far more likely to entertain both farmers and farm owners, and its surrounding farmers were far more likely to live on their land and be engaged in their local communities. The latter were more stable towns, more refreshing in their aesthetics, more nurturing in their culture than those of the Westside. And how odd—or rather how predictable, given the innate human desire for beauty—that the great suburban development of the last two decades in Central California centered on the west, rather than the east, side of the Valley.

How strange that we now uproot orchards and vineyards in places like Fowler and Dinuba only to call them Orchard Knolls and Vineyard Estates, only to leave largely undeveloped the corporate environs of a Mendota or Tranquility. Captains of agribusiness may resent such facile generalizations, but they themselves are more likely to live on the eastern rather than the western side of Central California. Self-proclaimed conservatives may object to such flip value judgments about the culture consequences of agribusiness, but very conservative developers choose to tear up eastern, rather than western, farms, knowing full well that would-be suburbanites prefer to live among the ghosts of yeomen rather than among the living flesh of corporate farms. Kingsburg really is a more livable place than Huron, and there are historical reasons why that is so.

California, for political, social, and aesthetic reasons, desperately needs a few of these often cranky voices of skepticism to remind us from their own daily ordeal with the elements that we are not born into (or deserve) constant entitlement; that we cannot always get our way from government or nature—or each other. We need to be reminded, as the Greeks knew, that farmland serves a role beyond the production of food; that it satisfies a very human need for beauty, continuity, and stability. This connection between family farming and reliable consensual government is also no romance of the present, but evident throughout the past.

Western civilization began with the rise of the Greek city-state in the eighth century B.C., and the *polis* itself was the result of the creation of family farming.[1] Earlier Hellenic civilization during the late Mycenaean era (1600–1200 B.C.) was based on an impressive palatial culture of two classes—master and serf—not three. Land was held collectively by palace grandees, themselves ensconced in fortified citadels, as laborers farmed according to state protocols and delivered their harvests to central clearinghouses to be redistributed by distant bureaucrats. While the Mycenaeans were able to sustain large populations and marshal thousands of workers to create vast palaces, tombs, and walls, theirs was an extremely fragile culture, one that vanished in a matter of decades when confronted with systematic foreign attack. Such are the wages of top-heavy regimes—the Aztec, Inca, Near Eastern, and Soviet dynasties are good examples—in which neither knowledge nor power is decentralized. And, of course, democracy, real literature, government apart from religion, free markets—what we call the Western paradigm—was unknown under the Mycenaeans.

The Dark Ages (1150–750 B.C.), which followed the abrupt collapse of the

Mycenaean palaces, was one of nomadism, feudalism, and stock raising, as a beleaguered population for some four hundred years scratched out a meager livelihood from an unforgiving Greek countryside. Prior overspecialization had left chaos in its wake, as the decapitation of nerve centers of Mycenae meant that there were no specialists left to arrange affairs in the countryside—and none in the countryside who had the expertise themselves to re-create the past elaborate farming regimes of their masters.

Yet by 700 B.C. some fifteen hundred autonomous communities had blossomed from the disorder of the Dark Ages; most were broadly-based governments of small property owners, characterized by written constitutions, civic militias, free markets, private property, and a general sense of personal freedom. Classical Greek civilization of the city-state was the creation of this new class of small farmers, who arose out of the Dark Ages to band together to protect their newfound autonomy as successful food producers. Real citizens appeared for the first time who determined the circumstances of their own economic and political life. The checkerboard of small farms in the countryside—we know of no classical Greek farm larger than one hundred acres—mirrored the seats in the assembly hall and the slots of the Greek phalanx on the battlefield, while a natural, not an enforced, egalitarianism among rural peers permeated landholding, political life, and military service. The result was that between 700 and 300 B.C.—the age of the free city-state—Greek culture established the foundations of Western civilization as evidenced from the sophisticated literature of epic poetry, Athenian tragedy, and Socratic philosophy to matchless achievement in art, architecture, urban planning, and natural science.

That classical renaissance slowly eroded with the rise of Macedonian hegemony and the establishment of Hellenistic monarchs in the period after the death of Alexander the Great (323–31 B.C.). Once again, as during the Mycenaean age, we see an era of great wealth, but also of power concentrated into the hands of kings and autocrats. Most interesting is the vast change in the conditions of land tenure of the ancient countryside that perhaps best explains the simultaneous transformations in political and economic life. Farms were consolidated, as bankrupt owners flocked to the cities—Alexandria, Ephesus, Antioch, and Pergamum dwarfed classical communities in size. Military service was largely mercenary, as huge armies employed destitute farmers in service to megalomaniac conquerors. Estates grew to enormous proportions—farms of thirty thousand to seventy thousand acres were not uncommon in Hellenistic Asia and Ptolemaic Egypt—even as the countryside itself became ever more uninhabited.

Ancient observers such as Polybius, Strabo, Plutarch, and Pausanias remarked of rural classical Greece that once prosperous farming communities had by their own times become desolate. With the demise of the autonomous yeomen, so too consensual government and local autonomy largely vanished. Literature and art revolved around the court and lacked the vitality of classical culture. If the Hellenistic World (321–31 B.C.) was a vast, bustling world of great wealth and urban construction, it was also an age of political autocracy, oppressive taxation, corporate agriculture, a restless and dependent urban population, and a dreary life of sitcoms and cheap entertainment for the masses, with arcane poetry and academic pamphleteering for the elite.

This continual cycle from the extremes of corporate *latifundia* to decentralized family farming was prevalent elsewhere in the history of Western civilization with all its attendant cultural ramifications, but perhaps most prominent at Rome, where clear fault lines divided Republican government from imperial autocracy. The later cosmos of the emperors (31 B.C.–A.D. 476) was largely a world of specialized large estates, just as an earlier Republican Italy in contrast for three hundred years (350–50 B.C.) had been a culture of tough small farmers.

What can such classical parallels teach us about farming in California? Obviously, contemporary conditions are vastly different from the ancient world, as the great divides across time and space make facile comparisons hazardous. Nevertheless, there are enough constants to give us concern, especially when the connections between farm life and larger culture were at the centerpiece of the astute cultural criticism of Plato, Aristotle, and Xenophon, who usually spoke of the human condition in terms of the ages rather than of the moment.

Quite simply, the loss of small farms and independent yeomen led to a dependent urban population that was far less likely to be either autonomous or free. And the ripples of the transformation went far beyond just the production of food or the conditions of land tenure, but in fact lapped upon the larger culture itself. Homer is dissimilar from the Hellenistic epic of Apollonius of Rhodes, as the Parthenon is a world away from the Colossus of Rhodes; as the small communities of classical Marathon were different from the later vast estates of Herodes Atticus, who came to own that entire *deme*. How did classical authors account for these radical cultural, literary, and artistic changes? And what in their view allowed an agrarian countryside to vanish, democracy to fail, and culture to deteriorate?

There is something about independent farming that, to use Xenophon's words, made it "the best life" and "the best tester of men."[2] In this ancient view, the daily struggle with nature to produce food on one's own, unaided by government, without an array of supporting clerks and bureaucrats, developed a unique citizen, who expected—no, demanded—the same degree of competence and responsibility in others. In contrast, ancient political philosophers also worried about the dangers of democratic government when married to an urban, often maritime, and increasingly affluent culture, since it put too much responsibility on too unprepared a citizenry. They felt that there was an inevitable tendency in the individual, once removed from physical work and the realities of nature—and without individual initiative and freed from personal responsibility for his livelihood—to seek comfort in consensus and uniformity. This pathology in their eyes could prove fatal for democratic government at large, which was after all an instantaneous reflection of what the average citizen felt on any given afternoon—in the case of Athens, vote to kill the residents of the island of Lesbos one afternoon, change your mind the next.

If consensual rule was only as good as those who provided a consensus, then it was of utmost concern to ensure the development of moral citizens who were confident in their own abilities, without envy, and independent without institutional support. Ancient authors are quite clear on this point of agrarian moral superiority. The poet Aristophanes concluded that "the farmers do all the work, no one else,"[3] while Aristotle felt that farming was "the best occupation" because it was "just" and "not at the expense of others." And he noted that agriculture was "the most honest of all occupations, inasmuch as wealth is not derived from other men," a calling he said, that "contributes to the making of manly character."[4] Likewise, Menander felt that "for all humans the farm is a teacher of virtue and of a life devoted to freedom."[5] In the mind of ancient political thinkers, it was as important to have social and cultural institutions that fostered moral citizens as it was a workable constitution.

Yet once that reservoir of yeomen were lost—Euripides reminded us that "the yeomen alone preserve the land"[6]—citizens were more likely to vote for government programs that they could not afford, to follow demagogues who promised lucrative but unwise foreign adventures, and to blame others more prosperous and stable for their own shortcomings. The result was soon a bankrupt society, with an unimaginative citizenry that soon was no citizenry at all. Without the desire or ability to govern, defend, or feed themselves the latter generations of the *polis* allowed others to fill the void, and the road to autocracy, mercenary service, and serfdom was inevitable.

California is obviously a postindustrial society, a world apart from classical Greece, with a diverse gross product of goods and services that represents 12 percent of our nation's total, and is itself the world's seventh largest economy. Yet if history has any relevance for the present, we should take note of the passing away of our state's yeomen class, which have served us well in ways that transcend the mere production of food. Our state is currently entering the most confusing period in the history of Western civilization. At the pinnacle of our greatest prosperity, we are in daily fear that our California's power grid may collapse. In a state dependent on the automobile, the cost of petroleum to ensure our transportation can nearly double in a matter of weeks. Entire cities of hundreds of thousands are cloned to arise out of desert and farm, even as their older exemplars of millions more are scenes of crime, social unrest, and incivility. The more affluent we suburbanites become, the more vulnerable the majority of us become to specialists in energy, transportation, and food, whose expertise we demand but cannot fathom.

The California electorate is ever more volatile, eager to legalize drugs one day, demand capital punishment the next, increasingly consistent only in its shared desire for ever more things at less costs. All the old political rubrics and labels mean little: self-proclaimed conservatives often engineer urban sprawl and destroy rural and traditional communities of generations, even as liberals are as likely to be corporate executives, ensconced in chic suburban estates, maintained by an array of immigrant gardeners and nannies. Yet through all this change and upheaval, California has been blessed this past century and a half with a bedrock community of tough independent farmers, in size small as to be almost indivisible, and yet vocal enough to knock the rest of us occasionally back to our senses. That we are now seeing the demise of this last check on our innate democratic excess should worry us—and scare conservatives most of all.

NOTES

1. I develop many of the following themes at greater length in my book *The Other Greeks* (Berkeley: University of California Press, 1999).

2. See Xenophon, *Oeconomicus*, trans. Sarah B. Pomeroy (Oxford: Clarendon Press, 1999), 6, 9–10.

3. See Aristophanes, *Peace*, trans. Robert Henning Webb (Charlottesville: University Press of Virginia, 1964), line 511.

4. See generally Aristotle, *Politics*, trans. Carnes Lord (Chicago: University of Chicago Press, 1984), bk. 6, pt. IV.

5. See Menander, *Menander's Georgos. A Revised Text of the Geneva Fragment*, trans. Bernard P. Grenfell and Arthur S. Hunt (Oxford, U.K.: Clarendon Press, 1898), (Kock), 481.

6. See Euripides, "The Suppliants," in *Euripides: Plays*, intr. J. Michael Walton, Frederic Raphael, and Kenneth McLeish (Portsmouth, N.H.: Heinemann, 1997), lines 244–245.

The Politics of California Public Education

Larry Peterman

The politics of California public education are a reminder that California politics are, perhaps, best viewed ironically. Things not only take unexpected twists and turns, they disappoint intentions and turn out opposite to what might be anticipated. Thus, to take two examples that have weighed heavily on California education, conservative objections to out of control property taxes in the 1970s led to property tax limitations—1978's Jarvis-Gann Initiative—which shifted educational financing in large part away from localities to the state, and at about the same time liberal objections to unequal local school funding led to a court decision—Serrano-Priest—which limited the ability of some districts to spend on innovations dear to them. The result is consternation among conservatives and liberals and a general dissatisfaction with the state's educational structure among other parties and factions that are not so easily labeled. The conservative leaning confront an enormous state-centered educational establishment and the liberal leaning are limited in what they can accomplish on the local level, even in those instances, rare as they may be, when resources are potentially available. On top of this, and affecting everyone, there is permanent sparring between local school districts and school boards, which actually run the schools, and the state, which attaches a variety of mandated programs to its financial support.

As if this situation was not sufficiently frustrating, educational decisions are complicated, as one observer puts it, by a "hopeless tangle of authority in which everyone has a say but no one has the final say."[1] At last count, a governor, a legislature, an education secretary appointed by the governor, a similarly appointed state board of education, and an elected state superintendent of pub-

291

lic instruction, all vie for influence over the direction the schools are to take and over how to implement even broadly supported policies.[2]

Given the competition for resources and control and the crisscrossing lines of authority that mark California public education, it is probably inevitable that different interest groups will try to take advantage. This is encouraged by the electorate's willingness to take a hand in the schools by way of the initiative process and the voting booth. In the recent past, for instance, Californians have responded to the urging of professional educators and seen to it that funding for schools will always have priority in the legislative process, have heeded the pleas of outraged parents and lay people and turned on the same professional educators to assure that English is the language of choice in the public schools, and, have followed the lead of Arnold Schwarzenegger to mandate the permanent appropriation of funds for after school programs.[3]

As the foregoing experiences with initiatives suggest, California politics also leaves a good deal of room in the educational process for mischief. Centralization of spending on schools and confused, overlapping, lines of authority provide openings in education, in this respect, to those with agendas that might be considered suspect if they were considered outside the educational context. A case in point, depending upon ones perspective, is provided by the California Teachers Association (CTA), the state union that represents upwards of 330,000 public school employees, including teachers and a variety of other nonsupervisory personnel. The CTA was founded almost one hundred fifty years ago but it is fair to say that, in another of those California political ironies, it came into its own politically after 1978 when the state took over so much of school spending. This concentrated power in Sacramento and allowed the CTA effectively to focus its financial clout, a process abetted by its informal, but open, alliance with the Democratic Party.

What this can lead to is exemplified by an attempt in spring 2002 to have the Democrat-controlled assembly pass a CTA sponsored bill, Assembly Bill 2160, that would have dramatically expanded the union's power over public education. Flexing its muscles—the union donates literally millions to politicians and political campaigns, mostly on the Democrat side—the CTA induced five Democratic members of the Public Employee's, Retirement and Social Security Committee, and eight Democratic members of the Education Committee to vote AB 2160 out of committee and on to the assembly floor. This was despite a fairly widespread public outcry, including those usually friendly to the CTA and educational causes. Thus, the *Sacramento Bee* likened the committee members acting at the behest of the union to the actions of "stooges."

AB 2160 was extraordinary. At its heart was a vast expansion of the collective bargaining process. The bill specifically added ten items to collective bargaining, including decisions on educational materials, including textbooks, local standards for achievement, course content, educational objectives, curriculum, and programs designed to encourage parental involvement in student education.

Locally centered interest groups took exception to almost all these features. The California School Boards Association (CSBA), for instance, argued that the plan would stretch the parameters of collective bargaining well beyond its intended scope, wherein teachers and school districts, in an adversarial process, represent their differing interests. In expanding the process as AB 2160 proposed, the argument went, the CTA would assume the right to represent students, parents, and others in the education community at the bargaining table. According to the CSBA, this was a recipe for disaster since the lesser interests would almost certainly be shortchanged as officials and teachers arranged the trade-offs upon which any successful collective bargaining agreement would depend. This likelihood, in turn, led the Small School Districts' Association to predict that the public would effectively be left out of public education and that the result of the bill would be an expansion of charter schools, private schools, and movements in favor of vouchers.

There were other complaints as well over what was variously described as a union power grab, an attempt to obstruct educational accountability—collective bargaining takes place behind closed doors, shielded from the public—and a purposeful obstruction to any attempts by outsiders to reform California public educations. Cost, for example, was a concern, since the money for a much more complex and lengthy bargaining process would have to come out of educational resources. There was also the worry that teachers, purportedly the beneficiaries of the expansion of collective bargaining, would actually pay a price for it. Whereas they already took part in most, if not all, of the considerations that AB 2160 would have included in collective bargaining, the naysayers on the bill argued that their views would be shunted aside in the future as professional union representatives and professional school administration officials took control of the entire bargaining process.

The CTA had responses to all these arguments, ranging from the position that teachers deserved a greater voice in deciding what was best for their students to offers to amend AB 2160 such that parents of pupils enrolled in public schools would be allowed to participate in committees that might be established through negotiations authorized by the bill. But even for the CTA the outcry had become too great, especially in light of the fact that the governor, particularly sensitive to public opinion in an election year, came out against the bill. The bill never came to a vote in the Assembly. In the final analysis, AB 2160 went further in the direction of putting barriers between the public and public education than was politically feasible, at least at that moment.

On the other hand, one senses that the forces to which AB 2160 responded are not done and that the question of who will command California education will remain politically charged into the foreseeable future. For instance, the CTA was the mustering agent for the groups that argued, albeit unsuccessfully, against the initiative that mandated the assigning of state funds to after school programs, the CTA's concern being that funding would drain money from programs that it would find more congenial. Again, as this is written, the sparring over the most recent California budget crisis has begun, and it is impossible to avoid CTA-sponsored advertisements that seek to insulate public education, or insulate it as much as possible, from the painful budget decisions that must be made. Beyond trying to protect its own turf, the CTA thus works toward further centralizing the politics of education, inasmuch as its advertisements make clear that Sacramento is, and presumably will remain, the focus of decision making about state schools. Its advertisements, for example, include no suggestion that switching control of educational resources out of Sacramento might mitigate the budget crisis.

This advertising campaign may also be said to signal an attempt through the political process to professionalize California public education, that is, to place the purveyors of public education in charge of the policies and decisions that govern it. The hope on the part of the CTA and its friends, in other words, is that eventually education will be in the hands of those who have daily responsibility for providing it. As the American Federation of Teachers, a national union ally of the CTA, put it when it came out in favor of AB 2160, under the bill there would be "enhanced cooperation between educators and administrators." This no doubt would have been true, but the concomitant would have been less room for nonprofessionals in the educational process.

The professionalization of education, in this sense, would mean the diminishing of lay or community influence on education. The result might be, thinking again of the ironic quality of California politics, an expectation that there would be more moves to make public education the object of the initiative process. The future is not transparent, but it seems reasonable that attempts to professionalize education might lead instead to a further fracturing of the educational structure as Californians, in the piecemeal fashion of the initiative process, demand input into public education at the polls. Whether or not this happens, however, it seems safe to assume that California education will retain its place at the center of California politics.

NOTES

1. See Daniel Weintraub, "Untangling All the Lines of Power in State Schools," *Sacramento Bee*, December 22, 2002.

2. The situation is widely recognized and as this is written, a new state school master plan is being considered in the legislature.

3. In order, Proposition 98 (1988), Proposition 227 (1998), and Proposition 49 (2002).

The Least Secure Right: Privately Owned Firearms in California

Daniel C. Palm

California stands without question as one of the nation's most restrictive states respecting firearms possession. A waiting period is imposed on all firearms purchases and transfers, and Californians are limited to one gun purchase per month.[1] While thirty-three states have passed laws since 1980 allowing citizens with no criminal record to apply for concealed handgun permits, California's government stands adamantly opposed.[2] California is one of only three states to have banned new sales of military-style semiautomatic firearms, and one of two to ban magazines holding more than ten cartridges.[3] While thirty-one states as of 2003 have passed legislation to prohibit lawsuits directed against firearms manufacturers—alongside numerous state and federal courts having dismissed such lawsuits—California's governor signed legislation explicitly permitting just such lawsuits in November 2002.[4] Beginning January 2003, California required a written test, thumbprint, and safe handling demonstration for each new handgun purchase, and is unique in limiting handgun sales to models from a list of approved models. Legislation is planned to register all firearms sold in the state, ban inexpensive handguns completely, and institute a "ballistic fingerprinting" database.[5]

It has not always been so. As recently as 1980, California resembled most other Western states in allowing relatively easy sale and transfer of privately held arms. In its turn toward increasing gun restrictions, California now more closely resembles New Jersey and New York than its neighbors, and the trend seems likely to continue. Does all this restriction make the state a leader in "sensible" gun control with a resulting lower degree of gun crime, or merely a leader in ineffective feel-good policy? Gun control is routinely mentioned as one of the top two or three hot-button policy issues by which Californians define themselves politically, and both sides recognize its importance as a strategic battleground in the national debate.[6] But gun control law presents more than just another policy issue, as it relates directly to the meaning and purpose of government. This, too, is recognized by both sides, and so the gun issue is fought in California with a stridency equal to that surrounding the debates about abortion and free speech. To understand why California's gun laws have taken this turn, it is necessary to understand the theory of government that informs California's Constitution, its peculiar history, and demographic changes it has lately experienced.

THEORY OF GOVERNMENT AND
AN INDIVIDUAL RIGHT TO ARMS

The Declaration of Independence presents to the world a philosophy of man's place in relation to government. That understanding holds that individuals are endowed with certain unalienable rights, and that "among these, are life, liberty and the pursuit of happiness." Government's task is a simple one, namely, "to secure these rights." A government that provides security enough so that people may go about their business, without constant fear for their lives and liberty, is a success. But the American founders recognized that government, like any human institution, could become corrupt, ceasing to secure rights: When "any Form of Government becomes destructive of these ends, it is the Right of the People to alter or to abolish it." Indeed, faced with despotism, argues the Declaration, "it is their right, it is their duty to throw off such government" and institute "new Guards" for the security of their rights. Operated as they are by fallible human beings, governments may become tyrannical.

The Constitution's Second Amendment fits easily with the Declaration's understanding of government.[7] If rights belong to the people, and government exists merely to secure those rights, arms privately held by law-abiding citizens stand as the people's ultimate recourse to protect their rights from tyranny, and the means for restoring rightful government. And, it may be offered, they stand as an effective deterrent to the imposition of despotism.[8]

With respect to individual protection, the founders follow classical Lockean political theory holding that when entering civil society, people surrender their right to punish wrongdoers.[9] But Locke is also clear that the right to protect self, family and other innocents, and property by force remains with the individual in the absence of law enforcement. Thus the Pennsylvania (1776) and Vermont

(1777) state constitutions, for example, include a provision "That the people have a right to bear arms for the defense of themselves and the State."[10] Nowhere do the founders deny an individual right to defend life, family, liberty, or property.

Neither California's first constitution, written in 1849, nor its second, written in 1879, includes a constitutional guarantee to keep and bear arms.[11] In the first instance, this can be attributed to the 1849 convention's close attention to the recently written Iowa and New York state constitutions, neither of which included a right to private arms.[12] The 1849 Constitution did, however, include a preamble asserting that,

> All men are by nature free and independent, and have certain inalienable rights, among which are those of enjoying and *defending* life and liberty; acquiring, possessing, and *protecting* property; and pursing and obtaining *safety* and happiness.[13]

A reasonable person reading the preamble might expect that Californians would not be forbidden the necessary tools—firearms being the most efficient—to allow defense of life and liberty, protection of property, and achieving safety.[14] The Constitutional Convention of 1879 retained the preamble, but did not discuss whether to include a right to keep and bear arms. "Public arms" received mention as the delegates considered the expense of the state militia, suggesting that privately owned arms are assumed, even if an explicit right is not mentioned.[15] The only other reference to arms at the convention is a proposed amendment that, "No alien who cannot become a citizen of the United States shall be allowed to bear arms."[16] This ultimately unsuccessful proposal, referred to the committee on Chinese affairs, reminds us of the intense anti-immigrant animus of the politically powerful Workingmen's Party. It is also worth noting that the 1879 California Constitution was written at the same time that state legislatures in the Reconstruction-era south were enacting "black codes," laws designed, in part, to restrict or forbid possession of arms by former slaves.[17]

Of greater ultimate importance to privately owned arms in California was the appearance at the 1879 convention of a new philosophy of government that stood opposed to the political principles of the American founding. A reporter observing California's 1879 Constitutional Convention for the Sacramento *Record Union* found a clear distinction between the delegates:

> There is the class who hold to the American idea, that the attainment of justice is the foundation of government; that the great problem of human government is how to combine the greatest good of the whole with the least practicable restraint

upon individual liberty; that the end of government is to protect men in their natural rights, without restraint upon natural capacities. Opposed to this is already seen a class favoring parental government, under which the confiscation of regulation shall be mandatory and constantly operative.[18]

What the reporter described as "parental government" is recognizable as the tendency toward centralized administration warned about by de Tocqueville. It is representative also of early Progressivism, built on Rousseau's understanding of the state as expression of the "general will," and a faith in political progress. History, according to this view, is moving society forward; there are no fixed principles or truths upon which to found government. Government should reflect the will of the people, and should be constituted to minimize any obstacles to its realization.

What does this mean in California as to the individual's right to keep and bear arms? First, the Progressive view holds that government can never become tyrannical—it is always an expression of the general will. There can thus be no conceivable need for the people ever to throw off government by arms. It comes as no surprise that politically liberal Californians deride this justification for private arms, as did California Supreme Court Justice Stanley Mosk in 1968 as "a psychotic fear of an impending Communist takeover which they are girding to resist by guerilla warfare."[19] Progressivism holds that we have advanced beyond the American founders' understanding of government. But gun rights are to California liberals more than an anachronism; they are philosophically offensive as representative of the idea that government can become a violator of individual rights.

As to the second use, Progressivism holds that individuals have no business attempting to protect themselves with arms. Law enforcement officers and the military—the agents of government—are solely qualified to possess and use arms. Others cannot be trusted to use them wisely.[20] Whereas the founders saw self-defense entirely justifiable, modern liberalism argues that self-defense with arms is unjustifiable and unsafe. The California Constitution's preamble and its understanding of rights is thus made meaningless.

For gun owners in California, the state's Progressive political philosophy means that there is no understanding of a right to keep and bear private arms. Moreover, California's gun owners can look for no protection from the Constitution's Second Amendment, according to the understanding laid down by California Attorney General Bill Lockyer in his comments of 2002 on the meaning and extent of that Amendment. Federal and state court decisions respecting the Second Amendment in California, he argues, leave us with two "clear and unambiguous" conclusions:

1) The Second Amendment limits only the powers of the federal government, not those of the states; and,

2) The "right to keep and bear arms" under the Second Amendment is not an individual right to possess firearms, but a collective right of the states to keep and maintain a "well-regulated militia."

And while I am personally convinced that the Second Amendment was indeed intended to provide *some measure of entitlement* for individuals to own firearms, the degree of that entitlement, and the extent to which it must be balanced with the *state's right and responsibility* to protect public health and safety, is still being interpreted by our nation's courts.[21]

The state's attorney general understands the state to have rights, while the citizens have only "some measure of entitlement," a view precisely the opposite of the American founders, but fully consistent with the progressive/liberal view of government. Californians are thus left with no right to arms whatsoever, and possess their privately held arms at the pleasure of their government, which might decide to ban all private arms at any time in the name of public health and safety.[22]

CALIFORNIA'S HISTORY AND PRIVATE ARMS

The popular image of frontier California and the West, thanks to Hollywood, is one of pervasive crime and mayhem at gunpoint. But research on crime and violence in pre-1900 California confirms that while guns were ubiquitous, the extent of crime depended on the makeup of the population. Gold Rush–era California was predominantly male; the census of 1850 reports that men outnumbered women in California by twelve to one.[23] Gun crime prevailed in those areas where numbers of unmarried males was highest. This was true even in the mining boomtowns of Aurora and Bodie, where crime was limited to young, transient males, and typically occurred in saloons or otherwise involved alcohol. Among ordinary citizens, gun violence was uncommon, despite easy access and near universal familiarity with firearms.[24]

The first restrictions on firearms in California, as in much of the West, were city ordinances not limiting ownership but directed against carrying concealed weapons or discharge within city limits. The Governor's Crime Problem Advisory Committee in 1932 recommended a greater emphasis on crime prevention, though it made no reference to limiting gun rights and generally remained focused on apprehension and punishment.[25] President Franklin D. Roosevelt and his attorney general Homer Cummings argued vigorously for national handgun registration, though Congress declined to include the idea in the National Firearms Act of 1934. That law had as its focus limitations on ownership of sawed-off shotguns, silencers, and machine guns, which California's legislature had already banned in 1927. In 1940, California imposed a forty-eight-hour wait on handgun purchases as a crime control measure, with that wait lengthened to three days in 1958, and five days in 1965, with the intent to stop crimes of passion.[26]

The Black Panthers's openly carrying rifles and shotguns in the streets of Oakland in 1967 led directly to the introduction of a state bill prohibiting open bearing of firearms in California cities; it passed quickly after twenty-six Panther representatives carried firearms into the state assembly to demonstrate against its passage.[27] Alongside the murder of Martin Luther King, Robert Kennedy's assassination at the Ambassador Hotel in Los Angeles on June 5, 1968, with a .22 caliber Iver Johnson pistol led President Johnson to press Congress for national gun registration and licensing for gun owners, and launched a nationwide crusade to ban handguns. In California, Proposition 15, a proposal to ban new sales of handguns in the state, was placed before the voters in November 1982. The measure was soundly defeated due to strong turnout among gun owners and little support from law enforcement.

Following this serious defeat, the gun control movement turned to the effort to ban military style semiautomatic weapons, which the media soon dubbed "assault weapons."[28] Several multiple murders and a bank robbery shootout in California proved crucial in the state and nationwide debate about these arms. James Oliver Huberty's firearms rampage at a restaurant in San Ysidro in 1984 killed twenty-two, and was followed in 1989 by Patrick Purdy's rampage in Stockton that left five children dead, twenty-nine wounded. These events, combined with urban gang violence of the 1980s and 1990s and Hollywood's amplification of the latter, served to link firearms with crime for large segments of the state's population. Combined with liberalism, which argued that gun control was essential to crime prevention, the way was paved for a wave of new restrictions on privately owned arms.

The California legislature responded to these events with bills introduced to ban new sales of "assault weapons," first by banning specific models in the 1989 Roberti-Roos Assault Weapons Control Act, amended in 1999 to the ban of weapons by identifiable features.[29] The Ninth Circuit Court of Appeals decision in *Silveira v. Lockyer*, delivered in December 2002, upheld the law, and included in its decision a lengthy discussion of the Second Amendment, concluding that the right to keep and bear arms is a collective right only.[30] Confusing matters somewhat, Attorney General Lockyer's statement on the decision seemed to support a right in California to private arms—so long as they don't resemble military weapons:

> I am pleased with the court's ruling upholding California's Roberti-Roos Assault Weapons Control Act. While I respect the rights of Californians to pursue hunting and sports shooting, and of law-abiding citizens to protect their homes and businesses, there is no need for these military-style weapons to be on the streets of our state.[31]

DEMOGRAPHIC CHANGE AND GUN RIGHTS

A final aspect of California's politics that bears heavily on privately owned arms concerns demographic change, particularly since 1980. First, California's population has grown dramatically, with most newcomers congregating in cities and rapidly expanding suburbs. Urbanization often bodes ill for the right to private arms: American cities tend to be liberal strongholds, with populations more likely to depend on "parental" government, unfamiliar with and unsympathetic toward hunting, and associating guns with crime.[32] A smaller percentage of Californians in rural areas means fewer Californians familiar with arms for hunting, pest control, and farm utility. Add to this that suburban growth has forced the closure of numerous public shooting ranges.

Secondly, the end of the Cold War also caused California to experience a massive shift in population. For decades prior to 1990 the state had been home to dozens of military bases and hundreds of military and aerospace contractors, together with their families and the service industries they depended upon.[33] This segment of the population, together with military veterans who settled here after 1945, tended toward political conservatism and were likely to associate private arms with national defense. Indeed, the federal government maintained significant programs to promote civilian marksmanship at California military bases, rifle clubs, and schools, supplying weapons on loan and ammunition at reduced cost.[34]

Finally, no aspect of California's politics can be understood apart from the continuous influx of legal and illegal immigrants at levels far higher than other states. During its first century of statehood, California's population was primarily American born, with a small percentage comprising foreign immigrants and their families, and assimilated within a generation or two. Great waves of new migrants begin arriving in the 1960s, so that as of 2002 one Californian in four was foreign born.[35] Since the 1970s, California has been the leading immigrant-receiving state, and one of the leading states where immigrants have settled.[36] Not only do these immigrants arrive in great numbers, but their assimilation, if it occurs, takes place at a time when their civic education includes virtually no discussion of the Second Amendment's connection to free government.[37]

Some of California's staunchest defenders of civil rights, including the right to private arms, are those who have emigrated from places where no such rights are recognized. On the other hand, de Tocqueville recognized that respect for rights in a democracy requires education and nurture among the citizens of a regime. For new immigrants this means a process of Americanization—a schooling in the history and political principles of their new home. If this civic education includes no attention to the connection between free government and a right to keep and bear arms, it should come as no surprise that understanding and appreciation for that right will decline. While a cursory exam in American government is administered to applicants for American citizenship, the test bank questions include none directly related to the Second Amendment.[38] It is thus fair to ask whether the state's high level of immigration, combined with the poor civic education new citizens receive, is responsible in part for the now precarious position of privately owned arms in California.

Some new citizens in California have come to appreciate their private arms under the worst of circumstances. During the April 1992 riots that followed the Rodney King verdict, Korean Americans, many of whose shops were adjacent to the worst areas, quite effectively defended their lives and property with arms. Some, however, learned a bitter lesson about the state's confusion about firearms wielded in self-defense:

> By Wednesday evening, we knew the mobs would soon reach Koreatown. Desperate calls for help to city authorities were not answered. Koreatown leaders thought they had many friends in City Hall. . . . At the time of crisis, no one provided us with police protection. We had to stand alone in times of danger. . . . Some veteran groups wanted to arm themselves in order to defend the town. Community leaders pleaded not to, that it would not be a right thing to do. Police handcuffed some armed defenders face down on the ground, while letting looters go.[39]

THE FUTURE FOR GUN
RIGHTS IN CALIFORNIA

Its political principles founded largely in Progressivism and marked by an overweening confidence in gun control as crime prevention, its recent history having included dramatic instances of gun violence, and a significant portion of its population unschooled in the principles of free government, the future of gun rights in California would appear bleak. And yet Californians continue to purchase firearms in the spirit of the state constitution's preamble, the better to defend life and liberty, protect property, and to guarantee safety, as well as for sport shooting and hunting. Outnumbered as they are, gun owners are reliable voters, politically organized, and politicians know that legislation to ban or restrict private arms will cost votes. Accidental deaths and injuries by firearms continue to decline in the state as in the nation. And it becomes increasingly apparent that in major U.S. cities, and in entire nations like England and Australia, restricting or even banning guns altogether is not only ineffective but also counterproductive.[40] With these factors at work, it is not impossible that some interesting and unexpected turns lie ahead for California's least secure right.

NOTES

1. The 1993 Brady Act requires that all states impose a five-day wait on handguns only. California's waiting period, ostensibly to run a more extensive background check on purchasers, presently stands at fifteen days for handguns, ten days for long guns.

2. California is one of fourteen "may-issue" states, allowing local law enforcement to issue permits at their discretion. Most states have adopted "shall issue" policies requiring issuance of a Carrying Concealed Weapon (CCW) permit to anyone meeting the individual state's requirements. See Clayton E. Cramer and David B. Kopel, "'Shall Issue': The New Wave of Concealed Handgun Permit Laws," *Tennessee Law Review* 62 (1995): 679.

3. The other is New York. New Jersey, Maryland, and Massachusetts have banned magazines holding more than fifteen cartridges. The 1994 Federal Crime Bill banned the further manufacture of magazines holding more than ten cartridges, but allows sale and transfer of those previously manufactured.

4. AB 496/SB 682.

5. George Skelton, "Backers of Gun Controls Preparing to Fire Another Round of Legislation," *Los Angeles Times*, December 16, 2002.

6. The Brady Campaign to Prevent Gun Violence (known as Handgun Control, Inc. from its founding in 1974 until 2001), for example, notes that "In 1999 . . . the bellwether state California passed the nation's toughest ban on assault weapons. . . . With your support, other states' legislatures can be convinced to emulate California and pass laws that will further reduce the availability and use of semiautomatic, military-style assault weapons in America." www.bradycampaign.org/facts/issuebriefs/assault.asp (April 7, 2003). Likewise, concerning two recent studies about the infeasibility of tracing crime guns through a firearms "fingerprinting" database, the Associated Press reports

that "Opponents of a national database have used the California studies to counter congressional proposals for a nationwide ballistics database spurred by last fall's sniper spree on the East Coast. Proponents, meanwhile, had hoped a California law would help spur similar databases in other states and, ultimately, nationally." "California Attorney General Says Firearms 'Fingerprinting' Premature," *San Jose Mercury News*, January 29, 2003 www.bayarea.com/mid/mercurynews/news/local/5060344.htm (January 30, 2003).

7. Sanford Levinson, "The Embarrassing Second Amendment," *Yale Law Journal* 99 (1990): 637–59.

8. "Before a standing army or a tyrannical government can rule, the people must be disarmed; as they are in almost every kingdom in Europe. The supreme power in America cannot enforce unjust laws by the sword; because the whole body of the people are armed, and constitute a force superior to any band of regular (or professional) troops that can be, on any pretense, raised in the United States." Noah Webster, "An Examination into the Leading Principles of the Federal Constitution Proposed by the Late Convention" in *Pamphlets on the Constitution of the United States*, ed. Paul Leicester Ford (Union, N.J.: Lawbook Exchange, 2000 [1888]). For additional material from the founders supporting this understanding of the Second Amendment, and refuting the idea that the right to keep and bear arms is not individual but belongs only to the organized militia, see *U.S. v. Emerson*, 270 F. 3d 203 (5th Cir.), and William Van Alstyne, "The Second Amendment and the Personal Right to Arms," *Duke Law Journal* 43 (1994): 1236–55.

9. Reference to John Locke, *Second Treatise on Government*, ed. Richard H. Cox (Arlington Heights, Ill.: Harlan Davidson, 1982]

10. Nelson Lund, "The Past and Future of the Individual's Right to Arms," *Georgia Law Review* 31 (1996): 59–63.

11. California is one of seven states with no constitutional protection for privately owned arms.

12. At the beginning of the 1849 Constitutional Convention, Iowa's state constitution was used as an example, but "as the session advanced, the constitution of New York was oftener consulted, and when the Convention finished its labors their perfected instrument resembled more that of the Empire State than any other." Franklin Tuthill, *History of California* (San Francisco: H. H. Bancroft and Co., 1866), 266–67.

13. Emphasis added. 1849 California Constitution, article I, section 1. Amended to refer to "people" instead of "men," and adding a right to privacy, the same words appear in the 1879 Constitution in its present form.

14. At least one pro-gun rights group is at work on an initiative to amend the California Constitution to include a right to keep and bear arms, to be put before the voters in the 2004 election.

15. For example, Mr. Harvey proposed an amendment to the Militia section to require "the safekeeping of the public arms, in such manner as may be requisite and necessary to best promote and make efficient this arm of the public service to cope with any emergency that may arise. . . ." E. B. Willis and P. K. Stockton, *Debates and Proceed-*

ings of the Constitutional Convention, vol. 1 (Sacramento, Calif.: J. D. Young, 1880–1881), 220.

16. Willis and Stockton, *Debates and Proceedings*, vol. 1, 285.

17. For example, Mississippi enacted as law that "no freedman, free Negro, or mulatto not in the military service of the United States government, and not licensed so to do by the board of police of his or her county, shall keep or carry firearms of any kind, or ammunition, dirk, or Bowie knife." As cited in Gregg Lee Carter, *The Gun Control Movement* (New York: Twayne, 1997), 25. See also Stephen P. Halbrook, *Freedmen, the Fourteenth Amendment, and the Right to Bear Arms, 1866–1876* (Westport, Conn.: Greenwood, 1998).

18. Sacramento *Record Union*, 30 September 1878, as reprinted in Carl Brent Swisher, *Motivation and Political Technique in the California Constitutional Convention 1878–1879* (Claremont, Calif.: Pomona College, 1930), 34.

19. Stanley Mosk, *New York Law Forum* 14 (1968): 697.

20. This is borne out by numerous statements from the anti-gun rights leaders: "For target shooting, that's okay. Get a license and go to the range. For defense of the home, that's why we have police departments." James Brady, *Parade Magazine*, June 25, 1994, and "Banning guns addresses a fundamental right of Americans to feel safe." U.S. Senator Dianne Feinstein, Associated Press, November 18, 1993. "Why should America adopt a policy of near-zero tolerance for private gun ownership? Because it's the only alternative to the present insanity. Without both strict limits on access to new weapons and aggressive efforts to reduce the supply of existing weapons, no one can be safer." "Taming the Monster: Get Rid of the Guns," *Los Angeles Times*, December 28, 1993, B6. Former San Jose, California police chief and spokesman for Handgun Control, Inc. Joseph McNamara, however, argued that certain classes of persons might be permitted private arms: "As much as I oppose the average person's having a gun, I recognize that some people have a legitimate need to own one. A wealthy corporate executive who fears his family might get kidnapped is one such person. A Hollywood celebrity who has to protect himself from kooks is another. If Sharon Tate had had access to a gun during the Manson killings, some innocent lives might have been saved." Joseph McNamara, *Safe and Sane* (New York: Putnam, 1984), 71–72.

21. Emphasis added. "Attorney General Position on the Second Amendment to the United States Constitution," No date. [caag.state.ca.us/firearms/2amend.htm] (April 7, 2003).

22. This appears to be exactly what has happened in England, the birthplace of the right to keep and bear arms, and Australia. See two books by Joyce Lee Malcolm, *To Keep and Bear Arms: The Origins of an Anglo-American Right* (Cambridge, Mass.: Harvard University Press, 1994) and *Guns and Violence: The English Experience* (Cambridge, Mass.: Harvard University Press, 2002).

23. James J. Rawls and Walton Bean, *California: An Interpretive History* (Boston: McGraw Hill, 2003), 112.

24. Roger D. McGrath, *Gunfighters, Highwaymen and Vigilantes: Violence on the*

Frontier (Berkeley: University of California Press, 1984), 199, and David Kopel, *The Samurai, the Mountie, and the Cowboy* (Buffalo, N.Y.: Prometheus Books, 1992), 327–29. Vigilantism, often a force toward law and order in areas without established police forces, could also become a problem, as happened with San Francisco's Vigilance Committee during the 1850s. See Ray Abrahams, *Vigilant Citizens: Vigilantism and the State* (Cambridge, U.K.: Polity Press, 1998), and Richard B. Rice, William Bullough, and Richard J. Orsi, *The Elusive Eden: A New History of California* (Boston: McGraw Hill, 2002), 211–16.

25. *Report of the Crime Problem Advisory Committee of California* (Sacramento, Calif., 1932), 9.

26. The wait was extended to fifteen days in 1976, the longest in the nation, and expanded to cover all firearms purchases. Wayne R. LaPierre, *Guns, Crime and Freedom* (Washington, D.C.: Regnery, 1994), 42.

27. "Heavily Armed Negro Group Walks into Assembly Chamber," *Los Angeles Times*, May 3, 1967, 13. Author David Horowitz notes that "As a street predator, [Black Panther leader Huey] Newton had studied law at night to develop his craft. Among his discoveries was that the law allowed citizens to bear firearms in public. Dressing his recruits in menacing uniforms of black leather jackets and berets, he invoked Mao's dictum 'It is necessary to pick up the gun.' Armed Panther 'field marshalls' patrolled neighborhoods to monitor arrests, making local police nervous and angry, and inspiring legislators to propose a change in the law. In the summer of the riots, the Panthers marched into a session of the State Assembly in Sacramento, shotguns aloft, to oppose legislation that would remove the privilege. Their demands were ignored, and the law about firearms was quickly changed." David Horowitz, *Radical Son* (New York: Simon & Schuster, 1997), 162. See also Clayton E. Cramer, "The Racist Roots of Gun Control," *Kansas Journal of Law & Public Policy* 5 (1995): 21.

28. Anti-gun rights activist Josh Sugarmann, head of the Washington, D.C.-based Violence Policy Center, authored a 1988 memo arguing that public interest in the handgun issue had waned, and that the movement should focus on banning military style semiautomatic weapons. He correctly predicted that the public would be frightened by their "menacing looks" and would be unable to distinguish between these arms and their fully automatic (i.e., machine gun) military counterparts. See Kopel, *Samurai*, 435. See also Jim Oliphant, "How the Gun Debate Died" *Legal Times*, October 22, 2002, www.law.com/jsp/article.jsp?id=103212879506(April 7, 2003).

29. "Court Upholds State Assault Weapons Ban," *Los Angeles Times*, December 6, 2002, A1.

30. U.S. Court of Appeals for the Ninth Circuit, *Silveira v. Lockyer*, 312 F. 3d 1052 (9th Cir. 2002). For an opposing view about the meaning of the Second Amendment, see U.S. Court of Appeals for the Fifth Circuit, *U.S. v. Emerson*, 270 F. 3d 203 (5th Cir. 2001).

31. Attorney General Lockyer Issues Statement on Federal Appeals Court Ruling Upholding California's Assault Weapons Ban, December 5, 2002 www.ag.ca.gov/newsalerts/2002/02–135.htm (April 7, 2003).

32. "On the state level, most of the current session's gun-control measures have come from urban Democrats, largely from Los Angeles." John Borland, "The Arming of California," *California Journal* 39 (October 1995): 39.

33. Forty military bases in California were closed 1988–1995. See A. G. Block, "History for Our Times: Pearl Harbor and the Birth of Modern California," *California Journal* 45 (November 2001): 8–19, and Herbert A. Sample, "Downsizing California's Military Industrial Complex," *California Journal* 39 (September 1995): 39–42.

34. The National Board for the Promotion of Rifle Practice was established by Congress in 1903.

35. William H. Frey, "Migration Swings," *American Demographics* (February 2002), 18–21. This is not to mention the state's illegal aliens, numbering an estimated 2.2 million as of 2000, a figure representing 30 percent of the nation's 7 million undocumented aliens. "Number of Illegal Migrants Growing," *Los Angeles Times*, February 1, 2003, A14.

36. Jeffrey S. Passel and Michael Fix, U.S. Population and Immigration [3] Hearing, U.S. House, Committee on the Judiciary, August 2, 2001 (Washington, D.C.: GPO, 2001), 10–11.

37. Legal immigrants into the United States number about 1.1 million annually, about 0.4 percent of the overall population, with approximately two hundred thousand new legal foreign-born immigrants settling in California annually. See James Goldborough, "Out-of-Control Immigration," *Foreign Affairs* 79 (September–October 2000): 89–101, and Ron Unz, "California and the End of White America," *Commentary* (November 1999): 17–28.

38. The Basic Citizenship Skills Examination Study Questions for the INS English/ Civics Exam lists only one question that would allow for mention of the right to keep and bear arms: "Name three rights or freedoms guaranteed by the Bill of Rights."

39. Sucheng Chan and Spencer Olin, eds. "Eui-Young Yu Offers a Korean American Perspective on the Los Angeles Civil Disorders, 1992," in *Major Problems in California History*, (Boston: Houghton Mifflin, 1997), 464. See also Seth Mydans, "A Target of Rioters, Koreatown Is Bitter, Armed, and Determined," *New York Times*, May 3, 1992, 1, and Elaine H. Kim, "They Armed in Self-Defense," *Newsweek*, May 18, 1992, 10.

40. "Taking Aim: Why Gun Control Won't Work," *California Lawyer*, January 2001, 46–49.

California's Political Mass Media

Richard H. Reeb Jr.

For many years political commentators were reluctant to describe as "political" that journalism we have all now become accustomed to calling the mass media. After all, citizens have had a century of imbibing Progressive sentiments in politics and accepting the related claim of "objectivity" in the press, both of which disdained mere "partisanship" as inadequate to the requirements of a modern age. The contention that newspapers, magazines, radio, television, and now the Internet, are "political" strikes the idealist as in bad taste and only the cynic as blatantly obvious. But as many students of politics have noted since the nation's founding, without a ubiquitous journalism dedicated to reporting reliable facts and presenting thoughtful opinions about matters of the common good, republican government cannot succeed. As James Madison once observed, a free nation without a free press is but the prelude to a farce—or a tragedy.

California, the most populous state in the Union with approximately 35 million souls (and counting) spread out over more than 158,000 square miles, could not function as a representative republic without free journalism. According to one online source (Abyz News Links), there are 492 news links in the state now available on the Internet, mostly daily and weekly newspapers. Of these, 366 are listed as newspapers of general interest, 63 as broadcast outlets (including 40 television stations), 52 as Internet, 26 as campus newspapers, 11 as magazines, and 6 as statewide media. Listed on another website (the Internet Press) are 218 radio stations and 53 television stations, but only 71 newspapers. The leading media markets of course, are in the largest cities, with 39 Internet-linked organs in Los Angeles, 31 in San Francisco, 25 in San Diego, 12 in Fresno and nine in San Jose.

Virtually all media pride themselves on their commitment to objectivity in news coverage, but business imperatives, as well as political ones, inevitably com-

311

promise this claim. All mass or general interest media want as large a market share as possible for maximum profit, so they rarely conspicuously flaunt their political views on the front page as they want regular customers from all parts of the political spectrum. At the same time, the media's politics tilt one way or another depending on the dominant political trends in the state and the local region. Today, the state is heavily Democratic and the urban areas are generally more liberal and Democratic than the suburban, small town, and rural areas.

The state's leading newspaper, the *Los Angeles Times,* published in the nation's second-largest city, has moved increasingly to the left in its political orientation, although observers with good memories or history books know that it was a strongly conservative organ in the past. Recently, it was purchased by the *Chicago Tribune,* which may or may not moderate its politics. Similarly, the *San Francisco Chronicle* was once a conservative newspaper, but that time has long past. The *Oakland Tribune* was a conservative source when it was owned by the Knowland family (William Knowland was a Republican senator in the 1950s), that has since passed into different and liberal hands. The *San Jose Mercury-News* and the *Long Beach Press-Telegram,* part of the Knight-Ridder chain, were once Republican organs, but they have also moved to the left.

The McClatchy chain, consisting of the *Sacramento Bee,* the *Modesto Bee,* and the *Fresno Bee*, still maintain a liberal editorial line, but the increasing conservative strength in the suburbs of these growing communities, has tempered each publication somewhat, and the chain's columnists, led by the redoubtable Dan Walters, are among the best in the state. The *Sacramento Bee*'s onetime conservative competitor, the *Sacramento Union,* could not garner enough advertising to survive (and was openly denounced by nationally prominent journalists as too partisan), but the *Bee* wants those former readers too.

The rise of the op-ed page in the late 1960s has introduced more variety into editorial opinions in the big urban markets, although the *San Diego Union* (the leading Copley Newspaper) and the *Orange Country Register* (the best known of the Freedom publications), have long been reliably conservative and libertarian respectively in their editorial views. Meanwhile, prominent syndicated conservative and liberal columnists are frequently found on the editorial pages of the state's medium and small-town newspapers, as well as editorials of differing ilk from the state's urban newspapers.

There is a solid readership for the editorial pages, but newspaper surveys reveal that this segment is never more than a minority, while the majority forms its impression of the newspaper—and therefore of politics and government— from the news sections, especially the front page. That is where politicians and their policies, not to mention their predilections and peccadilloes, more often rise and fall. It is more than a truism that, while news is regarded and often presented as a fungible product, not all newspapers have the same "take" on the state's news, however subtle the differences may be. Real choices have to be made, however conventional the whole process is.

For example, in their next-day Saturday morning coverage of Governor Gray Davis's long-awaited (and much-dreaded) almost $100 billion budget proposal on January 10, seven newspapers selected for comparison gave it various degrees of emphasis and contrasting angles. The liberal *Los Angeles Times,* serving an area that voted for Gray Davis's reelection, made painful choices the meat of its lead story: "Davis Budget of 'Hard Choices' Spreads the Pain: The governor says he has no option but to slash government services, raise taxes and impose fees. Republicans called his proposals a non-starter." In an apparent deemphasis of the rude budget awakening, the *Times* ran several other page-one articles—on the CIA, death-row pardons in Illinois, U.S. reaction to North Korean treaty withdrawal, and a thrill killer. (To be sure, this comprehensive organ had three full pages on the state budget deeper in the first section and another in the third section, for the more hardy and determined readers.)

By contrast, the *Sun* (a liberal Gannett newspaper) for San Bernardino County, a county that voted for Bill Simon, the governor's Republican challenger, devoted two-thirds of its front page to the budget news, declaring: "Davis wants cuts, tax hikes, layoffs: Governor proposes increasing sales, cigarette and income taxes, while trimming health care services and numbers of employees on state payroll." The only other front-page news concerned developments in North Korea and a local item. Another full page of state budget news appeared on page six.

The opening slant for the liberal *San Francisco Chronicle* front page was budget cuts. For readers in this heavily Democratic city (with a large Bay Area circulation), the headline was: "Davis proposes $21 billion in cuts: "$8.3 billion in higher taxes offered to fill budget hole." But this bad news took up only the top third of the page, with other articles on North Korea, U.S. job losses, body searches, Los Alamos firings, and Golden Gate Park's new dome. The budget story jumped to page 11 for two more full columns.

Finally, a newspaper in the largely Republican Mojave Desert (more precisely, the High Desert), the *Daily Press* in Victorville (Freedom chain), emphasized the increased taxes and the effects on local government: "Tax plan targets smokers, shoppers, wealthy: Plan puts wider range of local services on block."

Three national papers (which do not publish on weekends) treated the matter differently from the state papers and among themselves. Both *USA Today* and the *Wall Street Journal* kept the California budget story out of its Monday morning (January 13) news pages altogether, although the *Journal* included an op-ed piece entitled "California Drainin'," by Arthur Laffer, the man associated with the famous "Laffer curve" (that postulated an inverse relationship between tax rates and government income). Laffer criticized the tax increases and concluded that the state would have fiscal relief (along with other states) only if President Bush's tax plan is adopted and the national economy is thereby stimulated.

The *Christian Science Monitor* placed the story on page two: "The roots and ripple effects of Calif. deficit: Governor Davis urges tax hikes as part of a plan to fix a shortfall bigger than those of all other states combined" (only New York's budget is bigger). Indeed, the *Monitor* blamed California's current fiscal difficulty on the constitutional requirement for a two-thirds legislative vote for the state budget and the voters' right to propose ballot initiatives that place restrictions on state spending.

In each of these examples, there is plainly a common thread of information and interpretation, but the liberal papers stressed the disadvantages of budget cuts or simply downplayed the significance of the budget crisis, and the conservative papers (as well as those serving numerous conservative readers) more often emphasized the downside of tax increases.

Journalistic commentators have noted the decline in power of the editorial endorsement of newspapers, but the opinion vacuum is in such a manner regularly filled on the news pages. For politicians and policies, the most important asset is often press coverage, the more—and preferably the more favorable—the better, for that has the character of "fact" (found on the news pages) as opposed to "opinion" (found on the editorial pages). This is a misleading and even childish distinction, but there is no denying its practical force.

For the same reason, particularly with the imposition of political campaign contribution and spending limitations in the 1970s, political parties spent more and more of their money on the media. Campaign paraphernalia and precinct work, the heart and soul of political party campaigns for many years, were largely superseded by parties making media buys in major markets. Even though the distinction between news and advertising, not to mention news and entertainment, is supposed to be clear-cut, the truth is that media advertising, including especially so-called negative advertising, is highly effective, for the distinction between fact and opinion is more academic than real. Gray Davis's attacks on Los Angeles Mayor Richard Riordan in the state's earliest-ever primary (in March, formerly June) and then on Republican gubernatorial nominee Bill Simon in the general election, were highly effective in discrediting both men with the state's voters.

The "objective" *cum* commercial aspects of newspaper coverage are even more evident in broadcasting. The audiences are (at least potentially) even larger and more diverse than those for the print media, so every effort is made to appear impartial. Television news coverage can be riveting during events such as natural disasters and most emphatically the radical Islamic attack on the United States on September 11, 2001. But usually news programs fill up an hour or so with a little bit about a lot of things, not much of which is memorable. But here the mask slips a little too, as television news shows are generally liberal, although KTLA in Los Angeles has at times leaned to the right.

Even the news/entertainment distinction is hard to discern. One is struck, for example, by the glaring contrast between the lighthearted, devil-may-care, and downright flirtatious attitudes displayed by attractive local television news presenters, and the straight-faced, sober, and even serious coverage of the lifestyles of the rich and famous by equally attractive personalities on programs like *Entertainment Tonight*. Journalists who are at all thoughtful agonize over the superficial and even frivolous coverage that regularly characterizes television news programs (the long filming of the runaway white Bronco containing O. J. Simpson being the most egregious), but the requirement of "objectivity" and its evil twin of "market share" conspire to reduce journalism to the lowest common denominator.

In the mid-1980s a wholly new force was introduced into this bland and less than forthright mix: talk radio. When the Federal Communications Commission scrapped the Fairness Doctrine, the requirement of "equal time" went out with it. Opinionated radio commentary has proliferated, especially conservative viewpoints, which have consistently outdrawn liberal efforts. National figures like Rush Limbaugh, Michael Reagan, Michael Medved, and Hugh Hewitt, also figure prominently in California radio broadcasting. While the "mainstream media" still dominate the market as a whole, there is no denying that talk radio has provided bracing competition. And there are successful practitioners in local markets, such as John and Ken on radio station KFI in Los Angeles. (There are also so-called "shock jocks" who will do almost anything to get phone calls and lively audience attention.)

Talk radio isn't just more conservative; it is also more interesting, as liberal callers to these shows have confessed. Given the tendency toward blurring or obscuring political messages in the larger media outlets, the outspoken character of conservative talk radio has seized much of the public imagination. Whether this portends a fundamental change or merely a new journalistic niche for conservatives, remains to be seen. The "general interest" publications have too much at stake, professionally and commercially, to abandon their tried-and-true format. But the fact is that the mainstream media have less clout than before. Much is written these days about the need for diversity—in race, gender, and sexual orientation. In talk radio, the diversity in question is that of straightfor-ward political opinion. Can this be the true character of the media, or only a aberration? The debate has already begun.

An *EPIC* Legacy

Stephen Schwartz

In Brian P. Janiskee's and Ken Masugi's *Democracy in California: Politics and Government in the Golden State*, they refer to "the evolution of a Progressive state." But what does "Progressive" mean? For leftists, to be Progressive is to scream inane charges of genocide against President George W. Bush. But for California Democrats today it means a kind of particularly corrupt machine politics, even though, as Janiskee and Masugi point out, "early Progressives also despised the machine politics of their era" (i.e., of the period from 1905 to 1925). They quote the mordant observation of California's greatest Progressive author, the novelist Frank Norris speaking through a character in his novel *The Octopus*: "California likes to be fooled. . . . Indifference to public affairs—absolute indifference, it stamps us all. Our state is the very paradise of fakirs."

Today's California Democratic Party is not a legitimate heir of the Progressive tradition, which was created by Republicans, of whom the outstanding representative was governor and U.S. Senator Hiram Johnson, California's dominant political figure from 1910 to 1945. Those Progressives left the questionable, but beloved, legacy of the "initiative, referendum, and recall" system, which conservatives and other outsiders have more recently used to regain some influence over public policy. Its most spectacular incidence has doubtless been the gubernatorial recall effort of 2003.

By contrast, the origins of the contemporary California Democratic Party are to be found later, in the 1930s, paralleling those of the Democratic-Farmer-Labor Party in Minnesota. Both are, in effect, leftist cadre parties created by socialist radicals aligned with the Roosevelt New Deal, but very different from the New Deal in numerous ways.

The modern California Democratic Party emerged from the End Poverty in California or EPIC movement, a utopian uprising that swept the state in the

317

depths of the Great Depression, under the leadership of leftist writer Upton Sinclair, its gubernatorial candidate.

Sinclair gained the Democratic primary nomination for the governorship, defeating a favorite of the old guard leadership in the party, George Creel. The Sinclair triumph came at the end of August 1934, one month after the conclusion of a kind of labor insurrection in the maritime cities of the Pacific Coast: the "big strike" of longshoremen and seamen. Until 1933, Californians had paid attention to Sinclair, who enjoyed a worldwide reputation as an author, more as a literary than a political figure, even though nearly all his books represented lightly-fictionalized muckraking—his most enduring is his turn-of-the-century study of Lithuanian Socialists in the Chicago packinghouses, *The Jungle.*

He had been execrated by the California far left for his support of U.S. entry into World War I, but regained status as a hero in the early 1920s, when he defied the Los Angeles police during a premonitory labor battle involving marine workers who belonged to the ultraradical Industrial Workers of the World. He had been an occasional statewide candidate of the Socialist Party, once a major force in California, but by the 1920s a badly weakened, almost irrelevant organization.

In October 1933, Sinclair self-published a pamphlet titled *I, Governor of California, and How I Ended Poverty.* According to him, it sold one hundred fifty thousand copies in four months, at 20 cents per copy. It was, at the time, the greatest bestseller in the state's history, reaching two hundred fifty thousand copies by September 1934. The work's flamboyant promises of social transformation have earned it a reputation as a classic expression of irresponsible "Depression demagogy," although it was a surprisingly lyrical and moderate work, at least in tone.

Sales of *I, Governor of California, and How I Ended Poverty* became the foundation for the establishment of a network of EPIC clubs the length and breadth of the state. A month after his primary victory, two hundred fifty EPIC clubs had been set up. His Socialist comrades condemned him for abandoning their party to join the Democrats, which had never enjoyed a reputation for cleanliness or enlightenment in the state. But Sinclair was looking to Washington and the New Deal, rather than to the state's past. The social engineering principles proclaimed by President Franklin Roosevelt enabled him to graft a radical conception onto the existing party, which would, thereafter, never be the same. (It should be noted that the Communist Party, which was stuck in a period of ultra revolutionary extremism, violently condemned Sinclair and EPIC as "fascist." They offered their own candidate, a Russian functionary of cloudy legal status named Samuel A. Darcy).

Sinclair and EPIC appealed much more to the labor and agricultural rank and file in California than to the well-established radical elite in San Francisco, and even, to an extent, more to the southland of the state than the northern districts. His vision was more extreme than his vocabulary; he was an admirer of the Stalinist transformation of Russia, although not of the Communists themselves, at least as far as their local cadres were concerned. He was also a much more appealing and sincere candidate than most of the leftist intellectuals of his time. Having met him in his very old age, I can say he never lost his sense of humor.

Although Sinclair's proposals for the rescue of the state from economic disaster were, as shall be shown, far at variance from those commonly advanced in the Progressive era, his discourse echoed its bucolic and nostalgic themes. Western Progressivism had, in the final analysis, less to do with industrial or scientific ideas about progress than with yearning for a simpler and uncorrupted rural past in which the producer received a fairer recompense for his labor. *I, Governor of California, and How I Ended Poverty* begins, "Ever since the Civil War we have been governed by a business autocracy, and there has been a continuous struggle between the autocracy and our political democracy." This was much more the language of Andrew Jackson than of Karl Marx.

Nevertheless, the pamphlet evoked, in a minor key, a lyrical panorama of technology as the guarantor of the state's future promise: "a land ready to produce almost everything which humans need . . . machines of production, marvelous creations of human ingenuity . . . roads for distributing, the finest on the whole earth." But the pastoral was blighted: "A strange paralysis has fallen on this land. Here are fruits rotting on the ground, and vegetables being dumped into the bays because there is no market for them . . . thousands wandering homeless, and thousands of homes which no one is allowed to occupy . . . a million people who want work and are not allowed to work . . . another million being taxed out of homes and farms to provide the money to feed those starving ones, who would be glad to earn their food but are not allowed to! . . . The men who have made this condition are a little band of 'insiders,' the masters of our chain banks, railroads, and public service corporations."

Sketching out an imaginary "People's History of California, 1933–1938," Sinclair enumerated the innovations he would, if elected, bring to public policy:

- "Land colonies for the unemployed" (i.e., collective farms, run by the state, to operate alongside individual farming and large-scale agriculture). Unlike the Soviet system of collectivization, membership was to be purely voluntary.

- State operation of idle factories, employing those rendered jobless by the depression.
- Issuance of a separate state currency, combining scrip with $10 bonds redeemable on thirty days' notice.
- Financing of these measures by a state tax with a rate of 30 percent on income up to $50,000 per year, and 50 percent on inherited funds over $50,000.
- Homes occupied and farms worked by their owners, under a valuation of $3,000, would be exempt from taxation, but heavier taxes would be assessed on unimproved and uncultivated property assessed at more than $1,000 in value.
- Pensions of $50 per month for the indigent over sixty years of age, the indigent blind, the handicapped prevented from working by their condition, and widows with two dependent children, with $25 monthly for each additional child.
- Establishment of three public agencies to administer these programs: the California Authority for Land (CAL), the California Authority for Production (CAP), and the California Authority for Money (CAM).

In sum, the EPIC plan was a more extreme version of the New Deal. Where, in its early phase, the Roosevelt administration had adopted a "blue eagle" as its emblem, EPIC was symbolized by a bee, with the slogan, "I Produce—I Defend."

EPIC was not a welfare scheme; Sinclair condemned the notion that "people would be fed, but would not be allowed to grow their own food." His utopia more resembled the single tax ideology of Henry George (whose political career began in San Francisco) and of radicals active in the Mexican Revolution, than it did Soviet socialism.

Sinclair's running mate was Sheridan Downey, a Sacramento attorney. His ideal "brains trust" included such revered figures as Fremont Older, a crusading San Francisco newspaper editor and urban reformer, and J. Stitt Wilson, former Socialist mayor of Berkeley. A number of veteran Socialists soon succumbed to his appeal to change their political registration to Democratic. Others rejected the gambit, and the Socialists ran their own candidate for governor, Milen Dempster.

But Sinclair understood something that eluded the old-line Socialists; since the world war, socialist ideas had gained a wider popularity than the party itself ever enjoyed. This had little to do with either the allure of Soviet Communism or the sudden prestige of the New Deal. Sinclair argued that in the presidential election of 1924, when the Progressive candidate, U.S. Senator Robert M. La Follette of Wisconsin, was endorsed by the Socialists—and garnered 5 million votes nationally—the Socialists had indoctrinated the Progressives, and that the same phenomenon would be embodied in the EPIC capture of the Democratic Party. This insight was acute and accurate, with consequences seen today. EPIC also benefitted from the state's direct primary and ballot cross-filing. Legally, Sinclair could have cross-filed as a Democrat, Republican, Socialist, and even as a Prohibitionist.

EPIC may be said to have excited somewhat more enthusiasm from the left outside the state than within it. An editorial in *The Nation* commented, "If ever a revolution was due, it was due in California. Nowhere else has the battle between capital and labor been so widespread and bitter, and the casualties so large; nowhere else has there been such a flagrant denial of the personal liberties guaranteed by the Bill of Rights; nowhere else has authority been so lawless and brazen; nowhere else has the brute force of capitalism been so openly used and displayed; nowhere else has labor been so oppressed; nowhere else has there been a more false or more poisoned and poisoning press."

Sinclair and EPIC carried out a revolution in state politics, and especially in Democratic politics, even though he lost the election of 1934 to Merriam. (With its habitual levity, the *San Francisco Chronicle* headlined the news, "Merriam We Roll Along.") The story of his defeat has become something of a cliché; powerful business interests, including Hollywood, used faked newsreels to portray him as a dangerous, antireligious subversive and his supporters as aliens, eccentrics, and Communists—even though his political culture was thoroughly authentic and native to the state and, as he put it, the Soviets borrowed from his ideas more than he from theirs.

Nevertheless, his political heir, and the first Democratic governor of California since 1894, Culbert Levy Olson, won the state house in 1938. By then EPIC, the Democratic Party, and the state had undergone remarkable changes. After 1935, the Communists recognized their error in shunning EPIC, and poured into Democratic ranks. Thus, Ellis Patterson, lieutenant governor under Olson, was a close sympathizer of the Soviet network in the United States.

Olson, much more than Sinclair, typified an old-fashioned Western Progressivism. He was born in Utah and had worked as a cowboy, laborer, and railroad employee before graduating from Brigham Young University as a lawyer. Olson had served as a Utah state legislator and introduced such classic Progressive legislation as a workers' compensation law, a minimum wage, the initiative and referendum, and similar reforms reminiscent of the California model. He was elected as an EPIC standard bearer to the California state senate in 1934, leading the ticket in Los Angeles. Many Californians viewed him a safer and less controversial version of Sinclair. However, Olson had never actually been a member of the EPIC movement, although he became leader of the significant EPIC delegation in the state legislature.

Olson introduced EPIC measures into the 1935 session, including a "production-for-use" plan, a major tax bill, and others—which failed to pass. Such EPIC bills as did pass were mainly vetoed by Governor Merriam. But the indefatigable Olson campaigned for public ownership of utilities, more labor laws, old age pensions, regulation of the oil industry, and resettlement of the indigent on occupied farmland, among other schemes. Among Olson's first executive acts as governor was to release from prison a long-jailed labor radical, Tom Mooney.

Another change seen in California radicalism between 1934 and 1938 involved the emergence of a dubious reform movement, known as "Ham-and-Eggs." This was a variant of the Townsend Plan, a movement for old age pensions, based in Southern California and more fascist in spirit than progressive, regardless of the latter term's definition. As the Great Depression wore on the Townsend partisans gravitated toward right-wing populism. Nevertheless, in California leftist and liberal protest movements dominated the scene. In addition, right-wing populism, which elicited considerable enthusiasm in the Midwestern states during the Depression, ended up in the isolationist and even the pro-Axis camp with the approach of World War II. By contrast, the West Coast, where the trade union movement was the backbone of the left, generally despised totalitarianism and sympathized with the anti-Hitler allies.

Although Sinclair lost in 1934, his supporters had transformed the old, venal, and loosely organized Democratic Party into an ideological structure based on activist clubs. Its essence remains undiluted today; the only changes in its political style, over the years, have involved international issues. In 1939, Governor Olson, briskly repudiated the Stalinist-controlled "peace movement" and its alliance with Hitler; it would have been thrilling to see a major California Democratic leader, in 2003, come out against the fake pacifists' campaign to defend Saddam Hussein's regime in Iraq.

But the most recent Democrat governor, Gray Davis, was no Olson, and was anything but anxious to emulate the antitotalitarian Democrats of two generations ago. In 1948, prominent EPIC figures defected from the California Democratic Party to support the "peace" candidate for the presidency, Progressive Henry Wallace, and a new pattern was set for good. The Stalinist Progressives ran Vincent Hallinan, father of the contemporary San Francisco district attorney, Terence Hallinan, for president in 1952. Soon afterward, the pro-Communist defectors infiltrated back into the regular organization through a front group, the California Democratic Council, or CDC. In the 1960s, yet another leftist element emerged in the form of the San Francisco-based electoral machine headed by Phillip Burton. The outcome: a bureaucratic state party that today combines the exhausted heritage of EPIC with the mindless "peace" rhetoric of the Vietnam era.

It is thus that we must understand the faction of the California Democratic Party identified, as these lines are written, with House minority leader Nancy Pelosi, congresswoman from San Francisco—a human agglomeration that, as the old saw has it, have learned nothing and forgotten nothing. As the removal of Saddam Hussein approached, San Francisco was cheering—for the other side. The city used to glory in the nickname "Baghdad-by-the-Bay," which acquired a particularly repellent appropriateness. California had become a one-party state, just like pre-liberation Iraq, and with more characteristics in common with it than the outsider would imagine. Of course, there was no single dictator in the state, and there have been no massacres—call it Ba'athism without Bloodshed, or Tyranny without Tears.

Thinking about California's contemporary Democrats, I was also reminded of parallels with the former Yugoslavia, when Representative Pelosi acclaimed her state's delegation for its "extraordinary mix of diversity." The California Democratic leaders are diverse in exactly the way the Yugoslav Communist leadership was diverse: they are a group of token representatives of ethnic communities, brought together with identity as their main qualification. There seems to be, of course, no danger that California will arrive at the same violent end as its Yugoslav counterpart, but it seems certain that the California Democratic Party, like the Yugoslav Communist Party, is destined to disintegrate, because its time has long passed.

As I learned in visiting and reporting on the breakup of Yugoslavia, that country's Communists simply could not imagine that anybody did not share their beliefs and concerns, and the same is true of California Democrats. Pelosi has declared, "The issues we care about in California are the same ones people care about all around the country." If this kind of heedless devotion to a dead political form were to retain its hold over the national Democratic leadership, the party would truly be doomed; and if Pelosi wanted to save her party, she should have publicly acknowledged that the old ideology had failed, and turn a new page. But it seems Pelosi could not do this. The grip of the "dead hand of the past," as the once-dissident Russian poet Yevtushenko put it, was too strong. Certainly, it is absurd to believe that the majority of Americans share, with San Franciscans—because Pelosi is much more a San Franciscan than a Californian—a political agenda including officially-approved "teach-ins" against the war in Iraq to be led by high school faculty; designation of the grossly obese as a class to be protected from discrimination if they seek jobs as, say, exercise instructors; health coverage for municipal civil servants, and their partners, to obtain sex change operations; and a pressing need for debate over the legality of public urination and defecation by street people.

The first of these items was announced on television news at the end of 2002; the others are among the achievements of the mayoral administration of Willie L. Brown Jr., local satrap of the Democratic machine and Pelosi loyalist. Other Democratic ward heelers include Ted Fang, publisher of the *San Francisco Examiner*, who announced on national television, during a discussion of the Chinese Communist regime, that he didn't know what the word "democracy" meant. Fortunately, the TV host had put him up against Republican ex-congressman Bob Dornan, who immediately nailed Fang, thus rescuing the honor of, at least, the Southern Californians who voted for Dornan. It was a moment for a refugee from California like myself to savor. But the exchange was revealing, for it is entirely probable that Fang, if he expressed such a view at most levels of polite California Democratic society, would be met with hearty agreement. They don't know what democracy means, either, any more than they understand the real legacy of the word Progressive. If there is anyone in California politics, as these lines are written, who merits the title "progressive," it is Arnold Schwarzenegger. Hiram Johnson is chuckling from his seat in heaven.

Water, Water Everywhere and Nary a Drop to Drink

Ric Williams

The water problem in California is simple. The majority of the people live at distances far removed from the majority of the state's water supply. Currently, California's population is somewhere between 35.5 and 36 million. Roughly 85 percent of the total lives in six major metropolitan areas: the Los Angeles basin; the San Francisco Bay Area; San Diego County; and the Sacramento-Stockton, Fresno, and Bakersfield urban areas in the Central Valley. The LA basin, which includes the city of Los Angeles, the ninety-plus other cities in Los Angeles County, most of Orange County, the western portions of San Bernardino and Riverside Counties, and the southeastern portion of Ventura County, houses 17 to 18 million people or 45 to 50 percent of the state's population. The greater Bay Area or the ten counties (San Francisco, San Mateo, Santa Clara, Alameda, Contra Costa, Marin, Napa, Sonoma, Solano, and Santa Cruz) which surround the San Francisco Bay, has slightly over 7 million people or more than 20 percent of the state's total. The San Diego area contains just over 3 million people or 8 to 9 percent of the whole, and between 2 and 2.5 million people or roughly 5 to 7 percent of the state's population live in the Sacramento-Stockton, Fresno, and Bakersfield metropolitan areas. Outside of these six areas, the largest urban centers are the Palm Springs and Tahoe Valley resort centers and Redding, none of which have populations of over one hundred thousand.

Historically, the geographic distribution of the population was much different. The gold rush populated the northern half of the state with the growth of Southern California occurring later. For example, in 1900 the cities of San Francisco and Los Angeles had populations of 342,000 and 102,000, while in 1930, there were 634,000 people in San Francisco and 1,238,000 in Los Angeles.

What has not changed, however, is the fact that the major urban centers have occupied the arid and semiarid regions of the state. Since the 1880s when state-wide figures were first compiled, average annual precipitation (rainfall and snow-fall) has been as follows: in Los Angeles, 11 to 14 inches; in San Diego, 8 to 10 inches; in San Francisco, 19 to 22 inches; and in Sacramento, 18 to 20 inches. For almost a century, the fact that people have chosen to live in these regions has meant that local water supplies (river and well water) have not been able to meet the demand for water. Thus it has been necessary to "import" or transport water great distances from those areas of the state that have an average annual water surplus to those regions which have an average annual water deficit.

An annual surplus occurs when the amount of rain and snowfall exceeds the volume of water vapor which is drawn back into the atmosphere by the evapora-tive action of the sun, and an annual deficit exists when the sun draws more water out of the ground than is deposited by rain and snow. The surplus region forms a giant horseshoe with western and eastern arms and a northern bar or cap. The western arm is the Coastal Range with the greatest surplus area of that range lying north of the San Francisco Bay. The northern bar or cap stretches from Redding north to the Oregon border and is constituted by the Klamath and Cascade Mountain ranges. The Sierra Nevada Range, which runs from the Cascades in the North to the Tehachapis in the south, is the last or eastern arm of that horseshoe. On average around 200 million acre-feet of precipitation occurs in those areas. (An acre-foot of water, or the volume of water required to cover one square acre of land to a depth of one foot, equals slightly more than 325,000 gallons, and this means that we get around 650 billion gallons of pre-cipitation each year.) About 130 million acre-feet (roughly two-thirds of the total) are lost immediately through evaporation, which leaves some 70 million acre-feet available for us each year.

This is usable fresh water, for another irony of water in California is that while the world's largest body of water—the Pacific Ocean—washes onto our western coast, all of that water is unusable salt water. The technology for desali-nating water is simplicity itself. You can do it on your kitchen stove with a box of salt, a quart of water, two tea kettles, a tube to connect their spouts and an ice bag wrapped around that tubing. Boiling the water in one kettle produces steam; the steam condenses back into water when it passes the cold tubing, and fresh or desalinated water drips down into the second kettle. The problem, then, is not the technology; rather, it is the cost. About thirty years ago, that is, when our policy makers were still thinking seriously about such things, it was pro-posed to build a desalination facility on an artificial island somewhere off the western coast of the LA basin. But that proposal died in the planning stage because of the cost, which was calculated at some four times higher than what the Metropolitan Water District (MWD) was paying for the water which, since it was formed in the 1930s, it has been bringing into the basin from the water surplus areas.

Regarding the usable or potable 70 million acre-feet of fresh water, we are currently using between 40 and 45 million acre-feet per year. Sacramento, San Joaquin, Imperial Valley, and other agricultural users account for about 80 to 85 percent of that total, while industrial and domestic users consume the remaining 15 to 20 percent. Now, where all of those users are, none of the water is, and this means—as it has for almost a century—that large volumes of fresh water have had to be transported from the surplus to the deficit areas.

The Los Angeles aqueduct, which was built between 1910 and 1913, brings water about two hundred fifty miles from the Owens Valley in the southeastern Sierra Nevada Range to the San Fernando Valley. This was the first of what would turn out to be a continuous sixty-five-year effort to address our water distribution conundrum. At about the same time the LA aqueduct was being built the people of San Francisco turned eastward for water. After many delays the Mokelumne aqueduct was completed in 1929 and the Hetch Hetchy aqueduct was finished in 1932. Even before these projects were completed, planning had already begun on what would become the Central Valley Project. Serious consideration of this project began in 1921, but funding for it was not provided until 1933, that is, during the Great Depression. California turned to the federal government—which, in 1937, and as a part of the New Deal's economic recovery effort, made it a federal reclamation project. Work on the major element of that project, the Shasta Dam—about ten miles north of Redding—began in the late 1930s, but World War II put that effort on hold. In the decade following the war, the Clair Engle Dam (a few miles west of the Shasta Dam), the Friant Dam (near Fresno), and the north-south running Central Valley Corning, Tehama-Colusa, Delta-Mendota, Madera-Friant, and Kern canals, as well as the hydroelectric power plants and pumping stations that comprise the Central Valley Project were completed. Nor was Southern California idle during these decades.

The first great New Deal public works project, Hoover Dam, was completed in early 1936. About 32 million acre-feet of Colorado River waters are impounded behind the dam in Lake Mead. Water from the lake is drawn off by Nevada, Arizona, and California, and to deliver that water to Southern California, Parker Dam, the Colorado River, and San Diego aqueducts, and the All-American, Coachella, East Highline, and Westside Canals were constructed. As massive and expensive as all of these projects were, they nevertheless proved to be inadequate. Between 1910 and 1940, California's population had grown from 2.375 million to 6.91 million and industrial output and agricultural production had increased by even greater magnitudes. Census projections made in the late 1940s predicted that by 2000, the state's population would be somewhere between 20 and 25 million. However, the estimated long-term growth occurred much more rapidly and its magnitude was much greater than anticipated. According to the decennial census figures, the actual figures have turned out as follows: in 1950, 10.585 million; in 1960, 15.72 million; in 1970, 19.95 million; in 1980, 23.67 million; in 1990, 29.75 million; and in 2000, 34.65 million. Recently, the Demographic Research Unit of the California Department of Finance (DRU) estimated our population growth for the next forty years, and these were the numbers: in 2010, 39.957 million; in 2020, 45.448 million; in 2030, 51.868 million; and in 2040, 58.731. In short, we have experienced and, in all likelihood, will continue to experience a major and sustained growth in our population. But, let us return to the known past.

By 1960, the design, legislative authorization, and $1.75 billion financing for the California Water Project were in place. The major components of this project are the Oroville Dam on the Feather River, the San Luis Dam at the eastern end of the Pacheco Pass, and the almost four hundred fifty-mile-long California aqueduct. Work on the project was completed in 1973. But by this time it had become apparent that the sixty-plus year effort was still not enough, and between 1976 and 1980, the state legislature put together State Senate Bill (SB) 200, which was signed into law by Governor Jerry Brown in June 1980. Had SB 200 remained law, it would have created a five-phase, fifty-five-year program for building the dams, conveyances, power plants, and treatment facilities, which the state's ever-growing population would continue to need. However, less than two years after he had signed SB 200, Jerry Brown led the successful effort: the anti–Peripheral Canal referendum measure—Proposition 9—on the June 1982 ballot to repeal SB 200.

During his successful 1974 gubernatorial campaign, Brown's mantra was "small is beautiful" and "we are going to have to learn to live with less." At the time, nobody took him all that seriously; after all, he was Governor "Moonbeam." But 20–20 hindsight teaches us that we should have. Looking back on his election and the eight years of his administration, we now have a clear view of what at the time was only a small object on the distant horizon. We now know that the Jerry Brown years were a landmark or watershed era in California life and politics. For it was at this time, and without either public discussion or public authorization, that our public officials decided to abandon the consensus and agenda that had governed the state since the 1910 election of the Progressive Republican governor—Hiram Johnson.

Johnson's election marked the culmination of the almost two-decade long Progressive campaign against the Big Four Railroad Octopus that had its tentacles wrapped around almost every facet of state government and the institutionalized corrupt political practices of the boss-dominated party machines in San Francisco and Los Angeles. This campaign attacked the obvious forms of political corruption: bribery, kickbacks, graft, rigged elections, and the like. Beneath these well-publicized and very successful efforts was the Progressives's tacit equation of party or partisan politics with corruption. That is, the premise of the Progressive reform effort was that corruption was something like a necessity of the principle of party politics. Thus it followed that one could greatly reduce or even possibly eliminate political corruption by the expedient of greatly reducing or even possibly eliminating the governing role of the political parties.

The equation of corrupt politics with party politics was an inference from the Progressive notion that partisan politics was a "zero-sum game." In this they appeared to echo James Madison's observations in the *Tenth Federalist*. "The apportionment of taxes . . . is an act which seems to require the most exact impartiality; yet there is, perhaps, no legislative act in which greater opportunity and temptation are given to a predominant party to trample on the rules of justice. Every shilling with which they overburden the inferior number is a shilling saved to their own pockets." The Progressives broadened this "more for me means less for you" notion to cover the government's distribution of all of the burdens and benefits of citizenship, and they thus came to see party politics as not only corrupt but, beyond that, as inescapably tinged with injustice.

Their remedy was, in some sense, to take the politics out of politics, and at an institutional level, they both set out to and largely succeeded in eviscerating the political parties. Beyond that the Progressives also set out and largely succeeded in forging a new and long-term consensus as to what it is that is fitting, proper, and respectable for a responsible government to do. For the Progressives, responsible government was "trans-partisan" government. Trans-partisan government is based on the rejection of the idea that politics is a zero-sum game. Instead, a trans-partisan or responsible government is one that takes the lead in forging a public-private partnership dedicated to bringing about a more widely shared and higher level of economic prosperity. This notion that government's new and progrowth role was to be trans-partisan was based on the fact that the leaders and members of both the Democratic and Republican parties could—and, for a long time, did—join each other in affirming this Progressive responsibility of government. To put it another way, the Progressive era was not an era of limits. It was not a time when small was beautiful or when we were told to learn to live with less.

The Progressives reached out both to the rest of the country and the rest of the world with the pledge that if you come to California, life will be better for you, that in California you will find better housing, better educational and occupational opportunities, better transportation, recreation and entertainment facilities, and so on. Providing the infrastructure for all of this would not be an accidental or incidental consequence of the activities of government. Instead, the expanding infrastructure was the necessary and wholly intended consequence of this Progressive commitment, and until the 1974 election this Progressive conception and the commitment were the warp and woof of our public policy. As for the 1974 election, it was every bit as much a landmark election as the 1910 campaign, for as we are now painfully aware, it marked the end of the Progressive era and the beginning of anti-Progressive or antigrowth era. Since then, our public policy makers have deliberately and relentlessly been forcing us to in fact live with less. *The Wall Street Journal* used the acronym, BANANA or Build Absolutely Nothing Anywhere Near Anything, to describe this new political phenomena, at the center of which is the rhetoric of scarcity.

Scarcity: the drumbeat that we are running out of land, water, and various other natural resources, affordable housing, space for the ever-expanding population, and so on, has been the watchword of anti-Progressivism. Following hard on the heels of this relentless propaganda in behalf of scarcity has been an ever-expanding bureaucratic and regulatory apparatus whose ceaseless work has been the ever-expanding administrative effort and authority to ration or allocate these ever-diminishing resources. Now, it is the allocation of these and other scarce resources, which makes economics what economists describe as the "dismal science." But, dismal or not, we cannot not make decisions about the allocation of our scarce, that is, economic, resources. Thus, the only open question is simply this: who will decide? The contradictory answers given during the Progressive and anti-Progressive eras point us toward the core difference between them.

Many years ago, a leader of the post-Progressive or antigrowth movement announced that the aim of the movement was to replace the American Revolution with a new revolution that would replace the market economy with the moral economy. In the market or free-enterprise economy, decision-making authority is decentralized. That is, it is in the hands of countless private citizens whose millions of daily purchasing decisions determine what our scarce resources will be used to produce and the prices at which the ever-changing package products and services will be offered on the market. Conversely, in the moral economy, that authority is centralized or placed in the hands of that very small faction of our population who hold either elective or appointive public offices. That these few (relative, that is, to the state's entire population) decision makers hold public offices is decisive. Because they hold public office, they have available to them the power and authority of the law to compel obedience to their decisions and punish disobedience to their regulatory decrees.

In almost all cases the decision makers are bureaucrats or career civil servants who are allegedly accountable to our elected public officials. In fact, however, they are not. Rather, they constitute our largely invisible and almost entirely unaccountable "shadow" government. This has been quite acceptable to our elected officials who have been very content to preside over the silent transformation of government that has taken place since 1974. Unlike the architects of the Progressive era who openly articulated their reform agenda and who campaigned for and won the voters' initial authorization and many reauthorizations of that agenda, the devotees of BANANAism have gone forward under the cover of darkness. That they have been able to carry out their covert revolution is, in one sense, the result of the Progressives's success in transforming government from a political to an administrative enterprise.

Given the evisceration of the political parties, the public sentiment that party affiliation is insignificant and maybe even demeaning, the fact that successful candidates for public office are little beholden to their parties, and the failure of the Republican Party's leaders to articulate let alone campaign for an anti-BANANA agenda; it is little wonder that no public deliberation about the desirability of BANANAism has taken place. Now, it would of course be wrong to lay the whole problem at the feet of the Republican Party. After all, it has been Governor Brown's Democratic Party that persuaded first itself and then an entire generation of public officials not only to stop acting on but also to stop talking about and even thinking of that central responsibility of the state's governing bodies. In short and for a generation now, the formal pursuit of power has almost never been accompanied by any sense of public responsibility for dealing with our increasingly massive infrastructure problem.

Beyond this institutional void is that all-too-human love of power or the desire for preeminence and dominion, and any minion or minister of our current antigrowth agenda who claims to be innocent of this appetite is being simply disingenuous. But, however satisfactory it is to wield power over others, exercising power is never an end in itself. It is necessarily the means to some other end. In this instance, replacing the American Revolution with a new revolution has resulted in a government that no longer is shaped, guided, and governed by the interests, concerns, aspirations, and interests of that large middle class that was the sovereign ruler of the Progressive era. Since the 1974 election, and at the expense of that middle class for which it daily and relentlessly expresses its disdain, contempt, and even outright loathing; our government has set for itself the task of relieving "the disadvantaged" of the burdens of the oppressive discriminations which it is claimed they perennially or permanently endure at the hands of that "oppressive" middle-class or unenlightened and "petty bourgeoisie" majority that for too long had governed the state. The diversion of public attention, energies, and resources from the task of matching our ever-expanding population with the ongoing expansion of our infrastructure has been the wholly intended consequence of this revolutionary reconstitution of government.

This has been largely true of every component of our infrastructure, but it has been completely true in the area of water. Since 1973, our population has increased by some 13 million people, and over the next forty years (if the current projections are correct) it will increase by another 24 million. That we have not already run out of water is the result of good fortune, that is, of the fact that the Progressives built better than they knew. Because they did, we have been able to live on borrowed time, but at some point in the future, and as long as BANANAism defines our governing agenda, we will run out of both time and water.

Bibliography

Abrahams, Ray. *Vigilant Citizens: Vigilantism and the State*. Cambridge, U.K.: Polity Press, 1998.

An Act to Authorize the People of Missouri Territory to Form a Constitution. 3 Stat. 545 (March 6, 1820).

Adarand Constructors v. Pena, 515 U.S. 200 (1995).

Aitken, Jonathan. *Nixon: A Life*. Washington, D.C.: Regnery, 1993.

Alden v. Maine, 527 U.S. 706 (1999).

Amador Valley Joint Union High School District v. State Board of Equalization, 22 Cal. 3d 208 (1972).

Amar, Vikram David. "Indirect Effects of Direct Election: A Structural Examination of the Seventeenth Amendment." *Vanderbilt Law Review* 49 (1996).

Ambrose, Stephen E. *Eisenhower the President*. New York: Simon & Schuster, 1985.

———. *Nixon: The Education of a Politician 1913–1962*. New York: Simon & Schuster, 1987.

———. *Nixon: The Triumph of a Politician 1962–1972*. New York: Simon & Schuster, 1989.

———. *Nothing Like It in the World: The Men Who Built the Transcontinental Railroad 1863–1869*. New York: Simon & Schuster, 2000.

American Bar Association, Special Constitutional Convention Study Committee. *Amendment of the Constitution by the Convention Method Under Article V*. Chicago: ABA, 1974.

An American Citizen (Tench Coxe). "An Examination of the Constitution of the United States." In *Friends of the Constitution: Writings of the "Other" Federalists: 1787–1788*. Edited by Colleen A. Sheehan and Gary L. McDowell. Indianapolis, Ind.: Liberty Fund, 1998.

Anderson, Lindsay. *About John Ford*. London: Plexus, 1981.

Aristophanes. *Peace*. Translated by Robert Henning Webb. Charlottesville: University Press of Virginia, 1964.

Aristotle. *Politics*. Translated by Carnes Lord. Chicago: University of Chicago Press, 1984.

————. *The Politics*. In *Basic Works of Aristotle*. Edited by Richard McKeon. New York: Random House, 1984.

Arnn, Larry, et al. "A Difference of Principle: The Minority Report of the California Constitution Revision Commission, California Constitution Revision Commission, Final Report and Recommendations to the Governor and the Legislature." In *Final Report and Recommendations to the Governor and Legislature*. Sacramento, Calif.: Forum on Government Reform, 1996.

Bailey v. Drexel Furniture Co., 259 U.S. 20 (1922).

Baker v. Carr, 369 U.S. 186 (1962).

Bancroft, Hubert Howe. *History of California*. Vol. 5. San Francisco: The History Company, 1884.

————. *History of California*. Vol. 6. San Francisco: The History Company, 1888.

————. *History of California*, Vol. 7. San Francisco: The History Company, 1890.

Barnes, Fred. "California Doesn't Matter." *The Weekly Standard* (31 July 2000): 22–25.

Barone, Michael. "Nixon's America." *U.S. News and World Report* (20 September 1999): 21.

Bauer, K. Jack. *Zachary Taylor: Soldier, Planter, Statesman of the Old Southwest*. Baton Rouge: Louisiana State University Press, 1985.

Bean, Walton. *California: An Interpretive History*. 2nd ed. New York: McGraw-Hill, 1973.

Bell, Charles G. and Charles M. Price, "Pre-Legislative Sources of Representational Roles." *Midwest Journal of Political Science* 13 (1969).

Bell, Derrick A. Jr., "The Referendum: Democracy's Barrier to Racial Equality," *Washington Law Review* 54 (1978).

Berke, Richard L. "Bland but Tough, Gov. Wilson Uses Lessons of Nixon." *New York Times* (2 July 1994): 1.

Bestor, Arthur. "Constitutionalism and the Settlement of the West: The Attainment of Consensus, 1754–1784." In *The American Territorial System*. Edited by John Porter Bloom. Vol. 13. Athens: Ohio University Press, 1973.

Bethel, Tom. *The Noblest Triumph: Property and Prosperity through the Ages*. New York: St. Martin's, 1998.

Bliss, Michael. *Justified Lives: Morality & Narrative in the Films of Sam Peckinpah*. Carbondale: Southern Illinois University Press, 1993.

Block, A. G. "History for Our Times: Pearl Harbor and the Birth of Modern California." *California Journal* 45 (November 2001).

Block, A. G. and Charles M. Price, eds. "Local Government." In *California Government and Politics Annual, 1999*. Sacramento: StateNet, 2000, 68.

Bogdanovich, Peter. *John Ford*. Berkeley: University of California Press, 1978.

Bolick, Clint. *Grassroots Tyranny*. Washington, D.C.: Cato Institute, 1993.

Borland, John. "The Arming of California." *California Journal* 39 (October 1995).

Bowen, Don L. "Reshaping Special District Government in Arizona." *Arizona Review* 32 (1984).

Bray, Tom. "Reading America the Riot Act." *Policy Review* (Winter 1988): 34.

Brennan, William J. "The Bill of Rights and the States: The Revival of State Constitutions as Guardians of Individual Rights." *New York University Law Review* 61 (1986).

"The Brilliance of California's Founders." *Press-Enterprise* (Riverside-San Bernardino) (15 December 1997): A23.

Brinkley, Alan. *Liberalism and Its Discontents.* Cambridge, Mass.: Harvard University Press, 1998.

Brooks, Roger G. "Garcia, the Seventeenth Amendment, and the Role of the Supreme-Court in Defending Federalism." *Harvard Journal of Law & Public Policy* 10 (1987).

Browne, J. Ross. *Report of the Debates in the Convention of California on Formation of the State Constitution in September and October 1849* (1850).

Brownstein, Ronald. *The Power and the Glitter: The Hollywood-Washington Connection.* New York: Vintage, 1992.

Buchanan, Alfred Russell. *David S. Terry of California: Dueling Judge.* San Marino, Calif.: Huntington Library, 1956.

Buchanan, James and Gordon Tullock. *The Calculus of Consent.* Ann Arbor: University of Michigan Press, 1962.

Burke, Edmund. *The Works of the Right Honourable Edmund Burke.* Vol. 2. Boston: Little, Brown, 1866.

Burns, Nancy. *The Formation of American Local Governments.* New York: Oxford University Press, 1994.

Bybee, Jay S. "Ulysses at the Mast: Democracy, Federalism, and the Sirens' Song of the Seventeenth Amendment." *Northwestern University Law Review* 91 (1997).

California Fed. Sav. & Loan Ass'n v. City of Los Angeles, 54, Cal. 3d 1 (1991).

California Fed. Sav. & Loan Ass'n v. City of Los Angeles, 16.

California v. Eu, 54 Cal. 3d 492 (1991).

California v. Jones, 21 Cal. 4th 1142 (1999).

California Democratic Party v. Jones, 530 U.S. 567, 576 (2000).

California Senate, Local Government Committee. *What's So Special About Special Districts: A Citizen's Guide to Special Districts in California.* Sacramento: State of California, 1991.

Cain, Bruce E., Sara Ferejohn, Margarita Najar, and Mary Walther. "Constitutional Change: Is It Too Easy to Amend Our State Constitution?" In *Constitutional Reform in California: Making State Government More Effective and Responsive.* Edited by Bruce E. Cain and Roger G. Noll. Berkeley, Calif.: Institute of Governmental Studies Press, 1995.

Carey, George W. *In Defense of the Constitution.* Indianapolis, Ind.: Liberty Fund, 1995.

Carter v. Carter Coal Co., 298 U.S. 238 (1936).

Carter, Gregg Lee. *The Gun Control Movement.* New York: Twayne, 1997.

Chamberlain, John. *Farewell to Reform: The Rise, Life and Decay of the Progressive Mind in America.* Gloucester, Mass.: Peter Smith, 1958.

Chan, Sucheng and Spencer Olin, eds. *Major Problems in California History.* Boston: Houghton Mifflin, 1997.

Chandler, Alfred D. Jr. "The Origins of Progressive Leadership." In *The Letters of Theodore Roosevelt*. Edited by Elting E. Morison. Vol. 8. Cambridge, Mass.: Harvard University Press, 1954.

City of Boerne v. Flores, 521 U.S. 507 (1997).

Cleland, Robert Glass. *A History of California: The American Period*. New York: Macmillan, 1922.

Coalition for Economic Equity v. Wilson, 946 F. Supp. 1480 N.D. Cal. (1996).

Coll. Sav. Bank v. Fla. Prepaid Postsecondary Educ. Expense Bd., 527 U.S. 666 (1999).

Conine, Ernest. "Hiram Johnson Had It Right; '86 California Vote Supports His Faith in Grass-Roots Wisdom." *Los Angeles Times*, 10 November 1986, Metro, pt. 2, 5.

Controller of the State of California. *State of California Cities Annual Report, Fiscal Year 1997–1998*. Sacramento: State of California, 2000.

———. *Special Districts Annual Report, Fiscal Year 1997–1998*. Sacramento: State of California, 2000.

———. *State of California School District Annual Report*. Sacramento: State of California, 2000.

Cooley, Charles Horton. *Social Organization: A Study of the Larger Mind*. Glencoe, Ill.: Free Press, 1956.

Cooper, William J. *The South and the Politics of Slavery 1828–1856*. Baton Rouge: Louisiana State University Press, 1978.

"Court Upholds State Assault Weapons Ban." *Los Angeles Times* (6 December 2002): A1.

Coyle v. Smith, 221 U.S. 559 (1911).

Coyle, Dennis. *Property Rights and the Constitution*. Albany: State University of New York Press, 1993.

Cramer, Clayton E. "The Racist Roots of Gun Control." *Kansas Journal of Law & Public Policy* 5 (1995).

Cramer, Clayton E. and David B. Kopel. " 'Shall Issue': The New Wave of Concealed Handgun Permit Laws." *Tennessee Law Review* 62 (1995).

Croly, Herbert. *The Promise of American Life*. New York: Dutton, 1963.

———. *Progressive Democracy*. New Brunswick, N. J.: Transaction, 1998.

Crook, Sara Brandes. "The Consequences of the Seventeenth Amendment: The Twentieth Century Senate." Ph.D. diss. Lincoln: University of Nebraska, 1992.

Cross v. Harrison, 16 How., 57 U.S., 184–85 (1850).

Crowley, Monica. *Nixon Off the Record*. New York: Random House, 1996.

Darby, William. *John Ford's Westerns: A Thematic Analysis, with a Filmography*. Jefferson, N.C.: McFarland, 1996.

Davidson, Roger H. *The Role of the Congressman*. New York: Pegasus, 1969.

Davies, Gareth. *From Opportunity to Entitlement: The Transformation and Decline of Great Society Liberalism*. Lawrence: University Press of Kansas, 1996.

"A Debate on Initiative and Referendum: Haynes in Favor; Adams Opposed, a debate held on October 11, 1911 at the Commonwealth Club of San Francisco." In *California Controversies*. Edited by Leonard Pitt. San Rafael, Calif.: ETRI, 1985.

Delmatier, Royce D., Clarence F. McIntosh, and Earl G. Waters. *The Rumble of California Politics: 1848–1970.* New York: Wiley, 1970.

Dennison, George M. "Martial Law: The Development of a Theory of Emergency Powers, 1776–1861." *American Journal of Legal History* 18 (1974).

Dred Scott v. Sanford, 60 U.S. 393 (1857).

Eastman, John C. and Timothy Sandefur, "Justice Stephen Field: Frontier Justice or Justice on the Natural Rights Frontier?" *Nexus* 6 (2001).

Eaton, Allen H. *The Oregon System: The Story of Direct Legislation in Oregon.* Chicago: A. C. McClurg, 1912.

Eisenach, Eldon J. *The Lost Promise of Progressivism.* Lawrence: University Press of Kansas, 1994.

Elazar, Daniel J. *Building toward Civil War: Generational Rhythms in American Politics* Lanham, Md.: Madison Books, 1992.

Eldredge, Zoeth Skinner. *History of California.* Vol. 4. New York: Century History, 1915.

Elliot, Jonathon. *Debates in the Several State Conventions on the Adoption of the Federal Constitutions.* Vol. 2. Buffalo, N.Y.: William S. Hein: 1996.

Ellison, William Henry. *A Self-Governing Dominion: California, 1849–1860.* Berkeley: University of California Press, 1950.

The Employers' Liability Cases, 207 U.S. 463 (1908).

Erler, Edward J. "Independence and Activism: Ratcheting Rights in the State Courts." *Benchmark* 4 (1988).

———. *The American Polity: Essays on the Theory and Practice of Constitutional Government.* New York: Crane and Russak, 1991.

———. "The Future of Civil Rights: Affirmative Action Redivivus," *Notre Dame Journal of Law and Public Policy* 11 (1997).

———. "Immigration and Citizenship." In *Loyalty Misplaced: Misdirected Virtue and Social Disintegration.* Edited by Gerald Frost. London: Social Affairs Unit, 1997.

"The Essays of Brutus." In *The Complete Anti-Federalist.* Edited by Herbert J. Storing. Vol. 2. Chicago: University of Chicago Press, 1981.

Euripides, "The Suppliants." In *Euripides: Plays.* Introduction by J. Michael Walton, Frederic Raphael, and Kenneth McLeish. Portsmouth, N.H.: Heinemann, 1997.

Eyman, Scott. *Print the Legend: The Life and Times of John Ford.* New York: Simon & Schuster, 1999.

Farrand, Max, ed. *Records of the Federal Convention of 1787.* Vol. 1 and 2. New Haven, Conn.: Yale University Press, 1937.

Faulkner, Robert. *The First Liberal Democrat: Locke's Popular Government.* Forthcoming.

Fay, James S., ed. *California Almanac.* 6th ed. Santa Barbara, Calif.: Pacific Data Resources, 1993.

Fehrenbacher, Don E. *The Dred Scott Case: Its Significance in American Law and Politics.* New York: Oxford University Press, 1978.

Ferejohn, John. "Reforming the Initiative Process." In *Constitutional Reform in Califor-*

nia. Edited by Bruce E. Cain and Roger G. Noll. Berkeley, Calif.: Institute of Governmental Studies Press, 1995.

Fla. Prepaid Postsecondary Educ. Expense Bd. v. Coll. Sav. Bank, 527 U.S. 627 (1999).

Ford, Paul Leicester, ed. *Pamphlets on the Constitution of the United States.* Union, N.J.: Lawbook Exchange, 2000.

Franklin, William E. "Peter H. Burnett and the Provisional Government Movement." *California Historical Society Quarterly* 40 (1961): 126–29.

Freehling, William W. *Prelude to Civil War: The Nullification Controversy in South Carolina 1816–1836.* New York: Harper & Row, 1966.

Frey, William H. "Migration Swings." *American Demographics* (February 2002), 18.

Friedman, Lawrence. *A History of American Law.* New York: Simon & Schuster, 1973.

Gable, John Allen. *The Bull Moose Years.* Port Washington, N.Y.: Kennikat Press, 1978.

Galante, Mary Ann. "California Justices Face Own 'Executions': Bitter Campaign Focuses on Death Penalty." *National Law Journal* 3 (November 1986).

Gellman, Irwin F. *The Contender: Richard Nixon: The Congress Years 1946–1952.* New York: Free Press, 1999.

Gilmore, Grant. *The Death of Contract.* Columbus: Ohio State University Press, 1974.

Gimpel, James. *National Elections and the Autonomy of American State Party Systems.* Pittsburgh: University of Pittsburgh Press, 1996.

Goldborough, James. "Out-of-Control Immigration." *Foreign Affairs* 79 (September/October 2000).

Goodwin, Cardinal. *The Establishment of State Government in California 1846–1850.* New York: Macmillan, 1914.

Graham, Otis L. *An Encore for Reform: The Old Progressives and the New Deal.* London: Oxford University Press, 1968.

Gray, A. A. *History of California: From 1542.* (Boston: D. C. Heath, 1934).

Green, Roy. *The Profession of Local Government Management.* New York: Praeger, 1989.

Grimes, Alan P. *Democracy and Amendments to the Constitution.* Lexington, Mass.: Lexington Books, 1978.

Grivas, Theodore. *Military Governments in California 1846–1850.* Glendale, Calif.: A. H. Clark, 1963.

Grodin, Joseph R. "The Role of State Constitutions in a Federal System." In *Constitutional Reform in California: Making State Government More Effective and Responsive.* Edited by Bruce E. Cain and Roger G. Noll. Berkeley, Calif.: Institute of Governmental Studies Press, 1995.

Gunnison, Robert B. "Davis Says He Calls All the Shots: Legislature's Job Is to 'Implement My Vision.'" *San Francisco Chronicle* (21 July 1999): A1.

Halbrook, Stephen P. *Freedmen, the Fourteenth Amendment, and the Right to Bear Arms, 1866–1876.* Westport, Conn.: Greenwood, 1998.

Hall, Wallace Worthy. "The History and Effect of the Seventeenth Amendment." Ph.D. diss. Berkely: University of California, 1936.

Hamilton, Alexander. "The Federalist No. 1." In *The Federalist Papers.* Edited by Clinton Rossiter. New York: Mentor, 1961.

———. "*The Federalist* No. 59." In *The Federalist Papers*. Edited by Clinton Rossiter. New York: Mentor, 1961.

———. "*The Federalist* No. 71." In *The Federalist Papers*. Edited by Clinton Rossiter. New York: Mentor, 1961.

Hammer v. Dagenhart, 247 U.S. 251 (1918).

Hanson, Victor Davis. *The Other Greeks*. Berkeley: University of California Press, 1999.

Harlow, Neal. *California Conquered: War and Peace on the Pacific 1846–1850*. Berkeley: University of California Press, 1982.

Harrigan, John J. *Politics and Policy in States and Communities*. New York: HarperCollins, 1994.

Haynes, George H. *The Election of Senators*. New York: Henry Holt, 1906.

———. *The Senate of the United States: Its History and Practice*. Vol. 2. New York: Russell and Russell, 1938.

Hittell, Theodore H. *History of California*. Vol. 2. San Francisco: Stone, 1897.

Hi-Voltage Wire Works, Inc. v. City of San Jose, 24 Cal. 4th 537, 562 (2000).

Hoebeke, Christopher H. *The Road to Mass Democracy: Original Intent and the Seventeenth Amendment*. New Brunswick, N.J.: Transaction, 1995.

Hoff, Joan. *Nixon Reconsidered*. New York: Basic, 1994.

Holman, Craig B. and Robert Stern, "Judicial Review of Ballot Initiatives: The Changing Role of State and Federal Courts." *Loyola of Los Angeles Law Review* 31 (1998).

Horne, Gerald. *Fire This Time: The Watts Uprising and the 1960s*. Charlottesville: University of Virginia Press, 1995.

Horowitz, David. *Radical Son*. New York: Simon & Schuster, 1997.

Huber, Peter. *Liability: The Legal Revolution and Its Consequences*. New York: Basic, 1988.

Hunt, Rockwell D. *California and Californians*. Vol. 2. Chicago: Lewis, 1926.

Hyink, Bernard and David H. Provost. *Politics and Government in California*. 13th ed. New York: HarperCollins, 1996.

In re Heff, 197 U.S. 488 (1905).

In re Lance W., 37 Cal. 3d 873 (1985).

In re Neagle, 135 U.S. 1 (1890).

Interstate Commerce Act of 1887, 24 Stat. 379 (1887).

Iredell, James. "Answers to Mr. Mason's Objections to the New Constitution, Recommended by the Late Convention." In *Pamphlets on the Constitution of the United States : Published during Its Discussion by the People 1787–1788*. Edited by Paul Leicester Ford. Union, N.J.: Lawbook Exchange, 2000.

Jaffa, Harry V. *Crisis of the House Divided*. Garden City, N.Y.: Doubleday, 1959.

———. *Crisis of the House Divided: An Interpretation of the Issues in the Lincoln-Douglas Debates*. Chicago: University of Chicago Press, 1982.

———. *A New Birth of Freedom: Abraham Lincoln and the Coming of the Civil War*. Lanham, Md.: Rowman & Littlefield, 2000.

Janiskee, Brian P. and Edward J. Erler. "Crime, Punishment, and Romero: An Analysis of the Case Against California's Three Strikes Law." *Duquesne Law Review* 39 (2000).

Janiskee, Brian P. and Ken Masugi. *Democracy in California: Politics and Government in the Golden State.* Lanham, Md.: Rowman & Littlefield, 2002.

Jefferson, Thomas. "Letter to Edward Carrington (Jan. 16, 1787)." In *Jefferson: Writings.* Edited by Merrill D. Peterson. New York: Library of America, 1984.

———. *The Portable Thomas Jefferson.* Edited by Merrill D. Peterson. New York: Penguin, 1986.

Johnson, Phillip E. *The Court on Trial.* Santa Monica, Calif.: The Supreme Court Project, 1985.

Jones, Bill. *History of the Initiative Process.* Sacramento: California Secretary of State, 1995.

Kanner, Gideon. "California Judges' War on Property Rights, Camarillo, CA." *California Political Review* 9 (1998).

Kaus, Mickey. "Flipping the Bird." *New Republic* (15 April 1985).

Keller v. U.S., 213 U.S. 138 (1909).

Keller, Morton. "The New Deal and Progressivism: A Fresh Look." In *The New Deal and the Triumph of Liberalism.* Edited by Sidney M. Milkis and Jerome M. Mileur. Amherst: University of Massachusetts Press, 2002.

Kens, Paul. *Justice Stephen J. Field: Shaping Liberty from the Gold Rush to the Gilded Age.* Lawrence: University of Kansas Press, 1997.

Kim, Elaine H. "They Armed in Self-Defense." *Newsweek* (May 18, 1992): 10.

Kimel v. Fla. Bd. of Regents, 120 S.Ct. 631 (2000).

Knupfer, Peter B. *The Union as It Is: Constitutional Unionism and Sectional Compromise 1787–1861.* Chapel Hill: University of North Carolina Press, 1991.

Kopel, David. *The Samurai, the Mountie, and the Cowboy.* Buffalo, N.Y.: Prometheus Books, 1992.

Kurland, Philip B. and Ralph Lerner, eds. *Founders' Constitution.* Vol. 1. Chicago: University of Chicago Press, 1987.

Kyvig, David E. *Explicit and Authentic Acts: Amending the U.S. Constitution, 1776–1995.* Lawrence: University of Kansas Press, 1996.

Ladd, Everett Carll, ed. *America at the Polls 1998.* Storrs, Conn.: Roper Center, 1999.

LaPierre, Wayne R. *Guns, Crime and Freedom.* Washington, D.C.: Regnery, 1994.

Lence, Ross M., ed. *Union and Liberty: The Political Philosophy of John C. Calhoun.* Indianapolis: Liberty Fund, 1992.

Levinson, Sanford. "The Embarrassing Second Amendment." *Yale Law Journal* 99 (1990): 637–59.

Lewis, Paul G. *Local Government Structure in California.* San Francisco: Public Policy Institute, 1998.

Lincoln, Abraham. "First Inaugural Address." In *Collected Works of Abraham Lincoln.* Edited by Roy P. Basler. Vol. 4. New Brunswick, N.J.: Rutgers University Press, 1953.

———. *Collected Works of Abraham Lincoln.* Edited by Roy P. Basler. New Brunswick, N.J.: Rutgers University Press, 1953.

Linde, Hans A. "When Initiative Lawmaking Is Not Republican Government: The Campaign against Homosexuality." *Oregon Law Review* 72 (1993).

———. "Guaranteeing a Republican Form of Government: Who Is Responsible for Republican Government?" *University of Colorado Law Review* 65 (1994).

Linberry, Robert L. and Edmund P. Fowler. "Reformism and Public Policies in American Cities." *American Political Science Review* 61 (1967).

Lippman, Walter. *Essays in the Public Philosophy*. Boston: Little, Brown, 1955.

Little Hoover Commission. *Special Districts: Relics of the Past or Resources for the Future?* Sacramento, Calif.: Little Hoover Commission, 2000.

Lloyd, Gordon. "Nature and Convention in the Creation of the 1849 California Constitution." In *California Republic: Institutions, Policies, and Statesmanship*. Edited by Brian P. Janiskee and Ken Masugi. Lanham, Md.: Rowman & Littlefield, 2003.

Lloyd, Margie. "California's Golden Moment: The Latest Lost Opportunity to Heal Constitutional Ills." *California Politics and Policy* 49 (November 1996).

Locke, John. *Second Treatise on Government*. Edited by Richard H. Cox. Arlington Heights, Ill.: Harlan Davidson, 1982.

Lopez v. Unites States, 514 U.S. 549 (1995).

Lower, Richard Coke. *A Bloc of One: The Political Career of Hiram W. Johnson*. Stanford, Calif.: Stanford University Press, 1993.

Lowi, Theodore J. *The End of Liberalism: Ideology, Policy, and the Crisis of Public Authority*. New York: Norton, 1969.

Lund, Nelson. "The Past and Future of the Individual's Right to Arms." *Georgia Law Review* 31 (1996): 59–63.

Luther v. Borden, 7 How. 48 U.S. 1 (1849).

Macaulay, Thomas B. *History of England*. Vol. 2. New York: Washington Square Press, 1967.

Madison, James. *"The Federalist* No. 10." In *The Federalist Papers*. Edited by Clinton Rossiter. New York: Mentor, 1961.

———. *"The Federalist* No. 14." In *The Federalist Papers*. Edited by Clinton Rossiter. New York: Mentor, 1961.

———. *"The Federalist* No. 39." In *The Federalist Papers*. Edited by Clinton Rossiter and Charles Kesler. New York: Mentor, 1961.

———. *"The Federalist* No. 45." In *The Federalist Papers*. Edited by Clinton Rossiter. New York: Mentor, 1961.

———. *"The Federalist* No. 46." In *The Federalist Papers*. Edited by Clinton Rossiter. New York: Mentor, 1961.

———. *"The Federalist* No. 49." In *The Federalist Papers*. Edited by Clinton Rossiter. New York: Mentor, 1961

———. *"The Federalist* No. 51." In *The Federalist Papers*. Edited by Clinton Rossiter. New York: Mentor, 1961.

———. *"The Federalist* No. 63." In *The Federalist Papers*. Edited by Clinton Rossiter. New York: Mentor, 1961.

———. "Letter from James Madison to James Monroe (October 5, 1786)." In *Papers of James Madison*. Edited by William T. Hutchinson and William M. E. Rachal. Vol. 9. Chicago: University of Chicago, 1962.

———. *The Papers of James Madison.* Edited by William T. Hutchinson, William M. E. Rachal, Robert A. Rutland, et al. Vol. 14. Chicago: University of Chicago Press; Charlottesville: University Press of Virginia, 1962.

———. *Virginia Report.* Richmond, Va.: Thomas Ritchie, 1819.

———. *Writings: James Madison.* Edited by Jack N. Rakove. New York: Library of America, 1999.

Malcolm, Joyce Lee. *To Keep and Bear Arms: The Origins of an Anglo-American Right.* Cambridge, Mass.: Harvard University Press, 1994.

———. *Guns and Violence: The English Experience.* Cambridge, Mass.: Harvard University Press, 2002.

Marbury v. Madison, 1 Cranch (5 U.S.) 137, 176 (1803).

Marini, John. *The Politics of Budget Control: Congress, the Presidency, and the Growth of the Administrative State.* Washington, D.C.: Crane Russak, 1992.

Marx, Karl. "The Communist Manifesto." In *The Marx-Engels Reader.* Edited by Robert C. Tucker. New York: Norton, 1978.

———. "The Eighteenth Brumaire of Louis Bonaparte." In *The Marx-Engels Reader.* Edited by Robert C. Tucker. New York: Norton, 1978.

———. "The German Ideology." In *The Marx-Engels Reader.* Edited by Robert C. Tucker. New York: Norton, 1978.

Marx, Karl and Friedrich Engels. *Reviews from the Neue Rheinische Zeitung Revue, 1850.* *www.marxists.org/archive/marx/works/1850-nrr.htm (accessed 4 April 2003).*

May, Ernest R. and Janet Fraser. *Campaign '72: The Managers Speak.* Cambridge, Mass.: Harvard University Press, 1973.

Mazo, Earl and Stephen Hess. *Nixon: A Political Portrait.* New York: Popular Library, 1968.

McCoy, Drew. *The Last of the Fathers: James Madison and the Republican Legacy.* New York: Cambridge University Press, 1989.

McCubbins, Mathew D. "Putting the State Back into State Government: The Constitution and the Budget." In *Constitutional Reform in California: Making State Government More Effective and Responsive.* Edited by Bruce E. Cain and Roger G. Noll. Berkeley, Calif.: Institute of Governmental Studies Press, 1995.

McCulloch v. Maryland, 4 Wheat. (17 U.S.) 315, 406 (1819).

McGrath, Roger D. *Gunfighters, Highwaymen and Vigilantes: Violence on the Frontier.* Berkeley: University of California Press, 1984.

McLaughlin, Andrew C. *Lewis Cass.* Boston: Houghton Mifflin, 1891.

McNamara, Joseph. *Safe and Sane.* New York: Putnam, 1984.

McWilliams, Carey. *California: The Great Exception.* New York: Current, 1949.

McWilliams, Wilson Carey. "Standing at Armageddon: Morality and Religion in Progressive Thought." In *Progressivism and the New Democracy.* Edited by Sidney Milkis and Jerome Mileur. Amherst: University of Massachusetts Press, 1999.

Melendy, Howard R. and Benjamin F. Gilbert. *The Governors of California.* Georgetown, Calif.: Talisman, 1965.

Menander. *Menander's Georgos. A Revised Text of the Geneva Fragment.* Translated by Bernard P. Grenfell and Arthur S. Hunt. Oxford, U.K.: Clarendon Press, 1898.

Merk, Frederick. *Manifest Destiny and Mission: A Reinterpretation.* New York: Knopf, 1963.

Michigan v. Mosley 423 U.S. 96 (1975).

Milkis, Sidney M. *Political Parties and Constitutional Government.* Baltimore: Johns Hopkins University Press, 1999.

Miller, William Lee. *Arguing about Slavery.* New York: Knopf, 1996.

Morain, Dan. "Kaus to Retire from State Supreme Court; Deplores Strident Attacks on Justices in Anti-Bird Effort." *Los Angeles Times* (2 July 1985): pt. 1, 1.

Morel, Lucas. *Lincoln's Sacred Effort: Defining Religion's Role in American Self-Government.* Lanham, Md.: Lexington, 2000.

Morris, Roger. *Richard Milhous Nixon: The Rise of an American Politician.* New York: Henry Holt, 1990.

Morrison v. U.S., 120 S.Ct. 1740 (2000).

Mosk, Stanley. "State Constitutionalism: Both Liberal and Conservative." *Texas Law Review* 63 (1985).

Mowry, George. *The California Progressives.* Berkeley: University of California Press, 1951.

Moynihan, Daniel Patrick. *The Politics of a Guaranteed Income: The Nixon Administration and the Family Assistance Plan.* New York: Vintage, 1973.

Murray, Anthony. "Understanding Retention Elections." *California Lawyer* (September 1985).

Mydans, Seth. "A Target of Rioters, Koreatown Is Bitter, Armed, and Determined." *New York Times* (3 May 1992): 1.

Nalbandian, John. *Professionalism in Local Government.* San Francisco: Jossey-Bass, 1991.

Nat'l League of Cities v. Usery, 426 U.S. 833 (1976).

Nevins, Allan. *Ordeal of the Union: Fruits of Manifest Destiny 1847–1852.* Vol. 1. New York: Scribner, 1947.

New York v. United States, 505 U.S. 144 (1992).

Nixon, Richard M. "Annual Message to the Congress on the State of the Union, January 22, 1970." In *Public Papers of the Presidents, Richard Nixon 1970.* Washington, D.C.: Government Printing Office, 1971.

———. *RN: The Memoirs of Richard Nixon.* Vol. 1. New York: Warner, 1979.

"Number of Illegal Migrants Growing." *Los Angeles Times* (1 Feb 2003): A14.

Olin, Spencer C. *California's Prodigal Sons: Hiram Johnson and the Progressives, 1911–1917.* Berkeley: University of California Press, 1968.

An Ordinance for the Government of the Territory of the United States Northwest of the River Ohio. July 13, 1787. Reenacted August 7, 1787.

O'Sullivan, John. "As Goes California." *National Review* (25 September 2000): 42.

Pacific States Tel. & Tel. Co. v. Oregon, 223 U.S. 118 (1911).

Parmet, Herbert S. *Richard Nixon and His America*. Boston: Little, Brown, 1990.

People v. Frierson 25 Cal. 3d 142 (1979).

People v. Anderson, 6 Cal. 3d 628 (1972).

People v. Superior Court, 13 Cal. 4th 497 (1996).

People v. Teresinski, 30 Cal. 3d 822, 836 (1982).

Plyler v. Doe, 457 U.S. 202 (1982).

Polk, James K. *Messages and Papers of the Presidents, 1789–1908*. Edited by James D. Richardson. Vol. 4. Washington, D.C.: Bureau of National Literature and Art, 1909.

Porter, Douglas R., Ben C. Lin, and Richard B. Peiser. *Special Districts: A Useful Technique for Financing Infrastructure*. Washington, D.C.: Urban Land Institute, 1992.

Potter, David M. *The Impending Crisis 1848–1861*. New York: Harper & Row, 1976.

Potter, Philip. "Political Pitchman: Richard M. Nixon." In *Candidates 1960*. Edited by Eric Sevareid. New York: Basic, 1959.

Price, Glenn W. *Origins of the War with Mexico: The Polk-Stockton Intrigue*. Austin: University of Texas Press, 1967.

Printz v. United States, 521 U.S. 898 (1997).

The Public Papers of the Presidents, Richard Nixon 1969. Washington, D.C.: Government Printing Office, 1970.

The Public Papers of the Presidents, Richard Nixon 1972. Washington, D.C.: Government Printing Office, 1973.

Pure Food and Drug Act of 1906, 34 Stat. 768 (1906).

Quinn, Arthur. *The Rivals: William Gwin, David Broderick, and the Birth of California*. New York: Crown, 1994.

R.R. Retirement Bd. v. Alton Ry., 295 U.S. 330 (1935).

Raven v. Deukmejian, 52 Cal. 3d 336 (1990).

Rawls, James J. and Walton Bean. *California: An Interpretive History*. Boston: McGraw Hill, 2003.

Reichley, A. James. *Conservatives in an Age of Change: The Nixon and Ford Administrations*. Washington, D.C.: Brookings, 1981.

Reitman v. Mulkey, 387 U.S. 369 (1967).

Resolutions and Address Adopted by the Southern Convention. Nashville, Tenn.: H. M. Watterson, 1850.

Reynolds v. Sims, 377 U.S. 533 (1964).

Rice, Richard B., William Bullough, and Richard J. Orsi. *The Elusive Eden: A New History of California*. Boston: McGraw Hill, 2002.

Riker, William H. "The Senate and American Federalism." *American Political Science Review* 49 (1955).

The Ripon Society and Clifford W. Brown Jr. *Jaws of Victory*. Boston: Little, Brown, 1974.

Roche, John P. "The Passing of the Class of 1941." *National Review* (October 19, 1984).

Rogin, Michael P. and John Shover. *Political Change in California: Critical Elections and Social Movements 1890–1966*. Westport, Conn.: Greenwood, 1970.

Rohr, John A. *To Run a Constitution: The Legitimacy of the Administrative State.* Lawrence: University Press of Kansas, 1986.

Rolle, Andrew. *California: A History.* 4th ed. Arlington Heights, Ill.: Davidson, 1987.

Romer v. Evans, 517 U.S. 620 (1996).

Roosevelt, Theodore. *The New Nationalism.* Englewood Cliffs, N.J.: Prentice-Hall, 1961.

Rosenthal, Alan. *The Decline of Representative Democracy.* Washington, D.C.: Congressional Quarterly Press, 1998.

Roske, Ralph J. *Everyman's Eden: A History of California.* New York: Macmillan, 1968.

Ross, Jean. "Perspectives on Proposition 13: Flawed Reform." *California Journal* 28 (1997).

Rossum, Ralph A. *Federalism, the Supreme Court, and the Seventeenth Amendment: The Irony of Constitutional Democracy.* Lanham, Md.: Lexington, 2001.

———. "James Wilson and the 'Pyramid of Government': The Federal Republic." *Political Science Reviewer* 6 (1976): 113–42.

Royce, Josiah. *California: From the Conquest in 1846 to the Second Vigilance Committee in San Francisco, A Study of American Character.* New York: Knopf, 1948.

Runyon, John H., Jennifer Verdini, and Sally Runyon, eds. *Source Book of American Presidential Campaign and Election Statistics 1948–1968.* New York: Frederick Ungar, 1971.

Sabato, Larry J. *The Rise of Political Consultants: New Ways of Winning Elections.* New York: Basic, 1981.

Sabato, Larry J. and Glenn R. Simpson. *Dirty Little Secrets: The Persistence of Corruption in American Politics.* New York: Times Books, 1996.

Safire, William. *Before the Fall: An Inside View of the Pre-Watergate White House.* New York: Ballantine, 1977.

Salz, Debra F. "Note: Discrimination-Prone Initiatives and the Guarantee Clause: A Role for the Supreme Court." *George Washington Law Review* 62 (1993).

Sample, Herbert A. "Downsizing California's Military Industrial Complex." *California Journal* 39 (September 1995): 39–42.

San Antonio Independent Sch. Dist. v. Rodriguez, 411 U.S. 1 (1973).

Saunders, Myra K. "California Legal History: The California Constitution of 1849." *Law Library Journal* 90 (Summer 1998).

Savra, James H. "Conflict and Cooperation in Electoral-Administrative Relations in Large Council-Manager Cities." *State and Local Government Review* 31 (1999).

Schecter Poultry Corp. v. U.S., 295 U.S. 495 (1935).

Schrag, Peter. *Paradise Lost.* New York: New Press, 1998.

Scott v. Sandford, 60 U.S. 393 (1857).

Scott, John T. "The Sovereignless State and Locke's Language of Obligation." *American Political Science Review* 94 (2000): 547–61.

Sears, David O. and John B. McConahay. "Riot Participation." In *The Los Angeles Riots: A Socio-Psychological Study.* Edited by Nathan Cohen. New York: Praeger, 1970.

Secretary of State, State of California. *Official Voter Information Guide, General Election, Nov. 7, 2000*. Sacramento: State of California, 2000.

Sewell, Richard H. *Ballots for Freedom: Antislavery Politics in the United States 1837–1860*. New York: Oxford University Press, 1976: 193–94.

Seydor, Paul. *Peckinpah: The Western Films, A Reconsideration*. Urbana, Ill.: University of Illinois Press, 1980. *Sherman Anti-Trust Act of 1890*, 26 Stat. 209 (1890).

Silveira v. Lockyer, 312 F. 3d 1052 (2002).

Skelton, George. "Backers of Gun Controls Preparing to Fire Another Round of Legislation." *Los Angeles Times* (16 December 2002).

Small, Melvin. *The Presidency of Richard Nixon*. Lawrence: University Press of Kansas, 1999.

Smith, Elbert B. *The Presidencies of Zachary Taylor and Millard Fillmore*. Lawrence: University of Kansas Press, 1988.

Smith, Richard Norton. *Thomas E. Dewey and His Times*. New York: Simon & Schuster, 1984.

Starr, Kevin. *Americans and the California Dream 1850–1915*. New York: Oxford University Press, 1973.

Statistical Abstract of the United States. Washington, D.C.: U.S. Bureau of the Census, 2002.

Stegner, Wallace and Richard W. Etulain. *Stegner: Conversations on History and Literature*. Reno: University of Nevada Press, 1996.

Stephenson, Nathaniel Wright. "California and the Compromise of 1850." *Pacific Historical Review* 4 (1935): 114–22.

Still, Bayrd. "California's First Constitution: A Reflection of the Political Philosophy of the Frontier." *Pacific Historical Review* 4 (1935): 221–34.

Stolz, Preble. *Judging Judges: The Investigation of Rose Bird and the California Supreme Court*. New York: Free Press, 1981.

Story, Joseph. *Commentaries on the Constitution of the United States*. Boston: Hilliard, Gray, and Co., 1833.

Strauss, Leo. *Spinoza's Critique of Religion*. New York: Schocken, 1965.

Strober, Gerald S. and Deborah Hart Strober. *Nixon: An Oral History of His Presidency*. New York: HarperCollins, 1994.

Swift, Elaine K. *The Making of the American Senate: Reconstitutive Change in Congress, 1787–1841*. Ann Arbor: University of Michigan Press, 1996.

Swisher, Carl Brent. *Motivation and Political Technique in the California Constitutional Convention 1878–1879*. New York: Da Capo, 1969.

Syer, John C. and John H. Culver. *Power and Politics in California*. 4th ed. Toronto: Maxwell Macmillan, 1992.

"Taking Aim: Why Gun Control Won't Work," *California Lawyer* (January 2001), 46–49.

Testimony before Subcommittee on Education of the Committee on Education and Labor of the U.S. House of Representatives. Washington, D.C., March 19, 1969.

Thorpe, F. N. *The Federal and State Constitutions, Colonial Charters, and Other Organic Laws of the States, Territories, and Colonies*. Vol. 2. Washington, D.C.: Government Printing Office, 1993.

Tocqueville, Alexis de. *Selected Letters on Politics and Society*. Edited by Roger Boesche. Berkeley: University of California Press, 1985.

———. *Democracy in America*. Edited by J. P. Mayer; translated by George Lawrence. Garden City, N.Y.: Doubleday, 1969.

Tomlinson, T. M. and David O. Sears. "Negro Attitudes toward the Riot." In *The Los Angeles Riots: A Socio-Psychological Study*. Edited by Nathan Cohen. New York: Praeger, 1970.

The Trademark Cases, 100 U.S. 82 (1879).

Traynor, Roger J. "Law and Social Change in a Democratic Society." *University of Illinois Law Forum* (1956).

Tucker, St. George. *Blackstone's Commentaries: With Notes of Reference to the Constitution and Laws of the Federal Government of the U.S. and the Commonwealth of Virginia*. Philadelphia: W. Y. Birch and A. Small, 1803.

Tuthill, Franklin. *History of California*. San Francisco: H. H. Bancroft and Co., 1866.

Uelman, Gerald. "Shopping for Judges, California Style." *Los Angeles Times* (30 September 1986): Metro, pt. 2, 5.

U.S. Congress. *Congressional Debates*. Washington, D.C., 1824–1837.

U.S. Congress. *Congressional Globe*. 31st Cong., 1st sess. Washington, D.C., 1850.

U.S. Congress. *Congressional Record* 53. 7775 (1894).

U.S. Congress. *Congressional Record* 54. 1519 (1895).

U.S. House Committee on the Judiciary. *U.S. Population and Immigration [3] Hearing*, 107th Congress, 1st sess., 2 August 2001

United States Bureau of the Census. "Government Finances, No. 2." *1982 Census of Governments*. Vol. 4. Washington, D.C.: Government Printing Office, 1982.

United States v. Butler, 297 U.S. 1 (1936).

United States v. Dewitt, 76 U.S. 41 (1870).

United States. v. Emerson, 270 F. 3d 203 (5th Cir.) (2001).

United States v. Fox, 95 U.S. 670 (1878).

United States v. Nice, 241 U.S. 591 (1916).

Unz, Ron. "California and the End of White America." *Commentary* (November 1999).

Van Alstyne, William. "The Second Amendment and the Personal Right to Arms." *Duke Law Journal* 43 (1994).

Vitiello, Michael. "Three Strikes and the Romero Case: The Supreme Court Restores Democracy." *Loyola Law Review* 30 (1997).

Wabash, St. L. & P. R. v. Ill., 118 U.S. 551 (1886).

Wahlke, John C., Heinz Eulau, William Buchanan, and LeRoy C. Ferguson. *The Legislative System*. New York: Wiley, 1962.

Weatherson, Michael A. and Hal W. Bochin. *Hiram Johnson: Political Revivalist*. Lanham, Md.: University Press of America, 1995.

Weddle, David. *If They Move, Kill'Em!: The Life and Times of Sam Peckinpah*. New York: Grove Press, 1994.

Weintraub, Daniel. "Untangling All the Lines of Power in State Schools." *Sacramento Bee* (22 December 2002).

White, Theodore H. *The Making of the President 1964*. New York: Signet, 1966.

Wicker, Tom. *One of Us: Richard Nixon and the American Dream*. New York: Random House, 1991.

Wiebe, Robert H. *The Search for Order: 1977–1920*. Westport, Conn.: Greenwood, 1980.

Wiecek, William M. *The Guarantee Clause of the U.S. Constitution*. Ithaca, N.Y.: Cornell University Press, 1972.

Willard, Richard K. "Wheel of Fortune: Stopping Outrageous and Arbitrary Liability Verdicts." *Heritage Foundation: Policy Review* 36 (1986).

Willis, E. B. and P. K. Stockton. *Debates and Proceedings of the Constitutional Convention*. Vol. 1. Sacramento, Calif.: J. D. Young, 1880–1881.

Wills, Garry. *Nixon Agonistes*. New York: Mentor, 1970.

Wilson, Clyde N., ed. *The Essential Calhoun: Selections From Writings, Speeches, and Letters*. New Brunswick, N.J.: Transaction, 1992.

Wilson, James Q. "A Guide to Reagan Country: The Political Culture of Southern California." *Commentary* (May 1967).

———. "Reagan and the Republican Revival," *Commentary* (October 1980).

Wilson, Woodrow. *The New Freedom: A Call for the Emancipation of the Generous Energies of a People*. New York: Doubleday, 1913.

———. *The Papers of Woodrow Wilson*. Edited by Arthur Link. Vol. 5. Princeton, N.J.: Princeton University Press, 1966.

———. "Leaders of Men." In *The Papers of Woodrow Wilson*. Edited by Arthur S. Link. Vol. 6. Princeton, N.J.: Princeton University Press, 1969.

Xenophon. *Oeconomicus*. Translated by Sarah B. Pomeroy. Oxford, U.K.: Clarendon Press, 1999.

Yoo, John C. "The Judicial Safeguards of Federalism." *Southern California Law Review* 70 (1997).

Zimring, Franklin E. "Populism, Democratic Government, and the Decline of Expert Authority: Some Reflections on Three Strikes in California." *Pacific Law Journal* 28 (1996).

Zywicki, Todd J. "Beyond the Shell and Husk of History: The History of the Seventeenth Amendment and Its Implications for Current Reform Proposals." *Cleveland State Law Review* 45 (1997).

Index

right of revolution and, 3–31; slavery and, 12–14, 44–46, 48, 51–52; social contract and, 3–31, 98; the south and, 17–22, 22–23; suffrage, 42–43, 48–49; de Tocqueville and, 33–34, 55–56, 61; Whigs and Democrats' view of, 23; women, 47

Constitution, California (1879), xiii, xiv, xviii; administrative state and, 97–124; amendments to, xvi–ii, xviii–ix, 111, 127–29, 187–88; Article I section 24, 109–11; Article I section 27, 110; common good and, 97–124; Constitution of 1849 and, 54–57, 98–99; Constitution of the United States and, 101–119, Convention for, 299–300; direct democracy and, 54–57, 97–127, 151–52, 187–88; progressivism and, 151–52, 97–124, 187–88, 299–300; racism of founders, 57; right to bear arms and, 299, 305; special interests and, 98–99, 187–88; versus Constitution of 1849, 54–57, 98–99

Constitution, United States, 208, 259, 271, 299; Article I section 3, 78; Article 1 section 4, 79; Article I section 8 72–73, 86; Article V, 84–86; California statehood and, 3, 9, 20, 22, 25, 3–31; commerce clause, 68; Constitutional Convention 67–74, 299; due process clause, 40, 109 114; eighth amendment, 114; federalism and, 67–96; first amendment, 105; fourteenth amendment, 115, 118; guaranty clause, 101–7, 118; necessary and proper clause, 72–73; privileges and immunities Clause, 14, 45, 49; popular sovereignty and, 3–31; right of revolution and, 3–31; Second Amendment 300–303, 304; Seventeenth amendment and California, xviii, 67–96; slavery and, 3–31; south and, 3–31,

17–22; Taylor and 25; territories and, 9

Constitutional Convention of 1849, 12, 34, 36; amendment; 50–51; banking and corporations, 43; boundaries, 44–46, 51–52; Bill of Rights, 40–42, 47–48; calls for, 10–12, 17, 36, 37; convention of 1879 and, 54–57, 98–99; delegates to, 39–40, elections, 60; Europe and, 34, 35, 45; immigration, 49–50; issues surrounding 3–31, 34; legacy of, 57–62; literature on, 52–54; major issues of, 37–39; popular sovereignty and, 17, 48, 3–31; slavery and, 12–14, 44–46, 48, 51–52, 57; suffrage, 42–43, 48–49; table 2.1, *58–59*; women, 47

constitutionalism, constitutional government, xiii, xvii, 3, 17, 54; the South and, 17–22; 105, 208

Contra Costa County, 165

controller. See executive, California

Coolidge, Calvin, 248

Costco, xvii

counties. See local government

Coupal, Jon, xix

courts. See judiciary, California

Coxe, Tench, 69

Creel, George, 318

crime, 110, 112–14

Croly, Herbert, 205–7, 209–11, 213

Cromwell, Oliver, 219

Crowley, Monica, 228

Culver, California, 53–54

Cummings, Homer, 300

Custred, Glynn, 258–59, 261–62

Dailey, Peter, 226

Daily Press, 313

Dallek, Matthew, 237–40

Dark Ages, 285–86

Darwinism, 209

About the Contributors

Herman Belz is professor of history at the University of Maryland and author of several books and articles on constitutional and civil rights issues from the founding period to the present, including *Equality Transformed: A Quarter Century of Affirmative Action* and *A Living Constitution or Fundamental Law?: American Constitutionalism in Historical Perspective*.

Ward Connerly is a member of the University of California Board of Regents, the governing body of the UC system. He also is the founder and chairman of the American Civil Rights Institute. He was the principal proponent behind the voter-approved Proposition 209 (1995), the landmark California Civil Rights Initiative, which declared all race-based preferences in state and local government hiring unconstitutional. Mr. Connerly has been profiled on *60 Minutes*, the cover of *Parade* magazine, the *New York Times*, *Wall Street Journal*, *Newsweek* magazine, and virtually every major news magazine in America. He has also appeared on *The News Hour with Jim Lehrer*, *Crossfire*, *Firing Line*, *Hannity and Colmes*, *The Crier Report*, *Meet the Press*, *Rivera Live*, *Dateline*, *Politically Incorrect*, *NBC Nightly News*, CNN, and C-SPAN.

Jon Coupal is president of the Howard Jarvis Taxpayers Association, the organization that sponsored and promoted the watershed property tax reduction known as Proposition 13 in 1978. Proposition 13 became the basis for a property tax revolt that eventually swept the nation. Mr. Coupal's publishing record on matters of taxation is extensive. He is arguably the state's leading expert on property tax policy, a major political issue in California.

Edward J. Erler is professor of political science at California State University, San Bernardino. He is the author of *The American Polity* and numerous articles on constitutional law, crime, and affirmative action. Dr. Erler was the Director of Bicentennial Programs at the National Endowment for the Humanities in the Reagan administration and is a current member of the California Civil Rights Commission.

Steven B. Frates is senior fellow at the Rose Institute of State and Local Government at Claremont McKenna College. He has extensive experience in public policy analysis, with particular emphasis on local government finance. He has served as a senior advisor in municipal government, as director of a major metropolitan taxpayer association, and on the California Constitutional Revision Commission.

Victor Davis Hanson is professor of classics at California State University, Fresno, and a fifth-generation farmer. He is a regular contributor to the *National Review* and author of several books on agriculture and war in ancient Greece and Western civilization, including *An Autumn of War; Carnage and Culture: Landmark Battles in the Rise of Western Power; The Other Greeks, Warfare and Agriculture in Classical Greece; The Land Was Everything: Letters from an American Farmer; The Soul of Battle*, and *Mexifornia*. In addition, he was a featured commentator for the acclaimed television documentary, *The Rise and Fall of the Spartans*.

Steven Hayward is senior fellow of the Pacific Research Institute and former director of the Claremont Institute's Golden State Center for Policy Studies. A sought-after lecturer, he is the author of *The Age of Reagan* and *Churchill on Leadership*. He also has written extensively on the topics of regulation and environmental issues.

Brian P. Janiskee is assistant professor of political science at California State University, San Bernardino. He has written articles on local government, crime policy, and presidential elections. Along with Ken Masugi, he is coauthor of *Democracy in California: Politics and Government in the Golden State*, an innovative text that uses many ideas raised by Alexis de Tocqueville to analyze the current workings of California politics.

Harold Johnson is an attorney with Pacific Legal Foundation, specializing in property rights and individual rights. Before joining the Pacific Legal Foundation, Mr. Johnson worked as a journalist for several years. He was an editorial board member at the *Los Angeles Daily News, Rocky Mountain News*, and *The*

Orange County Register. Mr. Johnson has also served as West Coast editor of the *National Review*.

Brian T. Kennedy is president of the Claremont Institute. Mr. Kennedy has written on California public policy issues and national security affairs. He has served as the director of the Claremont Institute's Golden State Center for Policy Studies. He has also testified frequently before the California legislature on matters of state policy.

Gordon Lloyd is the John M. Olin Professor of Public Policy at Pepperdine University. He is coeditor of *The Essential Anti-Federalist* and *The Essential Bill of Rights*, among other works on the American political tradition.

John Marini is associate professor of political science at the University of Nevada, Reno. He received a White House appointment during the Reagan administration as a special assistant to the chairman of the U.S. Equal Opportunity Employment Commission. He has written extensively in the areas of American politics and public administration. He is author of *The Politics of Budget Control* and editor of *The Imperial Congress*.

Ken Masugi is director of the Center for Local Government of the Claremont Institute. Along with Brian Janiskee, he is coauthor of *Democracy in California: Politics and Government in the Golden State*. He is also editor of *Interpreting Tocqueville's "Democracy in America"* and coeditor of four other books on modern and American political thought.

Daniel C. Palm is associate professor of political science at Azusa Pacific University. He is the editor of *On Faith and Free Government*. His fields of research include American politics, foreign policy, and public policy.

Larry Peterman is professor of political science at the University of California, Davis. He is author of a variety of articles on political philosophy, family policy, and education. He is also the coauthor of *American Political Thought*.

John J. Pitney Jr. is associate professor of government at Claremont McKenna College and coauthor of *Congress' Permanent Minority?: Republicans in the U.S. House*, and the author of *The Art of Political Warfare*. He has served as research director for the Republican National Committee, and writes and comments frequently on politics for the press and electronic media.

Richard Reeb is professor emeritus of political science at Barstow College. He has published numerous articles on American politics and political philosophy. He is the author of *Taking Journalism Seriously*, which takes a critical view of the claims to political neutrality by the mass media.

Ralph A. Rossum is the Henry Salvatori Professor of American Constitutionalism at Claremont McKenna College and director of its Rose Institute of State and Local Government. He is coauthor of the *American Constitutional Law* and author of the *Politics of the Criminal Justice System* and *Federalism, the Supreme Court, and the Seventeenth Amendment*. He has also written on equal protection issues.

Stephen Schwartz is the author of *The Two Faces of Islam: The House of Sa'ud: From Tradition to Terror*. He is senior policy analyst and director of the Islam and Democracy Project for the Foundation for the Defense of Democracies in Washington, D.C. He was a staff writer for the *San Francisco Chronicle* for ten years and was secretary of the Northern California Newspaper Guild, AFL-CIO. His articles have appeared in most of the world's leading newspapers including the *New York Times*, the *Wall Street Journal*, the *Los Angeles Times*, the *Daily Telegraph* (London) and many more. He is a regular contributor to the *Weekly Standard* as well as to *Reforma* in Mexico City and leading periodicals in the Balkans.

Dan Walters is the preeminent political journalist in California. His *Sacramento Bee* column appears six days weekly and appears in syndicated form in dozens of newspapers throughout the state. He is the author of *The New California: Facing the 21st Century*.

Ric Williams is professor of government at Glendale Community College where, since 1971, he has taught philosophy, U.S. history, American government, U.S. foreign policy, and state and local government courses. He has authored various articles on subjects ranging from Shakespeare to American foreign policy. Professor Williams is currently finishing a commentary on Plato's *Republic*.

Scot J. Zentner is associate professor of political science at California State University, San Bernardino. He has published several articles on political parties, the presidency, and political philosophy. He is a frequent guest on California political talk shows and has published opinion pieces in such outlets as the *National Review*.